JUSCELINO KUBITSCHEK AND THE DEVELOPMENT OF BRAZIL

Map of South America showing countries and certain place names in Brazil.

JUSCELINO KUBITSCHEK AND THE DEVELOPMENT OF BRAZIL

by

Robert J. Alexander

Ohio University Center for International Studies
Monographs in International Studies

Latin America Series Number 16
Athens, Ohio 1991

The books in the Center for International Studies
Monograph Series are printed on acid-free paper ∞

Library of Congress Cataloging-in-Publication Data

Alexander, Robert Jackson, 1918-
    Juscelino Kubitschek and the development of Brazil / by
Robert J. Alexander
      p.   cm. – (Monographs in international studies. Latin
America series ; no. 16)
    Includes bibliographical references (p.).
    ISBN 0-89680-163-2
      1. Kubitschek, Juscelino, 1902-1976.   2. Brazil–Politics
and government–1954-1964. 3. Brazil–Politics and
government–1964-1985. 4. Brazil–Economic policy.   I. Title.
II. Series.
F2538.22.K8A83 1991
981.06'3'0973–dc20   91-22387
                                   CIP

To Dionir and Jordan Young

CONTENTS

PREFACE

I owe many debts of gratitude in connection with this book. First, I owe a major debt to the late Juscelino Kubitschek himself. He read an early draft of part of the book and made valuable criticisms. He also allowed me to question him at length on several occasions concerning aspects of his career. However, he was in no way responsible for any of the judgments which I express concerning him, his regime, or anything else. That responsibility is mine alone.

Edward Lacey, a young Canadian who was for some time Juscelino Kubitschek's English teacher and *amanuensis*, also contributed valuable criticisms of the first draft of the book. I owe him substantially for his insights concerning Brazil and the career of Juscelino Kubitschek. Lacey's successor, Edward Riedinger, an American, has been kind enough to make available to me transcriptions of some of his conversations with Kubitschek, as well as a copy of his book on Juscelino's presidential election campaign.

I should also thank Hope Hendricks for her meticulous preparation of the final manuscript and James L. Cobban, editor of the Monographs in International Studies, for his care in guiding this book through the publication process.

Finally, as always, I have to thank my wife Joan for bearing with me for so many years when I have talked perhaps too much about things Brazilian, and particularly about Juscelino Kubitschek. Her companionship during my two longest visits to Brazil and her own insights into that country and its people are undoubtedly reflected in the better parts of this volume. Many thanks too, for her preparation of the index for this volume.

INTRODUCTION

The origins of this book go back at least as far as the early months of 1956, when my wife and I travelled extensively in Brazil. Juscelino Kubitschek was newly in power, was not generally given much chance to remain long in office, and had not yet gotten under way his drive towards rapid economic development. However, I recall what in retrospect I see was a preview of what was to come, in the form of extensive praise in his native state of Minas Gerais for what he had accomplished in terms of pushing forward the economic transformation there during his recently ended administration as governor.

In 1959, I was back in Brazil again. At that time I visited Brasilia which was one vast construction site where building was going forward rapidly. There as well as in the coastal cities I was able to catch some of the spirit of excitement and exhilaration which Kubitschek was instilling into his countrymen.

Then in 1965-1966 my family and I were able to spend a full year in Brazil, thanks to a grant from the Rutgers University Research Council. During this year, I sought to become as thoroughly acquainted as possible with Brazil in all of its aspects. I visited twenty-one of its then twenty-two states, travelling most of the time by inter-city bus. I tried to find out not only about the country's political problems and the state of its economy, but also about its cultural development, its religious diversity, and its race relations.

By that time, Juscelino Kubitschek had been out of office for half a decade. He had become a pariah, deprived of his civil rights, and subjected to persecution by the military regime then in office. Yet one of my most vivid impressions during that year was the wide popularity which Kubitschek enjoyed among the great masses of his fellow citizens. It was clear that the source of this popularity was his great record of accomplishment during his five years in the presidency between 1956-1961.

Subsequently, Kubitschek's reputation continued to grow. Even the military, who continued to govern the country for almost two decades, came to give grudging respect to his achievements. They rendered him the sincerest of all kinds of flattery, by copying in many respects the kind of economic development program which had come to be associated with his name. Unfortunately, however, they did not copy his democratic style of government. Final testimony to his continuing popularity came at the time of Juscelino's death in 1976. The outpouring of people for his funeral was greater than that for any Brazilian public figure before or since.

I believe that any writer of relatively contemporary events has the obligation to let his readers know the biases or prejudices with which he begins, as a basis for judging what he has to say. Hence, I shall state mine. I am in favor of democratic government—a regime in which the rulers are selected by a majority of the electorate, and the minority is guaranteed its right lawfully to continue to try to convince the majority that they are wrong. I feel that the under-developed countries have little or no possibility of resolving their social and political problems unless they can find a way to increase their economies' ability to turn out goods and services, and thus to meet the material needs of their populations. I am convinced that Brazil is the giant among the Latin American countries, and is likely to emerge as one of the world's great powers.

Finally, I am convinced that Kubitschek presided over an administration which made a major contribution towards economic development of Brazil. His was the most democratic regime that the country has ever had. It was a regime which laid the basis for the emergence of Brazil as one of the world's major powers. I am, therefore, not impartial when looking at his career. However, I hope that I have been objective, capable of seeing his weaknesses and errors as well as his strengths.

Perhaps a word is in order about the use of proper names in this book. I have followed the Brazilian custom in this regard. It is common in Brazil, not only in conversation, but also in newspaper, magazines, and books, to refer to political leaders frequently by their first names or even their nicknames. Thus, Juscelino Kubitschek is often referred to merely as Juscelino, Getúlio Vargas as Getúlio, or João Goulart as Jango. This usage has the literary advantage of providing some diversity in references to individuals who are frequently mentioned. I have used it for this reason, and not to claim that I have been on a first-name basis with any of the individuals concerned.

Chapter 1

THE ROLE OF JUSCELINO KUBITSCHEK
IN BRAZILIAN DEVELOPMENT

The final verdict of history on the role of Juscelino Kubitschek in the development of modern Brazil is not yet in. However, we suggest that he will rank very high. His historical position was rising at the time of his death in 1976. Many political leaders and some intellectuals who had little or no use for Juscelino when he was in power were looking back to his tenure as president as a sort of Garden of Eden from which Brazil subsequently had fallen.

In retrospect, it is clear that Kubitschek made major contributions to his country and its history. His administration completed one phase of Brazil's economic development. He largely succeeded in getting the Brazilians to overcome their inferiority complex, and he gave them a confidence in themselves that previously they had not had. Finally, he gave the country an example of democratic government and tolerance, which stands in stark contrast to what came after him.

The Stages of Brazilian Economic Development

The economic history of Brazil presents a series of booms of varying length, of which all but the last collapsed after a period of time. In the early days of the Portuguese colonization of the country, beginning in the sixteenth century, the first Brazilian product that found a market in Europe was the famous *pau de Brasil*, wood which was in great demand as sturdy construction material and for dyes all over Europe. However, pau de Brasil was exceedingly heavy and bulky, a disadvantage in view of the relatively small ships that were available in the early decades of the sixteenth century.

By the middle of the century sugar had been developed. Sugar was Brazil's major export for at least two hundred years and left an

1

imprint on Brazilian society for an even longer period. The demand for sugar was growing in Europe. Portugal controlled not only Brazil, where the crop could be grown, but also the West Coast of Africa, from whence slaves for growing it could be obtained. Most of the Portuguese who migrated to the New World in that period did so with the object of having someone else earn their living for them. Thus, when Brazilian Indians fled to the interior rather than submit to servitude, the Portuguese brought in Negro slaves from their African colonies to work in their colony in Brazil.

The sugar industry was important not only because it provided the colony's major export for two centuries, but also because it set a pattern of race and class relations for the country. The master-slave relationship, in which the latter was subordinate to and dependent on the former for all of his needs, and was more-or-less completely subject to the master's orders, was succeeded in a later period by a patron-client system which bore a close similarity to the social system of the slave days.

Precious metals succeeded sugar as Brazil's most important export in the latter part of the seventeenth century. With this change, there was also a shift in the geographical center of the country's economy from the northeast to the center-south, where the mineral-rich province of Minas Gerais was located. Rio de Janeiro, also in the center-south, became the principal port and ultimately the capital of the colony. After the middle of the nineteenth century, another change occurred in Brazil's economy. Coffee production first located on a large scale in the Rio Paraiba valley in the province of Rio de Janeiro, moved southward to São Paulo, establishing that province's dominant position in the national economy.

Meanwhile, Brazil had become an independent nation, first as an empire in 1822, and with the overthrow of the second emperor, Pedro Segundo in 1889, as a republic. The advent of the republic marked the shift of the political center of power to the central-south part of the country, where its economic heartland had been for a generation. The states of São Paulo and Minas Gerais dominated the so-called "Old Republic" between 1889 and 1930.

During the Old Republic Brazil experienced yet another economic boom, this time based upon rubber and which was very short-lived. Between about 1890 and World War I, Brazil had a near monopoly of the natural rubber market. The product was tapped from the trees which grew wild in the Amazon jungle. It was

2

collected, processed, and sold in Manaus, one thousand miles up the Amazon, and at Belem, at the head of that great river's delta. Both cities became glittering centers of nouveau riche civilization during the short rubber boom.

The relative prosperity brought by coffee and rubber created a sufficient national market to give some encouragement to the growth of manufacturing within the country. By World War I Brazil possessed a substantial textile industry, as well as food processing and clothing industries, and some light metallurgy. During the war when Brazil was cut off from her customary sources of supply of manufactured consumer goods these rudimentary manufacturing industries received considerable impetus to expand.

In 1922 the Brazilian government formally adopted a program of tariff protection for national manufacturing.[1] However, it was not until the advent to the presidency of Getúlio Vargas in the Revolution of 1930 that there came to power an administration which was committed firmly to the industrialization of the country. Manufacturing proved to be the last of the historical waves of economic development, and the one which ended the total dependence of the Brazilian economy on the ebb and flow of its principal exports.[2]

During his campaign for the presidency before he was "counted out" in May 1930, Vargas had promised to encourage the industrialization of the country. He particularly stressed the idea of establishing a substantial steel industry, a project which he did not undertake until he had been in office for almost a decade. He began a period of almost three decades during which the government of Brazil followed a deliberate policy of import substitution industrialization.

The Import Substitution Strategy of Development

Import substitution is a strategy of industrialization and general economic development based on establishing industries which produce manufactured goods which formerly were imported. For the strategy to work, a country must have a substantial amount of imports. Substantial imports are possible if the growth of one or more major exports provides the foreign exchange necessary to pay for these imports. Brazil had developed such a source of foreign exchange in its coffee industry. A second prerequisite for import

3

substitution is protection of local manufacturing industries. As we have noted, Brazil had formally adopted a protective tariff policy in 1922. Getúlio Vargas and subsequent presidents augmented tariff protection and also used exchange controls and other measures for protective purposes.

Import substitution has certain corollaries. For one thing, it establishes a kind of natural priority for the establishment of industries. The first ones set up are those which constitute the bulk of the country's imports, usually light consumer goods and construction materials. As the market grows through industrialization, import substitution becomes possible in such areas as heavier consumer goods and some types of machinery used to make light consumer goods. Finally, the production of these second-stage consumer goods and simple capital goods may give rise to sufficient imports to justify not only the establishment of heavy industries such as iron and steel and petrochemicals, but even industries producing machine tools and heavy machinery. This third stage is possible only if the domestic economy is large enough, which the Brazilian economy was.

Although the completion of this third phase does not by any means bring an end to import substitution, it does indicate the end of import substitution as the major motor force for development. Thereafter, new strategies are needed, including a turn back to the development of agriculture, and the stimulation of new exports, particularly of manufactured goods in which, after the import substitution phase, a country has come to have a comparative advantage.[3]

In the Brazilian case, the progress of import substitution was clear. Between 1930 and 1945 the country became largely self-sufficient in light consumer goods; between 1945 and 1955 it developed the beginnings of a modern steel industry and a sector producing the nation's requirements for heavy consumer goods such as radios, washing machines, and the like. It was the task of the Kubitschek administration to complete the third phase of import substitution between 1956 and 1961.

Import substitution sets up certain geographic priorities in development. Since natural resources are limited, it is not possible to develop a whole country all at once. The import substitution process, based on domestic markets which already exist, makes it economically rational to concentrate investment principally in those parts of the country in which most of the national market is located. For the most part, new manufacturing industries will be established in or near those cities the population of which makes up the bulk of the national market for manufactured goods.

Similarly, government expenditures in infrastructure will tend to be concentrated in this same area. Thus, most expansion of electric facilities will be for the purpose of providing the power and light necessary for the new industries and the urban centers in which they are located. Roads will be built principally to tie together the major cities which make up most of the national market. Schools and health services will be concentrated in these same cities, where expanding manufacturing and service industries have a growing need for healthy, educated workers. In the Brazilian case, this meant that until the end of the Kubitschek period, the major impact of industrialization and the infrastructure to serve it was felt in the south-central part of the country.

Another corollary of import substitution is a considerable development of the urban industrial part of the economy without any major conflict between this modern sector and the traditional large landholding rural segment. Since there already exists a market for the products of new industries created by imports, the fact that the large landholding system keeps a large part of the rural population out of the market as subsistence farmers does not prevent the establishment of new import substitution industries. Also, since import substitution "saves" foreign exchange, making available foreign currency which was formerly spent on importing goods which are now produced in the country, some foreign exchange can be used to bring into the country foodstuffs and agricultural raw materials which retrograde large landholding agriculture cannot produce. This occurred in Brazil. From 1930 on the government encouraged the development of manufacturing, but at the same time took no steps to destroy the system of large landholding in the rural parts of the country. Even Kubitschek, who pushed forward the final phase of import substitution, did not challenge the rural large landholding system while in office.

The Great Depression of 1929 contributed strongly to the import substitution process. The depression hit Brazil with particular severity. The country's exports of coffee, the main earner of foreign exchange, dropped drastically. As a result, the country was unable to purchase abroad the textiles, processed foodstuffs, building materials and other products which made up most of the nations imports. Brazilian national industries took up much of the slack. For more than generation, manufacturing had been growing, and it possessed considerable excess capacity. For half a decade, this excess capacity was used to provide many of the consumer goods needed by the Brazilian population but which it was impossible to import. Thereafter, the government of President Vargas permitted the importation of substantial amounts of new machinery and equipment. This in turn allowed a considerable expansion in Brazilian industry.

The Vargas government also followed policies which maintained the purchasing power of the Brazilian market for consumer goods and construction materials. In an effort to keep up the income of the very important coffee producing sector of the economy, the Vargas regime undertook the purchase of the national coffee crop, in order to maintain its price in "milreis," then the national currency. As a result, the coffee producers, their workers, and everyone involved in handling the purchase and storing and export of coffee beans, was assured a continuing income in milreis, which made it possible for the single most important element in the national economy to continue to purchase the manufactured goods which they were accustomed to buying now produced to a large degree in Brazil rather than abroad.

The Vargas System

During his first fifteen years in power, President Vargas developed an institutional framework which controlled most of the tensions which might have been expected to appear during the process of rapid industrialization. This framework has been dubbed the Vargas System. Vargas did not develop this system deliberately. To the contrary, it emerged from a series of decisions which the president made in a quite pragmatic fashion for the purpose of keeping himself in power, or strengthening his position of power.

A fundamental aspect of the Vargas System was to leave the rural part of the economy and society alone. Vargas did not try to destroy the traditional large landholding system, and only slightly modified the political system based on "coroneis" or "colonels" (local political bosses), which had characterized Brazil during the Old Republic before 1930. He confined himself to substituting pre-

Vargas coroneis for those who were opposed to his regime, but made no effort to challenge this system for controlling rural Brazil. A second element of the Vargas System consisted of stimulating the development of the urban economy and society. Various institutions were established for this purpose. Not only was the tariff system strengthened, and an exchange control mechanism established which favored industry, but an Industrial Loans Office was set up within the semi-government Banco de Brasil, to lend money to industrialists.

A third aspect of the Vargas System was an institutional arrangement for controlling the conflicting interests created by the process of industrialization. Vargas began its establishment right after becoming president of Brazil in October 1930. He set up a Ministry of Labor and enacted a law which for the first time legalized workers' and employers' trade unions. As a result of this government patronage, several thousand new unions came into existence, in spite of the opposition to the new system of government-recognized labor organizations on the part of both communist and anarchist leaders of the pre-1930 trade unions.

With his coup d'etat of 10 November 1937, through which he established the semi-fascist Estado Novo (New State), President Vargas brought about a complete reorganization of the trade union movement, and its total subordination to the government. Every recognized union was forced to apply for re-recognition which could only be obtained on stringent terms. The government determined the jurisdiction of each union. It asserted its own authority closely to supervise union finances and to control union elections. At the same time, a "trade union tax" was imposed, consisting of one day's pay per year from each Brazilian worker. Most of this money was given to the recognized unions, on condition that it be spent on medical, dental, educational, and other similar projects and not for collective bargaining activities. Thus, the labor unions were largely converted into social welfare organizations. At the same time, a virtual end was put to collective bargaining. A system of labor courts, which not only passed upon unions' requests for wage increases and other benefits, but also dealt with an individual worker's grievances against his employer, was established to take the place of direct negotiations between the employers' and workers' organizations. The right to strike was abolished.

7

Meanwhile, President Vargas enacted by decree a large amount of labor and social legislation during the period of the Estado Novo. This included limits on working hours, establishment of minimum wages, the organization of a very extensive if unwieldy social security system. Since the Estado Novo (1937-1945) was a rigid dictatorship, Vargas was in a position virtually without opposition to picture himself as the patron of the country's working classes. One of the favorite phrases used to describe him by the official propaganda machine was that of "father of the poor." Large numbers of workers who had never enjoyed the benefits of real trade unionism came to believe Vargas' propaganda, and to regard him as the great defender of the country's humble citizens, and particularly of its wage workers. He thus became a kind of great *patrao* on a national scale, taking the place of the owner of the rural *fazenda* from which many of the new city dwellers had come.

Parallel organizations to those of the workers were established for the employers within the framework of the Estado Novo. In theory at least, all employers were brought into *sindicatos*, federations, and confederations. Like their working-class counterparts, these organizations were financed by special taxes upon all employers. They specialized in organizing a variety of social welfare and vocational education projects for the workers. The other, more licit, device for tying the industrialists to the government was the Industrial Department of the Banco do Brasil. It became the principal source of financial capital for the industries which were growing rapidly throughout the Estado Novo period, and continued to play this role for some years after the disappearance of the Estado Novo.

Much more effective in establishing control over the employer segment of the national economy than the institutions of the Estado Novo, was the government's role as the principal source of funds for the new industrial sector. These funds became available to industry through two principal sources. One was the extensive corruption which characterized the first Vargas regime. Although Getúlio himself had the reputation for being very honest financially, he did little to exercise control over the rapacity of those who worked with him. Through many devices, particularly those involving the exchange control system of the Banco do Brasil, people associated with the government were able to make substantial fortunes. In not

8

a few cases, these fortunes were used to establish and expand industrial enterprises.

During the closing months of the Estado Novo dictatorship in 1945, a new element was added to the Vargas System. Because of the popular reaction against the dictatorship, along with pressure from the armed forces, Vargas was forced to call elections for the end of 1945. In order to contest those elections, he had to organize his own followers. He first established the Partido Social Democrático (PSD), by the simple device of sending out orders to the appointed municipal mayors and state governors to establish branches of that party within their jurisdictions. The new PSD got wide support from the pre-Vargas coroneis and from many of the industrialists who had profited from the Vargas regime. However, the Partido Social Democrático did not have much appeal to the workers, who had become Vargas' most numerous constituency. As a result, he instructed the Director General of Labor, José Segadas Viana, to establish a second party, the Partido Trabalhista Brasileiro (Brazilian Labor Party—PTB). It was organized by the Ministry of Labor and the trade union officials who owed their posts to the Ministry. It became the principal rival of the revived Communist party among the ranks of the country's urban workers.

This series of institutions served for a considerable period of time to ameliorate or sublimate conflicts among contending groups in the urban sector of society. As long as the Estado Novo remained in existence, it prevented all open clashes, while granting enough concessions to both employers and workers to make them look upon the government, and particularly Vargas, as their chief benefactor. However, even after the formal end of the Estado Novo, with the overthrow of Vargas in October 1945, the framework of the Estado Novo institutions remained intact—as it largely did until the late 1980s.

Kubitschek and the Vargas System

Kubitschek was in a real sense a product of the Vargas System. His early political career began just before the Estado Novo. With the establishment of the pro-Vargas Partido Social Democrático, Juscelino became its secretary general in Minas Gerais. Subsequently the PSD elected him to the federal Chamber of Deputies, to the governorship of Minas Gerais, and to the

9

presidency of the republic. During his period as president of Brazil, however Kubitschek made less use of the Vargas System than any of his predecessors or successors. During his administration, the government interfered very little in the internal affairs of the workers' and employers' organizations. The Ministry of Labor refrained from interfering in the elections of these groups. Furthermore, the government abolished the provision that union officials could not take office until the Ministry of Labor gave assurances that they were not criminals, Communists or otherwise "subversive." The Kubitschek administration made greater use of the employers' sindicatos and gave them new responsibilities, particularly in determining allocation of scarce foreign exchange resources. Thus, employers had greater incentive to join the sindicates.

The workers and employers organizations had more freedom and ability to act on their own than they had possessed during the governments of Presidents Dutra, Vargas, or Café Filho, or were to have under Presidents Quadros or Goulart and their military successors. Although Kubitschek took few if any steps to destroy the legal structure of the Vargas System, he used it very sparingly. He relied largely on his power to inspire the people with his own vision of the Brazil of the future to rally the support which was necessary to carry out his program. Hence, he had little interest in trying to mobilize them mechanically through the legal instrumentalities of the Vargas System.

Kubitschek and the Brazilian Inferiority Complex

Perhaps of more importance in the long run than Kubitschek's completion of the import substitution phase of Brazilian economic development and his ignoring of the Vargas System was his contribution towards overcoming a feeling of inferiority which long characterized the Brazilians. The exuberance and enthusiasm and the unbounded faith and optimism demonstrated by Kubitschek not only served to make vast numbers of Brazilians conscious of the very substantial accomplishments which their nation already had to its credit, it also generated among them an excitement for what they were then doing, and an optimism about what their country might achieve in the future.

In trips made to Brazil between World War II and the Kubitschek period, the writer was impressed repeatedly with the deep pessimism which seemed to be characteristic of most Brazilians. They tended to depreciate themselves, to argue that Brazilians eschewed hard work, were not as bright as they ought to be, were doomed to remain second-rate. There was a widespread tendency to scoff at the already substantial accomplishments in such fields as literature, music, and architecture, and to compare these unfavorably with what had been done in other countries. There was very little popular awareness of the economic development which had taken place during the previous generation and which was going on virtually under their eyes in the post-World War II period.

Together with this there was a tendency to look abroad for models and inspiration. In an earlier day, the foreign models had tended to be Great Britain or France, whereas after World War II, the most important one was the United States. Sometimes this tendency to look outside the country reached the point of virtually slavish respect and deference for the foreign country involved. There were times when the tendency to look abroad took a perverse turn. Foreign elements—sometimes specified and named, more generally talked of in a more or less abstract fashion—were credited with immense power to keep Brazil backward and with having an unaltered determination to do so.

Kubitschek was by no means the first person to try to fight against this pervading spirit of pessimism about Brazil and its prospects. Since the 1920s, the country's novelists and poets had looked inward to find themes connected with the country's history and development and to underscore the virtues as well as the vices of the nation. The great pioneer Brazilian sociologist, Gilberto Freyre, had developed in his writings the theme that Brazil was in the process of engendering a unique tropical civilization. While borrowing from Europe, Africa and even Asia it was emerging as something which was not only very special but was remarkable because of the way Brazilians had overcome the challenge of their environment.

Even Vargas during his two periods in power clearly demonstrated his faith in the future possibilities of the country through his program for economic development and industrialization. However, the emphasis of his oratory and propaganda was generally directed more towards his presumed role as the patron of the more defenseless elements of the national society than towards an attempt to inspire his people with a new and more optimistic view of that society's possibilities. His suicide letter in 1954 reflected a deep pessimism, underscoring the hopelessness of anyone fighting for the nation's humble and for the country's welfare and progress.

By the middle 1950s the widespread pessimism of the Brazilian still persisted, but by the early 1960s it had largely disappeared. The change came during the administration of Kubitschek, to a very large degree because of his efforts. Spectacular progress in pushing forward Brazilian industrialization, rapid construction of the new capital Brasilia which dramatized brilliantly the whole process of economic development, and a sudden flowering of cultural life, all help to explain the new-found optimism. Equally important, vast numbers of Brazilians suddenly became aware of what their country was accomplishing and of its potentialities. This awareness was due not only to the actual material changes which were occurring, but also to the constant exhortations and expostulations of Juscelino himself. The peripatetic president, who sometimes gave the impression of being everywhere at once, tirelessly pointed out in endless speeches and conversations what was being accomplished and the plans ahead, while inciting his fellow countrymen to raise their sights to their nation's future, which he pictured in the brightest colors. The optimism which was engendered during the Kubitschek administration was not transitory. In spite of all of the difficulties which the country and its people experienced in the years immediately following the end of Juscelino's term, by the late 1960s the country had returned to a high rhythm of economic development. Large segments of the Brazilian population by then were convinced that it was only a matter of time until their country would emerge as one of the world's great powers.

Democracy of the Kubitschek Regime

Certainly another contributing factor to the optimism which characterized the Kubitschek regime was that politically it was the most democratic period in the nation's history. The rights of freedom of speech, the press, and assembly were intact during the period. The institutions of government—the congress, the courts, and the public administration—functioned normally throughout Kubitschek's five years in power. There were no political prisoners.

Elections were held in an orderly fashion. Although Juscelino had to confront attempted mutinies by disgruntled military men on several occasions, it was typical that sentences on those guilty were light, and generally were commuted by the president almost immediately. The military as an institution interfered little in political affairs, although large numbers of military officers held civilian jobs in the public administration, as had been true before Juscelino became president. The government interfered with the functioning of private organizations, such as labor unions, employers organizations, and professional societies less than any of its predecessors since the Revolution of 1930.

Of course, Brazilian political democracy continued to have certain limitations even under Kubitschek. The franchise was restricted only to those who could read and write Portuguese. Large segments of the population were virtually outside of the political process. The Kubitschek administration was not one of reform, but rather one stressing development. Juscelino was no more willing to risk his tenure in office by pushing drastic political reforms than he was ready to put it in jeopardy by sponsoring drastic social changes. But within that definite limitation Brazil had rarely if ever experienced another period during which democratic rights were as respected as was the case when Kubitschek was president.

The apparent democratic stability of the Kubitschek administration was all the more notable because of the crisis atmosphere which characterized the period before he assumed office, and the sharp contrast between the Kubitschek period and the decades after he left office. Constant military pressure upon the second regime of Vargas (1950-1954) was climaxed by his suicide in August 1954; the succeeding regime of President João Café Filho was overthrown by the military. Similarly, four chief executives held office during the single presidential term succeeding that of Kubitschek. In 1964 a military dictatorship assumed power, and remained in control for two decades.

Hence, as Brazilians looked back to the administration of Kubitschek from the vantage point of the years after he had left office they regarded his regime not only as a period of rapid economic development, but as one of great freedom and respect for the will of the electorate. Although economic development was renewed subsequently, political democracy of the type which existed under Juscelino remained for two decades after he left office and a decade after his death, outside the grasp of the Brazilian citizenry.

Kubitschek's Perspective

With characteristic optimism, Kubitschek expected to be president more than once. Therefore, he did not see what he was trying to do and what he was actually accomplishing as something which stood alone. It was a part of a longer process, over at least a second part of which he hoped to preside. It is in this light that one must understand Kubitschek's emphasis on economic development during his administration. This was to be the first phase of a longer process. Industrialization was to be complemented later by agricultural development, to be accompanied by certain social and political reforms which he knew were necessary, but which were not politically feasible during the 1956-1961 period. Thus, what Juscelino actually did achieve during his five-year span was incomplete so far as he was concerned. However, his role in Brazilian history must rest principally upon what he accomplished in what he had hoped would be only the first period of his tenure in power.

Chapter 2

THE HISTORICAL BACKGROUND OF
THE KUBITSCHEK ERA

By the time Kubitschek became president of Brazil, he was a seasoned politician. He had gotten his start during the fifteen-year first regime of President Vargas, and rose to national prominence in the decade following the overthrow of Vargas in 1945. The advent of Vargas to power had marked the end of the so-called Old Republic and the launching of the New or Second Republic. It marked a substantial shift in power from the landlord class which had dominated Brazilian political life from the days of independence, to the urban middle class, which from then on controlled the executive branch of government. However, the traditional ruling class continued to have a veto power on matters which directly concerned them.

The Colonial Period

During the more than three hundred year colonial history of Brazil, the Portuguese had a fundamental problem. The population of the "mother country" was very small, insufficient adequately to populate the vast territory which Portugal claimed in the New World. The Portuguese crown used various measures to try to deal with this problem, including making large land grants to favorites of the court so that they might undertake the settling and occupation of large parts of the South American coast. The principal result of these *donações* was that they continued to be political subdivisions of the colony, and ultimately became the provinces of the Brazilian empire and the states of the republic.

In part, the labor problem in Portuguese America was met by bringing into the area large numbers of Africans. The Portuguese had found that the native Indians were very unsatisfactory workers

15

when they were impressed into the service of the Portuguese. Indians either died or fled into the interior. Since the Portuguese had no intention of doing hard manual labor themselves, they imported Africans to take the place of the indians. Thus began a process which made the descendants of Africans one of the two basic elements of Brazil's population.

The Portuguese claim to part of the South American continent was based at least in part on a proclamation by Pope Alexander VI soon after the discovery of America. The proclamation granted half of the non-European world to the Spaniards for purposes of missionary activity, and the other half to the Portuguese. However, Brazilian explorers, particularly the *bandeirantes*, the adventurous residents of São Paulo, had vastly extended Portuguese claims beyond the original limits set by Pope Alexander VI, by their expeditions throughout the colonial period into the interior. In this way, Portugal asserted her claim by right of discovery and at least of token occupation to half of the South American continent, the territory which became the independent nation of Brazil.

During the colonial period, a socio-psychological system was established, the remnants of which still exist. The large sugar plantations of the northeast, which were owned by people of European descent and cultivated by African slaves, were patriarchal establishments. The *fazenda* owners completely dominated their landholdings and all of the people who lived on them. They ruled their families with an iron hand. The work force was the property of the landlord and the church on the fazenda was often staffed by male relatives of the owner. Even the defense of the fazendas was in the hands of militia units officered by members of the plantation owner's family with the rank and file consisting of the slaves and other dependents of the fazendeiro. This dependency relationship extended to other areas of Brazil. This was particularly true in Minas Gerais, when fazendeiros moved their families and dependents south in the eighteenth century to exploit the newly discovered precious metals and diamonds there, and to the area around Rio de Janeiro, the port from which the mineral wealth of Minas Gerais was shipped to Europe.

The imprints of the slavery and fazenda system of the colonial period persisted long after Brazil obtained independence. Slavery survived for more than sixty years thereafter. The persistence of attitudes molded by the slavery system continued after the abolition of slavery in the form of the "patron-client" relationship. It continued to be true that members of the humbler classes turned to their prosperous fellow citizens for patronage and help. A complicated system of mutual obligations developed between the patrons and their clients.

The Empire

Unlike Spanish America, the Portuguese part of the New World emerged from the colonial period as a single country. There were undoubtedly many factors which led to this difference. The mountainous and divided terrain, the well-developed and distinct Indian cultures of parts of Hispano-America, the greater distance from the mother country, and the relative inaccessibility of the Pacific areas, contributed to centrifugal tendencies once the movement towards independence had begun in the Spanish colonial domains. However, the different ways in which the two areas achieved their independence was certainly a major factor in the splitting up of Spanish America and the unity of the Portuguese part of the hemisphere. Whereas, the Spanish colonies had to fight for a more or less extensive period for their independence, in Brazil the heir to the Portuguese throne proclaimed the separation of the colony from Portugal. Within a year all Portuguese troops which objected to their proclamation of independence had been sent back home.

Independence was proclaimed by Pedro I. However, within less than a decade he had quarreled with his Brazilian advisers, abdicated, and returned to Portugal. Pedro I was succeeded by his infant son, Pedro II, as emperor of Brazil. Pedro Segundo became a man of extraordinary talents. In addition to possessing great political sensitivity and tact, he was a natural scientist of considerable ability, and a man of wide general learning. He ruled for almost sixty years and during which time Brazil enjoyed a political stability such as did not exist in any other Latin American country.

The Brazilian Empire rested principally upon the support of the rural landlord class, particularly that of the northeast. The rural landlord remained virtually sovereign within his domain during most of the imperial period. He not only continued to control the land and to own the labor force, but remained the principal supporter of

17

the Church in his area and the commander of the local militia unit which kept law and order in the vicinity of his fazenda. However, as the empire approached its end, the absolute domination of the land-lord declined, as the result of the country's economic development and the impact of modern ideas on Brazil. The stability of the empire was reinforced by the backing of the Roman Catholic Church until the 1880s. However, in that decade the emperor lost this backing because of his anticlerical attitude which led him into serious conflicts with the ecclesiastical hierarchy.

The military became a menace to the imperial regime only after the War of the Triple Alliance (1865-1870) during which Brazil bore the main burden in the struggle against the dictatorship of Paraguayan President Francisco Solano López. This conflict vastly increased the size of the regular Brazilian armed forces, and gave them an esprit de corps which they had never had before. It also resulted in many of the officers gaining sympathy for the cause of abolition of slavery as the result of serving with many ex-slaves who had been promised their freedom in return for service in the war. A number of officers also became believers in republicanism.

The monarchy lost the support of its most important backer, the landed oligarchy, as the result of the abolition of slavery early in 1888. Princess Isabel, acting as regent for her father Pedro Segundo while he was away in Europe, signed the Law of Emancipation with the full support of her father. Because of this, the oligarchy felt that it had no longer any particular interest to be served by supporting the continuance of the empire.

As a result of these factors, the monarchy fell without a struggle on 15 November 1889. Pedro Segundo, who was reported to have predicted that he would be the last Brazilian monarch, accepted his deposition without question, and went into exile in Europe, where he died shortly afterward.

The Old Republic and Its Downfall

The Old Republic, which was established with the downfall of Pedro Segundo, differed in subtle but important ways from the empire. It still was dominated largely by the rural oligarchy, but the center of gravity of national politics shifted from the traditional northeast, upon which slavery and the plantation system had set a pattern of patron-client relationship to the center-south, and particularly the states of São Paulo and Minas Gerais. During most of the period, leaders of these two states alternated as presidents of the republic. In addition, the landlord class was not as completely dominant in the Old Republic as it had been in the empire. The typical political figure of the former was the *coronel* or colonel, a kind of rural political boss, whose main function was to act as an intermediary between the rural landlords and the state governors. The *coroneis* depended on the state governors to provide them with the patronage and the favors for the local landlords which served to maintain their position. The state governors depended upon the coroneis for their own continuance in power. The president of the republic, in turn, depended upon the state governors, who were his principal constituency.

In a number of other ways, too, the Old Republic differed from the empire. The republican regime was a relatively loose federation in which the states had a wide degree of autonomy, in contrast to the centralized administration under Pedro Segundo. The army played a much more significant role in politics than it had done previously. The first two presidents were army officers, and another military leader was elected president shortly before World War I. The political importance of the army, however, was not that it provided presidents. Rather, it resided in the widely recognized "right" of the armed forces to function as ultimate guarantors of the constitution and of the republic itself. Under certain circumstances this right involved the prerogative of the military to oust the incumbent government by force.

The electorate remained tiny, consisting principally of the rural landlords and such of their dependents as they wished to allow to vote, and middle and upper class elements in the cities, with a growing number of literate manual and white collar workers joining the electorate as time went on. In addition, elections were thoroughly rigged, seldom if ever being won by the opposition on either a national, state, or local level. There was little or no concern upon the part of the government for social problems, or the plight of the less fortunate members of the society. This was symbolized perhaps by the famous remark which has been attributed to several leading figures in national politics during the 1920s that "organized labor [was] an affair for the police."

In the 1920s there began to develop serious opposition to the social, economic, and political system represented by the Old

19

Republic. This opposition was both nationalistic and social. It argued that the governments of the Old Republic had been excessively subservient to foreign interests, particularly foreign economic interests. It also sympathized with the plight of the urban workers and peasants who had virtually no participation in the politics of the Old Republic. This opposition found particular support in the younger officer ranks of the army. It found expression in two insurrections, one in 1922 and another in 1924. The first of these fizzled out in Rio de Janeiro after a short battle between elements of the garrison of the artillery base at Copacabana and loyal army units. However, in the 1924 uprising the rebels gained control of the city of São Paulo for a week, after which they retreated to the western part of the country and carried on guerrilla warfare against the army and local state police. These military rebels were popularly known as the *Tenentes* (lieutenants), since most of them were junior officers in the armed forces. They continued to conspire against the government after the collapse of their rebellion, drawing some civilians into their activities in the late 1920s.

Discontent with the institutions and ways of the Old Republic also had become evident with the growth of a labor movement. Before World War I, a national labor confederation had been established under anarchist influence. Trade unionism spread markedly during the war, and there were several major strikes during this period. In the 1920s the labor movement expanded further, and some elements turned to political activity, with local labor parties being established in several cities. The Communist party, founded in 1922, came to be the dominant political element within the ranks of organized labor.[1]

The stirrings of revolt, which were felt in politics during the 1920s were reflected in the cultural field. Samuel Putnam has noted that Monteiro Lobato's *Urupes*, a collection of sketches published in 1918,

> set Brazilian writers upon a new track. . . . The thing that made the volume remarkable was the new note of "caboclismo" that it struck, a fresh and different emphasis upon the "mestizo" of the interior. Here was not the noble and romantic savage of Gonçalves Dias the José Alencar, but rather the individual resembles Lobato's character Jeca Tatu, who spends a good part of

20

his life squatting on his heels, smoking his pipe and letting the world go by him, forgotten by a government that is supposed to be concerned with his welfare and with the task of making him ever into an intelligent and useful citizen.[2]

The Week of Modern Art, held in the Municipal Theater of São Paulo in 1922, from which there originated a general call by a group of young intellectuals and artists for a new approach to the plastic arts, with greater concentration on Brazilian themes and experimentation with new and original forms of expression, had its repercussions also in the field of literature. There began to develop in the late 1920s new trends in the novel as well as in non-fiction writing.[3] Samuel Putnam quotes Mário de Andrade, whom he calls the "Pope" of the modernist movement. He said that

> manifesting itself especially in the realm of art but also reacting violently upon social and political customs, the modernist movement was the forerunner and herald and in large part the creator of a national state of mind. The transformation of the world, with the gradual weakening of the great imperial powers, the introduction of new political ideas in Europe, the rapidity of transportation, and a thousand and one other causes of an international character, together with the development of a new spirit, called for a re-verification and even the remodelling of the national intelligence.[4]

One of the first signs of this new literary wave was the 1928 publication of the first novel of José Américo de Almeida, *A Bagaçeira*. José Américo, as he is commonly known, was a young man who already had gained considerable experience in the political life of his native state, Paráiba. His novel was the first to deal extensively with the economic, political, and sociological problems of the northeastern states. It set a pattern soon to be followed by a number of other writers who were to constitute the so-called Northeastern School of Brazilian literature.

21

The Revolution of 1930

The 1930 election brought a major split to the ranks of the political groups which had dominated the Old Republic. Outgoing President Washington Luíz decided to break with the tradition that political leaders from Minas Gerais and São Paulo alternated in the federal presidency. Himself from São Paulo, he decided to name a fellow Paulista, Governor Julio Prestes, as the official candidate to succeed him. As a result, the powerful political machine of Minas Gerais broke with the president. For tactical reasons, it threw its support behind the governor of Rio Grande do Sul, a state of secondary but growing political weight, as the opposition nominee. This was Getúlio Vargas, whose career had included considerable service in the state and national legislatures, as well as a short period in Luíz' cabinet. The great majority of the Tenentes also threw their support behind Vargas. Although they had little faith that the government would allow the opposition to win, and most of them favored a violent overthrow of the regime, the Tenentes saw the 1930 campaign as a vehicle for mobilizing much wider civilian support for their opposition to the status quo.

As was expected, the opposition was "counted out" in the election of May 1930. The only states which it carried were Minas Gerais, Rio Grande do Sul, and the northeastern state of Paráiba, from whence came Vargas' vice presidential running mate, João Pessoa. Vargas at first accepted his defeat, sending a congratulatory telegram to his victorious rival. However, there were serious pressures within Vargas' camp to try to reverse the results of the election through a military movement against the government. The Tenentes were strongly in favor of such a move, as was the man who had served as Governor of Rio Grande do Sul during Vargas' presidential campaign, Osvaldo Aranha. After the murder of João Pessoa in August (probably for non-political reasons), the pressure for a revolt became irresistible.

The revolution began on October 3. The state police force of Rio Grande do Sul defeated or won over the units of the federal army stationed in the state, and within a few days the Rio Grande forces had secured control of the northern neighbor of Rio Grande, the state of Santa Catarina. By the last week of October they had also occupied the next state, Paraná. Meanwhile, in the northeast and Amazon regions, the Tenentes had organized a successful rebellion and seized control of the whole northern two thirds of the country. The state police was also defeated in Minas Gerais. At this point, the military commanders in Rio de Janeiro decided to accept what by then appeared to be inevitable. They arrested President Luíz and the President-elect Julio Prestes, and put them on a ship destined for Europe. At the same time, they invited Vargas to come to Rio to be sworn in as the new chief executive.[5]

The Vargas Era

Vargas remained in power for fifteen years. It is unlikely that anyone would have predicted at the time he came into office that he would be able to remain for so long. During his first two years in the presidency, he was largely at the mercy of the Tenentes. They had military power, and they organized strong civilian pressure groups to make their wishes known to the president. However, Vargas proved to be a master politician in dealing with the Tenentes; over a period of two years he succeeded in dividing them, and finally winning complete supremacy over them. The subordination of the Tenentes was sealed with the three-month-long rebellion of the state of São Paulo in the middle of 1932, which served as the excuse for reinstating strict military discipline in the armed forces and reestablishing the army hierarchy, within which the Tenentes still remained junior officers. Meanwhile, Vargas had begun the task of developing a strong civilian constituency of his own. One of his first moves was to establish a Ministry of Labor and Industry. A few months later, he enacted a decree-law which provided for legal recognition of trade unions for the first time. He also began to establish an extensive social security system, which by the time he left office in 1945 covered virtually all wage and salary earning groups in the population.

Late in 1933 a constituent assembly met and wrote a new constitution. The assembly's last act was to choose Vargas as the first president to serve under the new constitution. He governed under it for another three and a half years. However, on 10 November 1937, in the midst of an election campaign to choose his successor, the president executed a coup d'etat, suspending the Constitution of 1934, and proclaiming a new one, closing congress permanently, and establishing strict censorship and other controls over the freedom of action of the citizenry, particularly the

23

politicians. This coup was executed with the support of the military leaders, particularly Minister of War Eurico Dutra and Chief of General Staff Góes Monteiro, as well as with the connivance of many civilian political leaders. The new constitution enacted on 10 November 1937 established the Estado Novo. This was a regime modelled on the fascist states then prevalent in Europe. It put all legislative power in the hands of the president, and established the framework for a corporative state, the Vargas System, which was discussed in the previous chapter.

The Estado Novo differed in a number of ways from the European fascist systems. It had no peculiar ideology of philosophy. No elite party was ever established to lead and control the system. There was certainly none of the racism which characterized many of the European fascist regimes. In fact, the Estado Novo was a very personal dictatorship of Vargas. No legislature was ever chosen under the Estado Novo. Vargas enacted laws by decree throughout the period. He exercised extremely strict control over all organs of public expression, his secret police ferreted out opposition, and he used the government's very substantial propaganda apparatus principally to sing his own praises.

The president appointed all of the governors of the states, who were given the title of *interventores*. These in turn appointed the heads of the municipalities within their jurisdictions. The hitherto very powerful state police forces—which in most states had been larger and stronger than the units of the federal army in the individual states—were drastically reduced in size. The president presided over a public ceremony at which the flags of the states were burned, symbolizing the subordination of the states to the nation. During the Estado Novo period, Vargas consolidated his support among the country's wage workers. He greatly extended the social security system which he had begun to establish soon after the Revolution of 1930, enacted a system of minimum wages, and decreed a variety of other measures for protection of the workers on their jobs.

The Return to Democratic Constitutionalism

Brazil participated actively in World War II, which it entered on the Allied side, soon after the attack on Pearl Harbor in 1941, when it became clear to Vargas that his interests and those of Brazil would be best served by aligning with the United States. A Brazilian division formed part of the United States Fifth Army in Italy, and took a very active role in the closing months of its campaign. Much enthusiasm was aroused among the rank and file citizenry for the exploits of the Brazilian soldiers. There is little doubt that this Brazilian participation in the war contributed greatly to bringing the Estado Novo to an end. It became increasingly incongruous for Brazil to be participating in a war in Europe to end fascism there, while it continued to have a fascist political structure at home. The incongruity became particularly obvious to the soldiers who participated in the war in Europe. As a result, early in 1945, Vargas was forced to promise to have elections before the end of the year. His pledge to do so was reinforced immediately by statements of leading military figures to the effect that the honor of the armed forces would stand behind the promise of elections.

Even before this, however, the rigors of the dictatorship had been somewhat relaxed. A quite public opposition began to develop, under the aegis of the National Democratic Union (União Demo-crática Nacional), a loose coalition which brought together virtually all elements of the opposition ranging from the communists to the conservative elements of the pre-1930 regime. As a result of this renewal of competitive political activity, numerous political parties sprang into existence in 1945 and the years immediately following. Generally, these tended to be aligned in terms of being pro-Vargas or anti-Vargas. Only a handful were not clearly on one side or the other.

As we have already noted, there were two political parties which the government itself organized while Getúlio was still president, the Social Democratic party (Partido Social Democrático—PSD), and the Brazilian Labor party (Partido Trabalhista Braileiro—PTB). Other parties which were fundamentally pro-Vargas included a number of splinters from the PTB, as well as the Partido Social Progresista, organized principally by Adehmar de Barros, an aspiring politician from São Paulo, who for some time had served as interventor in that state during the Estado Novo period. It had strength principally in São Paulo and one or two of the smaller Northeastern states.

The largest anti-Vargas group was the União Democrática Nacional. Early in 1945 it had been converted from a broad united front into a political party. Also generally anti-Vargas was the

Partido Socialista Brasileiro, established in 1948, which originated as a left-wing breakaway from the UDN. The Partido Republicano, organized as a revival of the parties of similar name which dominated the various states during the Old Republic, was also generally in the anti-Vargas camp, as was the Liberating party (Partido Libertador), centered principally in the state of Rio Grande do Sul, whose major point of doctrine was advocacy of the parliamentary form of government. Finally, the Christian Democratic party (Partido Democrata Cristão), organized in the late 1940s, was also basically anti-Vargas.

Not particularly pro or anti-Vargas was the Partido Comunista Brasileiro (PCB), led by ex-Tenente Luíz Carlos Prestes, and closely aligned with Moscow. Between May 1945, when Prestes was released after more than nine years in jail, and the overthrow of Vargas late in October, the PCB supported the continuance of Vargas in power. However, this alliance was one of convenience, and the PCB did not associate itself with him after he was ousted. Similarly, the Partido de Representacão Popular was not particularly concerned with the Vargas/anti-Vargas division of popular opinion. It was the revival of the fascist Accão Integralista party which had gained much strength in the 1930s, until it was suppressed along with all other parties by Vargas soon after he established the Estado Novo.

The Dutra and Second Vargas Administrations

The armed forces finally drove Vargas out of office late in October 1945. They claimed to have done so because they suspected that he did not intend to fulfill his promise to hold elections. Vargas' supporters, on the other hand, insisted that the military overthrew him because they feared that he would launch a large-scale program of economic and social reform, to which the military was opposed.[6] Elections were finally held in December 1945, with the two major candidates being General Eurico Dutra, former Minister of War under Vargas, running on the ticket of the Social Democratic and Trabalhista parties; and General Eduardo Gomes, founder of the Brazilian airforce, ex-Tenente, and principal organizer in 1944 of the UDN. Although Vargas withheld his endorsement of either candidate until the penultimate moment, he finally gave grudging support to Dutra, whose victory was generally attributed to this backing from the ex-dictator.

26

The Dutra administration (1946-1951) generally was marked by a return to constitutional government. Most of 1946 was spent in writing a new constitution, a task completed by the constituent assembly which had been elected simultaneously with Dutra. Thereafter, Dutra bit by bit put into effect the provisions of this new document, reestablishing the court system, returning the autonomy of the states through elections in January 1947, generally establishing the autonomy of the three traditional branches of government. He made no effort to dismantle the parts of the Vargas System which had established strict government control over organized labor and relations between workers and employers. On the contrary, on the excuse that the communists were gaining too much strength, he suspended all further union elections in 1947, and they were not renewed until after he went out of office. The Communist party was again outlawed by the Dutra government.

Dutra pushed forward a relatively modest economic development program. Although he announced ambitious plans for massive development planning, very little came of the plans. However, he did make a major contribution to the growth of the economy by beginning construction of the Paulo Affonso dam, which ultimately supplied electric power for a large part of northeastern Brazil.

President Dutra was succeeded by Vargas. As the 1950 election approached, Vargas accepted nomination by the Partido Trabalhista Brasileiro, and carried on a very energetic campaign. He promised among other things to expand the freedom of the labor movement, and to halt the inflation which had become serious during the Dutra administration. He also promised to take steps to halt the spread of foreign control of the Brazilian economy.

Vargas succeeded in rallying support of virtually all of the country's labor leaders, even those who had opposed him in the past. He also received the backing of the now illegal Communist party. However, he was not supported by the Partido Social Democrático, which he had formed. It put up a rival candidate, Christiano Machado. Vargas succeeded in defeating Eduardo Gomes, who was again the nominee of the União Democrática Nacional, and was Getúlio's principal opponent. The PSD nominee came in a poor third. There was some hesitancy in the ranks of the military to allowing Vargas to return to office. However, General Dutra himself insisted with the head of the armed forces that Vargas had been duly and clearly elected by the people and that

27

therefore he had the right to take office. Dutra reminded the military leaders that their duty was to guarantee respect for the constitution, not to violate it.[7]

The second Vargas administration was turbulent throughout. The military leaders were generally suspicious of the ex-dictator, and on several occasions intervened to force him to take steps he did not particularly want to take. The most serious incident of this kind—before Vargas' suicide—arose over his young protege João Goulart, whom he had named Minister of Labor in early 1953. Goulart owned a fazenda next to that of Vargas near São Borja in Rio Grande do Sul and the two men had come to know one another very well during the five years that Vargas was out of office spending most of his time in his native state. In state elections in 1947 Goulart succeeded as PTB candidate for the Rio Grande do Sul legislature, and subsequently became Secretary of Justice in the state government. In the 1950 election, Goulart ran successfully for the Federal Chamber of Deputies.[8]

During the year that Goulart was Minister of Labor, many observers felt that Vargas made it clear that he looked upon Goulart as his political heir, although subsequently members of the Vargas family maintained strongly that this was not his intention.[9] It was clear, however, that Goulart used his post as Minister of Labor to build up an extensive personal political machine in the labor movement. He was accused of encouraging strikes, which he then settled in favor of the workers. Finally, it was alleged that he had developed more or less close relations with President Juan Perón of Argentina. Already suspicious of Vargas' intentions, the military was particularly upset by Goulart's behavior in the Ministry of Labor. They finally forced Vargas' hand and made him "accept Goulart's resignation," which he did early in 1954. However, Vargas made it quite clear that Goulart was resigning under pressure and that his exit from the government in no way decreased the regard in which he was held by the president. For his part, Goulart warned Vargas that if he accepted military pressure to oust Jango, he himself would be the next victim of his enemies in the armed forces.[10]

In the meantime, President Vargas had taken several steps to stimulate the country's economic development. The foreign exchange control system was reorganized. More important was the establishment of the Banco Nacional de Desenvolvimento Económico

(National Bank of Economic Development). It was to become the principal source of funds not only for government development projects, but also for private industrialists. Another important economic step the establishment of Petroleos Brasileiros (Petrobras). The initiative for setting up this government petroleum firm came from President Vargas. This project did not provide for a monopoly on oil exploration and exploitation for Petrobras, an attribute introduced into the law by more radical nationalist congressmen.

A few months after the forced resignation of Goulart as Minister of Labor, the final crisis of the Vargas administration took place. The dismissal of Goulart had not diminished the hostility of many of the principal military leaders. In August 1954 an Air Force major was killed by one of Vargas' palace guards, in an unsuccessful attempt to assassinate newspaperman, Carlos Lacerda, editor of *Tribuna da Imprensa*, and a violent opponent of the Vargas regime. The military leaders then presented the president with a species of ultimatum, demanding that he go on an "extended vacation" until the end of his term of office.

Vargas summoned a meeting of his cabinet to discuss the issue. He listened without comment as each of his ministers gave his ideas on what the president should do. Some suggested that he fight, others argued that he should concede to the pressure of the military. The Minister of War pledged his support to the president, but admitted that he was not sure that he could impose his point of view on the men who were under his command. Vargas said virtually nothing. He seemed to be doodling, or perhaps writing something, during the discussions. When it was over, he dismissed his ministers and soon afterwards returned to the living quarters of the presidential palace, and to his bedroom.[11]

The next morning Vargas was found dead, having shot himself sometime during the night. Near his body there was found a suicide letter, asserting that he had spent most of his adult life fighting for the humble Brazilian citizenry and for the defense of the country against unspecified foreign and domestic interests. He argued that his enemies had now gotten the best of him, and he was sacrificing his blood in the cause of those for whom he had always struggled. He ended with the phrase, "I leave life to enter history."[12]

Vargas' suicide, ironically, reestablished his reputation. His prestige had been slipping badly during the period since his reelection, as a result of his inability to curb inflation and resultant unrest among his labor followers. However, the tragic nature of his death, and his suicide letter, which was immediately published, established Getúlio Vargas as a martyr to his country and to its humbler citizens—at least in the eyes of these citizens. As a result, those whose loyalty to Vargas had been slipping were reinforced in their belief in him. Consequently, Brazilian public opinion continued to be divided basically between Vargas an anti-Vargas elements for another decade, until sometime after the military coup d'etat of March-April 1964. Kubitschek became the principal spokesman for the pro-Vargas forces.

Chapter 3

YOUTH AND EARLY CAREER OF
OF JUSCELINO KUBITSCHEK

Juscelino Kubitschek de Oliveira, who became president of Brazil at the end of January 1956, as the victorious candidate of the pro-Vargas political forces, was no political neophyte. He had been active in politics for more than twenty years, had served as a state cabinet minister, as mayor of the capital of his state, twice as a federal deputy, and had just recently finished most of a four-year period as governor of one of the country's largest states. He had a well-earned reputation as one of the most personable, dynamic, and capable Brazilian politicians, although he was not without his enemies.

Family Background

Throughout his political career, Juscelino used his mother's family name, Kubitschek, rather than his father's, Oliveira. In part this was probably because his father died when he was very young, and he had been brought up by his forceful mother. Furthermore in Brazil Oliveira is a relatively common name, like Jones or Smith in the United States, whereas Kubitschek is very distinctive, and hence easy to remember.

In his book *A Experiencia da Humilidade*, Juscelino wrote that the Brazilian Kubitschek was a Sudeten German immigrant, a carpenter from what many decades later became Czechoslovakia. His first name was Johann and he arrived in Brazil about 1835. For reasons which remain obscure, he settled in the interior of Brazil, in the town of Diamantina, in the state of Minas Gerais. He was the great grandfather of the future president of Brazil. The peasants of the Minas Gerais *sertão* found Johann's family name, which his great grandson said "aroused interest and curiosity," impossible to

31

pronounce, and so he came to be widely known merely as "João Alemão," that is, John German.[1]

Johann Kubitschek had two sons, João Nepomuceno and Augusto Elias. Juscelino said that the first of these was a literary figure of some reputation in Minas Gerais, as well as being a politician of local distinction, a founder of the Republican Club of Diamantina, member of the first republican constitutional convention of the state, and its vice governor. Augusto Elias Kubitschek, Juscelino's grandfather, was a farmer in the municipality of Diamantina, and became proprietor of the Fazenda do Bueno. Augusto's grandson was to visit this farm on many occasions. Although he was not a particularly active politician, Augusto did have strong opinions. His grandson recorded that Augusto was "so integrated in liberty and law that he could be, and in a certain violent municipal election, was the *only* elector to vote for the candidate of the opposition."[2]

It was Augusto's daughter Julia who married João César de Oliveira and became the mother of Juscelino Kubitschek de Oliveira. João César has been described as an "authentic son of the region," being of old Mineiro stock, and the son of Teófilo Gomes de Oliveira who, typically enough for the area, was a dealer in precious stones.[3] Juscelino's father died when Juscelino was little more than a baby. In his memoirs, Kubitschek wrote that

> to tell the truth I hardly knew my father, and at that age could hardly have much memory of him. My image of him as a human figure must therefore be largely phantasy. The few memories are based on stories of my mother and the relatives, on the contemplation of photographs which were in the house, and later, on the confidences of friends and information from people who had known him. (EH.14)

However, Juscelino seems to have inherited a number of his personal characteristics from his father. Juscelino noted that his father was "extroverted and communicative," and that he always wanted company when he ate his meals, even going to the extreme of inviting friends or even just acquaintances in off the street to lunch with him when his wife was not home. Kubitschek added that "This was, without doubt, one of the many traits which I inherited

32

from my father. I never could sit down at the table without having at my side a companion, whether during my obscure period as a student or later as a doctor and politician" (EH.15,16).

João César held many jobs. However, by the time that Juscelino was born he was a travelling salesman. On one of his business trips into the interior he fell ill, and had to be transported home to Diamantina in a litter. During the last five months of his life, he lived apart from his family, fearful that his wife and two small children might contract his fatal tuberculosis. Juscelino and his sister Naná (Maria da Conçeição), could only peer at him from the street through a barred window (EH.14). Juscelino's father died in January 1904, when the boy was less than a year and a half old.

Childhood and Early Youth

Juscelino was born on 12 September 1902. His childhood was difficult, because upon the death of her husband, his mother was forced to become the sole family breadwinner, and to support Juscelino and his elder sister Maria. Sra. Julia de Oliveira was a school teacher. At first her school was quite unofficial, each student paying a small sum which went to the support of her family. However, after the visit of the state governor to the school it was made part of a state institution, and Sra. de Oliveira got a salary of 100 milreis a month (EH.37). Soon after her husband's death, Julia moved her small brood into the building in which she gave classes. They sat on the floor of the classroom playing, while their mother taught her two sessions of classes until they themselves were old enough to be numbered among her students.

Kubitschek wrote that his mother had efficient methods to educate and teach. "We were allowed to play at will," he wrote, "but only after learning our lessons. An imperative norm was that a job begun must be a job concluded. No pupil was permitted to interfere with his studies to watch a procession pass in the street. For her duty was always of first importance." This dictum was fixed in his subconscious through repetition and became for him the basis of his philosophy of life. Kubitschek summed up his mother's character thus: "Kindliness, tenderness, firmness and discipline— those were the qualities marking the character of my mother. It is indispensable to combine them to present with exactitude her true and curious personality" (EH.23).

33

So long as his mother lived, Juscelino's relations with her were always very close; after her death he revered her memory. I recall that when I met Kubitschek in Belo Horizonte in 1972, and we were going to go for lunch to Pampulha, he had the car stop on the way at the cemetery, where his mother was buried. He told me that he made it a practice to visit her grave every day that he was in the Minas Gerais capital. In his very early years Juscelino rose early, a habit which he kept throughout most of his life. His mother arose at 6 A.M., soon afterwards waking her children, so that they could all get to the schoolroom on time. In later years, starting his day's work almost at sunrise was to be the bane of many people who worked with Kubitschek.[4]

Years later his mother would tell a story about his primary school years which she thought presaged his later career. On one occasion he left their house without permission, to go to the railroad station to join a crowd which was there to greet the mayor of Diamantina, who was returning from a considerable sojourn in the state capital. When she asked Juscelino why he had disobeyed her, he replied that he had to see how the mayor behaved on such an occasion, since he intended one day to be mayor himself.[5]

Secondary School

At the age of eleven, soon after he had finished primary school, Juscelino entered the Seminary of the Archdiocese of Diamantina. As he explained many years later, this was the only way that a poor boy could continue his education, since there was no government secondary school in the town, and it would have been necessary otherwise for him to go to school in Belo Horizonte, something which the family finances would not permit.

Kubitschek explained that he "had no vocation for the religious life, and only for those who were candidates for the priesthood was there free tuition. [His] mother was not in a condition to pay the fees." However, some friends suggested that in order to get free studies the boy should inscribe in the seminary as one who was intending to become a priest, and it was agreed that he would do so. Kubitschek explained what happened next: "But at the moment of inscription, I could not lie. Asked, as was customary, by the secretary of the establishment, I answered with absolute sincerity, forgetting the consequences which could result, 'No, I have

34

no desire to be a priest. I want to study to be a doctor'" (EH.25). As a result, Juscelino was unable to go to the seminary. He sought to find work, but was unsuccessful. As a consequence in his words: "I did absolutely nothing . . . I joined with other poor kids of my age, none of whom was studying. We passed the time . . . throwing stones at parrots, fishing in the river, or playing in the street" (EH.39).

Aware of her son's frustrations, Juscelino's mother finally made an appeal to the head of the seminary to allow her son to attend the school without charge, even though he did not intend to become a priest. Although she did not succeed entirely, she did get a reduction of the tuition for Juscelino. The family was able just barely to afford this charge, although it meant that four-fifths of Sra. de Oliveira's salary each month went to pay the tuitions of her son and daughter, leaving only twenty milreis a month for all of the rest of the family's expenses (EH.40).

During his secondary school years Juscelino became an avid reader. His interests ranged very widely, and he was given special privileges to use the library of the seminary, the principal if not only large collection of books in the city. During his years of secondary schooling he is said to have read hundreds of books, and in future years it is reported that his acquaintances were often surprised at the variety of his knowledge on a wide range of subjects.[6] Juscelino himself commented that in the seminary: "I learned to discipline my reading, which before had been very disordered and confused" (EH.46).

Juscelino's Fight for Further Education

When Juscelino finished his course in the seminary, he still had little preparation to make a living, since the seminary was not officially recognized by the state as a secondary school, and graduating from it did not give one any qualifications for a job requiring secondary education. However, at about the time of his completing his seminary studies, Kubitschek became aware of a competition to be held in Belo Horizonte for posts as telegraph operators. He was sure that he could pass the examination, since he had spent much time with friends who worked in the Diamantina telegraph office, and had learned their trade.

35

With great strain on the family finances, he went to Belo Horizonte, passed the exam, but then was told that even having passed it, he still had to take a course in Morse Code, which he already knew. It was arranged that he could do this in Diamantina, but a year had to pass before he would be officially "qualified." Meanwhile, he spent most of his nineteenth year also studying for examinations which would qualify him for entry into the university. By the time he arrived back in Belo Horizonte, his Morse Code studies behind him, he had successfully passed most of the university entrance examinations.

However, his troubles were not yet ended. Even with all qualifications for the telegraph job completed, he still did not obtain the post he was seeking. It was not until he had spent several months more in Belo Horizonte, with a subsidy from his mother and sister (who was now a school teacher), that with the help of the political boss of Diamantina he was finally able to get an official appointment as a telegrapher. As he wrote about this in his memoirs: "This appointment was a kind of 'Open, Sesame' for me. I could stay in Belo Horizonte, without more sacrifice by my mother. And, doing so, I could easily finish my examinations, and enter the Faculty of Medicine" (EH.65).

During most of the next five years, until December 1927, Kubitschek studied at the University of Minas Gerais, and held his job in the telegraph office. However, he did take six months off during his fourth year in the medical school, spending the time resting in Diamantina. He had become ill, and he and his doctor feared that he might have contracted tuberculosis, which had been fatal for his father. Although it turned out that he did not have this disease, the doctor nonetheless suggested that he was overworking himself, and that he had better take a vacation, which he did.

At the university, Kubitschek had as his schoolmates a considerable number of people who were to make names for themselves subsequently, and he notes that these were "more or less my friends." Among these men were Milton Campos, later governor of Minas Gerais and cabinet member; Pedro Aleixo, future vice president of the Republic; Bilac Pinto, who was to be a distinguished jurist; Adauto Lucio Cardoso, who would be a leading politician and supreme court justice; Francisco Negrão de Lima, future politician and diplomat; and Carlos Drummond de Andrade, whom Kubitschek refers to as "one of the great poets of the Portuguese language" (EH.81).

When Juscelino had almost finished his course in the Faculty of Medicine, his sister Naná married one of the finer young surgeons of Belo Horizonte, Julio Soares. The wedding was held at her mother's house in Diamantina, and Kubitschek, together with all his cousins who were studying in Belo Horizonte, returned home for the occasion. Juscelino later commented that the union of Naná and Julio Soares left him most contented, adding that he soon came to regard Julio Soares almost like a brother, and commenting that the best way to describe Soares was by an old Minas Gerais saying: "God made him and then broke the mold" (EH.80). Kubitschek finally graduated from the Faculty of Medicine of the University of Minas Gerais on 17 December 1927. His mother, sister, and brother-in-law were all in attendance for the great occasion. But Kubitschek also noted that "still more important [he] succeeded in getting a certain young lady for whom [he] had affection" also to attend. This was Sarah Gomes de Souza Lemos, who in due time became Senhora de Kubitschek (EH.83).

Beginning of Kubitschek's Medical Career

Upon graduation from the Faculty of Medicine, Kubitschek received considerable help from his brother-in-law, Dr. Julio Soares, in getting started in his career. Soares secured him a position as assistant in the third ward of the surgical clinic of the Belo Horizonte Hospital. He also offered Juscelino a post as his assistant in his own private practice, a move which, as Kubitschek later wrote, meant that he was not to remain semi-inactive, in a deserted office, waiting for problematic clients. Under the supervision of Soares, Juscelino performed his first operation, the successful amputation of a leg. Within a short while he was doing three operations a week, which as he commented "was an excellent number for a recently graduated assistant" (EH.87).

Belo Horizonte was one of the major centers of the Brazilian medical profession in the late 1920s. It had many of the country's leading physicians and surgeons, and they made it a point to keep abreast of medical developments in Europe, and particularly in Paris. Working with many of these doctors, Kubitschek was in a position to learn a great deal about his profession during those first years. For two years he worked hard as a physician and surgeon. Also, for the first time in his life he was making a decent living, and was able to save a substantial amount of money.

During this period, Kubitschek took only passing interest in politics. He listened to discussions among some of his colleagues who were strong partisans of one or another of the leading politicians of Minas Gerais, but apparently did not take any active part in these discussions. In fact, Juscelino did not even vote until the fateful election of 1930. At that time, as he reported many years later, he cast his first vote for Getúlio Vargas (EH.89).

First Trip to Europe

After a little more than two years of activity in his profession, Kubitschek had saved enough money to afford an extended trip to Europe. The excuse, if not the reason, for this voyage was to go to Paris, then one of the world's great centers of medical study, to attend a course which would add to his professional knowledge. Undoubtedly, the lure of travel and adventure was also a prime motive for the young man to undertake a voyage which members of his family, particularly his mother, thought "crazy."

Kubitschek left Brazil late in April 1930 greatly enjoying the long sea voyage, and finally reached Paris. He settled down in a small hotel near the Hospital Cochin. There he inscribed in the course in urology given by Maurice Chevassu, then one of the most famous doctors in the French capital. He also registered for courses in anatomy and surgical techniques in the School of Medicine. These courses lasted three months. Regarding Chevassu, he noted that

> Chevassu must be included in the list of demanding professors. However, once the natural strangeness of the first contact had been overcome, the apprenticeship became fascinating. After the classes, the techniques discussed were debated. Each one gave his opinion with the greatest frankness. It was a pleasure to attend those discussions, given the humility with which the illustrious scientist listened and cleared up the doubts of the students. (EH.103)

Although Juscelino worked hard for the eight hours a day of classes during these three months, his time was by no means totally taken up with studying. As he wrote many years later: "With the end of the study period, I went out to enjoy myself, with the other students, in long discussions in the small bars of the neighborhood." He met a number of other Brazilians there with whom he became friends, including Cândido Portinari, who was later to become Brazil's most famous painter (EH.101). Kubitschek also took advantage of his stay in Paris to sightsee, and to become imbued with the history of the French capital. He not only visited all of the famous buildings of the city, but also read some French history.

Once his courses in Paris were successfully completed, Juscelino took an extended trip around the Mediterranean. He visited Italy, Egypt, the Holy Land, and Turkey. He then went up through Central Europe, visiting Vienna, Budapest, and Prague, and ending up in Berlin, which was another major center of medical research and practice. He intended to spend two months there also sitting in on medical courses. However, soon after Kubitschek reached Berlin, word came of the beginning of the 1930 revolution in Brazil. He cut short his stay in the German capital, quickly visited one or two of the other cities which he had planned to see in Germany, and returned to Paris. There, he and other Brazilian friends received word that the revolution had triumphed in their homeland.

Kubitschek recorded in his memoirs his great surprise at the victory of the 1930 revolution. He attributed this surprise to two things, "the belief which [he] had then in the stability of governments and from knowing that the movement in Minas was headed by governor Olegario Maciel" (EH.123-24). Once the revolution had triumphed, Juscelino and his friends were anxious to get home as soon as possible. Perhaps with the wisdom of hindsight, Kubitschek wrote several decades later in his memoirs about the sensations which he experienced regarding the prospect of returning home under the changed circumstances.

> On leaving the Embassy, walking down the Avenue des Champs Elysees, still perplexed, in asking myself what would be happening in Belo Horizonte at that moment, I had the sudden sensation, in a kind of mysterious premonition, that not only Brazil had changed its

destiny, but also I, in my simplicity. And it is true that the course of my life was to receive from that day on, under the influence of the victorious Revolution, a profound transformation. (EH.126)

Marriage

Upon the return to Brazil, Juscelino again threw himself energetically into his professional duties. He at first renewed his practice together with his brother-in-law, Julio Soares, but after a few months established his own office on a different floor of the same building. He also returned to the service which he gave gratis to the charity hospital, the Santa Casa, as well as to a position as doctor in the Medical Service of the Official Printing Office. Finally, he again took up his post as assistant in the Medical Physics Department of the university, and began studying to enter a competition for a professor's post in the Faculty of Medicine. Kubitschek summed up his life after his return home as follows: "Intense Life. Assured medical practice. Extension of my reputation as a doctor" (EH.136).

However, Kubitschek also had something else on his mind. When passing through Rio de Janeiro on his way home, he had seen Sarah, who was spending some time with one of her brothers in the capital. They had decided to get married sometime in 1931, the fixing of the date to depend on the reorganization of his clinic (EH.136). The date was finally set for 30 December 1931. Juscelino's bride-to-be came from a very distinguished Minas Gerais family. She was the daughter of Jaime Gomes de Souza Lemos, who had been a federal deputy for thirty years. Her mother was the daughter of an important figure of the empire period, José Duarte de Costa Negrão, a very wealthy landowner. On both sides, she had other distinguished ancestors. As a result of his marriage, Kubitschek came to be related to a number of Minas Gerais' leading political figures.

Juscelino and Sarah decided to be married in Rio de Janeiro, rather than in Belo Horizonte, as might have been expected. He explained that the reason for this was that they wanted to have it an intimate wedding, with only the members of the immediate family present. This would have been impossible in Belo Horizonte, in view of the large circle of relatives in Sarah's family (EH.143). The couple spent their honeymoon in Copacabana, at a hotel on the Avenida Atlantica one block from the beach. After celebrating New Year's Eve at the Copacabana Palace Hotel, they returned to Belo Horizonte and moved into a house which Juscelino had rented with two floors, and enormous garden, near Liberty Square. In his memoirs, he summed up his situation writing: "New house. New life. And consequently, more extensive projects for the future" (EH.159).

Kubitschek and the Constitutionalist Revolution of 1932

One of the many jobs which Kubitschek had undertaken upon his return to Belo Horizonte was that of being a medical captain in the Minas Gerais State Police (Força Publica). Although this was normally a position which required very little of his time, in July 1932, he was called into active service and for three months played a role in the civil war which had been launched by São Paulo on 9 July 1932.

The São Paulo uprising was the culmination of almost two years of growing disenchantment among São Paulo political leaders with the revolution of October 1930. It was launched in the name of "constitutionalism," the demand that the provisional government of Getúlio Vargas give way to an elected regime. There was widespread sympathy in other states for this demand. Kubitschek noted in his memoirs what his own attitude had been: "In my heart . . . I felt that São Paulo was right. Two years had passed since Washington Luíz was deposed, and it was time to reestablish the democratic regime, with full constitutional guarantees for the people" (EH.164). However, after some hesitation, the government of Minas Gerais decided to support the federal regime against the Paulista rebels. When São Paulo troops invaded Minas Gerais, a combination of Força Publica and federal troops was rushed to the vicinity of Passa Quatro (also known as the Sector of the Tunnel), to confront them. Captain Kubitschek was mobilized to go with the Força Publica troops.

When he arrived at the front, Captain Kubitschek was ordered to set up an emergency hospital in Passa Quatro. The only medical facility there was a small charity ward for first aid, run by a nun. There was very little medical equipment and the facilities were totally inadequate. However, Kubitschek, with the help of the nun and some volunteers, quickly established a small hospital which

41

included an operating room. The first operation he performed used the services of a veterinarian as anaesthetist. With the arrival of a medical train, with more or less adequate equipment and a staff of physicians, surgeons, nurses and other technicians, some of the pressure was taken off of the little improvised hospital which Kubitschek had established, although it remained in service throughout the three months of the battle in that sector. Kubitschek however, spent much of that time actually at the front, taking care of wounded soldiers and of others who had become ill.

This experience at Passa Quatro was of great importance to Kubitschek, both in his profession as a physician and surgeon and as a major step in initiating his political career. His services as a doctor were recognized in the official report of Dr. Magalhães Góis, chief of the Health Service of the military police of the state. He wrote that

> Dr. Juscelino Kubitschek—Surgeon of the Hospital of Passa Quatro—temperament of a Slav, calm, very modest, extremely disciplined, resistance of steel, in one day treated more than forty wounded, without respite, was a great revelation for the health service. He showed himself a most excellent surgeon, an improvisor of the means of helping the badly wounded of the war, with impeccable education, intelligence and discrete manner. His praise can be summed up by noting here the request of officers of the Army, leaving for the front, to have him as the surgeon, in case of being wounded in battle. (EH.190)

Kubitschek himself said of this experience that

> it is curious to note how little facts sometimes have profound consequences, and even come to modify in a surprising way, human existence. In my case, coming to the Sector of the Tunnel represented one of these "little facts." I was at Passa Quatro only to be a doctor. However, good luck smiled upon me. I won friends. I saved human lives. I confronted difficult situations and, to overcome them, was obliged to call upon forces which

existed within me in a latent state and which I really didn't know I had. (EH.190)

Kubitschek added that

The Sector of the Tunnel—I don't know by what strange reason of fate—ended up being the seedbed of a new generation of politicians. . . . A colonel of the Army—Eurico Gaspar Dutra—would be minister of war and president of the republic. Three state governors emerged from the trenches of Maniqueira: Captain Ernest Dorneles, of Rio Grande do Sul; Captain Zacharias Assumpcão, of Pará; and the Chief of Police of the Sector, Benedito Valadares, of Minas Gerais. And finally—a medical captain of the Força Publica of Minas as governor of his state and president of the republic. (EH.190-91)

This last, of course, was Kubitschek himself.

First Steps in Politics

One of the friendships which Juscelino made during his short military career, that with Benedito Valadares, led directly to his initiation into politics. In September 1933, Olgario Maciel died. He was the only elected state governor who had not been replaced by a presidentially-named interventor after the revolution of 1930. As a result, President Vargas got the opportunity to name an interventor in Minas Gerais to take his place. After much maneuvering, Vargas finally chose Valadares for that post. Shortly after taking office, Valadares asked Kubitschek to serve in his cabinet as "Chief of the Civil Household." This post involved working very closely with the interventor, and being in general charge of organizing the work of the state administration.

Kubitschek at first refused the post. He had absolutely no intention of abandoning his medical practice. He feared that the job as chief of the civil household would make it impossible to continue with his profession, since he would have to devote virtually full time to the new work. However, Valadares refused to take no for an answer. Three days after Kubitschek's refusal of the post, the interventor used the occasion of a ceremony in the military hospital of the Força Publica, at which Juscelino was present as one of the hospital's surgeons, to comment that he had such a high regard for the staff of the military hospital that he had chosen one of its doctors to be the head of his civil household. In the face of that announcement, Kubitschek felt that he had no alternative but to take the post. It was arranged with Valadares that he would continue some of his medical practice, particularly his work as a surgeon (EH.213).

This introduction into the political life of the state of Minas Gerais gave Kubitschek an opportunity to become very well acquainted with both the problems of the state and the political leaders on all levels. Valadares turned over to Juscelino the handling of relations with the mayors and other officials of the various municipalities of the state. They regularly came to the capital to present to the state government the problems of their towns and cities, and to ask for financial help and other kinds of aid to solve them. It was Kubitschek who handled these matters for Interventor Valadares.

Aside from being an indication of the trust which the interventor had in Kubitschek, this work was a major contribution to Juscelino's political education. In his memoirs, he commented that

> in those interviews, which were exhaustive, I succeeded before long, in penetrating the secrets of the rivalries in the hinterland. After a few months, I knew all of the municipal situations of the State and I could, without any hesitation, propose realistic alternatives, which would contribute to regional pacification. (EH.222)

The presence of Kubitschek in the state cabinet proved to be a godsend to the people of Diamantina. The political boss who had dominated that part of the state for a generation had been ousted as a result of the revolution of 1930, and the political leadership of the area was in great disarray. In addition, the town and its environs had deteriorated economically since Juscelino had left it fifteen years before. With his elevation to a key post in the state administration, Kubitschek was deluged with requests for aid from the local politicians and rank and file citizens. He was able to make resources available to start the process of reconstructing the public buildings and the general economy of the region. In the process, he converted himself into a popular political figure in the Diamantina area.

Valadares' confidence in Kubitschek was demonstrated in other ways. For one, the interventor had his chief of civil household accompany him on frequent trips, not only around the state, but to Rio de Janeiro and elsewhere. On one of these occasions, Kubitschek had his first encounter with Vargas. He accompanied Valadares to the summer capital at Petrópolis to confer with the president. From the way in which Juscelino later remembered it, it would appear that the usually very reserved Vargas and the extroverted and voluble Kubitschek found one another's company enjoyable, and each developed considerable respect for the other's capacities (EH.217).

Meanwhile, the process of "reconstitutionalization" of Brazil was moving forward. In May 1933 a national constitutional assembly was elected, and by early 1934 it had finished its work. One of its last acts was to choose Vargas as the first "constitutional president" to govern under the new constitution. In accordance with the new situation, further elections were necessary for the federal Chamber of Deputies and for state constitutional assemblies, which would write new state constitutions, and also choose new governors and members of the federal senate. These elections were held in 4 October 1934.

Once more, Interventor Valadares indicated his confidence in Juscelino in September 1934, when Kubitschek was named Secretary of the Progressive party (PP), to conduct the final work of the election campaign. Kubitschek noted years later that his "party affiliation had nothing to do with any doctrinal conviction; it was imposed by the ties of friendship. Further, none of those parties had an authentic program or supported a specific cause." The PP had been organized in February 1933 to bring together most of the state's major political figures and was, as Juscelino described it, a "political 'bag full of cats'" (EH.232).

Kubitschek was also named a candidate of the PP for the federal Chamber of Deputies. In the 4 October 1934 election, he won, along with most of the other Progressive party candidates, and received the highest vote of any of its nominees for the Chamber (EH.233).

Deputy Kubitschek

For about three years, Kubitschek served as a member of the federal Chamber of Deputies. However, he was not one of the members of Congress who drew wide national attention. He was very assiduous in attending meetings of committees, but seldom took the platform in plenary sessions of the body. He showed particular concern for the welfare of the postal and telegraph employees and with problems of public health. However, by his own admission, Kubitschek was hesitant and bashful during those years in the Congress, handicaps which he agreed that he outgrew in subsequent years. Later, he attributed his reticence in Congress to his humble origins.[7] However, although a member of the federal Congress, which met in Rio de Janeiro, Kubitschek continued to be secretary of the Progressive party, which meant that he had to spend a large part of his time in Belo Horizonte and elsewhere in his native state.

In mid-1936 he was asked by then Governor Benedito Valadares to undertake a new task, both pleasant and difficult. The opponents of the Progressive party tended to be predominant in Juscelino's native district of Diamantina. The governor wanted to change this situation. In pursuance of the reconstitutionalization process, the first municipal elections in Minas Gerais since 1930 were planned for June 1936, and Governor Valadares asked Kubitschek to undertake to lead the cause of the Progressive Party in those elections. The result would be, if he was successful, that he would become the *chefe politico*, or political boss of that part of the state. Juscelino finally agreed to undertake the task.

The job was far from being an easy one. Juscelino had not lived in Diamantina for fifteen years, and had visited it only very occasionally in the interim. His political supporters when he began the municipal campaign were largely confined to members of his admittedly quite extensive family, and a few politicians whom he had been able to favor from his position as chief of the civil household of the interventor. However, Kubitschek threw himself very energetically into the campaign in Diamantina. The experience was a very new one for him, and it contributed substantially to the development of the political style which was later to come to characterize him. It was the first time that he had really had to campaign, since his job as chefe da casa civil was an appointive one, and his election as deputy had come about more because of the general triumph of the list favored by the interventor than because of his own exertions.

Kubitschek himself admitted many years later that the style of campaigning which he adopted was a new one for Diamantina. In the past, representatives of the dominant party in the state had been accustomed to bringing in the state police and using other methods of coercion to "convince" people to vote for the candidates of the party. But this was not Kubitschek's way of doing things. Spending two months in the campaign, Kubitschek started a door-to-door effort, throughout the town of Diamantina, and in the twelve rural districts which were part of the municipio of Diamantina. He particularly sought the support of the humbler voters, and in one case won over the principal maid of one of his most rabid political opponents. He for the first time put into effect the hand shaking and personal conversation techniques which were to become his hallmarks later in his political life. He visited people in their homes and accepted their humble hospitality at a meal or for just a cup of coffee.

During his excursions into the interior of the municipio, his being a medical doctor stood him in good stead, at least politically. People lined up by the scores if not hundreds in the isolated villages he visited, to get free medical advice and treatment from the visiting doctor—and hopefully to vote for his candidates subsequently. However, it was not just Juscelino who campaigned. His wife Sarah and his sister Naná, recruiting Juscelino's several aunts to help them, also campaigned vigorously, concentrating particularly on work among the housewives of the area.

The last event of the campaign was his first public speech, at the Clube Flamengo in the center of Diamantina. In his memoirs, he described that speech as follows:

> When I began to speak, I felt cold sweat. But the voice, in the beginning hesitant, soon became sure. I spoke about peace and progress. I promised the conservation and restauration of Diamantina, as an architechtonic relic. I announced the construction of roads, of bridges, of schools, and of hotels. But I did not do so vaguely, as was the practice at the time. I cited the name of each road, indicating its course and its length. I gave the number of bridges and said where they would be

constructed. I spoke of schools, indicating the place where they would be built, and how many students they would hold. And, concerning the hotel, I proclaimed its need since, if I was victorious at the ballot boxes, I would convert Diamantina into a center of tourist attraction. It was a developmentalist message, albeit in embryo. (EH.254)

Juscelino's candidates won by 120 votes. The Progressive Party elected eleven of the fifteen members of the municipal council of Diamantina. The victory coverted Kubitschek into the official political leader of the district, although his friend Joubert Guerra was named the prefect (mayor) of the municipality.

Prelude to Coup d'etat

As the end of Vargas' term as constitutional president approached, the democratic regime entered into crisis. Vargas did not want to give up the presidency, and intended to avoid doing so, if at all possible. However, there were a number of important political figures who stood in the way of what Kubitschek called in his memoirs "continuismo," the maintenance of Vargas in the presidency in defiance of constitutional provision. One of these was Antônio Carlos de Andrada, ex-governor of Minas Gerais, and one of the principal architects of the revolution of 1930 which had put Vargas in power. Antônio Carlos had run unsuccessfully against Vargas when the constitutional assembly had elected the first president under the constitution of 1934. In 1936, he was the leader of the Minas Gerais bloc in the Chamber of Deputies and president of the chamber as well.

Another major impediment to Getúlio's remaining in office was the governor of Rio Grande do Sul, José Antônio Flores da Cunha. He, too, had been one of the main organizers of the 1930 revolution, and for several years had been the dominant figure in Vargas' home state. He undoubtedly had presidential ambitions of his own. In Rio Grande do Sul, there was the additional inconvenience, insofar as Vargas was concerned, that General Lucio Esteves, the commander of the Second Army based in Rio Grande do Sul, and the largest element in the Brazilian armed forces, was not favorable to "continuismo."

In the face of this situation, Vargas moved very cautiously. He allowed the campaign to elect his successor to proceed, and by the middle of 1937 there were three candidates. One was Armando Sales, the governor of São Paulo and clearly an opposition nominee. Another was Plinio Salgado, head of the fascist party Acão Integralista Brasileira, who was a participant in the plot to keep Vargas in power. The third nominee was José Américo de Almeida, who for some months seemed to be the government's candidate to succeed Vargas. Also a major participant in the revolution of 1930, José Américo was one of the principal political leaders of the Northeast. His candidacy was orchestrated by Benedito Valadares, governor of Minas Gerais, and a known confidante of President Vargas.

The Role of Benedito Valadares

By the time the election campaign began, Valadares had already cooperated in removing Antônio Carlos from any positions in which he might be able to offer resistance to the president's planned coup d'etat. First, he had engineered the removal of the ex-governor as chief of the Minas Gerais delegation in the Chamber of Deputies, and then he had succeeded in bringing about the defeat of Antônio Carlos for reelection as president of the Chamber. Although at first apparently believing that Vargas intended to go ahead with an election, at some point Valadares was won over to the idea of Getúlio's continuing in office, and to the idea of the coup d'etat which the president was planning to achieve that end. He played a major role in the final stage of preparation for the coup, by dispatching Francisco Negrão de Lima, one of his closest associates in Minas Gerais politics, to visit all of the governors of the north and northeast—except Carlos de Lima Cavalcanti of Pernambuco and Juracy Magalhães of Baia, who were known to be against Vargas' continuing in office.

It was Negrão de Lima's job to outline to each of the governors the nature of the new fascist constitution which Vargas was planning to issue. He was told not to talk to anyone except the governors, but word got out very quickly concerning what was about to take place. Negrão de Lima said many years later that this fact proved very embarrassing to several of the governors, and removed the element of complete surprise from the coup itself. After his trip

49

to the north and northeast, Negrão de Lima also went to São Paulo to explain what was going to happen to the man who had succeeded Armando Sales as governor of that state. Governor Cardoso de Melo Neto told Negrão de Lima that he wanted nothing to do with the coup, although he understood the necessity for President Vargas to carry it out.[8]

By the time of Negrão de Lima's trips, the last really major center of possible opposition to the coup in Rio Grande do Sul had been removed. First, General Lucio Esteves was replaced by General Daltro Filho, an officer who was apparently aware of and supported the coup plans which were afoot. Then on 16 October, General Daltro Filho decreed the incorporation of the state military police of Rio Grande do Sul into the federal Army, whereupon Governor Flores da Cunha resigned and fled to Uruguay.

Kubitschek and the Preparations for the Coup

Kubitschek played at best a minor role in the developments leading up to the Vargas coup of 10 November 1937. Of course, he owed his political career to Benedito Valadares, and so cooperated with him in the first stages of Valadares' involvement. However, Valadares obviously did not take Juscelino into his confidence once he, Valadares, was clearly launched as a participants in the plot to bring about a coup d'etat from the presidential palace. In his memoirs, Kubitschek insisted that

> my attitude had been clear and defined from the beginning. Various times I discussed the matter with Benedito Valadares—who was our leader. In the interviews, I indicated my opinion with the greatest frankness. I thought that the regime should be consolidated through free elections, with the rulers succeeding one another in accord with the sovereign wishes of the people. (EH.310)

As a result of his attitude, Juscelino was not taken into Valadares' confidence as the plotting moved ahead. However, Kubitschek had played some part in events earlier in the year. For instance, he supported the move to replace Antônio Carlos as leader of the Minas Gerais delegation in the Chamber. The announcement

50

of the change in the Chamber gave rise to spontaneous demonstration of support among the deputies for Antônio Carlos as president of the body. Kubitschek noted many years later that

> in that sea of shouting voices, of raised arms, of vehement protests, only the Minas government party bloc, of which I was a part, remained seated, shocked by what was happening in the room. So many years later, I still remember, with regret, that day so crucial for us . . . Our attitude was in accordance with an absolute duty of party discipline, since Benedito Valadares had decided, and we, his fellow party members and friends, could not fail to give our support. (EH.269)

Kubitschek also played a role in launching the candidacy of José Américo de Almeida as the supposed pro-government candidate. As intermediary between Valadares and José Américo, he succeeded in obtaining from the latter a promise that if elected, he would support whoever was chosen by Valadares to be his successor as governor of Minas Gerais.

By early November 1937, Juscelino was aware, as were virtually all the other political leaders, that a coup was going to be made by the president. He therefore returned to Belo Horizonte, had his license plate which had the initials CN (Congreso Nacional) on it replaced by another—an action noted in the local press—and took steps to return to his medical practice. He was sure that he would not be a deputy for much longer, and that his political career would be over in the wake of the coup which was virtually inevitable. On the morning of 10 November 1937, hearing rumors that something was under way, Juscelino went to the governor's palace, the Palacio de Liberdade. As he entered Governor Valadares' office, the governor greeted him, "God day, my dear ex-deputy!" (EH.313). So ended the first stage of Kubitschek's political career.

Chapter 4

MAYOR OF BELO HORIZONTE

With the advent of the Estado Novo dictatorship on 10 November 1937, Kubitschek returned to his activities as physician and surgeon. For almost two and a half years he was again immersed in intense professional activity, as well as trying his hand with mixed results at being a businessman. However, in April 1940, Juscelino's political career was once again renewed, this time as mayor of Belo Horizonte, a post in which he was to develop many of the attitudes and policies which were later to characterize him as governor of Minas Gerais and as president of Brazil.

Return to Medicine

With his return to medical practice, Juscelino reopened his private doctor's office, where he took care of his patients each afternoon. The mornings he spent either at the Military Hospital, where he reassumed the functions of Chief of Urology Service, or at the Charity Hospital, the Santa Casa. At both hospitals his duties were mainly in the operating room as a surgeon.

However, Kubitschek soon found that the three years of political life had had negative effects upon his technique as a surgeon. He found himself working too slowly and frequently hesitating, "two weaknesses with unforeseeable effects in certain situations, where the time and rapidity of action were elements of greatest importance."[1] He felt that it would not be appropriate for him to try to solve this problem by returning as a student to the Medical School. Instead, he made arrangements with the director of the Medical School to be given access in the evenings to the anatomic amphitheater, where medical students practiced surgery on cadavers, so that he could practice his surgical skills with no one to observe him and without any danger of hurting a patient. For three months he continued these somewhat erie nocturnal visits, until, as he recounted, "I reacquired my former skill and became accustomed once again to anatomical practice" (EH.333).

Although his professional activities kept him very busy, there was time for relaxation. Juscelino became an habitué after his afternoon office hours of a restaurant on the main street of Belo Horizonte, the Confeitaria California, where he would have an aperitive with friends. He commented that the attendance there "was always large, but inconstant. There were only three assiduous participations, Milton Campos, Pedro Aleixo and I" (EH.348). The family life of the Kubitschek household was much more regular than it had been when Juscelino had been a deputy. He was generally home in the evenings, sometimes bringing friends home with him for dinner, which Sarah would prepare. This was in great contrast to his years as a congressman when, as he was to admit in his memoirs, he "was a João César de Oliveira, deputy, reliving the life of the travelling salesman in the era of the automobile and the airplane" (EH.330).

When he abandoned his role as a politician, he not only ceased to be a deputy, he ceased to be the *chefe politico* in Diamantina. However, he by no means lost his interest in his native town. In March 1938, when Diamantina celebrated the hundredth anniversary of its foundation, Juscelino was invited to participate in the festivities. All the members of the family resident in Belo Horizonte—including Juscelino's mother, who was then living with her daughter in the capital—took the long train ride to their provincial home town. There were several days of dancing, speech giving, fireworks, and other activities. The high point was the dedication of a plaza, the Praça Juscelino Kubitschek, in front of the court house. Among the speeches on this occasion was one by Juscelino himself, after which he led the whole crowd in singing the traditional folksong *Peixe Vivo* (Live Fish), which had been his theme song two years before in his campaign to become chefe politico of Diamantina (EH.337-38).

Kubitschek the Businessman

It was during these years of return to the medical profession that Kubitschek laid the basis for the small fortune which he was to acquire. His medical practice was quite lucrative, and it provided him with considerable funds to invest. He put these funds into two different kinds of activities, one of which proved to be very profitable, the other of which was a disaster.

Kubitschek's profitable investments were in land, company stock, and apartments. In his memoirs, he noted that

> Belo Horizonte was then going through a phase of intense real estate speculation. The city was growing, and many bet on its future. What was bought today could be worth twice as much in a year. Subdivisions were being laid out in the nearby area. And I was to be found among the buyers. What I acquired in that period, rising in value with time, gave me later a situation of economic independence. (EH.346)

However, all of Kubitschek's investments were not successful. One of these was a commercial enterprise, a wholesale warehousing company, in which he, his brother-in-law Julio Soares, and a friend, Dorinato Lima, became partners. All being very busy doctors, the three partners turned the management of the business over to a person in their confidence who had carte blanche to act. Unfortunately, this individual proved not to be worthy of the partners' trust, and they finally liquidated the enterprise, sharing the loss equally among themselves.

Subsequent events tended to prove that this was indeed the period, when he was out of politics, that Kubitschek laid the basis for his modest fortune. Virtually throughout his subsequent political career, Kubitschek was to be accused by his political enemies of having gotten rich through the corrupt use of public office. In his memoirs, Juscelino mentions the occasion for one such accusation, his campaign for the presidency in 1955. However, much later, during the presidency and afterwards the same charges were made against him, by word of mouth and sometimes more openly.

However, the most serious effort to develop a case against Kubitschek as an allegedly corrupt politician was made in the years immediately following the coup of 1964. His military enemies, who then controlled the government and were exceedingly anxious to prove charges against him of both subversion and corruption, were unable to come up with any evidence sufficient to bring any formal charges against him. Indeed, they sought evidence in at least three countries—in Brazilian company and bank records, and in similar sources in the United States and in Europe—but were unable to come up with anything convincing even before a hostile military court. One is therefore left with the conclusion that Kubitschek was correct when he claimed that it was in the period of the late 1930s that, with funds which he earned from his medical practice, he was able to make certain real estate and other investments in and around Belo Horizonte which proved quite profitable subsequently, and were the basis of whatever fortune he possessed.

Juscelino Named Mayor of Belo Horizonte

Kubitschek remained on friendly personal terms with his political benefactor Benedito Valadares, who continued to be governor of Minas Gerais—the only state chief executive to continue to hold that title—after the establishment of the Estado Novo. From time to time, Juscelino went to see his friend in the Palacio de Liberdade and exchanged views with him on the course of national and international politics. Early in 1940, Valadares called in Juscelino to tell him that he wanted to name him as mayor (prefect) of Belo Horizonte, a post which under the then existing order was at the disposal of the governor. Kubitschek refused the offer, saying that he did not want to abandon once again his medical practice, and that he had no aspiration to seek a permanent career in politics.

This was certainly one of the reasons which made Juscelino hesitate to accept a new political position. Another may have been his disapproval of the Estado Novo regime, an issue which we shall discuss shortly. Finally, he certainly had doubts about working in a position which depended so directly on Governor Valadares. The governor was an imperious man who was not very much inclined to delegate authority, and who quite often interfered with the details of administration which were supposed to be the province of those working under him.

However, Juscelino's lifetime friend, José Maria Alkmin, whom he informed of the offer, urged him to accept. He insisted that the nature of the mayor's position was such that Valadares, who had no great interest in municipal affairs in any case, would not be likely to interfere. Alkmin also argued that being mayor would not preclude Juscelino's continuing with his medical practice, albeit on a reduced scale. As Kubitschek summed up this argument in his memoirs, he "could be a doctor-prefect or a prefect-doctor, whichever was more convenient for [him]" (EH.350).

Nevertheless, Kubitschek persisted in resisting the offer. Governor Valadares then played the same kind of game with him that he had done when he had named him Chefe da Casa Civil several years earlier. He ordered that there be printed in the state's official bulletin of 16 April 1940 a decree naming Kubitschek as prefect of Belo Horizonte. Under these circumstances, Kubitschek accepted the nomination, and served for the next five years as the chief executive of the capital city of Minas Gerais.

A Democrat Serving a Dictatorship?

In accepting the post of mayor of Belo Horizonte, did Kubitschek betray his own democratic principles? Before looking in some detail at his career as mayor, it is of interest to raise this question, and to determine why a professed democrat would consent to serve in a position of considerable responsibility in a regime which was clearly an oppressive dictatorship.

Certainly, Kubitschek was quite aware of the nature of the Estado Novo regime which Vargas had established on 10 November 1937. In his memoirs, he recorded his own reaction to the setting up of the Estado Novo. He wrote as follows:

> As far as I, an ex-deputy was concerned, what was my intimate reaction? The same as that reflected in everyone's face. Disillusionment. Despondency. Desperation. Until November 10, I had been part of the representative machinery of a democratic regime. I carried out, therefore, like many others, the role of delegate of thousands of electors, spread through all the regions of Minas. And suddenly, everything had changed. . . . In this situation . . . I did not succeed in escaping the pessimism which was the characteristic of the collective consciousness. In reality, the reaction in Minas to the institution of the Estado Novo had been very bad. (EH.318)

Nor does Kubitschek in any way defend the Estado Novo in his memoirs. He says of it that "The Estado Novo carried out, with apparent security, its mission of anaesthetizing the national conscience. The people were not informed of anything. And the solutions, when they became known to the public, were presented as accomplished facts. Getúlio Vargas had not altered his traditional political line. His objective was the strengthening of his personal authority" (EH.339).

In his book *A Escalada Politica*, Kubitschek summed up the Estado Novo thus: "Brazil . . . had in its internal organization a totalitarian structure: an imposed Constitution; suppression of the two legislative houses; dissolution of the political parties—in summary, a dictatorial regime, with the suspension of all individual guarantees and rigid censorship of the press."[2]

Nor was Juscelino unaware of the importance of the question which we have raised. In a conversation with me in 1972, he recognized the validity of the issue, and said that it should be answered. He gave two explanations at that time for having agreed to become an important official of the Estado Novo. One was that when he first rejected Governor Valadares' offer of the mayoralty, in part on the grounds of his disagreement with the Estado Novo, Valadares had told him that Vargas was coming to Minas Gerais soon to make a speech in which he would announce both elections and a return to democratic government. Valadares added that the real reason he needed Kubitschek in the mayor's post, therefore, was to organize the voters for the forthcoming elections.[3] Kubitschek repeated this account in his memoirs and said there that Valadares' explanation almost convinced him, added that "It was a good chance to attempt to collaborate for the return of the democratic regime in Brazil, being in a leading position and being able to exert influence in political circles" (EH.349). Of course, Vargas never did make that speech.

Kubitschek's second explanation to me was that during his years as mayor of Belo Horizonte he remained loyal to his democratic beliefs and continued to advocate the need to return to a democratic regime.[4] The validity of that claim is impossible to check. There were probably at least three other factors which influenced Juscelino to accept and continue in the job of mayor of Belo Horizonte. One was his personal relationship with Valadares. The governor had been his political sponsor since he had entered politics. Furthermore, they remained personal friends, and Juscelino continued to visit him in the governor's palace from time to time.

He felt that public opinion in Minas Gerais, and particularly in Belo Horizonte, had been unduly harsh in condemning Valadares' role in the events preceding 10 November 1937 and as governor under the Estado Novo. Juscelino thus very much sympathized with his friend on a personal basis, and wanted to help him as much as he could.

Another factor which probably weighted in Kubitschek's decision to accept the mayor's post was that he had found that he liked the political life during the three years that he had so far engaged in it. He mentions this several times in his memoirs. Furthermore, Juscelino almost certainly saw the mayor's job as a challenge. He summed up this aspect of the question when he said in his memoirs

> If Brazil was under the regime of exception, which was repugnant to my democratic background, I consoled myself with the nature of the post which I would occupy. An administrative post, par excellence. Until now, I had worked on the human organism. Henceforward, the material with which I was going to deal would be a city. It was also an organism consisting of similar organs. Streets which were arteries and veins. A respiratory system. Traffic network which was a kind of blood circulation. Parks which were similar to the lungs. Only my work would be different. As a doctor, I always had as the objective the welfare of the patient. But as prefect, I would be curing urban infirmities, looking after the well being of hundreds of thousands of people. (EH.355)

Kubitschek's Style of Government

It was as mayor of Belo Horizonte that Kubitschek first developed the style of government which he used as both governor of Minas Gerais and president of Brazil. This style had many different aspects. Among the most important of these were having a clear vision of what he wanted to accomplish, being willing to try to do things which other people thought were impossible, spending exceedingly long hours and intense concentration on the job, being in constant contact with the people whom he was governing, and keeping aware of how the programs of his government were being carried out.

As Belo Horizonte's prefect, Juscelino had a very clear view of what he wanted to accomplish. When he took over its direction, the state capital was a relatively new city, having been founded only in 1897. It was also a planned city, but a grave error had been made by its early planners. They had laid out a city for 25,000 people, whereas by the time Kubitschek became mayor it had grown to about ten times that size. As a result, the center of the city was planned, although the fulfillment of the original projects was not yet complete; outside of the center city, however, Belo Horizonte had grown chaotically. Furthermore, it was already archaic, having originally been conceived of as a "horse and buggy" city, before the advent of the automobile.

Kubitschek saw his task as being one first of finishing work on the city center, and second of bringing order out of the chaos in the areas beyond the heart of the metropolis. He also sought to make Belo Horizonte a city adapted to the motor age, which meant building streets wide enough to accommodate automobile traffic, and constructing a series of "entry-ways" for the city, which ultimately would connect with highways leading to all parts of the state and to the major cities immediately beyond its borders. But Juscelino's vision went beyond that, influenced as it was by his experience as a medical doctor. He wanted to construct what he called "lungs" as well as "veins and arteries" in the city. He wanted to have areas where the people could get away from daily cares, could relax, could enjoy recreation and other facilities. In a word, he wanted to make Belo Horizonte not only a place to work but a place enjoyable to live in.

Kubitschek combined audaciousness with his vision of what needed to be done for the city. He frequently showed himself willing to undertake projects such as beginning to pave the main street of the city during his first week in office, and constructing a great recreational area on the edge of the city, which other politicians and many technical experts said were impossible. As he did later as governor and president, he showed that it *was* possible to accomplish many "impossible" things, although it might be difficult to do so.

Another integral part of Kubitschek's style of government as he first developed it in Belo Horizonte was his constant contacts with the people of all social and economic levels. This was a revolutionary innovation insofar as the governing of Belo Horizonte was concerned. He succeeded to the degree that, as he proudly said many years later, he was often hailed by boys in the streets with a cheery "Hi, Juscelino!" as he passed by. Kubitschek made it a policy to keep track of the many programs which he got under way. He never contented himself with just receiving reports from his subordinates about how things were progressing, but insisted on going out to see for himself, sometimes certainly to the consternation of those whose work he was inspecting.

Juscelino's Vision

One of Kubitschek's Brazilian biographers has observed that it was as mayor that he adopted the philosophy of what constituted a good administrator: that anyone holding such a job should be expected to maintain the routine services which depended on it, but that the hallmark of a good mayor (or governor or president) was the degree to which he went beyond just routine administration, and built for the future.[5]

Kubitschek certainly had a clear vision of the future direction that he wanted Belo Horizonte to take. He had grown exceedingly fond of the city, and recorded in his memoirs that he owed a great debt to the city, since it had made it possible for a very poor boy who arrived there with little more than the clothes on his back to become first a successful doctor, and then to have a political career of consequence. He sought to repay this debt by providing Belo Horizonte both with the infrastructure which would facilitate its daily life, and with the services which its people needed. When he came into office the city was lacking woefully in both of these things, and by the time he left the mayor's job, he had succeeded in making very great strides in converting what had been a rather backward and overgrown provincial town into a modern city.

Kubitschek himself has commented on his penchant for trying to do things which other people proclaimed to be unattainable. He wrote that there "always predominated in my personality . . . an interior impulse—perhaps the remnants of the mentality characteristic of mining prospectors—which always brought me to run a calculated risk, and in doing so, to have the satisfaction of seeing success finally crown my audacity." He goes on to note that Otavio

60

Dias Carneiro, "one of the most powerful minds that [he knew]," called this trait of Juscelino "the Kubitschekian instinct." That instinct he defined as one which impels a person in a certain direction independently of his will and at a certain moment, even when a thousand voices are heard denouncing the temerity of the step to be taken (EP.21). There were numerous instances of the "Kubitschekian instinct" during Juscelino's period as mayor of Belo Horizonte. Several of his major street building projects, his planning of whole new housing developments, and most of all his construction of the Pampulha recreation project, fell into this category. Certainly, the Kubitschekian instinct was closely associated with Juscelino's vision of what the city should be when he was finished being its mayor and for a long time thereafter. In order to fulfill that vision, he was willing and able to attempt many things which a person less willing to run risks would not have attempted.

Contact with the People

Another characteristic part of Juscelino's style of government as mayor of Belo Horizonte was his maintenance of constant contact with his constituents. He began this immediately upon taking office. He found that previous mayors had been virtually inaccessible to the general public, people having to pass through many anterooms, each with personnel to impede their progress, before getting to the mayor's office. Only politicians and personal friends ever succeeded in seeing the city's chief executive. Juscelino changed this immediately. He converted a large waiting room into his office, and began the practice of having office hours there from four to six each afternoon, during which time anyone wishing to see the mayor could do so. When the lines of prospective visitors got too long, he reversed the procedure, going out (accompanied by a secretary) to where they were waiting, and talking to each person there in succession. His secretary took notes of what problem each visitor had and the mayor tried to do what he could to help them with these problems.

However, his contacts with the people of Belo Horizonte went well beyond these meetings. He took advantage of his constant inspection tours of city projects to talk with passersby. Upon occasion, he did personal lobbying for one or other of his projects among people who were involved. One such case occurred in an

61

area in which he wanted to put through and pave a street, which would require the expropriation of some property from people living on both sides of it. The normal procedure would have been condemnation proceedings, which might have taken years to complete. Instead, Kubitschek opted for personal conversations with all of the people involved, and he succeeded in convincing all of them to sell the city the portion of their land needed to complete the project.

In the latter part of his period in office, Juscelino organized neighborhood committees throughout the city. The purpose of these committees was to keep the mayor informed about problems in their areas, and to undertake with some help from the city administration, projects which they could carry out themselves. These committees proved to be of great political help to Kubitschek after the end of the Estado Novo.

A Long Working Day

Still another characteristic of Juscelino as mayor of Belo Horizonte was his long hours of work. As a boy he acquired the habit of rising early. He now took advantage of this habit. He arose about 6 A.M., and after taking some coffee, he went out to inspect construction projects and other government programs around the city. In the late morning he went to the Military Hospital or the Santa Casa to perform one or more operations, and then at 1 P.M. returned home to have lunch with Sarah. The afternoons and early evenings were devoted to mayoral paper work and to receiving people who wanted to see him. Only after this work was done did Juscelino relax. He and his wife frequently had guests for dinner, either personal friends or political associates, and would often go to parties, receptions or dances later in the evening. Only after the birth of their child did they begin to limit this late evening social life. The furious pace of Kubitschek soon drew the attention not only of his fellow politicians, but of many of his constituents as well. As a result of it, he got the nickname "The Hurricane Prefect," which was to stick with him as long as he was mayor (EP.27,45).

Keeping Track

From the very beginning of his administration, Juscelino made it a practice to see for himself how the various projects of the city government were progressing. Workers became used to visits by the mayor to virtually any kind of city activity. These visits were made not only to construction sites, but to garbage collection centers, "popular" restaurants maintained by the city, administrative offices, and almost any other part of the municipality's activities. He would talk with the workers involved, conferring with those directing whatever it was he was inspecting. He wanted to know any problems which might have arisen, to help clear up difficulties if he could, and generally to encourage the workers and supervisors alike to work as well and as rapidly as possible. Mayor Kubitschek had a paternalistic attitude toward the city employees. In discussions with them during his visits of inspection, he frequently asked about their families as well as about the work in progress. Twice a year he sponsored large parties for the municipal employees and their families. He was always present, getting better acquainted with the workers themselves, and with their spouses and children.

That he had gained the confidence of at least many of the workers was demonstrated on the occasion of one of the few strikes which took place in the Belo Horizonte region during the Estado Novo period. When Juscelino was visiting Diamantina, he was summoned back to Belo Horizonte with great urgency by Governor Valadares, because the municipal garbage collectors had quit work. After conferring with his cabinet, Kubitschek decided to go to the garage where the strikers were assembled, to talk with them personally. Although tempers were running high among the strikers, he finally got them to name one of their number to explain what their grievances were. The most pressing was the wages which they received, which Juscelino immediately agreed were entirely too low.

Kubitschek was finally able to solve the situation by promising that their wages would immediately be increased, although he did not specify by how much. He asked them to trust him to resolve also as many of their other grievances as he could. They did trust him and went back to work. Juscelino's decision to parley with the workers first, while they were still on strike, rather than taking his cabinet members advice not to talk with them until they had returned to work was successful (EP.59-60).

Making Belo Horizonte a City of the Auto Age

When Kubitschek became prefect many of the streets in the old center of the city were still paved with cobblestones, and virtually none of the streets outside the center were paved at all. In addition, there were few if any city streets which could serve as links with highways, which did not yet exist but which certainly would have to be built, to connect the Minas Gerais capital with other parts of the state and country. Juscelino set out to change this. His first major project, for which he signed the construction contract only nine days after taking office, was the paving of Avenida Afonse Pena, which ran through the center of the city. He undertook to pave the whole length of this street, first doing the right side of the Avenida, and then the left. At the same time, he laid new sewer and water pipes and new electricity and telephone wires.

Juscelino admitted in his memoirs that this project disrupted traffic in the middle of the city for some months, and at first ran into considerable protest. He conceded that he was very lucky that Governor Valadares was out of the city for the first two months of the operation, and so did not see what was going on, although he heard reports about it. Fortunately Valadares was too busy hosting and politicking President Vargas to pay much attention to the Avenida Afonse Pena. Otherwise, Kubitschek said, he probably would have ordered the work suspended. By the time the governor got back to town, however, it was near enough to completion that suspending it was out of the question (EP.24).

Another early street building effort was one connecting the center of the city with the thoroughfare which ran all around the original city, separating it from the outlying areas which had grown up subsequently. This work required a massive landfill operation, to get the road across a large depression, as well as the building of two canals to channel streams which ran down this depression. The city did not possess enough trucks to haul the dirt which was needed for this landfill so Kubitschek advertised for private mule carts. Very quickly he had obtained the services of 10,000 mules, carts and their drivers. Observing them at work one day, Juscelino commented about the hard working mules that "they [were] the 10,000 most loyal workers that the Prefecture has" (EP.26)

Outside of the old center of the city, Mayor Kubitschek undertook to lay out new streets, the paving of many of those that had arisen during previous years, and the laying out of various new developments. These were important contributions to bringing some of the benefits of a modern city to the inhabitants of Belo Horizonte.

However, the street building project of which he was perhaps most proud was that which connected the city proper with the Pampulha recreation area. The plans which his municipal engineers presented him for this road by no means satisfied the prefect. In his memoirs, Juscelino commented that

> they had suggested a common means of communication, like the other roads existing in the state. There was no greatness in the project. . . . [He] proposed a road with a total length of 8 kilometres and a half, 25 meters wide in the urban perimeter, and 25 meters in the rural area. It would not be, then, only a road, but a true *boulevard*, of the type that I had seen in Paris, with separated lanes, with flower gardens, grassy shoulders, wooden seats for those who wished to relax on them, and above all, wide open spaces, pleasant to the view and relaxing to the nerves. (EP.46-47)

It was along these lines that the road was constructed.

Other Municipal Projects

The construction of streets was only one of many types of projects which Kubitschek undertook during the five years that he presided over Belo Horizonte. Very early he was interested in fostering real estate developments, both low cost housing estates and luxurious projects. One of his first successes in this regard was to interest the Industrial Workers Social Security Fund in building a housing development for the benefit of their worker members in the newer part of the city. This was one of the first such schemes to be constructed by the various social security funds anywhere in Brazil. Subsequently, Juscelino succeeded in getting several similar projects constructed by other social security funds (EP.32). Of quite a different type was what was called Garden City (Cidade Jardin) also constructed in the newer part of Belo Horizonte. It was designed to be luxurious. The city prescribed that there must be large yards, and that these must have trees and various other kinds of plants, and there were various other requirements which were laid down by the city administration. Although there was considerable skepticism expressed concerning whether prospective residents would in fact be willing to buy and build in the area, given all of the conditions which surrounded the project, such fears proved to be groundless. Very soon Garden City was a very prestigious place in which to live, with people competing to buy and build there (EP.72-73).

One of his Brazilian biographers has cited Juscelino's accomplishments in several other fields. He observed that Juscelino "renewed and tripled the sewer system; he doubled the water supply; [and] he reequipped the garbage disposal department."[6] Kubitschek himself noted other accomplishments in his memoirs such as the building of the Municipal Hospital with 306 beds, the establishment of a series of popular restaurants by the city where people could buy cheap but wholesome meals, and the taking over by the city of a small private School of Architecture which was about to go bankrupt. This school later became part of the University of Minas Gerais, and became a major center of architecture and allied studies in Brazil (EP.73). He also had all Belo Horizonte real estate reassessed, bringing much property beyond the original planned city onto the tax rolls for the first time, thus substantially increasing the income of the municipality (EP.42).

Pampulha

However, the project which Kubitschek undertook as mayor, the project which was dearest to his heart, was the establishment of the Pampulha recreation area. One of his predecessors had begun an effort to dam two small rivers some miles from the city to form a lake. However, when Juscelino became prefect, only the foundations of the dam had been constructed, and there were no plans for what would be done with the area around the lake which the dam would create. The area was relatively wild. There were woods, some open areas, and virtually no construction anywhere near the prospective lake. Characteristically Kubitschek was very much enchanted with the possibilities of the region. He saw it as providing a place to which the people of Belo Horizonte could come to relax, play sports and games, row and canoe, dance and otherwise enjoy themselves. He also saw the possibility of complementing nature's beauty with buildings which would be both useful and beautiful. He took a deep and abiding interest in the construction of Pampulha, and perhaps aside from Brasilia, was prouder of it than of anything else during his political career.

Kubitschek first consulted his municipal architects who presented him with quite uninspired plans for the buildings: a yacht club, a large restaurant (casino), a ballroom or dance hall, and a church. He then turned to a young architect, who had been recommended to him by Rodrigo Melo Franco de Andrade, director of the Department of National Historic Patrimony of the Ministry of Education in Rio de Janeiro. This young architect, Oscar Niemeyer, and his sponsor both came to Belo Horizonte, and Mayor Kubitschek took them out to the dam site, and sketched to them in words his concept of what should be done with the area and the buildings which he wanted constructed there.

The next morning at 10 o'clock, de Andrade called the mayor and asked him to come to the Grande Hotel, where he and Niemeyer were staying. When Kubitschek got to their room, he found it in chaos, with sheets of paper strewn all over it. However, once the mayor sat down, Niemeyer, who had been working all night on his sketches for the Pampulha buildings, explained to him in detail what his conceptions were. Kubitschek was enchanted and intrigued by what Niemeyer showed him, and agreed on the spot to have him be the architect for the project. They agreed on a schedule for Niemeyer to present him his completed plans for each of the proposed buildings. This was the beginning of a long and fruitful association of these two men, one an incumbent politician and the other destined to become one of the world's great architects.

Meanwhile, Kubitschek pushed forward with completion of the dam. In due time, Niemeyer completed the buildings. Perhaps the most notable of these was the church, and to decorate this Kubitschek commissioned Cândido Portinari, whom he had met many years before in Paris, to design and paint murals. He also commissioned a young Brazilian sculptor Cheschiatti to provide the baptismal font and other statuary for the church. Portinari's murals depicted along the side walls of the church the various stations of the cross. Behind the altar, he painted a picture of St. Francis, who was to be the patron of the church. However, instead of having St. Francis accompanied by a wolf, as was traditional, Portinari substituted a dog, since wolves are virtually unknown in Brazil. For both Niemeyer and Portinari, their work on Pampulha was a major landmark in their professional careers. Another artist who also laid the foundations of a world-wide reputation in this project was Roberto Burle Marx, the landscape architect, who Mayor Kubitschek commissioned to lay out the grounds of the Pampulha project.

Although when they were opened to the public the buildings of Pampulha were vastly admired by painters, writers, and ordinary citizens, the church did not arouse the admiration of the archbishop of Belo Horizonte, Antônio Cabral. He professed to be shocked by the spectacle of a dog being painted with St. Francis behind the altar. This was, he declared, "a mockery of religion." He therefore refused to consecrate the building. The archbishop persisted in this refusal for the remaining seventeen years that he stayed in his post. It was not until 1959 with the advent of a new archbishop, João de Resende Costa, that the church finally was consecrated. Kubitschek, by then president of Brazil, was especially invited for the occasion. In turn, he succeeded in getting the mayor and council of Belo Horizonte to turn over ownership of the church building to the archdiocese (EP.65-66).

Mayor Kubitschek and Governor Valadares

As prefect of Belo Horizonte, Kubitschek had strong support from Governor Valadares. Indeed, he would not have remained in the post if this had not been the case, since under the Estado Novo it was an appointive one, at the free disposition of the governor. Rather more surprising than the fact that the governor continued to support him during the five years that Kubitschek was mayor was that Governor Valadares seems to have given Juscelino a completely free hand to run the state capital. In spite of the fact that Valadares had a reputation of not being willing to delegate authority, he did so with Kubitschek.

It would appear that there was only one occasion in which Governor Valadares sought to impose his will on Kubitschek, one which the mayor successfully resisted. This was less than a year after Juscelino had taken his post. The group which had been organized to run the Yacht Club which was about to be constructed at Pampulha had had an election for its first president and had, on Kubitschek's recommendation, chosen his friend Osvaldo Penido, for the post. Upon hearing this, Valadares, who was then in Rio de Janeiro, dispatched a telegram to Juscelino indicating that he disapproved of the selection of Penido. Furious as much because of the cold way the governor had chosen to show his displeasure as by his interference in what Kubitschek thought was none of his business, Juscelino quickly went to Rio to confront the governor.

Kubitschek told Valadares his objections, indicating that the members of the Yacht Club had every right to pick anyone they wanted. However, Valadares replied by ordering Juscelino to annul the election so that he, the governor, could appoint someone of his own choice. At that point, Kubitschek said, "That order you will have to give to the new prefect. I accepted the post, giving in to your virtual imposition, and I did so because I thought that, as your friend, I should not be wanting when you had need of me. . . . I shall turn over the post to whomsoever you name to take my place." However, a few hours later, when the two men were having supper together, Valadares backed down, and assured Kubitschek that he would not interfere in the Yacht Club election. If Kubitschek is to be believed, this was the last time in which his friend the governor tried to interfere with his management of the affairs of Belo Horizonte (EP.56).

Father at Last

During his years as Mayor of Belo Horizonte, Kubitschek and his wife had a more or less normal domestic life, in spite of his intense round of daily activity. Most evenings, after his day's work was completed, he was at home. Often friends were at the dinner table. The Kubitscheks were able to take short trips to Diamantina and elsewhere together, and to celebrate holidays with family and friends. However, for several years a child was lacking in the domestic life of Juscelino and Sarah Kubitschek. This was undoubtedly a cause of sadness and worry for both of them, but even more for Juscelino's mother. She frequently asked them when they were going to present her with a grandchild. One of her favorite comments was that "no home [was] complete without the crying of a child." Whenever Juscelino would have some success either in his medical or political career, she would comment: "This is all fine, my son, but when are you going to give me a grandson or a granddaughter?" (EP.46).

Finally, early in 1943, after more than eleven years of marriage, Sarah became pregnant. Perhaps because of being comparatively old to be bearing her first child, her pregnancy was a difficult one. As the date of delivery approached, Juscelino became increasingly worried about her condition, and as he records in his memoirs, for sometime he even cut down somewhat on his hectic activities. Finally, at midnight on 27 October 1943, Sarah began to experience the first pains of childbirth. After calling his sister Naná's house to alert her, their mother, and Naná's husband, Julio Soares, her husband rushed his wife to the São Lucas Clinic. Sarah's childbirth was as difficult as her pregnancy had been. After almost ten hours, her obstetrician, Dr. Lucas Machado, decided that it would be necessary for there to be a Caesarian birth. He invited Juscelino to assist him in the operation, which he did. Finally, at 10 o'clock on the morning of 23 October 1943, a healthy young baby girl was born. She was christened Marcia. In his memoirs, Kubitschek summed up his feelings about the birth of Marcia. He said: "A period of twelve years gives the impression of an eternity of solitude for a couple without children. But this all came to an end, with the birth of Marcia" (EP.51).

End of Medical Practice

It was during his period as mayor of Belo Horizonte that Kubitschek finally decided to abandon the medical profession for that of politics. This was early in 1945. He had been awakened at 3 A.M. by the wife of Eduardo Frieiro, a leading novelist and businessman of Belo Horizonte. Arriving at the Frieiro home, Kubitschek discovered that his friend had had a severe attack of appendicitis, and by the time he was able to operate the appendix had burst, and he was barely able to save the man's life. Several days later, it became necessary to operate once again, to deal with a rare inflection which had set in after the first operation.

About a week after this second operation, when Frieiro was finally able to leave the hospital, Juscelino told Frieiro's wife: "Today I am going to order two discharges, Dona Noemia. One to Frieiro, who is well and can return to his activity. And the other to me, because I am closing with the case of your husband, my professional activity." After recounting this conversation in his memoirs, Kubitschek wrote: "The choice which I had hesitated to make for so long, had just been made. Now I was not a doctor. But a politician" (EP.61-62).

The reason for this decision is clear. By this time the process of disintegration of the Estado Novo was obviously under way. The country was once more entering the path of constitutional government and electoral politics. In the face of these developments, Kubitschek made the choice which he had resisted for so long. He decided to throw himself completely into this new phase of political life, apparently believing that this time the democratic system would be secure enough that he would no longer need the option of his medical profession to fall back upon.

Chapter 5

KUBITSCHEK AND THE PSD OF MINAS

Kubitschek's reentry into electoral politics was as a member of the new Social Democratic party (Partido Social Democrático—PSD) in the state of Minas Gerais. Part of the national party which was for two decades the country's largest, "the PSD de Minas," as it was almost universally referred to, gained fame during those twenty years as being the best led political machine in all of Brazil. Its leaders were credited with a political sagacity, and an ability to maneuver and manipulate the strings of practical politics, as well as a thoroughness of organization, which was unmatched anywhere else in Brazil. Kubitschek was one of the principal organizers of the PSD de Minas, and his position of leadership in it was to be of key importance in his political career. It would first put him back in the Chamber of Deputies, then into the governor's Palacio de Liberdade, and finally was to be an essential element in his election as president of Brazil in 1955.

Kubitschek and the Sociedade de Cultura Inglesa

In his later years, Kubitschek always insisted that he had made it clear throughout the period of the Estado Novo that he thought that Brazil should return to political democracy. What discussion on this subject he had with his political intimates, it is impossible to say. However, it is clear that one post which he held during much of this period gave him an opportunity to stress publicly the virtues of democracy, at least by implication. This was his presidency of the Sociedade de Cultura Inglesa of Belo Horizonte, the bi-national center maintained in the Minas Gerais capital with British help to foster the study of the English language, and the propagation of British culture and ideas.

72

Kubitschek became president of the society in April 1941. In his speech on 11 June 1941 opening a new headquarters of the society, Juscelino noted that "England [had] been transformed into the bulwark of liberty in the world, and all those must turn to her for inspiration who live under oppression and who love, above all, the respect for the dignity of man." Kubitschek noted in his memoirs that this speech "was the subject of lively commentaries in state political circles." It also provoked a comment to him by the Chief of Police of Minas Gerais, Colonel Dornelles Vargas, to the effect that he liked Juscelino's democratic preaching, but that his speech was enough to make anyone lose his job.[1]

Kubitschek did not lose his job as mayor of Belo Horizonte, and he continued throughout the rest of World War II to be head of the Sociedade de Cultura Inglesa, in which post he sought to foster as many discussions of British culture and political life as possible. This seems to have been the extent of Kubitschek's public advocacy of a return to democratic life in Brazil, at least until the last months of 1944. Subsequently, Kubitschek's work on behalf of the British cause received public recognition from none other than Winston Churchill. The British prime minister first sent Juscelino a dagger made from parts of one of the bombs dropped on Britain, and then sent him a collection of his books, with a dedication in his own handwriting.

The Unravelling of the Estado Novo

It was World War II which prepared the way in Brazil for a return to democracy. Brazil was an active participant in the conflict, declaring war on the Axis powers a few months after Pearl Harbor, making naval and air bases along the northeast coast available to the Allies, and finally sending a Brazilian Expeditionary Force to be part of General Mark Clark's Fifth Army in Italy during the last ten months of the war. Inevitably, Brazil's participation in World War II was pictured as a contribution toward the worldwide struggle against fascist tyranny. The contradiction between being part of an alliance against fascism and having a fascist regime at home became increasingly glaring, and by the latter half of 1944 popular pressure for an end to the Estado Novo regime was reaching almost uncontainable limits.

Apparently one of the first of Vargas' close collaborators to suggest to him that he had to make some concessions to this mounting popular sentiment was Governor Valadares. He suggested to President Vargas that he should call elections for a constituent assembly which, as in 1934, after writing a new constitution would choose Vargas as the first president to govern under the new document. The suggestion of Valadares was backed by Francisco Campos, another Mineiro and principal author of the Estado Novo constitution. Finally, Vargas grudgingly suggested to them that they join with acting Minister of Justice Marcondes Filho to draw up a document calling elections for such an assembly.

However, events began to move faster than Vargas could control them. Both the Minister of War General Eurico Dutra and the Chief of the General Staff, General Pedro Aurelio Góes Monteiro, publicly called for an end to the Estado Novo. Furthermore, word soon got out that Marcondes Filho was working on a method whereby new elections could be held without Vargas vacating the presidency.

Finally, on 22 February 1945 there occurred the event which meant the definitive end of the Estado Novo. The Rio de Janeiro newspaper *Correio da Manha* published an interview of a young journalist, Carlos Lacerda, with José Américo de Almeida, who had been the government candidate in the ill-starred 1937 election campaign. In this interview among other things Américo called for new presidential elections and said that only three men should be ineligible to run in them, the two candidates of 1937—Armando Sales and himself—and Vargas. The government censors took no steps against *Correio da Manha*. This served as a signal that the Estado Novo was finished. Within a few weeks President Vargas declared a general amnesty of political prisoners, issued a new electoral law, and set the date for the election of a new president and a constituent assembly for 2 December 1945.

The opposition quickly put forth its presidential candidate, Air Force chief General Eduardo Gomes. It then became necessary for those politicians who still supported the government to decide upon a candidate of their own. As he had been in 1937, Valadares became one of the prime movers in selecting this nominee, General Eurico Gaspar Dutra. It was Valadares who suggested to Dutra that he be a candidate, and who then went to the presidential palace to convince Vargas to allow the launching of Dutra's candidacy. Vargas grudgingly agreed.

Juscelino Kubitschek and the End of the Estado Novo

Kubitschek, as an intimate friend of Valadares, had some role in these developments. He accompanied Valadares on the trip to Rio de Janeiro to convince Dutra to run for president and to get Vargas to give his approval to his candidacy, although Juscelino apparently was not himself present at either interview. Subsequently, Kubitschek also accompanied Valadares to a meeting in São Paulo, to arrange with the interventor of that state for the official launching there of the Dutra candidacy. Kubitschek was an active participant in the rather delicate negotiations with the São Paulo interventor, who had serious reservations about the naming of an official candidate, fearing that Vargas really did not want one.

Meanwhile, Kubitschek had thrown himself into the organizing of the pro-government forces in Belo Horizonte in preparation for the elections which now seemed likely. The capital of Minas Gerais traditionally had been a center of opposition to the government of the state. Kubitschek was anxious to change this. Preparations were underway for the establishment of a branch in Minas Gerais of a nationwide pro-government party. In Minas, as in the other states, this job fell principally upon the interventor. In Belo Horizonte the main person responsible for organization of what came to be the Partido Social Democrático was the mayor, Kubitschek. During the first months of 1945 there was organized in various parts of the city, a series of meetings to honor Juscelino for his contributions to the city while mayor. It is to be supposed that these meetings were not completely lacking in inspiration from the prefect's office. In any case, they served Juscelino as a platform from which to mobilize his supporters on behalf of the new party in embryo.

The first formal step in launching the PSD de Minas was a state convention, which was called for on 8 April 1945. Its organizers chose to hold the meeting in the Benedito Valadares Stadium in Belo Horizonte. However, once they had made this decision, they began to worry about how they would fill up such a large place. It was Kubitschek who solved this problem. He called each of the presidents of the neighborhood committees which he had established many months before, and asked them to mobilize as many people as

75

possible in their various localities to attend the meeting. As a result, the stadium was packed for the first convention of the PSD de Minas.

That meeting had two major items on its agenda. The first was to endorse General Dutra as the candidate for president of the republic in the forthcoming elections. The second item was the election of the first state committees of the PSD de Minas. Kubitschek was one of those elected. Kubitschek was chosen to be the chief executive officer of the new party, as he had been the secretary of the Progressive party in 1934. When Valadares asked him to accept this position, he commented to Juscelino: "It's your turn, Juscelino; and I hope that you won't disappoint me." Kubitschek adds, in his memoirs, that "The interventor need not have worried, in fact I would not disappoint him" (EP.82).

One of Juscelino's early steps as organizer of the PSD was to call together in the mayor's office the presidents of his neighborhood committees. He recounted the nature and results of this meeting:

> What I wanted to do was just to indicate to my friends the need for Belo Horizonte to give a demonstration of civic duty, preparing adequately, and with forethought, for the exercise on December 2 . . . of its right to vote. When I said to them that I was talking neither as prefect nor as secretary of the PSD, but as an old comrade in the struggle for municipal improvements, I saw that my words had reached their mark. Almost all—because there were exceptions and it was natural that there would be—indicated their unrestricted solidarity with me, hurrying to enter immediately the PSD. (EP.86)

However, the work of organizing the Partido Social Democrático was not easy. For one thing, it was being sabotaged by President Vargas. For another, Governor Valadares was himself hesitant about pushing the matter too energetically in Minas, both for personal reasons and for fear of the effect of President Vargas' attitude on the people of the state, and particularly of Belo Horizonte. As a result of this, the meeting for the official proclamation in Minas Gerais of the candidacy of General Dutra, with the presence of the candidate, was postponed several times. Finally, after a personal representative of Dutra demanded to know of Valadares and Minas party secretary Kubitschek when the meeting would be held, it was agreed that the meeting would take place on 1 September.

However, Valadares was skeptical as to whether it would be possible, as a result of Vargas' attitude to mobilize the workers of Belo Horizonte for a meeting with Dutra, since the workers tended to be strong supporters of Vargas. Juscelino assured Valadares that it would be possible to get out a large crowd to greet General Dutra. To that end, he held a meeting with the presidents of all of the unions in the city—many of whom wanted Vargas to stay in office—and urged them to mobilize their followers for the 1 September meeting. After vigorous debate, they agreed to do so, but on the condition that none of them should be asked to speak, and that no one else would pretend to speak on behalf of the workers. In his memoirs, Kubitschek noted that

> it was with pleasure that I awaited September 1. Everything had been prepared most meticulously, and I looked forward to a very successful meeting. And in fact it was. When I got to the Fairground Place, I was thrilled. I had expected that there would be a large turnout of people, but what I saw surpassed all my expectations. The plaza was a sea of heads. (EP.88)

"Queremismo" and the Fall of Vargas

Clearly, Vargas was very unhappy with the idea of leaving the presidency. He used various stratagems to try to make this unnecessary. On the one hand, he encouraged meetings of his working class followers held for the purpose of urging him to stay in office. The favorite slogans at these meetings were "Queremos Vargas!" and "Queremos Getúlio!" (We want Vargas, We Want Getúlio), from which his followers got the nickname *Queremistas*. On 19 August, he addressed a meeting of the queremistas and said that there was "a stairway which he would descend" to join them "to find the road . . . to the happiness of Brazil." This statement was widely regarded by the press as an indication that he did not intend to step down or to allow the election of his successor (EP.87).

Vargas' apparent desire to stay in the presidency received support from what might be regarded as strange quarters. Luís Carlos Prestes, leader of the Communist party, who had been kept in jail for nine years by Vargas, and whose German wife and child had been turned over to the Nazis by him, sent Vargas a telegram, urging the postponement of the presidential election until after the constituent assembly had finished its work (EP.86). At the time, there were widespread rumors that before Vargas had released Prestes from jail, in May 1945, he had sent an emissary to see the communist leader, and that an agreement had been reached that in return for his release and Vargas' granting legalization of the Communist party and giving it complete freedom of action, Prestes would support Vargas' continuance in power. Even some of the communist leaders suspected that there had been negotiations between Vargas and Prestes before the latter's release. Astrogildo Pereira, one of the party's founders, even suggested to me that the likely intermediary had been the ex-Tenente João Alberto (in 1945 chief of the police), an old friend of both men. However, Pereira insisted that whatever negotiations there may have been were not the cause for the attitude which the Communist party assumed then towards Vargas.[2] José Segadas Viana, Vargas' ex-director general of labor, on the other hand, suggested that Agamemnon Magalhães, who had held several ministerial posts under Vargas, was the intermediary with Prestes.[3]

When I interviewed Prestes in 1946 he denied that there had been any conversations preliminary to his release or any deal with Vargas. He insisted that it just happened that the policies of Vargas and of the communists had been parallel in 1945. Vargas was against a military coup because it would depose him, the communists were against one because it would probably turn violently against them, since the Army was primarily in the hands of "fascist" elements who hated the party. So, he said, they both worked to keep Vargas in power and to have free elections.[4] Another communist leader of the time, Agildo Barata, the party's treasurer, explained the communist support of Vargas on the basis of their very strong support of the Allied cause during the War, and their approval of Vargas' having taken Brazil into the conflict.[5]

In any case, it is clear that Vargas gave extensive support to the queremistas of all kinds. Thus, when he was offered the presidency of the new national Partido Social Democrático, which had endorsed General Dutra's candidacy, he turned it down, saying: "My mandate is approaching an end, and when it is concluded, I shall return to Rio Grande" (EP.80). Subsequently he accepted the presidency of the Brazilian Labor party (Partido Trabalhista Brasileiro) which was organized by the queremistas.

Vargas adopted another stratagem which he had used successfully in 1937. He spread word among his friends that neither of the candidates, generals Dutra and Gomes, would be able to take power. The first, he claimed, was a lackluster nominee, who stood no chance of winning; and if Gomes were to be elected, the military would not let him take power because of his violent campaign oratory against the Estado Novo and against Vargas himself. Vargas therefore suggested that both nominees ought to retire from the scene, to give way to a third who could be supported in both camps.

Vargas involved Valadares in this ploy. On September 12, he called in Valadares, gave him his talk about the unsuitability of both Dutra and Gomes, and suggested to Valadares that he would be the perfect "third candidate," and that as such he would have the full support of Vargas. Valadares was enchanted with the idea.

Valadares immediately summoned Kubitschek—both men had apartments in the same building in Rio de Janeiro, where they were staying at the time. He told Juscelino what had happened, and his delight at the idea. Kubitschek recorded what happened then:

> Benedito told me all that, expecting that I would accept the idea with enthusiasm. I was his friend and, as such, it was my duty to alert him to the dangers of that attitude. I disagreed with the idea with delicacy but firmly. I said, textually, that this was *a crazy idea*. What would General Dutra think of the politicians of Minas and of our publicly assumed commitments? Benedito Valadares fell into a chair and remained in silence. (EP.91)

Valadares was not easily dissuaded from his dream of the presidency. He tried to convince General Dutra to resign his candidacy, which Dutra, after conferring with other Minas Gerais political leaders (not including Kubitschek), refused to do. Meanwhile, the press got wind of what had occurred and denounced it, thus cutting short the president's maneuver. Vargas continued his encouragement of the queremistas, addressing more of their meetings, and repeating the idea that although he was having to leave the presidency, he would be ready from his home in Rio Grande do Sul to come back and lead the people once again. One particularly large queremista meeting was held in Rio de Janeiro on 3 October, and another one was planned for 26 October. Using the excuse of disorders which had taken place during the 3 October meeting as an explanation, Rio police chief João Alberto banned further outdoor meetings.

On 10 October, President Vargas issued a revision of the election law, providing that there would be elections on 2 December not only for president and a constituent assembly, but also for governors and state legislatures. At the same time he authorized the interventors in the various states to issue new constitutions for them. This served to confuse the election very greatly, something the maneuver was intended to do. On 22 October, João Alberto was called into the office of Minister of Justice Agamemnon Magalhães, and was informed that the president planned to name him interventor in the Federal District, thus removing him from direct control of the police. However, when Alberto told Magalhães that he had a pact with Minister of War General Góes Monteiro whereby if either of them was removed from office, the other would resign, the minister postponed the removal of Alberto.

Finally, on the morning of 29 October, Alberto was told personally by Vargas that he was to be "promoted" to interventor and that Vargas' own brother Benjamin was to be his substitute as police chief, while Góes Monteiro also was to be replaced. The actual transfer of the police job took place at 11 A.M. Meanwhile, Alberto had notified Monteiro, informing him of President Vargas' actions. Soon afterwards there was a meeting in Monteiro's office of the top officers of the armed forces, together with the minister and the two presidential candidates, General Dutra and Brigadier Gomes. At that meeting they decided to depose President Vargas, something they accomplished during the afternoon of the same day (EP.89-106).

Ex-Mayor Juscelino Kubitschek

Kubitschek had been kept informed of much of what was transpiring during the weeks before the ouster of President Vargas.

After the decree of 10 October providing for elections of governors and legislatures on 2 December, Kubitschek had been informed along with other PSD leaders by Valadares that he, Valadares, would not be a candidate for the governorship. On 23 October at a meeting of the executive commission of the PSD de Minas the governor announced that the selection of candidates for the 2 December election would have to be postponed for at least a week, until he had had time to issue the state's new constitution.

Kubitschek noted in his memoirs that at this PSD executive meeting, Valadares reiterated that he would not be a candidate, because to do so he would have to resign in conformity with the electoral law; this would interfere with the campaign on behalf of General Dutra in the state. Juscelino added that

> none of those present believed in the sincerity of the words of the governor. Benedito Valadares was impressed with the confusion reigning in the political scene and believed that, in spite of the resistance of the Armed Forces and of the political leaders, Getúlio Vargas would still find a solution for the impasse, and that this might well be what the chief of the Government had confidentially suggested to him: his own selection to be the *third man*. (EP.97)

At 3 P.M. on 29 October, Governor Valadares summoned Juscelino to the Palacio de Liberdade. Dutra has just informed Valadares by phone that Benjamin Vargas had been named Rio police chief and that he, Dutra, was "putting on his uniform and going to act." Valadares, as he told Kubitschek, had replied: "I am with you, general." At that point, the colonel of the Twelfth Regiment of the Army entered Valadares' office, and asked Valadares to provide transport to move his troops to Juiz da Fora to reinforce the defenses of the State. When Valadares replied that he not have such transport available, Juscelino volunteered the trucks belonging to the prefecture of Belo Horizonte.

After dispatching the city's trucks to army headquarters and signing what proved to be his last decree as mayor, Juscelino was back in the governor's palace at seven o'clock that evening. This was just in time to hear on the radio the announcement of a proclamation which Valadares had just issued expressing his support for the

Army's move in ousting President Vargas. Juscelino wrote years later that he was shocked at this proclamation, and was reminded of Julius Caesar's famous question "Et tu, Brute?" (EP.101). As a result of the events of 29 October, which brought the installation to the presidency of José Linhares, chief justice of the Supreme Court, the new administration decided that all of the state interventors would be replaced. Valadares failed in his attempt to have himself excluded from this decision. In Minas, as in all of the other states, the governorship was turned over to the ranking judge of the state. With the ouster of the interventor of Minas Gerais, it was only a matter of a day or two before not only the members of his cabinet, but all important officials appointed by the interventor, also would be removed. These included Kubitschek.

Juscelino the Campaign Manager

Before the fall of Vargas, the Partido Social Democrático in Minas Gerais had named its candidates for the federal Senate and Chamber of Deputies, and Juscelino, along with Valadares, José Maria Alkmin and various other party leaders were among the candidates for deputy. In addition, as general secretary of the PSD de Minas, it fell to Kubitschek to organize and lead the party's electoral campaign. Characteristically, Kubitschek threw himself with all of his energies into the contest. He opened the party headquarters each day at six in the morning, and seldom left before ten o'clock in the evening. He wrote many years later: "The correspondence was copious. The telephone rang every minute. People came and went, asking for and carrying away instructions. And there were the meetings in which I participated, and the circulares that had to be issued. I lived, then in the midst of commotion. But always I felt fine in the eye of the tempest" (EP.107).

Juscelino gave particular attention to the campaign in Belo Horizonte. He converted his famous neighborhood committees into local committees of the PSD. He attended numerous campaign meetings in the capital, and often after them campaigned in the vicinity, ringing doorbells and soliciting votes for the party. He commented that what he wanted to do was to make friends, to establish personal relationships, and to project a cordial image of a candidate who was accessible to all. That policy of fraternization soon produced results: in many families of political adversaries, a member appeared who resolved to break domestic unity and to give him his vote (EP.108). During one of the early meetings of the campaign he first heard the slogan "Juscelino for governor!" uttered by an old lady in the front of the crowd. He recorded somewhat disingenuously that after the meeting that he "went to embrace her, not for what she had said, but for the civic spirit she revealed." However, he did ask her why "she wanted to throw him in the fire," and he recorded her answer as being, "You are going to be governor, my son, so that the poor can improve their lives" (EP.108).

The PSD suffered considerable disadvantage in the campaign. After its leaders had for many years been the "ins" they were suddenly the "outs" after 29 October. The new government tended to side with the National Democratic Union (União Democrática Nacional—UDN), the anti-Vargas party, after the dictator's ouster. Partly because of this, the UDN leaders were absolutely convinced until after the votes were counted that they would win by a landslide. However, this did not prove to be the case. Kubitschek credits the failure of the UDN, and the consequent success of the PSD and the PTB, to two things. First, the majority of the workers were still under the influence of Vargas, and since the UDN appeared to be the gainers from the overthrow of Vargas, the workers tended to incline towards the opponents of the UDN. He commented that "they did not vote in favor of Dutra but against the UDN" (EP.109). When Vargas finally came out and endorsed Dutra's candidacy only four days before the election, that was conclusive. In addition, candidate Gomes had made some disparaging comments about Vargas' labor followers which very much rankled many of them.

In the state of Minas Gerais, Kubitschek "came to be the principal target of the UDN batteries." However, he remarked that "there are evils which come out for the best. . . . The hatred of the adversaries did not succeed in tarnishing my reputation, but, on the other hand, caused great irritation in PSD circles. As a result, the electors, in the face of injustice, closed ranks around my name" (EP.110). As it turned out, the UDN failed to carry Minas Gerais. Juscelino was particularly pleased that the PSD candidates won in Belo Horizonte, seats which the UDN had taken particularly for granted. He also had reason for satisfaction in the fact that he

83

received the second highest vote for deputy in the state; only Vargas, who ran on the PTB ticket, received more votes than he.

Marcia's Illness

With his election once again to the Chamber of Deputies, Kubitschek moved his small family to an apartment in Copacabana, half a block from the beach. His three-year-old daughter, Marcia, did not take well to the move. In June 1946 she fell seriously ill with bronchial pneumonia. She ran a high temperature and for several days her parents feared that she might not survive. Even after her temperature broke, it was four weeks before it had completely disappeared. Although Marcia recovered physically, she seemed to remain very depressed. Juscelino and Sarah noted that the only time she seemed to get back to her former cheery disposition was when small cousins of about her own age were brought in to play with her. Seeing this, the Kubitschek decided that since Sarah could not have any more children it was necessary for them to adopt another little girl about Marcia's age.

A few months later, when they were spending the hot summer months in Belo Horizonte, they were able to carry out their decision. The parents of eleven children in a town in the interior of the state were willing to allow the Kubitscheks to adopt one of their youngest offspring, Maria Estela. Juscelino noted that "she and Marcia understood one another on their first encounter. They became friends. And a few days later, they were already sisters—the sister that Marcia had been awaiting anxiously for three years."

There was a sequel to this, which Juscelino Kubitschek recorded in his memoirs as follows:

It will be just to record a fact which made me very proud. We never made any distinction between them. Both were daughters with the same rights and the same attention. The only difference was that Marcia called us *papa* and *mama*; and Maria Estela treated us as god-parents. That situation did not cease being painful for me. On 10 December 1957—when Maria Estela was about to be fifteen and I was president of the Republic— I prepared a decree, permitting adopted daughters to have the same rights as legitimate ones, including the

84

use of the family name of their respective parents. With the decree completed, I gave it to Sarah, asking her to take it to Maria Estela and say that it was my present for her birthday. Sarah made Maria Estela aware of the terms of the act and talked about its implications. She asked her not to hurry in giving her reply. Upon finishing reading it, Maria Estela took her decision. She went to my office and kissing me, said: "Thank you, papa." (EP.122)

Kubitschek and the 1947 Campaign for Governor

Soon after Vargas' overthrow, the new president cancelled Vargas' decree calling for gubernatorial and state legislative elections at the same time as those for the national congress and the president. As a result, the state elections were postponed until 19 January 1947. These elections caused a major crisis in the PSD de Minas, bringing about its only defeat on a statewide level until 1962.

Carlos Luz, one of the more important figures in the PSD de Minas, selected by Dutra to be Minister of Justice, decided that he could take advantage of his position in the federal cabinet to be chosen as PSD candidate for governor of Minas Gerais. However, Valadares, Kubitschek, and a majority of the executive commission of the PSD de Minas rejected his candidacy, on the grounds that it was being imposed by the president. As yet, they did not have a nominee of their own, although Bias Fortes was one who had substantial backing. Luz sought to gain supporters among the majority of the executive commission, including Kubitschek. The two men had a conversation that lasted for an hour and a half, during which Juscelino made it clear to Luz that the Minas Gerais PSD leaders would not accept what they thought was an imposition by the president of the republic, even though he was a fellow member of the PSD.

President Dutra meanwhile, sought to disentangle himself from the quarrels over PSD gubernatorial nominations—his support was not only being sought in Minas but in many of the other states as well—and turned this task over to General Monteiro, the Minister of War. Monteiro thereupon called in Valadares and Kubitschek, and sought to convince them to support the Luz candidacy. However, both men refused. Finally, Monteiro asked Juscelino:

"You mean to say that even being recommended by the president of the Republic, this nomination runs the risk of not being accepted?" Kubitschek replied: "Exactly, general" (EP.126). Although opposing the Luz candidacy, the Valadares-Kubitschek forces did not as yet have a nominee of their own. At one point, Valadares apparently circulated the name of Kubitschek as a possible nominee. This idea was also picked up by Juscelino's old neighborhood committees, which organized a campaign of wall graffiti and posters proclaiming "Queremos Juscelino." Kubitschek finally got in touch with the heads of the committees and asked them to end their campaign, because by that time he had pledged to work for the nomination of Bias Fortes.

Later Kubitschek looked back at his action in discouraging this campaign on his behalf as an example of the "Kubitschek instinct." He noted that "If [he] had agreed to be a candidate at that time, and if by any chance [he] had obtained the support of the electorate, at the end of the gubernatorial term [he] would certainly have been a candidate for the presidency of the republic, and the man whom [he] would have had to face in the dispute for the popular vote would have been none other than Vargas, an adversary impossible to defeat at the polls" (EP.144).

Meanwhile, General Monteiro desisted in his efforts to push the Luz candidacy, and the idea developed to name a third person. Once convinced that he could not get the nomination, Luz threw himself into this campaign, mobilizing his supporters to back Venceslau Brás, former Minas Gerais governor and ex-president of the republic. For a while, Valadares seemed to accept the idea of the Brás nomination. He spoke to both Monteiro and President Dutra in support of the idea. The ex-interventor was not really happy about the nomination of the ex-president. When the delegates to the PSD state convention, which would finally pick a candidate, were already gathering in Belo Horizonte, Valadares, from his headquarters in the Grande Hotel "carried on conversations day and night—behind closed doors—in his apartment. And the more he conversed, the larger came to be the number of those who did not think that the candidacy of Brás was a happy one" (EP.138).

Finally, Valadares called in Kubitschek and José Maria Alkmin, and told them that he wanted to talk to every convention delegate, and asked them to organize this. They did. The upshot of these conversations was the reemergence once again of the name of

Fortes. When the convention finally opened, it was tumultuous. But the efforts of Valadares, Kubitschek, and Alkmin had been successful: Fortes received 191 votes, Brás only 24, with six blank, and 16 votes annulled. As Kubitschek commented: "The Valadarista victory was overwhelming" (EP.140).

Although Valadares and his allies were able to carry the PSD convention, they were unable to elect the party's candidate. A coalition against the PSD was formed behind the candidate of the União Democrática Nacional, Milton Campos. It included not only the UDN, but also the Republican party of ex-President Arthur Bernardes, the Christian Democrats, the National Labor party, and the Carlos Luz wing of the PSD. Campos was elected with a majority of 59,724 votes. Nevertheless, the PSD received more votes than any other single party, surpassing the UDN by more than 80,000 votes (EP.141).

Travelling Deputy

In his memoirs, Kubitschek passed over almost completely his experiences as a member of the Chamber of Deputies from 1946 until 1950. In private conversation, he told me that his duties as secretary general of the PSD de Minas largely prevented him from being very active in the Chamber.[6] However, one initiative of President Dutra which he did strongly support in Congress was the so-called SALTE plan, the first approach to attempting to plan Brazil's economic development.[7] Kubitschek does write extensively in his memoirs about two trips he took during his tenure in the Chamber, one of them official and one unofficial. These were of considerable importance in the evolution of his ideas and in developing in his mind the kind of program which he would seek to apply when he became governor of Minas Gerais and then president of the republic. These voyages were to the Northeast and Amazon areas of Brazil, made as a member of an official congressional mission, and to the United States and Canada on a purely personal basis.

The first trip was carried out in a plane of the Ministry of Aviation, and Juscelino was a member of the high-sounding Parliamentary Commission for the Economic Evaluation of the Amazon Region. The group of senators and deputies visited the Territory of Amapá, where the exploration for manganese, which was to hasten the development of that relatively remote part of the country, was just getting under way. They then flew to Belem, at the head of the Amazon delta, and down the coast to the cities of Teresina, San Luis de Maranhão, Fortaleza, Natal, João Pessoa, Recife, Maceio and Salvador. Kubitschek says of this voyage that it "was the first time that [he] entered into contact with a Brazil different from that which [he] had habitually admired in the cities of the center and the south." He adds that he saw there "the drama of those disinherited populations, lost in the crannies of an immense territory and almost without effective connection with the capital of the republic."

Juscelino commented on the effect on his thinking of what he saw in the north and northeast: "Seeing that socioeconomic fragmentation, which transformed the country into a real archipelago, sowed in my spirit the tender roots of a preoccupation, which would later become overwhelming; that of linking all of the states—one to another, and all to the center of the country—through an extensive network of highways, so as to establish by land what aviation was just establishing, albeit so far very timidly, by air" (EP.147).

The trip to the United States and Canada which Juscelino and Sarah took in the company of two friends also made a great impression on Kubitschek and helped to mold his thinking. They took a ship to New York. After seeing that city, they rented a car and drove to Montreal. From there they drove across Canada, then back to the United States through Detroit, Chicago, and Washington and subsequently to Philadelphia and back to New York City where they boarded a plane for a thirty-hour flight to Rio de Janeiro (EP.153). Kubitschek was impressed with much that he saw in North America. But he was particularly fascinated by Washington, D.C., a city built to be the capital of the nation. In summing up the effect which his first visit to North America had had on him he said in his memoirs that

> the spectacle of those two functioning civilizations—that of the United States and that of Canada—aroused in me the feeling for the needs of Brazil. I saw the road which we must follow. The effort which must be made. And, still more important, the sense, the direction, the route

which the governments of our country had to take towards our progress.

I understood the role which Brazil could represent in the world if its development was oriented towards industrialization. . . . The image which I had of Brazil was that of mediocrity of governmental initiatives. It worked on a lilliputian scale, when dealing with a giant country. That is why we never moved from the same place.

It was then that I understood the importance of having audacity so that the giant could be awakened . . . the dream must be converted into reality, and for this one needed courage, audacity and determination. . . . Courage, audacity, determination—three qualities that were never missing in me. As for the dream—Dream, with a capital D—that was a characteristic that I had from the cradle. (EP.153-54)

The Issue of the Presidential Succession

When Kubitschek arrived home from the United States in the latter part of 1948, discussion of the 1950 election was already underway, both for the presidency and the governorship of Minas Gerais. Juscelino soon got deeply involved in both of these issues. The great problem with regard to the election of a successor to President Dutra, according to most of the country's political leaders, was the possibility that Vargas would attempt to make a comeback. He was constitutionally eligible, he still had the support of a large part of the working class, and he had ready at hand the Brazilian Labor party (PTB) which would nominate him. The leaders of most Brazilian parties wanted to block the election of Vargas. They thought first, therefore, in terms of trying to reach agreement on a single candidate, who would be backed by all of the parties except the PTB. This proved easier to say than to do.

The politicians of Minas Gerais played a major role in the effort to form a united front against the prospective Vargas candidacy. In April 1949, Juscelino, as secretary general of the PSD de Minas, conferred with the leaders of the UDN and other parties in Minas, with the idea of working out a common basis for the campaign, and if possible agreeing on a single candidate that they

89

could all support. It proved impossible at that time to reach an accord, but this did not end the effort which was transferred to the national level.

A Committee of the Big Three was established in Rio de Janeiro, consisting of the heads of the national PSD, UDN, and Republican party, that is, Nereu Ramos, Prado Kelly, and ex-President Arthur Bernardes. It was their job "to coordinate the different political current, and give them a single orientation, looking towards the presidential succession" (EP.161). When the Committee of the Big Three seemed to make no progress, the Mineiro politicians decided to enter the scene once again. In August 1949, representatives of the UDN, Republican party, and Juscelino for the PSD drew up and signed a manifesto designed to serve as a basis for unity of all the parties opposed to Vargas' candidacy. The statement was endorsed by all of the parties in Minas except the PTB. However, it did not resolve the problem of who should be the coalition candidate, an issue thrown again into the hands of the Big Three.

Finally, at the end of September, President Dutra became impatient. He dispatched Valadares and Kubitschek to Belo Horizonte to try to get the Minas political leaders to agree on a single candidate. They failed. On 22 October 1949 the Big Three also recognized their failure to reach agreement, and from then on each party set about to name its own nominee for the presidency. Meanwhile, on 20 September, Vargas officially launched his campaign as candidate of the PTB.

The PSD was in a particularly difficult situation. Not only were there several possible nominees, but in Minas Gerais there continued the old split between the majority of the party led by Valadares, and the minority, known as the liberal wing. These problems resulted in continued postponement of the selection of a PSD presidential nominee. It was only on 15 May 1950 that PSD nominee was selected in a quite informal fashion, to be ratified later by the party convention. At a meeting in an apartment in Rio de Janeiro, organized by the Rio Grande do Sul leaders of the party, and attended among others by General Monteiro, now a PSD senator from Alagoas, representatives of the various state PSD organizations discussed the different candidates. The Rio Grande do Sul representatives finally put forward the name of Cristiano Machado, a member of the liberal wing of the PSD de Minas. His name was accepted finally, even by Valadares who was present representing his wing of the PSD de Minas (EP.155-66).

The Struggle for the Governorship

Valadares had been shrewd in supporting the nomination of Machado as the PSD presidential candidate. With the national nominee from the liberal wing, the choice of the candidate for governor of Minas Gerais fell logically to the Valadares wing of the party there. Valadares himself appears briefly to have had some aspirations to seek his old job again. Very quickly, the contest for the PSD nomination for governor of Minas Gerais centered on Fortes, the candidate in 1947, and Kubitschek. Both men had certain factors in their favor. Fortes was a close personal friend of President Dutra, who for some time used his influence on behalf of Fortes. On the other hand, Juscelino continued to be popular with large segments of the population of Belo Horizonte; during his five years as secretary general of the PSD de Minas he had built up very good relations with the party leaders of the various municipalities of the state.

The selection of a nominee did not prove an easy one. The choice was supposed to be made by the executive commission of the state PSD. When it met on 15 June 1950, Kubitschek felt that he clearly had the support of the majority of the commission members. However, in the face of strong pressure from the presidential palace on behalf of Fortes, the executive commission decided to postpone its decision and to name a sub-commission of five to make a recommendation. Three of the five people selected were favorably disposed to Juscelino.

Presidential pressure continued, exercised principally through Senator General Monteiro. Twice he summoned Juscelino and Valadares to his apartment in Rio, the first time to suggest openly to Kubitschek that he withdraw his candidacy, the second time to suggest that the sub-commission turn the task of choosing a candidate back to the full executive commission without any recommendation. At the first meeting, Kubitschek refused absolutely to withdraw his name; but in the second he accepted the idea of leaving the decision up to the executive commission, although that meant considerable risk for his candidacy.

91

Juscelino felt that he must do everything possible to end the pressure from the presidential palace on the delegates to the executive commission. He sought and received an interview with Presidential Dutra, and spoke quite frankly to him, reminding him of his own efforts on Dutra's behalf in 1945 including opposition to Valadares' attempt at that time to get Dutra to withdraw his presidential candidacy and his own role of some propensity to help finance Dutra's campaign in Minas Gerais. He strongly urged the president to stop trying to use his influence to determine the PSD nomination for governor of Minas. Dutra finally agreed. Nevertheless, when the executive commission finally met again on 20 July, no one knew which man would be named. There were twenty-five members of the commission, but both Forte and Juscelino agreed not to attend, and so there were only twenty-three votes to be cast. Each member of the commission deposited his vote in a sealed ballot box. Then Alkmin and Euvaldo Lodi, supporters respectively of Kubitschek and Fortes, acted as tellers. By the time twenty votes had been counted, the two candidates were tied. As the members of the commission pressed around the ballot box, the last three votes were taken out and all three were for Kubitschek (EP.180).[8]

The Gubernatorial Campaign

Even before his nomination by the PSD, Kubitschek had been negotiating with ex-president Arthur Bernardes and his son, Arthur Bernardes Filho, to obtain the backing of the Republican party (PR), which until then had been allied with the UDN in Minas. After his nomination, Juscelino quickly completed these negotiations, accepting a PR leader, Clovis Salgado, as his running mate for vice governor. He also received the backing of the National Labor party (PTN), which was headed by his friend, Octacilio Negrão de Lima, the mayor of Belo Horizonte. Thus, Juscelino started his campaign as the nominee of three parties. Several other small ones subsequently threw their backing to him (EP.191-92).

The great unknown insofar as the Minas gubernatorial campaign was concerned was the attitude which Vargas and the PTB would adopt. Gabriel Passos, the UDN candidate, had long been a friend of Vargas, and the UDN had great hopes that the ex-president would endorse their candidate. In characteristic fashion, Vargas said nothing about the matter through much of the campaign. However, Vargas finally summoned Kubitschek to meet with him in Rio de Janeiro. He there explained to Juscelino that after looking at the campaign in Minas he had come to the conclusion that his own situation in the presidency—which he fully expected to win—would be stronger if Kubitschek was governor of Minas, and that therefore he intended to endorse Juscelino, and have the PTB support him.

Getúlio was undoubtedly surprised—although Juscelino indicates in his memoirs that he gave no indication of just how he felt—when Kubitschek told him that such an endorsement would be highly inconvenient to him on personal and moral grounds. As the secretary general of the PSD de Minas he was duty bound to support the candidacy of Cristiano Machado, and an endorsement by Vargas would make it appear that he was foreswearing that duty. He suggested to Vargas that instead of endorsing him, Getúlio should leave the PTB voters free to vote as they pleased in the gubernatorial race, adding that he was sure that given his own close contacts with the unions of the state particularly those of Belo Horizonte he would receive the votes of most of the PTB members. Vargas finally agreed to this (EP.197-200).

There were only two months left in which to campaign. During this period, Juscelino visited 168 municipalities, made 207 speeches, and listened to 1,032 others. On one day, he gave a speech in Carancola at 2 A.M., and on another day, he spoke in the town of Corinto at 9 A.M.[9] Juscelino's campaign for governor was fought on a program of what came to be known as "developmentalism." His slogan was "Two Words: Energy and Transport." He worked with Lucas Lopes, Alkmin, Julio Soares, and Cristiano Martins to develop a detailed program of the things which he proposed to accomplish during his five years in office, and presented these ideas to the electorate during the campaign. The election was finally held on 21 December 1950. Insofar as the state of Minas Gerais was concerned, it was an overwhelming victory for Kubitschek. He received 714,364 votes, against 554,086, obtained by his rival and brother-in-law Gabriel Passos (EP.210).

Chapter 6

GOVERNOR JUSCELINO KUBITSCHEK

The administration of Kubitschek, governor of Minas Gerais (1951-1955), presaged the administration of Kubitschek, president of Brazil (1956-1961). As chief executive of Brazil's second largest state, Kubitschek gave priority to economic development, with major emphasis on the development of power resources, transportation facilities, and manufacturing, as he was later to do as head of the federal government. Although he by no means ignored such problems as education, public health, and the administration of justice, and had some notable achievements to his credit in those fields, he felt that his primary objective was to develop the economy of the state, so that it could bear the cost of social programs.

Governor Kubitschek, in a speech to the Commercial Association of Rio de Janeiro on 4 March 1953, gave an exposition of his program and its rationale, which he could as easily have given several years later to explain his policies as president of the republic. He commented as follows:

> To provide Minas the resources to transform and enrich its production was the only path to follow for the good of the people of Minas and of Brazil. And we would have betrayed the most sacred urgings of our conscience if, once in the government, as we now are, we were to relegate to a secondary plane those objectives, and in a mediocre way, undertake a program of pure appearances which would give us easy fame and popularity. We are spending more than a billion cruzeiros on our electrification plan—with less than half of this we could construct five hundred new schools, which Minas needs, passing into history as the great friend of education, although within ten years our successors would have to

94

close them, because of inability to pay the teachers. On a single contract for constructing roads we are spending five hundred million cruzeiros—and half of this would suffice to construct two hundred sumptuous new courthouses for towns of Minas, which would give us fame as the government of justice, although our successors would encounter terrible difficulties in maintaining them. We are going now to invest nearly two hundred million in the first packinghouse for Minas—and with this we could equip dozens of new hospitals, gaining the aura of patron of the people's health, although within five years these hospitals could no longer offer their services, for lack of drugs and of doctors and nurses. It was necessary, I repeat, to strike out on new paths. To renounce easy glory and put our hands resolution to the work of salvation. We shall succeed in giving Minas energy and transport, exchanging its future without hope for one in which honest labor can be fairly rewarded.[1]

Governor Kubitschek and President Vargas

In his development efforts in the state of Minas Gerais, Kubitschek had considerable aid from the federal government. Juscelino was elected governor of Minas Gerais at the same time that Vargas was reelected president of the republic. As soon as his own election was officially confirmed, Kubitschek sought out Vargas. In his memoirs, he explained how and why he made contact, as governor-elect, with the president-elect. He noted that the UDN was making efforts to have Vargas' victory annulled on the grounds that Getúlio had not received an absolute majority of the votes cast in a four cornered race, and that among the parties of Minas Gerais not a single voice had been raised in protest. Juscelino wrote that because of that situation he felt it his duty to substitute for the missing parties and to himself visit the president-elect in a bid for solidarity.

Kubitschek arrived at Vargas' fazenda in São Borja, in the state of Rio Grande do Sul, on 2 January 1951. Vargas told Kubitschek that he was anxious to give Juscelino all of the help that he could in his new post. Kubitschek naturally thanked him, but said that he did not quite understand Getúlio's gesture since he,

Juscelino, had had some profound differences of opinion with Getúlio. Vargas then told him that he himself had changed, that he had become convinced of the value of democracy by the 1950 campaign, in which the most powerful interests had opposed him, but he had been elected by the workers and his assumption of office was being guaranteed by elements favoring close adherence to the constitution.[2] He promised Juscelino that in his second term he would adhere strictly to the constitution, which had made it possible for him to return to power.[3]

Vargas honored this pledge to support Governor Kubitschek. In the years that followed, the federal government, and President Vargas personally, gave political and financial support to a number of the development programs of Kubitschek's state administration. Juscelino noted that this help was concentrated in five categories:

1. devolution to the Union the financing of the Minas Road Network
2. guarantee of the Banco do Brasil of our external loans raised by the State
3. asphalting of the Juiz de Fora-Belo Horizonte highway
4. channeling of immigrants to us to stimulate agriculture
5. providing Minas with a large iron and steel plant, so as to dissipate the resentment generated by the installation of a large plant at Volta Redonda in the State of Rio, when all of the mineral consumed by its was furnished by Minas (EP.219)

In later years, Kubitschek even had some reason to believe that Vargas looked upon him as the best man to succeed him in the presidency. Juscelino noted in a conversation with me in 1972 that Alzira Vargas had told him of a discussion among Getúlio and several members of his family, in which the subject of the political succession was discussed. After several names had been mentioned, Vargas commented: "Don't overlook the *moço* [young man] from Minas," meaning Kubitschek.[4]

On various occasions during his governorship, Kubitschek invited President Vargas to come to the state, usually to participate in the inauguration of one of the state administration's projects. The last such visit was made early in August 1954, about two weeks before the death of Vargas, to help open the first phase of the

Mannesmann steel plant in Belo Horizonte. The final crisis which was to drive Getúlio to suicide had already begun. He went to Minas Gerais in spite of advice of his closest associates, including members of his family, who feared that the military might carry out a coup during his absence from Rio de Janeiro. Also, after dedicating the Mannesmann plant, Vargas refused to rush back immediately to the national capital, instead staying overnight in the Palacio de Liberdade, as Governor Kubitschek had invited him to do.

In his memoirs, Kubitschek stressed his belief that Vargas really enjoyed this stay, in spite of the preoccupations of that period. His popular reception in Belo Horizonte was very enthusiastic, and the official activities marking the occasion were very agreeable to the president. Juscelino noted: "Upon embarking, when he said goodbye, he said to me, visibly moved: 'Thank you, governor, I won't forget the happy hours which you have given me'" (EP.300).

Juscelino's Strategy of Development

By the time he took office, Kubitschek had a clear strategy which he intended to carry out as governor. First, he put primary emphasis on the development of the infrastructure of the Minas Gerais economy. This meant major efforts to expand the state's power resources and to extend its road system. Kubitschek and his advisers felt that the development of the electric power resources of the state was essential for its future growth. Only with abundant quantities of electricity would it be possible to attract sizable manufacturing industries, and to further the development of agriculture, grazing, and small local industries and services. In a radio address to the people of Minas on 25 August 1951, the governor underscored the importance which he thought the provision of electricity would have for much of the state. He noted that the availability of electricity

> in one of these localities will be an authentic impulse for progress, bringing into use energies which have hitherto been unused: a local carpentry shop which installs a tiny motor for its lathe, a butter factory which will be established, a small metal store which will be transformed into a mechanical workshop, without speak-

ing of the civilizing function of electricity, which inside homes, through the radio and small comforts which it makes possible, all this will have a legitimate mission of enlightenment and creation of incentives. (QA.28)

Roads were the second part of the infrastructure to which Juscelino gave particular attention. A substantial part of the population of the state lived in virtual isolation, having little or no contact with the rest of Minas Gerais or Brazil. Living under conditions of subsistence agriculture, these people participated little in the general economy, unable to get their products to market, and not themselves constituting a market for other sectors of the economy. Kubitschek thought it essential to establish roads which would begin to provide the basis for the creation of an integrated state economy, linked to that of Brazil as a whole. Early in his term as governor, Juscelino indicated the prime importance which he gave to the problem of roads. He commented that "In commercial language, I signed a promissory note, with fixed date of liquidation, and without possibility of extension. I based my election campaign on these numbers—simply on these numbers. Certainly these goals, two thousand kilometers of roads and two hundred thousand horse power, were the backbone of my election, the substance of a gruelling campaign" (QA.11).

Second only to electricity and roads, Governor Kubitschek placed in his strategy of development the establishment of new manufacturing industries in the state. Although the possibility of establishing such industries depended mainly on his success in extending the state's infrastructure, he did not wait for such success in order to begin the task of large-scale industrialization. In his speech to the Rio de Janeiro Commercial Association on 4 March 1953, Governor Kubitschek underscored the importance which he placed on industrialization. He commented that "wealth does not come today merely from tilling the soil, but from the work of production and transformation, greater benefits coming from the finished product, to which is added the value of the energy spent, the perfection of the product by the machines, and the technique of man" (QA.12).

A third element in his strategy for the development of Minas Gerais, was the establishment of definite goals or *metas* for the various sectors of the economy. Very general goals had been suggested during his election campaign, but once in the governor-ship, Juscelino brought together groups of experts and practitioners in the various fields to lay out detailed plans and projects for electric power, road building, and other sectors, plans which involved not only physical aspects but details concerning how the various programs were to be financed. Although no overall *Programs de Metas* (Plan of Goals) such as he offered as president was established while he was governor, there was very extensive sectoral planning.

The administration of Governor Kubitschek also sought to mobilize not only the resources of the state government, and whatever help could be gotten from the federal administration, but also the largest possible participation of private enterprise in programs for the development of the state. The principal instrument for encouraging private participation was the "joint company," which was set up by the state for a particular project, but in which private investors were invited to buy shares. Such companies were established for electric power enterprises and for several industrial enterprises launched by the administration. At the same time, encouragement was given to private firms through the establishment of industrial parks and other devices.

The Incident with Mr. Russel

Kubitschek put considerable emphasis on obtaining more or less extensive private investment in the mixed companies. Sometimes he was not above using arm twisting to get it. One such occasion was when he sought to obtain the participation in the Centrais Eletricas de Minas Gerais, S.A. (CEMIG) of the St. John del Rey Mining Company, a British-owned gold mining concern operating in Morro Velho. The manager of the mining firm was a W. Russel, whom Kubitschek described as follows:

> An Englishman with all the peculiarities of his eccentric compatriots. He lived like a lord in his castle in the countryside of Kent or the Country of Wales. He dressed in a smoking jacket to dine, only read news-papers from London, and to the parties which he organized occasionally in his residence, he only invited subjects of His Britannic Majesty. He did not know and

99

had no desire to have contact with the Brazilians who
worked in the organization. . . . He was an authentic
feudal lord who, through the windows of his inaccessible
fortress, observed with unhidden contempt the villeins
who entered and left the mine. (EP.232-33)

One of those Brazilians whom Russel despised was the
governor of Minas Gerais. When Juscelino called him on the phone,
the Englishman would not receive the call because he was having
lunch and would not be disturbed. Hanging up the phone,
Kubitschek then called the British Consul in Belo Horizonte, a
friend of his, Mr. S. Walter, and informed him that despite their
friendship, he would no longer be able to receive him, or any other
British subject in the gubernatorial palace. When the consul asked
for an explanation, Kubitschek informed him of the incident with
Russel.
    That same afternoon, Consul Walter sent an intermediary to
Kubitschek to beg the governor's pardon and to explain that Russel
did not speak any Portuguese (after living in Brazil for twenty
years), and had misunderstood his servant about the phone call from
the governor. The messenger also reported that Russel was now in
Belo Horizonte, and would stay until the governor could receive
him. Kubitschek, in recounting this story, commented that he "was
never capable of fomenting misunderstandings and even less of
cultivating hatred." So he called in Russel immediately, who "after
hearing from [him] about what CEMIG would be, without discussing
the matter, subscribed the amount which [he] had suggested"
(EP.233).

Kubitschek and "Fiscal Irresponsibility"

Governor Kubitschek had the policy of not being afraid to add
to the state's debt burden for productive enterprises, an attitude
which he also had as president of the republic. However, this did
not mean fiscal irresponsibility on the part of the state government,
since it was accompanied by a rationalization of the public
administration, a very substantial increase in tax revenues, and
conversion of much short-term borrowing into a long-term funded
debt. The philosophy of the Kubitschek regime in Minas Gerais, as
later in Brazil as a whole, was that there was little to fear from an

increased burden of debt, so long as the funds acquired were used to stimulate the economy and expand the future tax base.

Political Problems with a Development Program

The kind of overall development program for the state which the Kubitschek administration carried out was something completely new for Minas Gerais. It was an absolute break with political tradition, and it cost Governor Kubitschek considerable time and effort to accustom the local political leaders in the various municipalities of the state to this new way of conducting affairs. Traditionally, the local political leaders associated with the state administration occupying the Palacio da Liberdade had been concerned principally with obtaining patronage from the governor and his associates. Most particularly, they sought to have friends of theirs named as the local police chief, and to be able to dismiss teachers from the local schools and replace them with others who were politically aligned with them.

Kubitschek disrupted this ancient political patronage ritual. From the very beginning, when a local political chieftain came to him, requesting the traditional kinds of patronage, Kubitschek refused. He suggested instead that the local politician ask for a school, a new bridge, a medical dispensary, anything else which would contribute to the economic and social progress of his municipality. Juscelino explained to them that they would gain from this. He later wrote as follows:

In the beginning there was a reaction, followed by resentment. Afterwards, when the bridge was inaugurated, or the medical dispensary began to function, my position improved. With the bridge constructed, the travellers did not have to trudge through the mire, and when they came to the town, they always had a word of praise for the local political chieftain who put an end to the problem with that bog. With the dispensary functioning, he saw with pride, opening the window of his house, the scores of patients obtaining medical treatment . . . without him having to spend anything. Miserliness allied with vanity contributed, after a while, to changing the rules of the game. (EP.290)

In conversations with the local political leaders he preached the message "that the time of patronage has passed, and prestige is acquired not by the truculence of a police chief but by the construction of works of real interest to the community." He was particularly resistant to demands for a change in local teaching staffs, saying: "Ask me for a bridge, a school, a loan, but absolutely not for the removal of a teacher" (EP.290).

The Electrification Program

As soon as he took office, Governor Kubitschek began to put into effect his program for expansion of the state's electric power network. A semi-official account of the Kubitschek regime notes that

> a few days after taking office, Governor Kubitschek had the technicians busy who were going to aid in the formulation and execution of the plan for electrification. It was necessary to carry out something more than a mere reinforcement of what was under way; the possibility of industrialization would only exist when the state could assure an abundant supply of energy on a long-range basis. The initial plans provided for expansion. (QA.18)

This same source noted that the studies undertaken by the administration took into account projects which were already underway. It also involved the study of other projects which it would be possible to push to conclusion during the new administration.

Once the basic planning of the electrification program had been completed, Kubitschek undertook the establishment of several regional mixed companies in various parts of the state, to get started on individual projects. The first of these was the Companhia de Electricidade do Medio Rio Doce (CEMRD), the Electric Company of the Middle Rio Doce. With a total capital of 27 million cruzeiros, it had a private contribution of 13,400,000 cruzeiros, or 49.5 percent (QA.32). The second regional company to be launched was the Companhia de Electricidade do Alto Rio Grande (CEARG), or Electric Company of the Upper Rio Grande, which had a total of 100 million cruzeiros in capital, of which only 12 million cruzeiros were supplied by private investors. In the Central Eletrica do Piau, a private company, the state acquired 50 percent of the total capital of 15 million cruzeiros (QA.33).

The overall control of the electric power development of the state was soon put in the hands of a holding company, Centrais Eletricas de Minas Gerais, S.A., generally known by its initials, CEMIG. The government of Minas Gerais transferred to CEMIG the 488,517 shares of stock which is possessed in various subsidiaries. The 378,368,526.70 cruzeiros contributed by the state represented 37.8 percent of the authorized capital of one billion cruzeiros (QA.34). However, effective control of CEMIG was in the hands of officials named by the governor.

Although most of the projects undertaken by CEMIG and its subsidiaries during the Kubitschek administration were of relatively small size, the ultimate impact of the government's efforts in this sector was very substantial. A semi-official account of the Kubitschek regime in Minas Gerais summed up the administration's accomplishments in the following terms: "Minas Gerais passed in fact from having 200,000 kilowatts to 605,000 kilowatts, of which 405,000 kilowatts were added between 1951 and 1955. Some 225,000 kilowatts were built directly by the government of the state, the rest being provided by private initiative, with effective help from the state administration" (QA.168).

Several large-scale projects were also commenced during the period that Kubitschek was governor of Minas Gerais. The most important of these was the Tres Marias Dam on the São Francisco River. With a capacity of 520,000 kilowatts, this project was worked out as part of the program of the Federal Commission of the Valley of the São Francisco, in conjunction with CEMIG, and was financed largely by the National Bank of Economic Development. The actual construction was entrusted to CEMIG, which also had a minority share in financing it. It was completed in the early 1960s (QA.88).

Most of the electrification effort of the Kubitschek administration in Minas Gerais was designed to bring into existence a state-wide electric grid. For this purpose, much of the effort and expenditure of CEMIG and its subsidiaries was directed towards construction of long-distance transmission lines from the various hydroelectric projects they constructed to the principal consumption centers. The governor did not overlook the many isolated towns and villages for which connection to the grid was impossible. For many of these, CEMIG provided small diesel powered motors of from fifty to five hundred horsepower (QA.27).

By the end of the administration of Governor Kubitschek, CEMIG controlled the third largest electric power complex in the country. Sometime earlier, Juscelino had indicated the significance of his administration's accomplishments in the electric power field when he commented to the Commercial Association of Rio de Janeiro that

> to evaluate the size of the undertaking, we must point out that at the end of 1950 the installed potential in Minas was 180,000 horsepower, which included plants for industrial use and the small rural plants. Instead of these 180,000 horsepower of 1950, the people of Minas Gerais will have at the end of 1955 at least 600,000 horsepower at their disposal. The significance of this total of 600,000 horsepower to the Minas economy can be judged by the fact that today the industrial colossus of São Paulo, which made that state the pioneer in our progress in 1952, disposed of a total of 680,000 horsepower.[5]

However, Kubitschek's electrification plans were not confined to what could be accomplished in his own five-year term as governor. He wrote as follows about CEMIG in his memoirs:

> The expansion of the firm was projected far beyond my government, and the goals established were attained within the time limits stipulated. During the period 1952 to 1956, CEMIG carried out the establishment of its electric system for the service of industries; in the subsequent period, that is from 1956 to 1960, it extended its services to the cities and towns of the Minas interior; and then in the five years between 1961 and 1965, it came to provide energy to the fields and farms, in fulfillment of its phase of rural electrification. (EP.235)

Road Building

As in the field of electrification, the administration of Governor Kubitschek considerably exceeded the promises which Juscelino had made with regard to road construction. By the end of his period in office, his government had constructed 3,013 kilometers of road, compared to his original goal of 2,000 kilometers. The road building effort was carefully coordinated. The first six months of the administration were taken up largely with reorganization of the Departmento Estadual de Estradas de Rodagem (DER), the state highway department, and with planning the network of highways which it was proposed to construct. The reorganization of the DER was a major factor in the success of the road building program. A new headquarters for the department was built in the state capital, Belo Horizonte, which not only had extensive office space, but also modern garages for road building equipment, repair facilities, and storage space for equipment which would ultimately be required by the various regional headquarters of the DER. Several subdivisions of the DER, notably its Bureau of Soils, were strengthened with new technical personnel and equipment (QA.114-15).

The system of regional headquarters of the DER was considerably strengthened. It was these decentralized units of the department which were to have the actual job of constructing the new roads. The idea of this kind of decentralization did not originate with the Kubitschek administration, but many of the existing regional headquarters had been inoperative when it took office. One of the major efforts of the first few months of the administration was the reorganization or establishment of some twenty-six different regional headquarters spread throughout the state. Each regional office of the DER had its resident regional chief and resident construction engineer, as well as other technical personnel (QA.111-12).

Much new construction and associated equipment was purchased, part of it from a loan negotiated in France by Governor Kubitschek. In 1951 eighty new machines of various types were added to the DER's equipment pool, in 1952 some two hundred and twenty more, and in 1954 an additional eighty-two machines. By the end of that year, some twelve hundred vehicles of various types were being used and maintained by the repair facilities in the various regional headquarters and the central repair depot in Belo

Horizonte (QA.118-19, EP.246-47). Careful planning was also an element in the success of the road building effort. Governor Kubitschek himself commented in the middle of 1952 that "the execution of the highway program was only begun after careful elaboration of plans, which required several months of observation and study" (QA.112).

There was careful coordination also between the DER headquarters and the various regional offices. The semi-official account of the Kubitschek administration in Minas Gerais commented as follows:

> We have already seen that the field work would be totally controlled by the regional headquarters, in radio contact with the DER in Belo Horizonte. The DER, in Belo Horizonte, is thus the center of all studies and all preparatory schemes. Planning was done in the offices, execution in the field. When doubts arose, the men who worked on the cartographical maps also went out into the field—and when these doubts were of major importance, the Governor himself accompanied the technicians charged with clearing them up. (QA.113)

Highway construction was conceived as taking place in three steps, in conformity with the growing traffic which was expected on each road. When a highway first was opened, "it followed as closely as possible the undulations of the landscape, maintaining an angle of inclination of 6 to 7 percent, and a minimum width of the road base of several meters and sixty centimeters. The construction thus was more economic, in time and money, long stretches being completed in a relatively short time and in more favorable financial conditions" (QA.115). The second phase, when traffic conditions required expansion of the highway, saw a widening of the road base, to accommodate the larger number of vehicles. The third phase involved the paving of a highway, at which time a road base would be further widened, grades would be reduced, and, preferably, materials available in the locality would be used for paving purposes.

Sixteen different highways were built during the Kubitschek administration, extending into virtually all parts of the state. The largest of these, going in a north-easterly direction from Belo Horizonte, was over nine hundred kilometers in length. Generally, the roads were built outward from the capital city, taking off from the "exit" streets Kubitschek had had constructed when he was mayor. The city served as the axis for the state's entire road system. Usually, too, efforts were made to link the state highway system with the existing and growing federal highway network (EP.245-46).

As in the case of its electrification efforts, the Kubitschek administration planned for road building which would take place long after Juscelino's term as governor. Kubitschek noted in his memoirs, that

> in 1951, some 1,947 kilometers were investigated in the zones of the state most needing expansion, and during my term there were projected 6,654 kilometres of highways. This study of the conditions of the soil involved many complex operations. The analysis was necessary in order to carry out the stabilization of certain portions, and to consolidate the cutting and particularly the excavation in clay areas. . . . The earth over which the roads were going to be built was treated by the technicians as something live. It underwent a complete medical examination, such as a patient is submitted to before undergoing a surgical operation. (EP.246)

The Mannesmann Project

Governor Kubitschek saw the development of the infrastructure of the Minas Gerais economy as a necessary precondition for the state's becoming a major industrial center. However, he did not wait for the completion of his expansion program for the infrastructure before undertaking to augment the manufacturing sector. The most spectacular new industry established in the state during the Kubitschek term of office was the Mannesmann steel plant. Perhaps more clearly than any of the other industrial projects launched during the Kubitschek period, it illustrated the key importance of the infrastructure development program of Juscelino's state administration.

President Vargas informed Kubitschek in the middle of 1951, only a few months after taking office, that the Mannesmann Company of Dusseldorf, West Germany, was contemplating the establishment of a large plant for the production of steel tubes somewhere in Brazil, and that it had some interest in locating this plant in the state of Minas Gerais. The firm listed a number of requirements, the fulfillment of which would determine the location of the plant. Among the requirements laid down were housing for 1,200 workers, including 150 German technicians, an area of 500,000 square meters in a region amply supplied with water, and most essential of all, the immediate availability when the plant opened of 12,000 horsepower of electricity, and the ultimate availability of 70,000 horsepower. In a number of ways, Belo Horizonte was an ideal location for the new plant. It had the required water supply, a new industrial park was under construction outside of the city where the installation could be located, and there was an ample labor supply in the vicinity. However, more difficult was the electricity requirement. As of 1961, the amount of electric power needed by Mannesmann represented almost half of that then available in the whole state (QA.267).

In seeking to get the Mannesmann firm to establish its plant in Belo Horizonte, Kubitschek provided a characteristic example of his willingness to take risks, if he thought them to be justified. Lucas Lopes, president of CEMIG, was quite unwilling to commit the firm to providing the electricity required by Mannesmann at the times the Germans specified. He refused to sign a document giving such guarantees. Juscelino wrote in his memoirs: "I was not accustomed to conforming to solutions which limited my freedom of action. The installation of Mannesmann in Minas represented a great step— already foreseen—towards fulfillment of my plan to take the state out of its agropastoral phase and to put it surely on a path of intensive industrialization." Therefore, he summoned the Mannesmann officials to his offices, and "asked them if, instead of a guarantee of the president of CEMIG, a document signed by [him], as governor, would serve to assure the installation of the steel plant in the State. The reply was affirmative" (EP.237-38)

The first phase of the plant opened before Governor Kubitschek left office. It involved a steel production and lamination mill with a capacity of 70,000 tons a year, using a Krupp-Renn furnace which could use Brazilian coal. It also called for the installation of an electric furnace, a lamination mill for the production of tubes, and an extrusion press operating with a special Mannesmann process. It was particularly designed to produce tubing needed for the petroleum industry.

Construction of the plant got underway in April 1952. The first phase of the installation was inaugurated some two years later, on 12 August 1954, in a ceremony attended not only by Governor Kubitschek but also by President Vargas. On that occasion, Juscelino noted that

> precisely four years ago, in his electoral campaign, the present governor of Minas promised the people to give our state, if elected, the elements necessary for the transformation of its economy from one based essentially on agriculture and grazing, to one in which a sizable portion of its income would come from industry. Therefore, our euphoria on this occasion is justified, when the government and the people see today marked by tangible evidence of that dreamed-of transformation. The four years of struggle which have passed are crowned this morning by a spectacle which we shall see in a few moments when the first flow of incandescent metal will proclaim in its smoke that we, the Mineiros, have achieved an industry typical of our era and of great importance. (QA.272)

The Mannesmann plant was only the larger of two steel industries established in the state during the Kubitschek period. The second was set up by Brazilian entrepreneurs of the Jafet combine.[6]

Other Industrial Projects

The state government of Minas Gerais itself undertook two important industrial projects during the Kubitschek administration. For this purpose, two mixed firms were established, with private participation, but a majority of government ownership. These were the Companhia Frigorificos de Minas Gerais S.A., known popularly as FRIMISA, organized to build packinghouses, and Fertilizantes Minas Gerais S.A., FERTISA, a firm for the purpose of manufacturing fertilizer. The idea of establishing a large commercial packinghouse under state ownership was projected first by Governor Antônio Carlos in 1928. However, the onslaught of the Great Depression and other factors had intervened, and it was not until the Kubitschek administration that the state government once more gave serious study to the idea. FRIMISA was officially established by State Law No. 833 of December 1951; in the middle of the following year the governor ordered the preparation of a detailed study for the establishing of the plants which were to be built by FRIMISA.

It was decided to build the first FRIMISA plant in the vicinity of Belo Horizonte, since that city was so located that it was relatively easily accessible to most of the grazing sections of the state and provided the largest market in the state. Financing for the enterprise, which represented an investment of 300 million cruzeiros, came partly from the federal government, partly from the state, and partly from credits advanced by the Companhia Mineira de Engenheria, which undertook to construct the plant. Some parts of the packing plant began operations in 1955, but in August of that year a fire destroyed much of what had been constructed. As a result, it was not until 1959 that the first FRIMISA packinghouse entered fully into operation (QA.247-57).

Kubitschek saw the establishment of a fertilizer plant as an essential ingredient in any effort to rehabilitate the agriculture of Minas Gerais. The worn out soils of the state resulted in very low productivity; the availability of relatively cheap and abundant fertilizer was essential to rebuild agriculture in the state. Minas possessed reserves of phosphate raw material for such a plant at Araxa, and of potassium at Poços de Caldas. It was decided, therefore, that FERTISA which was established by Law No. 1,007 of 5 November 1953 would undertake to establish plants at both places to exploit these raw materials. Although the installations of FERTISA were not finished during Juscelino's governorship, most of them were opened during the administration of his successor, Bias Fortes (QA.258-66).

In addition to projects in which the state government had a direct interest, Kubitschek sought to do as much as possible to encourage the establishment of private industries. One major effort in this regard was the completion and expansion of an industrial park on the outskirts of the capital, which had been planned originally by Governor Valadares. Kubitschek later noted that many of the industrial firms which had already been established in that park expanded their installations during his administration. In addition, as he noted, "factories of different kinds—such as the Mafersa firm, making railroad material, and others making stoves,

110

flour, distributors of petroleum and its derivatives, abrasives and laminated iron—were being erected, and through this constellation of new firms, developing upon a solid basis the process of industrialization of the state" (EP.282).

The Kubitschek Administration's Work in Other Fields

Although the governor's greatest attention was centered on his electrification, road building, and industrialization programs, his administration also brought the state substantial progress in a number of other fields. One of these was public health in which Governor Kubitschek as a medical doctor by profession had particular interest. His Brazilian biographer José Moraes has noted that

> in the public health sector, in his travels as a candidate for governor, he found that in sixty Minas municipalities there was not a single doctor to take care of their inhabitants, and as a result, judging medical dispensaries as the most practical means of bringing health care to the poor, he announced his intention of creating one hundred such dispensaries throughout the state. He ended up creating one hundred twenty, all installed by his government, many with specially constructed buildings.[7]

The expansion of public education was also an important objective of the Kubitschek administration in Minas Gerais. At the time he took office, school registration amounted to only some 680,000 students. Kubitschek at first promised to double the number of children in school, but as Moraes notes, "the technicians, more familiar than he with the difficulties of this sector, counselled him to promise an increase of only 300,000 places. He ended up surpassing this, since he left school registration in Minas Gerais at 1,100,000 students."[8]

Moraes also cites other achievements of the Kubitschek government in a number of other fields.

> He constructed 52 new airfields; constructed 137 new school buildings; constructed 37 new sports fields;

111

constructed 251 new bridges and left 257 others under construction; he installed two faculties of medicine, one of law, one of pharmacy and dentistry, five musical conservatories and one school of fine arts. And he left in an advanced state of construction the monumental state library, the organization of which he confided to the great Minas writer Eduardo Freire, and which he hoped would be the model establishment of its kind in South America.[9]

It is interesting to note that in the construction of the state library, Governor Kubitschek again employed the services of the famous architect Oscar Niemeyer, who was given several other commissions by Juscelino's state administration.

Kubitschek's accomplishments in fields other than those directly related to economic development would seem to indicate a somewhat wider range of interest and concern by Governor Kubitschek than that which was to characterize President Kubitschek. As federal chief executive he did not tend to provide as much in the way of resources and personal attention to social and cultural aspects of development as he did during his tenure as governor. Perhaps this reflects the different nature of the jobs of a state and a federal chief executive, or perhaps it reflects a substantial change in the emphasis of Juscelino's own thinking.

Financial Aspects of the Kubitschek Administration in Minas

The financial situation of the state government of Minas Gerais was close to being disastrous when Kubitschek took office. One of his more notable achievements as chief executive of the state was bringing order into its finances. He himself described the fiscal situation which he faced when assuming the governorship, in a radio address on 24 April 1951. It included a

floating debt, that is, debt for which prompt payment is required, with the creditors at the door every day, 800 million cruzeiros; promissory notes, 630 million cruzeiros; checks issued and not paid, 220 million cruzeiros; total of these urgent debts, 1,650,000,000 cruzeiros. This without speaking of the funded and consolidated debt, with fixed dates of payments, and definite interest due on designated days. There are obligations of 1,650,000,000 cruzeiros payable within a year, in a state which has to take care of its normal services—payment of wages, public works, schools, police, justice, and the teaching staff—to the amount of 1,531,000,000 cruzeiros and which in the last year took in taxes only one billion five thousand cruzeiros! The situation, consequently, is not good. (QA.172-74)

After extensive study of the problem of the state's finances, Kubitschek undertook a number of measures to improve them. These involved better tax collection, rationalization of the tax structure, restriction of unnecessary expenditures, and conversion of the floating debt into more long-term obligations. One of the earliest measures was the holding of a series of tax conferences in various parts of the state. Top officials of the Secretariat of Finances met with regional authorities charged with tax collection, both to stress the administration's determination to put an end to tax evasion, and to clear up problems concerning interpretations of the tax laws. The results of these conversations were felt almost immediately: in 1951 for the first time since 1947 tax receipts were larger than anticipated in the annual budget. Overall tax collections in the year were 495,612,507.20 cruzeiros larger than in 1950, of which 345 million had not been foreseen in the budget (QA.178). During subsequent years, tax collections continued to rise significantly, with the result that in 1954 the state collected 3,380,814,243.60 cruzeiros in taxes, compared with 1,916,261,802.20 in 1951, the first year of the Kubitschek administration. At the same time, tax rates were somewhat increased during 1951. Both sales taxes and levies on motor vehicles were augmented. A sliding scale was introduced in the motor vehicle tax, by which cars of greater power were taxed heavier than those with less. Expenses of the regular budget, as opposed to the items dealing with the administration's economic development program, were substantially curtailed. The semi-official study of the Kubitschek administration in Minas Gerais argued that over the four years of Juscelino's government, some 1,831,108,819.80 cruzeiros were trimmed from the ordinary budgets (QA.184).

Throughout the administration, Kubitschek followed the policy of consolidating the most urgent portions of the floating debt through the issuing of long-term bonds. The possibilities of doing this were limited by the admittedly narrow market for government obligations of any description which then existed in Brazil. As a matter of fact, both the floating debt and the funded debt continued to increase each year of the Kubitschek administration, although at a slower rate than in the previous one, insofar as the floating debt was concerned (QA.191). Extraordinary borrowing was resorted to in order to finance the development programs of the Kubitschek administration. For one thing, the state government entered into a *convenio* (agreement) in 1951 with a French firm IMPEX, which provided most of the construction equipment and electrical installations, for the liquidation of the cost of these over a period of several years. The total amount of money involved was some U.S. $20 million. On the other hand, in the middle of 1953 the state assembly passed a law authorizing issuance of a special series of state bonds totalling two billion cruzeiros, which funds were to be used specifically for the electrical and highway development programs.

One aspect of the increase in state indebtedness upon which the Kubitschek government placed great emphasis was the productive nature of the use of the state's funds. Thus, a semi-official study of the administration stressed that 75 percent of the debt resulted in increases in property belonging to the state. There were in four years more than two billion cruzeiros added to the state's property, in the form of real property, bank stock, highways, equipment of all kinds—resulting in rapid increases in the resources of the land and of social welfare (QA.194).

Thus, Kubitschek was able as governor of Minas, although faced in the beginning with the direst financial prospects, to find ways to substantially increase the state's tax revenue, to decrease its normal bureaucratic expenditures, and to obtain credit for the substantial economic development program undertaken by his administration. He showed the same conviction as governor that later he did as president, that the acquisition of an increased public debt burden was thoroughly justified if the proceeds received by the state from this debt increase was used for the purpose of broadening and strengthening the economy, and thus ultimately widening the tax base of the government. Certainly, the state was in as good if not a better financial condition when he left the governorship than it had been when he became governor.

Negative Aspects of Kubitschek's State Administration

Of course, the administration of Governor Kubitschek was not without its weak points. Edward Riedinger, an admirer of Juscelino, pointed out some of these. He noted that

> in comparison with the rest of the country, agriculture grew little during the period (in 1950, 70 percent of the population was rural); rural income declined and emigration continued. In spite of vigorous industrialization, the state did not improve relatively, since the internal consumption market grew little. This was the natural result of agrarian policy, which resulted in a diminution of middle sized landholdings, while large ones grew, stimulating the irrational use of already poor land. Although running rapidly, Minas remained somewhat behind.[10]

Riedinger went on to say that

> one cannot deny that the government of Kubitschek was economically and politically beneficial to Minas. Personally, too, it brought financial returns: the Kubitschek Group, a real estate firm, was established in Belo Horizonte during his term. But the administration of Juscelino was not exempt from criticism. With regard to several projects, corruption in the concession and execution of contracts was alleged. . . . Certain grave problems, such as the shortage of secondary school teachers, were ignored. Many projects were badly executed, or were not completed. Of the many highways constructed, none was asphalted, all were of earth or macadam.[11]

The Political Opposition

The Kubitschek administration in Minas Gerais certainly was not without opponents and even enemies. It met very vocal, although not particularly effective, opposition from the União Democrática Nacional in the state legislature, which was controlled by the administration's partisans. Both the legislators and the predominately pro-UDN press constantly attacked the supposed errors of both commission and omission of the Kubitschek regime.

The UDN could not very well attack the specific development projects of the administration, although they did accuse the governor of extravagance. However, one of the issues which the opposition did raise was concerned with the completion of a small retreat for the governor at a place called Mangabeiras. This building was pictured by the UDN members of the legislature as being a "sumptuary palace," and was strongly attacked on the floor of the assembly. Kubitschek thereupon asked deputy Ultimo de Carvalho of the PSD to organize a conducted tour of the "palace" by members of the state legislature making sure to have a number of the UDN members among those participating. According to Kubitschek, this tour, which showed the absurdity of the charge, ended the discussion of that issue (EP.230).

One continuing complaint of the opposition was the strong hold of the parties which supported the Kubitschek regime on the municipalities of the state. In his memoirs Kubitschek commented that "in reality, [his] electoral victory had resulted in profound modifications in municipal political representation. UDN control was broken, with the Chambers and the prefectures of the municipalities being turned over to representatives of the PSD or the PR." Kubitschek went on to explain that "there arose, then, local conflicts, district rivalries, and quarrels between political adversaries. Those incidents, generally of a personal character, had repercussions in the Legislative Assembly, giving origin to violent attacks on the government. They blamed [him] for everything, as if [he] had time to get involved in the municipal intrigues and disputes" (EP.250). At one point, the state president of the UDN gave an interview to a Rio de Janeiro newspaper in which, using these municipal quarrels as a basis for his charges, he "denounced to the Nation . . . the situation of insecurity which exists in the State." The pro-administration majority in the legislature responded by passing a resolution "lamenting the unpatriotic procedure of the UDN in promoting a campaign to discredit the Government of the State" (EP.251).

In later years, in the light of what had happened subsequent to his governorship, Juscelino was inclined to see the bitterness of some of the attacks upon him as governor as part of a much wider conspiracy of the national UDN and the military men allied with them, to oust from power not only Vargas, but all of that part of the national political leadership which was more or less associated with Vargas. In 1973 he told me that he was convinced that the center of that conspiracy had been the Superior War College (Escola Superior de Guerra), which he said became "a permanent center of conspiracy." Kubitschek attributed the Vargas suicide to this alleged conspiracy, and also some of his own problems both as governor and as president.[12]

In any case, the opposition inside and outside the legislature was not sufficiently strong to hamstring any of the essential projects of the Kubitschek administration in Minas Gerais. With a solid majority in the state assembly, Juscelino was able to pass whatever legislation his program required. With the backing of President Vargas, he was able to obtain extensive help not only from the federal government, but also from abroad. He had a style of government which put him in constant touch with large segments of the population and widened the political base of not only the governor personally, but of the administration as a whole.

Kubitschek as Supervisor and Inspirer

As governor of Minas Gerais, Kubitschek continued the pattern of governing which he had begun as mayor and was to follow later as president of Brazil. He worked indefatigably, and travelled around the state with great frequency, keeping in personal touch with the many programs which his administration was undertaking, and maintaining contact with people of all levels of society in all parts of the state. Kubitschek himself once described an average day of the governor when he was in Belo Horizonte:

> Coffee on the desk at seven in the morning, already with cabinet aides in front of me, reading papers and signing them; public audiences, more meetings with

officials, which never begin after eight and never end before one o'clock in the afternoon, and when I got to lunch at two or three o'clock it is always with four to ten people at my side and in front of me, to tell me what bridge is falling down, or that the teachers' pay needs to be increased, that the communists are shooting in Uberlandia, that the members of the police are without nightsticks or that Montes Claros needs a road. Afterwards more audiences and work in the office until dinnertime, after which, for variation, more office work or audiences. It is about eleven in the evening that the Palace begins to be empty and only then do I have the calm and tranquility to shut myself in my office with one or two aides, and until two or three in the morning study plans and projects, discuss general policies of the administration and lay plans for the future. (QA.383-84)

The furious pace which Kubitschek maintained for himself and those working with him soon won him the sobriquet "the jet governor" because he worked at the speed of a jet plane. He introduced many innovations in the customary conduct of Minas Gerais governors. Years later, he observed: "The use of the telephone was one of the many taboos which I broke. There was a prejudice in the palace against telephonic communications. To reinforce the fragile basis of this anachronism, there was cited the example of Getúlio Vargas . . . who never used the telephone to communicate with his ministers" (EP.220). Kubitschek went on to explain that he considered that "another factor decisive for the dynamism which existed in all sectors of my government was the practice of not imposing a rigorous schedule on the different types of work to which the governor was subject. The routine was obeyed until something new arose" (EP.221).

Much of the governor's time was not spent in the capital city, but in travelling in the interior of the state. On one occasion, in August 1952, he spent thirty days visiting twenty-one municipalities. From this trip there resulted twelve new schools, seven medical dispensaries, six new bridges, and a variety of other projects (QA.385). Many of his trips around the state were voyages of inspection of the many and varied projects which his administration had under way. It was his custom to appear suddenly in his small plane and have it landed right there on the project, a procedure which some of his accompanying aides thought was dangerous both for the governor and for themselves. Kubitschek noted in his memoirs, that "they thought that I should leave the airplane at some field nearby and continue in an automobile to the work center. I agreed with them, but always acted in a different manner." He added that "I wanted to exploit the psychological effect of a sudden arrival at the place, which always created an atmosphere of enthusiasm among the workers, favorable to the acceleration of the job."

Juscelino went on to observe that "the project chiefs of the secretariat of transport, highways or aviation, and the contractors working for the state lived with their eyes on the sky . . . in the worried expectation that my *Bonanza* might at any moment come out of the clouds. And those unexpected appearances occurred in the most disconnected work projects: now in the frontiers of Bahia, then in the south of Minas, today on the border with Goias, tomorrow in the endless stretches of the Minas Triangle" (EP.259). Elsewhere, Kubitschek stated what he thought was the most important advantage which came from his frequent travels about the interior of the state. It was, he said,

> the overall vision which they give to the head of the government, permitting him to understand the interrelationships and catch the thread which runs through them, so as to see clearly which undertakings and initiatives are of widest scope. That is, those which because of their basic effects, their fundamental and collective nature, will immediately or later contribute to the fulfillment of all the others, and accelerate the process of general enrichment. (QA.385)

He might have added that these voyages kept him in constant touch with the rank and file of the citizenry and with those who were responsible on the spot for carrying out the programs of his administration. Furthermore, they served to let his constituents know that things of great moment were really being accomplished by his administration. His constant travels certainly had the effect of arousing in the people of his state the mystique of "developmentalism," the idea that it was possible for the people of Minas to do much for themselves, to take charge of their own destiny, and to bring economic development and social and cultural progress to their native land.

Chapter 7

THE 1955 ELECTION CAMPAIGN

With the suicide of Vargas in August 1954, Vice President João Café Filho succeeded to the presidency. After trying unsuccessfully to arrange a one-candidate election, it was he who finally presided over the poll which made Kubitschek the Brazilian chief executive. Subsequently, suspicions that he might cooperate in an attempt to frustrate the results of those elections led to his removal by the military in November 1955.

Background of João Café Filho

Café Filho was an unlikely successor to Vargas. During virtually all of his political career he had been an opponent of Getúlio. Although he had participated in the Revolution of 1930, and after it had been named chief of police of Natal, the capital of the northeastern state of Rio Grande do Norte, he soon turned against what he conceived to be the dictatorial tendencies of Vargas. Café Filho was arrested by the Vargas government after the suppression of the communist-led National Liberation Alliance revolt in November 1935. He was exiled to Argentina and did not return to Brazil until 1938, when he retired from politics until the end of the Estado Novo. With the termination of the dictatorship he was one of the two principal co-founders of the Partido Social Progresista (PSP), along with Adhemar de Barros of São Paulo, who became the party's principal national figure. During the 1945-1950 period, Café Filho served as a PSP member of the Chamber of Deputies.

During his service in Congress, Café Filho gained a reputation for being one of the more militant and left-wing members of that body. He not only was very much concerned with social and labor problems, but was also associated with the still small but growing group of nationalistic congressman who were concerned about the supposed threat to national sovereignty represented by the country's heavy dependence on foreign investment. The nomination of Café Filho as Vargas' running mate in the 1950 election was the result of a deal between Getúlio and Partido Social Progresista leader Adhemar de Barros. Adhemar, who was himself very anxious to be president, apparently felt that if he would support Vargas in 1950 instead of also running in that election, Getúlio would reciprocate by backing him in the following presidential election in 1955. However, the price of Adhemar's support was the nomination of a member of the PSP as vice president on the ticket with Getúlio, who had been chosen for president by the Partido Trabalhista Brasileiro.[1]

Kubitschek never believed that Vargas would have backed de Barros in the 1955 presidential election. In a conversation with me in 1972, Juscelino recounted that after the gubernatorial election of 1951, when Lucas Garcez was chosen governor of São Paulo with Adhemar's support, Vargas had asked Kubitschek to help him to win Garcez away from his political association with Adhemar. Vargas' explanation for this request, Kubitschek said, was that he did not want to have to back Adhemar in the 1955 election, and so wanted to deprive him of his political base in São Paulo. Juscelino added that he thought it inconceivable that Vargas would have supported Adhemar whom, Kubitschek described as a "simple crook," citing Adhemar's famous slogan "I rob, but I accomplish things."[2]

In any case, Café Filho was the man selected as part of the 1951 Vargas-Adhemar deal. His choice was not unwelcome to Getúlio, since Café Filho at that time had wide popularity due to his energetic support of various measures on behalf of the urban workers and other underdog elements in the post-Estado Novo period.[3] During most of the second Vargas administration, Vice President Café Filho remained in the background. Although he presided over the Senate, as required by the constitution, he was not one of the close advisers or associates of the president. Indeed, he tended to have a good deal closer relations with some of the leading opponents of the administration that he did with the key figures of the second Vargas period. He took little part in such bitter controversies of those years as that centering upon the government oil firm Petrobras and that over João Goulart's tenure as Minister of Labor.

During the crisis which preceded the suicide of Getúlio, Café Filho was actively consulting with both sides in the dispute. At one point, he offered to resign jointly with Vargas, if the president decided that that would be the best solution to the crisis. He apparently felt that the removal of a vice president who was widely known to lack warm sympathy for Vargas might make Getúlio more willing to give up his post. Subsequently, he was accused by his former nationalist friends of having been part of a plot to get rid of Getúlio.[4] Kubitschek was also convinced that Café Filho's suggestion was part of the UDN's campaign to get rid of Vargas and all those associated with him.[5] Many years later on 2 December 1974, he told Edward Riedinger that he had spent the whole night of August 23/24 working on official business, while keeping constant contact with friends in Rio, fearful that a move against Getúlio would also mean his removal as governor of Minas Gerais.

Political Situation after Vargas' Death

When he learned of Vargas' death, Café Filho went to Laranjeiras Palace—since Getúlio's body was still at the Catete Palace where he had died—and assumed the duties of chief executive. There was no attempt on the part of the military men who had provoked the crisis leading to Vargas' suicide to keep Café Filho from assuming the presidency. The cabinet organized by President Café Filho was relatively conservative and with a few exceptions, distinctly anti-Vargas. However, the new president asked various people, including Kubitschek, for advice on his cabinet appointments. Juscelino suggested the name of Lucas Lopes, head of CEMIG, a suggestion to which a number of other PSD leaders objected, not wanting to collaborate at all with Café Filho. After some hesitation, the new president named Lopes as minister of transport (EP.310). Lopes stayed in the cabinet only until the sharp clash between Café Filho and Juscelino early in January 1955.[6]

Café Filho's most important cabinet selection was his choice of a minister of war. Brazilian historian Glauco Carneiro has indicated how this came about: "The Army, particularly, needed a pacifier. And the eyes of the President fell on Lott. There was a man for the moment: by the rules, hierarchical, dutiful, without party, without group, without intimates; forty years of discipline and military virtues."[7] In a word, General Henrique Teixeira Lott was chosen because of his reputation for being an apolitical military man, who was not associated with any of the cliques into which the leadership of the armed forces was then divided.

Because Vargas' unexpired term had less than year and a half to run when he took over the presidency, Café Filho did not launch any large new programs. In a written reply to questions submitted to him by the author on 8 June 1966, ex-president Café Filho commented as follows:

> I became president constitutionally on 24 August 1954, as vice president, after the suicide of President Getúlio Vargas, to complete his term, the duration of which was less than a year and a half. In view of the short time available, I preferred to continue certain projects already under way, not presenting them as my own, but seeking to fulfill them in a harmonic fashion. I governed during a period of transition and conformed rigorously to the legal limitations of a fully democratic regime.

The Café Filho administration generated a favorable impression among many foreign observers. Thus, an article in *Time* magazine of 6 December 1954, noted that

> besides providing a conspicuous personal example of candor and integrity, Café Filho is giving Brazil a government that is opposed to nationalism and favoritism, that is trying to work out the country's problems instead of conjuring them away. Said a member of Brazil's Chamber of Deputies: "Café Filho is setting a much-needed example. He is proving that an honest man with common sense can be more useful to this country than a glamorous personality."

The 1954 Congressional and State Elections

One of the first political decisions which President Café Filho had to make was whether or not to go ahead with congressional and state elections which were scheduled for 3 October, less than a month and a half after Vargas' death. According to Kubitschek, Café Filho was of the opinion that they should be postponed, and

124

he sounded out leaders of the various parties about the idea.[8] However, Juarez Távora, Café Filho's chief of the military household, maintained that both he and the president were strongly opposed to the postponement of the elections, as some of the leaders of the União Democrática Nacional were urging.[9]

Some PSD leaders, particularly those who were opposed to the possible presidential candidacy of Kubitschek, also thought the elections should be postponed. At a meeting of major PSD leaders in Rio de Janeiro, Etelvino Lins, then governor of Pernambuco, in particular insisted on the need for postponing the elections which he argued would disrupt public order. However Kubitschek was strongly opposed to postponing the congressional and state elections. As he wrote many years later:

> I presented the reasons which made me not agree with the suggestion. An election was not, and could not be, a reason for the perturbation of order, and if it was, we would be facing a real collapse of the regime. I emphasized that a postponement, in those circumstances, would be the equivalent of an attack against existing institutions. And, reinforcing that line of thought, I declared that, being governor of Minas I would use all the power that that post conferred on me to impede the alteration of the electoral calendar. (EP.314)

Kubitschek told me in 1972 that he felt that his strong opposition had been a major factor in convincing Café Filho not to postpone the scheduled elections.[10]

Café Filho's version of the discussion concerning postponing the 1954 elections differed from that of Kubitschek. Café Filho said in his memoirs that leading figures in the PSD as well as those of the UDN and other parties urged him to postpone the elections. However, he insisted with all of those who urged this upon him that it was not within his authority as president to do this, that it was his job only to preside honestly and fairly over the elections, and that if they wanted them postponed, they should go to Congress for that purpose.[11]

The elections were held on schedule, and their results were mixed. Because of the varying alliances of parties in different states, it was hard to say clearly whether the pro-Vargas or anti-Vargas forces had been the winners. However, from Kubitschek's point of view, the results were particularly favorable in Minas Gerais. He wrote in his memoirs that "That election clarified the horizon. . . . The PSD and the PTB won a majority of the mayors, as well as strong majorities in the National Congress and in the state legislatures." He added that "In Minas the numbers of votes were most eloquent: the PSD alone elected 320 of the 485 prefects. Those 320, added to those elected by the other parties which supported me in the state—the PR and the PTB—came to a total of 432, the opposition electing only 63. The same proportion was seen in the new Legislative Assembly and in the election of the Minas representatives in the federal Senate and Chamber" (EP.315).

As a consequence of the congressional elections, the Social Democratic Party had 114 deputies and 22 senators in the national congress, clearly the largest representation of all. Second came the União Democrática Nacional with 74 deputies and 13 senators, and the Partido Trabalhista Brasileiro followed, with 56 deputies and 16 senators. The fourth largest party was de Barros' Partido Social Progresista, which after the 1954 election had 36 deputies and four senators. The rest of the members of the two houses were divided among eight other parties with one independent member of the Senate.[12]

The Campaign for a "Single Candidate"

A presidential election was scheduled to take place a year after the October 1954 legislative ones. It seemed virtually certain that this would develop into a contest between the anti-Vargas forces—the UDN and its allies—and the pro-Vargas forces of the PSD, PTB, and several minor parties. Given the results of the 1954 elections, it seemed highly possible that the pro-Vargas forces would elect a new president and vice president in 1955. President Café Filho, the UDN, and pro-UDN elements in the armed forces wanted to avoid this at almost all costs. They suggested that in the 1955 election there be only one candidate who would be supported by all political parties in the name of national unity. If that idea were to be accepted, the UDN people and President Café Filho apparently felt that someone from their ranks, or at least someone who had no previous association with Vargas, could be agreed upon to become the "single candidate."

However, the great majority of the PSD, as well as the PTB and several smaller parties of the pro-Vargas camp, were strongly opposed to this idea. Kubitschek was particularly opposed to it, feeing that an uncontested election would be a negation of political democracy in Brazil. He also felt that the PSD, which was at that time the country's strongest party, had every right to test its strength at the polls in the 1955 presidential election. His objections certainly were influenced by the supposition that he was the most likely person to be nominated by the PSD, and would probably also be able to muster the backing of the PTB and several smaller parties.

Juscelino's position was well known. Therefore, President Café Filho sought to convince him to accept the idea of a single candidate. He summoned Kubitschek to Rio for a discussion of the subject. Kubitschek reported on the meeting as follows:

> I got to the presidential residence at noon, and only left at five in the afternoon. Café spoke during the whole time, now with enthusiasm, now with pessimism, but trying to be as obscure as possible. The thesis was the same: a single candidate, since that was what the military men wanted. During the interview I made myself remain silent. I could not say anything without consulting the leaders of the PSD. (EP.316)

Café Filho, writing about this same meeting, said: "I alluded to the gravity of the problems of the country, particularly in the economic-financial field. I could give him the testimony of my experience. Whoever would be my successor would need a sufficient base of support to be able to confront the difficulties, including the political ones." Café Filho went on to say that he pointed out the split then existing within the national PSD ranks, and that it might prevent Juscelino's getting his party's nomination. However, he noted that this did not seem to worry Kubitschek and added

> I don't know if he saw in a disunited PSD a field more propitious for his personal objectives. What I do know is that he showed me the way of making his candidacy prevail. He told me that, to obtain the government of

127

Minas Gerais, he went into battle in spite of the PSD. He would enter the campaign before any decision of the party. This would oblige it to accept him.[13]

There were those within the PSD who were won over to the idea that there should only be one candidate in 1955, on the theory that if the PSD were to win, the military would not allow its nominee to take power. Reportedly Juárez Távora, as Café Filho's chief of the military household, had told São Paulo Governor Jânio Quadros that such would be the case, and the PSD leaders knew about this. (Távora makes no mention of such a discussion in his memoirs.) One of the PSD leaders who was convinced that the PSD should not have its own nominee was Benedito Valadares, Kubitschek's old patron, and as Juscelino reported in his memoirs: "Within the PSD, Benedito Valadares carried on his usual antlike activity. He worked without noise, but with incredible efficiency" (EP.319). Café Filho confirms in his memoirs that attitude of Valadares towards Juscelino's candidacy and the reasons for it.[14] Understandably, the leaders of the PSD in Pernambuco, Santa Catarina and Rio Grande do Sul, who were for one reason or another opposed to Kubitschek's candidacy, also sought to commit the party to the single candidate idea.

Candidate to be Candidate

However, the majority of the national and state leaders of the PSD went ahead with the idea of the party putting up its own nominee, and agreed that this candidate should be Kubitschek. Particularly forceful in pushing this position was the national president of the PSD, Ernani Amaral Peixoto, who was also the husband of Vargas' daughter, Alzira. Kubitschek had some problems of his own to settle before he could make a final decision to fight for his party's nomination. His vice governor, Clovis Salgado, belonged to the Republican party, not the PSD. If Juscelino were to be a presidential candidate, he would have to resign as governor at least by 2 April 1955 in conformity with the constitution. He had no compunctions about turning the reins over to Salgado, but he did not want to do so until he was sure that the PSD-PR alliance would continue in the 1955 gubernatorial election, and that the candidate of the coalition would be from the PSD.

128

Juscelino negotiated with ex-president Arthur Bernardes, head of the Republican party, on this issue, but Bernardes insisted that the PSD-PR gubernatorial candidate should come from his party. Kubitschek then turned to Arthur Bernardes Café Filho, son of the ex-president and a senator, who pledged his support for Kubitschek as president and for a PSD nominee for governor, saying he would resign from the senate if his father did not agree with this. Probably conclusive in the discussion of this issue within the republican ranks was Vice Governor Clovis Salgado's promise that if the PR insisted on naming its own gubernatorial candidate in the 1955 election, he would resign, turning the governorship over to the president of the legislature, who belonged to the PSD. In any case, Kubitschek finally got agreement by the PR to support him for president and to back another PSD leader for governor of Minas Gerais (EP.320-23).

With this issue resolved, the National Directorate of the PSD met in Rio de Janeiro on 25 November 1954, and by a vote of 123 to 36 resolved to recommend to the national convention of the party that Kubitschek be the PSD candidate for president in 1955 (EP.323). It also agreed to a suggestion of Pernambuco Governor Etelvino Lins, that the convention not meet until 10 February 1955. Juscelino's opponents hoped that the intervening two months and more would be sufficient to get Kubitschek to retire from the contest (EP.326). Lins was an old opponent of Kubitschek's nomination. Even before the death of Vargas, he had been trying to work out a deal for a joint candidacy of the União Democrática Nacional and the Partido Social Democrático in the 1955 election. In his "political testament" Lins claimed that in January 1954 Juscelino had agreed to a joint ticket of Juárez Távora as presidential candidate and Kubitschek as nominee for the vice presidency.[15]

Once Vargas died, Kubitschek no longer felt himself committed to their agreement, according to Lins who attributed Juscelino's change of attitude to his assurance that he would have the support of the Partido Trabalhista Brasileiro in the 1955 election. On the day before the PSD executive committee meeting which was to propose a party candidate, Lins suggested to Juscelino that the PSD propose to the UDN a choice of three possible candidates for president: Kubitschek, Gustavo Capanema, and Lucas Lópes, who was at that time President Café Filho's minister of transport. Kubitschek said that he would let Lins know on the following day. The answer Lins received consisted of letters from Capanema and Lópes saying that they wanted nothing to do with such a deal.[16]

Juscelino had no intention of giving up the nomination. To strengthen his position in preparation for the convention, he made five trips to various parts of the country, visiting almost every state, conferring with the PSD and PTB leaders in the various states, and assuring himself of the support of most of them.

Once the PSD National Directorate had recommended Juscelino, Ernani Amaral Peixoto also set about to line up support from other parties. Almost immediately the Partido Trabalhista Brasileiro announced its backing of Kubitschek. The endorsement of the Republican party had already been obtained. So it was decided to establish an Interparty National Committee, with its headquarters in Rio de Janeiro, to take charge of the coming campaign. At the same time, Kubitschek organized "a group of technicians oriented by Lucas Lópes and Israel Pinheiro, charged with receiving suggestions, making studies, and suggesting solutions for the great problems which would have to be confronted" should he be elected president (EP.328).

Confrontation with João Café Filho

Meanwhile, the effort continued to convince Kubitschek to give up the PSD nomination and to allow the naming of a single candidate. Among those who tried to change Juscelino's mind was his old friend José Américo de Almeida, the government candidate in the 1937 election, and in 1954 the governor of Paraíba. When Juscelino went through that state on his campaign tour, Américo, although of the UDN, insisted that Kubitschek stay in the gubernatorial palace. They had a long conversation. Kubitschek recorded in his memoirs his reply to Américo's claim that an election campaign might generate a civil war: "Who is menacing Brazil with a civil war? Not I. I am defending the Constitution and the law. There will come no provocation from me. In my speeches to the electorate, I only appeal to them to go to the ballot box, and that the result of the voting he respected" (EP.337).

Finally, President Café Filho decided to intervene directly once again to try to achieve Kubitschek's withdrawal. The two men met in the Catete Palace in Rio on 20 January 1955, Kubitschek being accompanied by Senator Arthur Bernardes Café Filho. In his memoirs, Juscelino summed up the line of argument of the president: "the moment is very grave; his duty as president was very painful, since for long he had held me in high regard; but a national union was indispensable, with a single candidate" (EP.343).

Café Filho showed Kubitschek a document signed by the top officers of the armed forces, which demanded "a solution to the problem of presidential succession on the basis of understanding and interparty cooperation." *Time* magazine in its 21 February 1955 issue commented that "translated from the officialese, the message meant that the generals and admirals wanted the right and center parties to put up a joint candidate to swamp Kubitschek." Café Filho subsequently wrote that this was not the intention of all the military leaders; at least one suggested that Kubitschek might be considered as a possible "unity" candidate. Also, Café Filho insisted that he had had no hand in provoking the writing of the memorandum; it had come as a complete surprise to him.[17] Whatever the document's origins, Juscelino told the president that it was "an instrument of pressure, which conveniently exploited could give the impression that the Armed Forces, going contrary to their traditions, desire to frighten the electorate," and urged him not to publish it (EP.345).

Neither man convinced the other. Before Kubitschek and Bernardes Café Filho left, they agreed that the latter would write up quickly a summary of what had been discussed. João Café Filho and Kubitschek both agreed that it reflected what had transpired. The note read as follows:

> The object of my conversation with the president of the republic was, in fact, the problem of the presidential succession.
> It was for this purpose that we met.
> Examining the national scene in all of its aspects, the president of the republic indicated to me his desire which he considered to be his duty, to do everything so that the campaign for the succession proceed on a high plane, and if possible within a spirit of national unity.
> The proposals of his excellency received, in principle, on my part, full approval, since as I have indicated on various occasions that is my own desire.

131

I shall have to inform the leadership of my party of this conversation.[18]

This document signed by Juscelino was shown to a journalist from the newspaper *O Globo*. When Kubitschek showed it shortly afterwards to other PSD leaders, they told him that the statement did not make it sufficiently clear that he intended to stay in the presidential race. As a result, the following phrases were added at the end of the note, "and that I shall remain fully in the campaign, if my candidacy is ratified by the convention of my party."[19]

Kubitschek maintained that in accepting the original version of the note he had had no notion of indicating that he was withdrawing from the presidential campaign. He thought that it remained implicit that he was not retiring his campaign, but when his colleagues thought that it was open to other interpretations, he had agreed to appending the addition and issued the revised version of the note to the newspapers (EP.344). Café Filho claimed that Kubitschek had intended to have the note say that he was withdrawing his candidacy, and that its original version "was a loyal summary of the spirit of the conversation he had with [him]."[20]

A week after this meeting the president gave a radio speech in which he charged that "the prospect of a convulsed presidential succession was presented when one party launched a candidate without agreement with other political forces," and accused the PSD and Kubitschek of proposing "to restore the order of things tragically ended on 24 August 1954." The president also read the statement of the military which he had shown Kubitschek, and which Juscelino thought they had agreed would not be made public. Finally, he criticized Kubitschek for altering the statement about what had taken place at their interview (EP.345).

Juscelino answered the president in an interview with *Correio da Manha* in Rio, in which he began by saying that what the president of the republic said was not true. In his memoirs he explained why he responded so harshly, saying as follows:

> I did not think that I had committed any excess. Café Filho had acted towards me with undoubted impropriety, and I saw no reason for limiting myself to halfway measures, just because he was the chief of government. It was true that never before even in the

most turbulent phases of political activity had anyone called the president of the republic a liar; before Café Filho, none had incurred that fault. (EP.348)

Kubitschek also reaffirmed his intention to stay in the presidential race in a speech before the PSD of the Federal District a few days before the PSD convention. He said: "They have attempted to form a circle of iron around me, to make me renounce my candidacy. And while they invite me in the name of peace and the unity of Brazil to abandon the pacific field of struggle so far deserted, they do not wish to propose an adversary, they force me to persevere" (EP.350). This speech, which was reported verbatim in the press, won him the support of the Rio daily *Correio da Manha*, which until then had tended to be pro-UDN.

During these last weeks before the PSD convention, Kubitschek feared that the president might go so far as to have him arrested. Because of this fear, he wrote:

> I had my own security arrangements. They were the most simple possible. They consisted of an airplane, on the runway and ready to take off. . . . I gave orders to the crew not to leave the airport for an instant. If there was any hostile attitude on the part of the authorities, I would be advised in time by friends, and I would fly to Belo Horizonte. In Minas, no order of Café Filho would be carried out, and I would raise the State [in revolt]. (EP.351)

Although President Café Filho did not ever order the arrest of Kubitschek, there is no doubt that he was and remained very bitter towards his successor. In his memoirs, Café Filho wrote:

> His attitude which he continually affirmed, moreover, in fact frustrated my efforts at pacification. But it frustrated also, in time, the objectives of those efforts, to safeguard the normality of the democratic process in Brazil. The military men responded, in June 1964, to the attitude of Kubitschek, cancelling his mandate as Senator for Goyas and suspending for ten years his political rights.[21]

Candidate at Last

Until the meeting of the PSD National Convention on the evening of 10 February 1955, the pressure against Kubitschek's candidacy continued. Valadares had succeeded in getting the proxy votes of 100 delegates from Minas Gerais who could not attend the convention. All kinds of pressure was brought upon delegates from the other states. The majority of the delegates from Rio Grande do Sul, Santa Catarina, and Pernambuco were known to be against Kubitschek's nomination. Kubitschek's candidacy could therefore by no means be taken for granted when the convention met in the Chamber of Deputies building in Rio de Janeiro at 8 P.M. on 10 February. The last maneuver tried by Perachi Barcelos of Rio Grande do Sul, Lins, and Valadares was to try to postpone the convention for a day, in the hope that they could turn more votes against Kubitschek. They failed.

Amid considerable tumult, finally the convention opened. The first successful move made by the pro-Kubitschek elements was a resolution that the nomination be by roll-call vote, so that each delegate would have to make clear just how he voted. After speeches by Barcelos and by a supporter of Kubitschek, deputy Vieira de Melo, the voting commenced. One of the high points of the process was when Valadares was called upon to cast his vote and those of the hundred proxies he held. When he cast them for Kubitschek, a cheer went up among the delegates. Finally, Kubitschek's nomination was ratified by 1,646 in favor with 276 abstentions (EP.358).

Kubitschek was then called and was asked to come before the convention to accept the nomination. He did so after being introduced by Amaral Peixoto. In his peroration, Juscelino promised: "I swear and promise that I shall have no rancor for what I have suffered, for the offenses and injustices which I have had to support, and that I wish to work from now on for political peace, for the profound and living unity of the nation, for the elevation of the level of this campaign, for a full, generous and sincere general understanding" (EP.359).

João Goulart's Candidacy

The Partido Social Democrático represented only part of the pro-Vargas element in Brazilian politics. The other major part, the Partido Trabalhista Brasileiro, was headed after the death of Vargas by João Goulart. He was his party's logical candidate for president. However, it was clear that the PTB had no chance to win on its own, and the only result of Goulart's candidacy would be the election of an anti-Vargas nominee. Therefore, negotiations took place between the PTB and the Partido Social Democrático.

The elements opposed to Kubitschek's candidacy did what they could to try to dissuade the PTB from joining forces with Juscelino. On 13 March, Juárez Távora, chief of the military household of President Café Filho, met with Goulart for this purpose. The meeting was not an easy one for Távora. He recorded in his memoirs that Goulart insisted on talking against a change in the electoral law which the government was pushing. Távora wrote: "I permitted myself to return to the previous explanation, of the conciliation guaranteeing him that if this was obtained, the Armed Forces, cohesive in support of their chiefs, would guarantee the new government, upon being installed, a loyal and decided support. . . ." He added that "Goulart abstained, prudently, from any observations on the matter. . . . I did not touch on his negotiations with the PSD about the Kubitschek candidacy, nor did I judge it opportune to provoke him on this matter."[22]

An agreement between the PSD and PTB was finally reached. The PTB endorsed Kubitschek, and the PSD agreed to have Goulart as Juscelino's running mate for vice president (EP.367). This arrangement was based on a patronage accord. It was agreed that in the future Kubitschek government, the Partido Trabalhista would have the portfolios of minister of labor and minister of agriculture, and would also have control of patronage in the social security institutes.[23] Maria Victoria de Mesquita Benevides has stressed the importance of this PSD-PTB alliance not only in winning the 1955 election, but also in providing the relative stability of the Kubitschek regime, contrasting so sharply in that regard with those which preceded it and immediately followed Juscelino in office.[24]

The Other Candidates

For some time it appeared as if Jânio Quadros might seek the presidency. He had been elected governor of São Paulo in 1954 and was undoubtedly one of the most popular figures on the Brazilian scene. A Brazilian newspaperman, Newton Carlos, associated with Carlos Lacerda's *Tribuna de Imprensa*, summed up the strength of Jânio at the end of 1954 as follows:

> Quadros' mass support is a symptom of the popular reaction against both Vargas and his traditional opponents, who were generally conservative. Quadros, who was supported by the young Brazilian Socialist party, opposed both the "laborism" of Vargas and the false "Populism" of Adhemar de Barros, former São Paulo governor and the perennial presidential candidate. The popularity of Quadros and of journalist Carlos Lacerda (these are the two men most prominently in the news at the moment) marks the onset of a new political generation and the end of the rule of the politicians who have dominated Brazil since the overthrow of President Washington Luiz in 1930. The popular feeling behind this new generation makes the election of Juscelino Kubitschek or any other conservative candidate most unlikely.[25]

Although Carlos proved to be a misinformed prophet insofar as Kubitschek's eventual victory was concerned, he was quite correct in analyzing the strength of Quadros, who was the first politician who was not either pro-Vargas or anti-Vargas. Carlos was also right when he predicted that it might well be that he would wait until 1960 before seeking the presidency. Quadros ended up supporting the candidacy of General Távora in 1955. Távora, chief of the military cabinet of President Café Filho, was first approached late in March 1955, by leaders of the Christian Democratic party, who told him that their organization wanted to nominate him as their candidate for president. At that point, he told them that he could not accept. The previous December the military leaders, including him, had promised that none of them would run for the presidency. Furthermore, until Kubitschek resigned as governor of Minas, thus making himself constitutionally eligible to run, all hope of getting a single candidate should not be abandoned. Café Filho indicated that once Kubitschek had acted, he might change his mind.[26]

Távora was almost legendary. He had been one of the principal figures in the revolt of the tenentes in the 1920s, and one of the chiefs of the so-called Prestes Column. He led the revolution of 1930 in the northeast, and during the first two years of the Vargas administration had been, because of his military backing, perhaps more powerful than the president himself. However, with the outbreak of the 1932 revolution in São Paulo, he had returned to active service in the Armed Forces, and had risen by the middle 1950s to the rank of full general. He still had a certain flair as a popular orator and had a reputation for honesty and integrity.

Early in April, after Kubitschek's resignation as governor, Távora conferred with the other military leaders who had signed the December 1954 document. They all agreed that in the light of Juscelino's definite candidacy, they were all freed from the pledge made in the document not to run. Távora then notified the Christian Democrats, as well as President Café Filho and Governor Quadros of São Paulo of his willingness to run.

In the face of Távora's attitude, Quadros indicated his willingness not to launch his candidacy under certain conditions. These were the inclusion in Café Filho's ministry of two São Paulo political leaders, and the naming of Paraná Governor Munoz da Rocha, a political friend of Quadros although a member of the Republican party, as Távora's running mate. He demanded a reply from Café Filho within forty-eight hours, so that if it was not forthcoming, he could resign as governor and become eligible as a presidential candidate on 2 April. Quadros and Café Filho quickly reached agreement, and took for granted that Távora would concur with their decisions. On 3 April Távora demurred; two of his friends were to be the ones replaced in Café Filho's cabinet by the Paulistas. Furthermore, the selection of his running mate by the president and governor was an imposition upon the political parties which might be willing to support his candidacy.

In the face of Távora's withdrawal, the UDN, the Partido Libertador, and the dissident wing of the PSD agreed to nominate Lins, the PSD ex-governor of Pernambuco, as their candidate against Kubitschek. Lins was a weak nominee, relatively unknown and had little possibility of drawing support outside of the three groups which had declared their support for him. Among other things, he lacked the backing of Governor Quadros, backing which was crucial for anyone who sought to defeat Juscelino. Therefore the Christian Democrats and the Socialist party again approached Távora. Quadros also sent feelers to sound out Távora's availability. Finally on 10 May 1955, he decided to run with the backing of the Christian Democrats, Socialists, and the probable backing of the Partido Libertador. He hoped that ultimately Lins might withdraw, and the groups supporting him would throw their backing to Távora.[27]

Távora not only accepted the support of the Christian Democrats and Socialists, he also agreed to a platform which was distinctly in favor of basic reforms in the economy and society, which had been largely drawn up by the Socialists.[28] It advocated agrarian reform and supported the oil monopoly of Petrobras in spite of Távora's former opposition to the idea. He chose as his electoral slogan "revolution through the vote."[29] On 26 June Lins retired from the race. The UDN endorsed Távora on 13 July. At the same time it named Minas ex-Governor Milton Campos (of the UDN) as his running mate. On 18 July the dissident PSD groups of Pernambuco and Rio Grande do Sul also endorsed Távora. The party in Santa Catarina headed by Neuru Ramos decided to support Kubitschek.[30]

The most radical anti-Vargas elements in the UDN were not in favor of backing Távora and thought that the elections should not be held at all. Thus, Carlos Lacerda wrote in the 30 January 1956 issue of *The New Leader* of New York reflecting the position he had held in the campaign:

> Café also insisted that the presidential election be held on 3 October 1955, as scheduled, instead of doing what democrats are now doing in Argentina: disinfecting the entire structure of government. That is to say, Café's cardinal error was to call elections before cleaning out the Vargas gang. . . . Against the dictates of common sense, the elections were held.

Kubitschek tended to see the candidacy of Távora as the objective which President Café Filho and the UDN had been seeking all along. In his memoirs he wrote the following:

138

Meanwhile, the adversaries were untiring. Since the *single candidacy* had not prospered, and the *military veto* was proven to be non-existent, they judged that the time had come to drop their mask. On 9 May, Juárez Távora, in a letter to his partisans, published in the press, admitted the possibility and even indicated the intention of being a candidate. That was the final result of the maneuver elaborated for so long. The *military veto* and *single candidacy* finally gave way to the hidden objective of that tricky campaign of national pacification. The Juarez Távora candidacy was its objective. Like the other two maneuvers, that one also had its origins in the Catete Palace. (EP.373)

In addition to the two major candidates—Kubitschek and Távora—there were two other nominees in the 1955 presidential race, neither of whom had a chance of winning. The first of these was Plinio Salgado, head of the successor to the old fascist party, Açao Integralista, now known as the Party of Popular Representation (Partido de Representaçao Popular). Kubitschek wrote of this nominee that

for a long time it had been known that he would be a candidate, and under these circumstances, the quicker his candidacy could be launched, the better perspective would the political problem of the country have. With the existence of two candidates, it would not be possible any longer to argue the removal of my name to assure the antidemocratic formula of the single candidacy, vehemently advocated by Café Filho. (EP.370)

As a result, soon after his own formal nomination, Juscelino contacted Salgado urging him to hurry up the announcement of his candidacy. The fourth candidate was Adhemar de Barros, running with the support of his own Partido Social Progresista (PSP). His nomination undoubtedly hurt Kubitschek, because in São Paulo, with the largest number of voters of any of the states most of the generally pro-Vargas workers tended to be supporters of Adhemar and his PSP.

Juscelino's Campaign

As had become customary with Kubitschek, he campaigned exceedingly hard, visiting virtually all parts of the country. He travelled 205,307 kilometers, the equivalent of five times around the world. Some 196,000 kilometers he traversed by air, 9,000 by train or automobile, 292 by river launch, and 15 kilometers on horseback. He gave 1,000 speeches and listened to 2,500 others. He participated in over 100 television programs and 300 round-tables. He gave approximately 500 press interviews. Some 100 deputies and 30 senators accompanied him on his various campaign swings (EP.372).

His campaigning techniques were unusual for Brazil at that time. In most of his campaign meetings, after giving a short speech he would go down into the crowd, talking with individuals, questioning them about the problems of their part of the country, and receiving questions about details of his program. As a result of these exchanges, his program tended to evolve somewhat as the campaign progressed. As a consequence of new information he acquired while travelling the emphasis would change and new things might be added to the program. One of these new points was the construction of Brasilia.

The campaign program, ultimately the Kubitschek government's program, was first elaborated under the title Program of Goals (Programa de Metas) by his economic and technical advisers. There were thirty of these goals at first—Brasilia being added as the 31st—and in the beginning they tended to be stated in very general terms. However, at Kubitschek's insistence, his advisers worked out very specific numbers for the most important goals. As a result, in his meetings he could "adopt the practice of having a dialogue with the listeners—[he] did not announce that there would be highways, ships, factories, automobiles, that the production of petroleum would increase and the fabrication of steel would be expanded. On the contrary, [he] cited figures. [He] established targets which would be attained" (EP.371). Thus, the whole stress of Kubitschek's 1955 campaign was on what was being called "developmentalism," the conviction that the country's first priority was its economic development. Juscelino summed up this idea in his slogan, "50 years' progress in 5."

The Issue of Communist Support for Juscelino

During the eight months of the campaign, various efforts were made by Juscelino's opponents to divert him from his principal task of getting out among the voters. One of the first of these diversions arose over the endorsement of Kubitschek by the Communist party (PCB). The Communist party had been formally outlawed in 1947 and many of its leaders had gone into hiding. However, the party continued to function and in 1958 was reported to have about 9,000 members.[31] It had its own press and was active in the labor movement and various front organizations. For the purpose of the 1955 election campaign early in June, the communists established the Movimento Nacional Popular Trabalhista (MNPT). It was ostensibly led by a non-communist trade unionist Ari Campista, but in fact was run by the veteran communist labor leader Roberto Morena.

According to Juscelino's one-time English-language secretary, Edward Riedinger, the MNPT had decided to support the Juscelino and Jango ticket by the end of June, although this was not announced until the Movimento's convention early in August.[32] The formal endorsement of Kubitschek and Goulart by the MNPT brought a steam of denunciations from the supporters of Távora, who accused Juscelino and Jango of having made a deal with the communists to obtain their support, agreeing to legalize the party once they had taken office.[33] Years later, Moises Vinhas, a major figure in the Communist party in 1955, also claimed that Juscelino had promised the PCB leaders that he would legalize the party, a promise on which he reneged.[34]

However, Riedinger has written that "Kubitschek really met with the communist leaders, anxious for the support which they might be able to give. . . . What he promised the party was more cautious and less infuriating than was alleged, but even so it was more than the party could negotiate with any other candidate with a chance to win." Riedinger continued: "As president, Kubitschek would not legalize the party, but he wold permit it to function as freely as any other. Publicly, he would not reject the support offered by the PCB, accepting it as something normal in a democratic campaign. Finally, the resources distributed by the PTB would not be limited, as was customary, only to that party, but would be channeled also to the communists."[35] The communists further

141

complicated the situation, however, by issuing an Election Manifesto in their newspaper, expressing support of Kubitschek and Goulart. In his memoirs, Kubitschek noted that "the incident had been created, following Moscow's best technique."

The MNPT's formal endorsement of Kubitschek had provoked a rapid return of the candidate to Rio from the campaign trail. At that point, Minister of War Henrique Teixeira Lott issued a statement to the effect that "support by the communists of the Kubitschek-João Goulart ticket has aggravated the crisis, leaving [him] practically incapable of controlling the reactions of certain military circles." To this, Kubitschek replied with a statement denying any agreement with the communists, and ending with the comment that "he was a disarmed man, but like the minister of war, [he] shall not retreat one step in the defense of legality" (EP.382-83). The incident passed. The campaign against Kubitschek on the issue of communist support became difficult for the UDN to maintain when Távora, their own candidate, pointed out that "by law, every elector is obliged to vote," and that it was impossible in the ballot box to distinguish the vote of a communist from that of any other citizen (EP.408).[36]

Early in September, the government outlawed the MNPT. Riedinger has noted that "Kubitschek maintained a cautious distance from that repression. He did not condemn it, to avoid aggravating allegations about his 'deal' with the communists; but he also did not approve of it, already carrying out his agreement for future tolerance of the party whose votes he needed."[37] Estimates varied wildly concerning the number of votes the communist endorsement brought to Kubitschek. Some UDN sources claimed that it accounted for 400,000 of the votes that Juscelino received. However, Tancredo Neves, Kubitschek's long-term close associate, estimated in an interview with Maria Victoria de Mesquita Benevides that the communists probably delivered about 150,000 votes to the PSD candidate.[38]

The Issue of Juscelino's Finances

Another serious move of Kubitschek's opponents which threatened to end his campaigning completely was a storm raised concerning Juscelino's personal finances. Upon launching his campaign, Távora had submitted to the Chamber of Deputies an accounting of his finances.[39] The UDN members of the Chamber then insisted that Alkmin, chairman of the PSD bloc in the Chamber, present the body with a detailed statement of Kubitschek's financial status. Such a statement was drawn up and submitted as requested. Then the UDN deputies alleged that the statement was false, and demanded establishment of a congressional committee of inquiry on the matter. They won the support of Carlos Luz, president of the Chamber of Deputies, who, although a member of the PSD, had not been a friend of Kubitschek since the 1947 gubernatorial campaign in Minas Gerais. If the congressional committee had been established, it could have required Kubitschek to leave the campaign trail to answer questions. However, through skillful use of parliamentary procedure, his friend Alkmin was able to get the hearings of the committee postponed until after the election date, which made the whole subject moot.

The most serious of the diversionary efforts of the UDN against Kubitschek's campaign was the move only twenty days before the election date to change the kind of ballot which would be used. Theretofore, each party had prepared its own ballots, containing its list of candidates. Each voter got the party's ballot which he preferred and deposited it in the box. The suggestion, which had first been made by the Electoral Tribunal, was for a single ballot, to be prepared by the Tribunal. Many months before, the UDN had introduced into Congress a bill providing for this and many other things, but the PSD-PTB majority succeeded in holding it up. As the election approached, however, pressure from the military and other sources for change in the ballot became irresistible. Finally, an agreement was reached by the Electoral Tribunal and the party leaders on a law providing for a single ballot, to be issued and distributed by the Tribunal.

A single ballot had many grave drawbacks insofar as Kubitschek's campaign was concerned. The PSD-PTB combination had its support principally among the humbler and less informed citizenry. Therefore, the base organizations of the two parties—4,000 of the PSD and 3,000 of the PTB—spent much of their efforts in instructing their supporters how to vote with the ballot which they presumed was going to be used. Although in parliament the PSD and PTB were able to prevent the alterations which would have done their candidates most damage (particularly the distribution of ballots by the Ministry of Justice instead of the electoral Tribunal,

143

and the issuing of four different ballots, each having the candidates listed in a different order), they were not able to prevent the issuing of a new type of ballot, only a few days before the election. This meant that the educational job of the base units of the PSD and PTB had to be done all over again in a very short period of time. Kubitschek estimated that this change of the ballot cost him at least one million votes on election day (EP.399).[40] Kubitschek was the winner by about 450,000 votes from a total of nine million cast. Paulo Singer (who in 1955 had supported Távora) noted that "the victory of Juscelino, like that of Getúlio in 1950, resulted in a popular protest, in this case, against the coup of August 1954. It was also a vote in favor of economic development, at any cost, which Juscelino succeeded in personifying. Since economic development fell during 1955, due to the economic policy in practice . . . the Juscelinista message encountered ample support."[41]

Chapter 8

"AS NOVEMBRADAS" OF 1955
AND AFTERWARDS

Kubitschek had received only about one third of the total votes, and his coming to power on 31 January 1956 was no by means certain. Indeed, the inauguration of Kubitschek did not become assured until after two military coups and complicated political maneuverings between 10 and 21 November 1955. The Brazilians refer to these events as "As Novembradas" of 1955.

A Conspiracy Against Kubitschek's Taking Office?

President Café Filho, in answering written questions of mine on 8 June 1966, insisted that the cause of the November 1955 events was not to be found in any attempt to keep Juscelino from becoming president. Café Filho wrote as follows:

> There was no conspiracy to prevent Kubitschek from taking office. The elections of 1955 for president and vice president of the republic and for some state governors, were the freest possible, with the government allowing the people to show their choice, and with the executive power, headed by me, maintaining a position of absolute neutrality with regard to the candidates. This neutrality was recognized by all, including candidate Juscelino Kubitschek, in a visit to me which he made in Catete Palace. The problem of counting the votes was handled by the judiciary and not the executive, that is, was under the control of the Superior Electoral Tribunal.

145

What existed to explain the military movement of November 1955 was a purely military question, which reached a crisis during the period I took leave from the presidency, hospitalized, for treatment for a heart condition, and under medical orders for complete repose. This was the military situation. Insofar as the political situation was concerned, those who had been elected, and their partisans, feared the results of the scrutiny by the specialized court of the votes they had received, since it was claimed that there had been frauds in various states, as well as active, ostensive and confessed participation by the communists in the 1955 campaign. Juscelino received a little more than 33 percent of the votes counted in 1955 and only a small advantage over General Juárez Távora, which aroused doubts as to the legitimacy of his election, a doubt which only the electoral court, judging the objections which had been presented to it, could clear up. This did not occur, because of the military coup of November.[1]

Kubitschek, however, denied to me that the recount issue had anything to do with the "counter coups" of November 1955.[2] He was convinced that forces opposed to his candidacy, particularly the leaders of the União Democrática Nacional, were determined that he should not come to power. In his memoirs, he wrote: "If everything had been done to prevent my becoming a candidate, now, after the elections, forces were mobilized to prevent the leadership of the country being turned over to me. The solution of the political problem on an electoral basis, unfavorable to them, brought the Udenistas to try a military coup as the way out."[3]

Café Filho's "Illness"

Exactly a month after the election President Café Filho had a heart attack and was rushed to a hospital. His doctor, a leading figure in the UDN, announced that the president was too ill to be visited by any political leaders, although he would recover after some period of rest.[4] His illness, however, did not prevent Café Filho from sending a handwritten note dated 7 November to Carlos Luz, president of the Chamber of Deputies, announcing to Luz that he was taking a temporary leave of absence and that Luz, the constitutional successor, should serve as acting president during that period. Nor did it prevent him on 6 November from talking at length to Minister of Agriculture Munoz da Rocha and Minister of Justice Prado Kelly, although he was "too sick" to see Minister of War Lott on that same day.[5]

Then and afterwards, Kubitschek felt that the president's heart attack was what might be called a diplomatic illness, designed to get him out of responsibility for the coup which was about to take place, and to which he was a party. Kubitschek's argument was that the only major impediment to the coup, which was designed to cancel the results of the 3 October election, was General Lott, who strongly favored the inauguration of the electoral victors. It was necessary, therefore, to dismiss Lott.

Like Kubitschek, Lott was from Minas Gerais. Kubitschek stated that

> this might give rise to an exacerbation of the localist sentiment which was very marked among the mineiros, leading to an armed reaction in the state. . . . As a measure of prudence, the conspirators decided then upon an evidently diversionary maneuver. Café Filho would take a leave and would pass the Government to Carlos Luz. In this way, the danger that Minas might feel aggrieved would be avoided, since it would all appear as an *affaire* among three Minas public men, or just a family quarrel. (EP.415)

Some credence to Juscelino's view that Café Filho's illness was feigned is given by Juárez Távora. He wrote in his memoirs that, on visiting Café Filho, only three days after he entered the hospital, he found the president "well disposed and in a good humor." When he asked Café Filho when he would return to the presidency, Távora records that "his reply was only an enigmatic smile."[6] General Lott, the principal mover in what happened in November, speaking after the events, confirmed the view of Juscelino. In an interview with Ubiratan de Lemos, a reporter of *O Cruzeiro*, which appeared in the 26 November 1955 issue of that magazine. Lott explained that he felt that his resignation as minister of war had been forced, in order to pave the way for cancellation of the results of the elections.

According to his account, Lott had serious grounds for believing this. The ministers of Navy and of the Air Force had argued with him at some length, urging him to demand of the Superior Electoral Tribunal that it declare the results of the poll null and void, on the grounds that no candidate had won an absolute majority. Lott had refused to join the other two military ministers, saying that he was not a lawyer, and hence was not capable of interpreting the law, and that it was the duty of the soldiers to uphold the right of the Tribunal freely to decide who had won the election.

UDN Threats of Coup

It is certainly clear that some of the Udenistas and their allies, including Carlos Lacerda, were willing to seek almost any alternative to prevent the assumption of office by president-elect Kubitschek. They particularly insisted that a candidate had to win an absolute majority in order to be elected president. However, in 1964, when the military government of President Humberto Castelo Branco was proposing to write this requirement into the constitution, thus imperilling his own ability to be elected president, Lacerda admitted that he had supported that idea in 1955 only as a maneuver to prevent Kubitschek from assuming the presidency.[7]

One scheme elaborated by Lacerda, Carlos Castilho Cabral, and other politicians and military officers, called for a Federal Council to take the place of the presidency. According to this proposal, which its authors presented as a solution for the crisis, this Federal Council would consist of "two representatives of the Army, one of the Navy, one of the Airforce, the president elected 3 October (doubtless it would be Kubitschek), his opponent Távora and two other 'big names' such as Otavio Mangabeira and Raúl Pilla, or even Neuru Ramos."[8] There is certainly little question that Lacerda called for a coup d'etat to prevent Kubitschek's coming to power. At one point, shortly before the events of 11-21 November, *Tribuna da Imprensa* went to the extreme of proclaiming that such a coup was going to take place within forty-eight hours.[9] It is also clear from various references in his memoirs that Távora suspected during and after the campaign that there would be a coup to keep Kubitschek from taking office.[10]

The Ouster of General Lott

The sequence of events of November 1955 is somewhat complicated. It was a funeral oration of Colonel Jurandir Mamede at the bier of former Chief of Staff General Canrobert da Costa which finally precipitated the crisis. In this speech the colonel, in addressing the corpse and those assembled to honor it, asked:

> Will not a presidential regime which, given the enormous amount of power in the hands of the Executive, can consecrate the installation of the highest representative of the nation, through a victory of a minority, be an undoubted democratic lie? Will it not also, perhaps be a patient pseudo legality that which seeks to legitimize itself by intransigent defence of a mechanism deliberately prepared to assure fully the vote of the illiterates, prohibited by Law?[11]

The Minister of War, General Lott, interpreted this speech, which openly suggested a repudiation of the election results, as being a subversive political discourse and therefore subject to punishment. However, Mamede was at the time a professor at the Escola Superior de Guerra. So Lott ordered him transferred back to his ordinary army duties, an order which was ignored by the commander of the Escola, an admiral. Nor would the Joint Chiefs of Staff of the Armed Forces move in the case. This suddenly converted a purely internal military affair into a political one, which served to precipitate a constitutional crisis.

Before Lott had a chance to insist with President Café Filho that he punish Mamede, the president had his heart attack, was confined to bed, and was ordered by his physicians not to see anyone on official business. Carlos Luz became acting president. General Lott insisted in his interview with *O Cruzeiro* that from the moment Luz took office, rumors spread that Luz favored an "illegal" solution to the problem of the election results. After Luz's first cabinet meeting, Lott had a private session with the new president, confronted him with these rumors, and although Luz denied them, Lott claimed not to be reassured.

At 5 P.M. on 8 November, Luz was sworn in as acting president. The next morning he presided over a short cabinet meeting, but General Lott was unable to raise the Mamede issue with him. They did discuss it later in the day.[12] Finally, on 10 November, General Lott was summoned to the presidential palace by acting president Luz to discuss again and decide about the case of Colonel Mamede. Luz kept the minister of war waiting for two hours in a large anteroom before receiving him, a fact which came to the attention of newspapermen assigned to the Catete Palace. During the second hour, a local radio statio announced every five minutes: "General Lott is still waiting in the anteroom" (EP.430).

When General Lott was finally admitted to the acting president's office, Lott presented him with five alternative ways of handling the Mamede situation, four of which involved some kind of punishment for the recalcitrant colonel, the fifth of which was to accept his own (Lott's) resignation on the grounds that he was unable to exercise his authority. The acting president, said Lott, quickly accepted the fifth alternative. During the discussion which followed, the acting president's nominee to succeed Lott, General Fiuza de Castro, entered the room. When Luz suggested that he assume the post of minister of war, Fiuza de Castro accepted. The two generals then arranged that the transfer of office would take place the following day, 11 November at 3:00 P.M.[13]

Café Filho wrote in his memoirs that not only was he not consulted on the dismissal of General Lott, but he was only informed of it after it had taken place. He said that

> the notice of that decision of my provisional substitute, entirely unforeseen by me, not only because I had not been consulted in advance about it, but also because I was ignorant of the evolution of the crisis, surprised me and alarmed me. I did not think that a minister of war could not be dismissed. But never in that way and under the circumstances of its being done by a substitute. Since I am very reticent about making a judgment of this kind, I continue to prefer not to comment on the ethical aspect of the dismissal in my absence of my minister of war, during a governmental interregnum caused by my illness under strict medical orders of absolute repose.[14]

Soon after his meeting with the president, General Odilio Denys, Commander of the Western Zone, waited for General Lott at his home and informed the minister of war that he and a number of other top officers were convinced that Luz was plotting to cancel the results of the election and that they were determined to use force to prevent this. General Denys invited Lott to take the leadership of the movement to depose Luz. General Lott took several hours to decide. Later, in the interview with *O Cruzeiro*, he described his indecision at that moment as a "shock of conscience," and said that "I asked myself: Where is my duty? What is legality?" Finally, at 1:30 A.M. on 11 November, he decided to accept the leadership of the movement against acting president Luz.

The "Counter-Coup" Against Carlos Luz

Once decided upon, the deposing of the acting president was quickly carried out. The Army seized most of the important buildings in the capital, and the leaders of the coup received pledges of support from virtually all Army units in the interior. Lott sent a telegram to all state governors, ministers, and troop commanders, justifying the actions of the Army leadership in the following terms:

> Taking into account the solution given by President Carlos Luz to the case of Colonel Mamede, the chiefs of the Army, judging such an act to be pure provocation to the Army, undermining the principle of discipline, decided to undertake to interpret the anxieties of the Army, seeking to return to the normal functioning of the existing constitutional regime. We believe we have the solidarity of the comrades of the Navy and the Air Force and we call upon all of the state governors, asking support for that attitude.[15]

One temporary stumbling block which arose in the early morning of 11 November was the choice of the successor to the deposed acting president. The indicated person was Neuru Ramos, the president of the senate, who was constitutionally the next in line of succession. A PSD leader from Santa Catarina, who had originally opposed Kubitschek's candidacy for president, Neuru Ramos was summoned to the Ministry of War, from which the "counter-coup" of General Lott was being carried out. However, he refused to accept the presidency. Alkmin, who was working closely with the minister of war suggested that they try to get through to President Café Filho on the phone, asking him to return to office and to promise to leave his ministry intact (that is, not dismiss General Lott). However, Alkmin could not get Dr. Raimundo de Brito, Café Filho's physician, to let him have access to the president.

Rather desperate, and fearing that if no constitutional successor to Carlos Luz was found soon, General Lott would do as some of his Army aides were urging, and establish a military dictatorship, Alkmin finally suggested that José Linhares, chief justice of the Supreme Court, who had served as president upon the deposition of Vargas ten years earlier, and was now again the next after Ramos in constitutional line, be asked to assume the presidency. Hearing that suggestion, Ramos changed his mind. In his memoirs, Kubitschek noted that "Neuru Ramos became palid. What he most feared was just what Alkmin had suggested. In his opinion, anyone could be president except Justice Linhares. In addition, the summoning of that magistrate would end once and for all his own chance to be president, exactly at the moment when he was only two steps from the Catete Palace" (EP.441). Ramos agreed to assume the post of acting president. The next day, the actions of the Army leaders were given constitutional sanction by Congress. Meeting throughout much of the day of 11 November, the Chamber of Deputies by a vote of 185 to 72, and the Senate by a vote of 44 to 9, declared Carlos Luz "disqualified from exercising the presidency of the republic." Ramos was immediately inaugurated as the acting president of the republic.[16]

The Incident of the *Tamandaré*

While the Army was being mobilized against him, President Luz had succeeded in getting away from the Catete Palace and reaching the Ministry of the Navy, where Lacerda and other civilians had already arrived. After hurried discussions, it was decided that the president and his supporters would board the cruiser *Tamandaré*, which was in dry-dock nearby undergoing repairs, but was in a condition to travel. They hoped to get to the state of São Paulo, which they had heard was still loyal to the deposed president.

On the morning of 11 November, the *Tamandaré* steamed out of the Rio de Janeiro harbor. Aboard, in addition to the regular crew, were the deposed president and five cabinet members, Justice Minster José Eduardo de Prado Kelly, Agriculture Minister Bento Munoz da Rocha, Chief of Civil Household José Monteiro de Castro, Transportation Minister Marcondes Ferraz, and Minister of the Navy Amorim do Vale, as well as the Commander in Chief of the Fleet, Admiral Carlos Penna Botto, and various other civilians and military men, including Lacerda and Colonel Mamede. Meanwhile, Luz's air minister, Eduardo Gomes, had taken off from the Galeão airport for São Paulo, hoping to align the armed forces there with Luz. Before leaving, he had telephoned Governor Quadros asking for and thinking that he had received promises of support from him. As it headed out to the open sea, the *Tamandaré* was fired upon by coastal batteries from the Duque de Caxias and Copacabana coastal artillery forts, but without any damage being inflicted upon the cruiser. Those on board had been informed that the navy base at the São Paulo port of Santos had remained loyal to Luz, but by the time the ship arrived there, the Santos garrison had changed its mind.

In the face of this situation, and the failure of any movement on behalf of Luz to develop in the state of São Paulo, Luz ordered a cessation of all resistance to the new government of Ramos. The *Tamandaré* returned to Rio and dropped anchor in the harbor on 13 November. Ovidio de Abreu went aboard as a representative of President Ramos, and obtained a letter of resignation from Luz as president of the Chamber of Deputies which was, in effect, a resignation as acting president of the republic. Those aboard were then allowed to disembark, and only one of them, Lacerda, sought refuge in a foreign embassy, but a few days later thought better of it, and left the embassy to return to his journalistic and political activities.[17] The effort of Luz and his supporters to establish their government in São Paulo failed basically because Governor Quadros did not support the move. Kubitschek later described Jânio's attitude: "In São Paulo, Jânio Quadros issued successive communiques, all very ambiguous, without any definition of position" (EP.447).

The "Counter-coup" Against Café Filho

The events of November 1955 were not yet completed. Café Filho had not resigned from the presidency. During the ten days from November 11 to 21, Alkmin tried to act as intermediary between the forces which had deposed Luz and the hospitalized president. He suggested that Café Filho return to the presidency, but that he agree to keep intact the military group then in command of the armed forces. Arguing that he was the legitimate president and could not compromise his authority, Café Filho refused to accept any conditions surrounding his return to office.[18] On 20 November, Café Filho sent messages to both houses of Congress, to acting President Ramos, and to the Supreme Court announcing that he was returning to the presidency. However, both the military and civilian elements which had been involved in the deposition of Luz were not ready to allow him to return to office, fearing that the efforts to organize a coup to cancel the results of the election, which they were convinced they had frustrated on 11 November, would be renewed if Café Filho returned to office. Steps were taken, therefore, to prevent this from happening.

Troops again took control of many of the important buildings of Rio. At the same time, the edifice in which Café Filho had his private apartment, to which he returned late on 20 November, was blockaded by soldiers and no one was allowed to leave or enter. On the following day, both houses of Congress declared that President Café Filho was deposed and replaced by Ramos. President Ramos then requested the Congress to declare a state of siege, which it did. In his memoirs, Kubitschek recounted his view of the political effect of that measure: "The Nation returned, thus, to its habitual tranquility. The Udenistas, fearful of the suspension of constitutional guarantees implicit in the state of siege, judged it more prudent to restrain their enthusiasm. The press, following the example of its inspirers, also adopted a discrete attitude" (EP.453).

Café Filho made one last effort to return to office. He sought from the Supreme Court a ruling that his deposition had been unconstitutional. Although at first refusing to rule on the matter so long as the state of siege existed, as soon as it was temporarily suspended, the Supreme Court turned down Café Filho's motion (EP.453).[19]

Juscelino Kubitschek During the November Events

Kubitschek spent most of the time in Minas Gerais while the events of November 1955 were unfolding. He felt that he was safer there, and furthermore, he was busy organizing possible civil and military resistance if a coup were attempted which was designed to prevent him from becoming president. Early in the crisis, Kubitschek "worked out with Clovis Salgado, governor of Minas, various precautionary measures, designed to frustrate the sinister undertaking of the sowers of disorder." Juscelino explained that

> I had conversations with distinguished chiefs of the Armed Forces, recognized as legalists, and reinforced my bases in Minas, through a concentration of the troops of the state police. I fact, I was not going to permit a cancellation of the results of the voting. The Minas people, almost unanimously had enthusiastically supported my candidacy, and through consultations with various state leaders, I was certain that Minas would consider it an affront to see their son prevented from taking office. . . . To this end, I had laid plans for a counter-coup, supported by strong military sectors, and I waited tranquilly the evolution of events. (EP.414)

Kubitschek was kept in constant touch with what was going on in Rio de Janeiro by Alkmin and other friends in the capital. However, he seems to have played no direct part in those events. In Belo Horizonte, he worked very closely with his successor, Governor Clovis Salgado. As events reached a climax on 10-11 November, Governor Salgado "wrote a note, in his own handwriting, directed to the people of Minas. He mentioned the facts of what was happening in the capital of the Republic, and revealed in it, his decision to fight in defense of legality. . . . The state military police were on the alert, night and day, and in the interior, there developed a movement of resistance among the people, with nuclei organized in the municipalities" (EP.443). Kubitschek took it upon himself to negotiate with the commander of the federal troops stationed in Minas. He happened to be General Jaime de Almeida, who had been an artillery captain during the 1932 contitutionalist revolt, upon whom Captain Kubitschek had operated when he had

155

been wounded. Kubitschek wrote that the general "was frank and positive. He would defend the Constitution, remaining at the side of General Lott" (EP.444).

Juscelino was not in Minas Gerais at the time of the deposition of Café Filho. On 18 November he had had to go with his mother-in-law to São Paulo, where she underwent an operation for cancer on 21 November, at nine in the morning. She died on the operating table. It was only after the operation, at which Kubitschek was present, although not operating, that he found out that the deposition of Café Filho was under way. Even so, he took his friends' advice and left São Paulo the next day, with his mother-in-law's body, to return to Minas Gerais. There was some fear that Governor Quadros might take some step against Kubitschek. In his memoirs, Juscelino notes that the governor was the only important political figure in São Paulo who did not send him condolences on the death of his mother-in-law (EP.450).

Kubitschek as President-elect

Juscelino stayed in Minas Gerais until just before Christmas time. For one thing, he had much work to do in preparing for his program upon being sworn in as president. For another, his relations with President Ramos were at best problematical, and so he felt that it was best to carry on those reactions with him at a distance (EP.457). After the Christmas season, which he spent in Rio de Janeiro, Kubitschek left on a three-week trip to the United States and Europe. The avowed purpose of this voyage was to get away from the Brazilian political situation, so as not to get involved in any new problems which might arise, and to meet political leaders and businessmen in the countries which he visited, seeking to sound out possibilities for getting help and cooperation in the economic programs which he intended to launch upon entering the presidency.

One typically Kubitschekian incident occurred during the planning for this trip. Since he had not yet been formally proclaimed president-elect by the Supreme Electoral Tribunal, he was informed by the United States government that he would not be hosted in Blair House, and by the British government that he would not be received by the Queen. So he cut the two countries off his itinerary. In both cases, that was enough to get the governments involved to change their minds. When they did, he did (EP.460). Kubitschek returned to Brazil only a few days before the date of his inauguration. He had one major task to complete, the selection of the members of his first cabinet. Before leaving on his trip abroad, he had conferred with João Goulart concerning the two posts which were assigned to the Partido Trabalhista Brasileiro, those of Agriculture and Labor. There was no problem in agreeing on the first of these, Ernesto Dornelles, governor of Rio Grande do Sul and a cousin of Vargas.

The selection of the minister of labor was more difficult. But Juscelino and Jângo knew that there was grave suspicion in the armed forces of Goulart as political heir of Vargas. Both also remembered that the military had forced Vargas to remove Goulart from the cabinet. Therefore, Kubitschek wanted a PTB leader for the ministry of labor who would not create new areas of controversy. In looking over the list of possible ministers which Goulart had submitted to him, Kubitschek chose Senator Parsifal Barroso, a "practicing Catholic, representative of the PTB in Ceará." Juscelino noted that "he would be an excellent candidate for minister, although he would certainly not be among the first rank of the names indicated by João Goulart." However, when Kubitschek suggested Barroso, Goulart accepted him as minister of labor (EP.458). Many years later, Parsifal Barroso told me that General Lott had had some influence in his selection by Kubitschek. He said that the general had advised the leaders of the Partido Trabalhista Brasileiro not to select anyone for the Ministry of Labor who was a demagogue. Since Barroso was not one, but was a good member of the PTB, he was a logical choice (he said) for the position.[20]

Even more important than the Ministry of Labor, however, was the Ministry of War. There was considerable logic in Kubitschek's asking General Lott to continue in the post. Lott had, at considerable personal risk and with certain moral qualms, carried out military actions to depose two presidents to assure, as he saw it, the inauguration of Kubitschek. He could therefore be expected to have a personal interest in the maintenance of the Kubitschek regime in power, and in its general success. On the other hand, Kubitschek, with Lott in charge of the armed forces, would in some sense be a prisoner of his minister of war, to whom he owed such a large and obvious debt, and whose prestige in and control of the military was so clear.

Nonetheless, Kubitschek was anxious to have Lott as his minister of war. In view of the close relations between Lott and Alkmin during the November events, Juscelino first asked Alkmin to sound out the general on the subject. Lott refused to continue in office, saying that it was a moral issue with him, and he felt it his duty to return to active service in the Army. However, Alkmin sensed some possibility that the general might change his mind if Kubitschek would personally approach him on the subject. Juscelino did so. He later recorded that "I repeated, more or less, the same arguments used by Alkmin. I wanted to carry out an extensive administration program, but how could I do so if I had my attention diverted by the problem of maintaining order? I appealed to him, not in my own name, but in that of Brazil, which needed tranquility and order so as to work and progress." Finally, General Lott replied: "I understand your situation, Mr. President, and I am disposed to help you. However, I do not want to decide without first hearing from my comrades who stayed at my side during the events of last month. I will need twenty-four hours for these discussions. After this time, I will give you a definitive response" (EP.496). In due time, a positive response came.

The other posts to be filled were relatively easy. After some persuading, the retiring president, Ramos, agreed to become minister of justice. Ex-governor Clovis Salgado of Minas Gerais accepted the Ministry of Education, and various other posts were filled by members of the parties which had supported Kubitschek's candidacy, and by technicians (EP.497).[21] One person who turned down a preferred appointment was General Humberto Castelo Branco, to whom Juscelino offered the chairmanship of Petrobras, the government oil firm. Branco preferred to stay in the post of assistant chief of staff of the Armed Forces.[22]

In making his decisions concerning appointments to top posts in his administration, one thing Kubitschek had to keep in mind was a promise he had made to Jaime Cardinal Uamara, Archbishop of Rio de Janeiro. Shortly after his election, Juscelino had gone to see the cardinal, who, as Kubitschek told Edward Riedinger, disliked him very much. In their discussion, the cardinal told the president-elect that he would accept no divorced man in the cabinet. Juscelino agreed to concur with Don Jaime's wishes on this matter, explaining to Riedinger that he had done so out of respect for his mother's Catholicism.

Generally, he kept to his promise not to appoint any divorced man to high office. However, two years after taking office, when faced with an Air Force mutiny, he felt that he absolutely had to appoint Brigadeiro Mello as Air Minister, even though he was living with a woman who was not his wife, after having been separated from his wife. Kubitschek sought and quickly received from the cardinal an exception to his promise. As Juscelino told Riedinger many years later, the prelate "had come to be less afraid of me," by that time.[23] On 31 January 1956, Kubitschek was inaugurated as president of Brazil. In his memoirs, Juscelino summed up his feeling at that moment: "What preoccupied me was only the promise which I had made to those who had given me their vote: to make Brazil progress 50 years in 5. That promise I was determined to honor, at whatever cost" (EP.497).

Chapter 9

KUBITSCHEK'S DEVELOPMENT STRATEGY

Kubitschek was elected president of Brazil in October 1955 with a minority of the popular vote. He won less because he was Kubitschek than because the voters regarded him as a representative of the tradition of Vargas. He was the nominee of the Partido Social Democrático, a party founded by Vargas, and had as his running mate Goulart, who was widely regarded as Vargas' political heir and had succeeded Getúlio as head of the Partido Trabalhista Brasileiro.

At first very little was expected of Kubitschek. He was underestimated by friend and foe alike. Perhaps a typical opinion of many politicians was that of Plinio Barreto, UDN leader and former member of the 1946 Constitutional Assembly. In April 1956 he commented that he did not think much of Juscelino, that he was a pleasant man, good for talk and for attending balls, but that he had no idea about the problems facing the country and did not have the qualities of a statesman.[1] Indeed, there was a joke current during his first few months in office to the effect that the slogan "J & J," signifying Juscelino and Jango, which had been widely painted on walls by Juscelino's adherents during the 1955 election campaign, really meant "Janeiro a Junho" (January to June). It was often added that optimists thought that it meant "Janeiro a Julho" (January to July). Few gave Kubitschek much chance to remain in office for more than a few months.

Juscelino's Vision

Kubitschek not only stayed in office for his full constitutional term of five years, but by the end of this period he was the complete master of his administration, and left office with great personal popularity. In fact, he was regarded by many millions of Brazilians as a national hero. Furthermore, during his five years in office he

160

had quite literally changed the face of Brazil. In the light of the troubled years which followed his administration, even many of his erstwhile opponents looked back at Juscelino's presidency as a period of extraordinary achievement, almost as a golden age.

Tad Szulc, the *New York Times* correspondent in Brazil during much of the Kubitschek period, has given one view of the way in which Juscelino functioned. In his book, *The Winds of Revolution*, Szulc wrote the following:

> Vibrating with boundless enthusiasm for what he turned into a mystique of 'desenvolvimentismo'—'economic development'—the new president plunged into the task of remaking Brazil with a total and almost admirable lack of understanding of the mechanisms of economics and finance. His cavalier disregard of the country's financial capabilities and of consequent inflationary dangers led him to push such extraordinary projects as the building of the new capital in Brasilia and the crisscrossing of the vast and largely uninhabited territory with a wide network of highways slashing open the jungles and the savannas. Perhaps a man more versed in economics and less endowed with imagination would not have even attempted to carry out the program that Dr. Kubitschek drew up for himself. But Brazil needed a visionary and there was no stopping Dr. Kubitschek and his dreams. So, for five years Brazil lived through an amazing and exciting era of contagious enthusiasm that propelled the nation from its erstwhile inferiority complex directly to a new sense of manifest destiny. (p. 195)

Only a man with great political talent could have achieved this, but Kubitschek was much more than an accomplished politician. He was a very practical politician with a dream, with a soaring vision of the kind of a country he wished his nation to be. During his administration, he demonstrated the ability to begin to convert this vision into reality. During his election campaign, Kubitschek promised the voters that he would achieve "fifty years in five." Many Brazilians would agree that he came close to achieving this promise. The secret of Juscelino's success lay in three things: his ability to push his country rapidly along the road of economic development and industrialization; his capacity for transmitting to the great masses of the people his own optimism, pride in contemporary Brazil and the vision of the Brazil of the future; and his political astuteness.

Conciliation and Compromise

Celso Lafer has pointed out the socio-economic background against which Kubitschek carried out his development program. He has noted that in the first place there was a compatibility during the whole period of economic development through industrialization (1930-1961) between the interests of the traditional rural elite, based mainly on coffee production, and those of the new industrial elite thrown up by the development of manufacturing. He has argued that

> the industrial sector needed the foreign-exchange reserves that only the export-sector could supply to proceed with its expansion, and this expansion did not obstruct, in a significant way, the development of the export-sector, which was contingent on stimuli from the international market; stimuli which were sufficient to assure the absolute level of income of the sector, even with the use of the foreign exchange reserves by the industrial sector.[2]

Furthermore, the rise of industry brought about "the creation of investment alternatives without which the export-sector would have entered an uncontrollable crisis of over-production."

In addition, with the rebirth of democracy after the fall of the Estado Novo, the middle and working classes which through their votes elected the presidents and part of the Congress, also found the industrialization of the country to serve their interests. Lafer argues that

> in fact, the mobilized masses demanded an enlargement of job opportunities, which was an aim perceived as compatible with the aims of the members of the elite, concerned with industrial expansion, and not perceived as uncompatible [sic] with the aims of the members of

162

the elite concerned with the export sector. . . . On the other hand, industrial expansion served not only the needs of the new mobilized masses; it served even more the aims of the middle-classes, since it brought about the bureaucratization of enterprises, and consequently, the opening up of new and different jobs for the middle class.[3]

Thus, the basic direction in which Kubitschek led the nation was congruent with the interests of the four major social groups— rural elite, industrial elite, manual working class, and white collar and professional middle class—which were active in civilian politics during his period in power. However, his genius lay in his ability to set seemingly unattainable development targets, and to rally substantial segments of all of these class groups in what amounted to a national crusade to achieve them. At the same time, he was successful in neutralizing those elements among the civilian politicians and the military who were more motivated by the fatal division in politics that had been created by Vargas between those associated with him and those opposing him, than by class or economic considerations, and would have liked to block his efforts and even to overthrow him.

Broad Lines of Kubitschek's Strategy

When he came to the presidency, Kubitschek was of course in no way a neophyte in dealing with problems of economic development. He had had extensive experience in the field both as mayor of Belo Horizonte and governor of Minas Gerais. However, in addition, he had studied development very extensively and continued to do so as president. Kubitschek commented that he was certain that the first need for a political leader seeking rapid economic development was intuition, something which he felt he had.[4]

As president, Kubitschek had a strategy of economic development which was undoubtedly partly the result of intuition, and partly the consequence of study. Thomas Skidmore has noted that "the Kubitschek strategy deserves the label 'developmentalist nationalism' rather than simply 'developmentalism,' because of the manner in which it was presented to the Brazilian public. Underlying the government's statements and actions was an appeal to a sense of nationalism. It was Brazil's 'destiny' to undertake a 'drive to development.'[5] Kubitschek felt that the first priority was industrialization and the development of the infrastructure of the economy which contributed to industrialization, that is roads, electricity, and communication. This decision to concentrate on industry and infrastructure involved several other deliberate choices on the part of Juscelino and his closest advisers.

First, Kubitschek's policy meant the temporary relegation of most of the development of agriculture to a secondary plane. The thinking of the Kubitschek administration was that in order for the country to undertake the development of agriculture, it was necessary first to possess a heavy industry which would permit the production within the country of the agricultural implements and equipment. It also meant the need for a petrochemical industry which could provide the necessary fertilizers, insecticides, and other chemical products needed for agriculture. Without these industries, a long-range program for development of agriculture would involve a heavy strain on the balance of payments position of Brazil, and would be subject to the extensive fluctuations in the price of its principal exports.

Second, Kubitschek felt that doctrinaire nationalism should not be allowed to interfere with the process of industrialization. He believed that the matter of first importance was to have manufacturing industries established in the country, after which there would be plenty of time to be concerned with the problem of who owned such industries. Such discussions of ownership he felt to be futile if the industries did not exist in any case.[6] In practice, this meant that Brazil should accept capital and knowhow from wherever it was available, and provide the most favorable possible terms for both national and foreign firms to establish industrial plants in the country. The result of this policy was that most of the new automobile industry, the shipbuilding industry, and some of the new units of the steel industry were established by foreign firms or with foreign help.

The role of foreign investment in the Kubitschek development program should not be exaggerated. A study of O.J. Menezes comments thus on the question of investment sources for the industrial sector of the economy.

The sources of finance for these investments were the following. Retained profits fluctuated between US $300 millions and US $550 millions p.a. Capital issues . . . fluctuated between US $200 millions and US $300 millions p.a. The predominant portion of this volume of capital issues was accounted for by *closed* companies (that is, those without shares held by the general public). Thus, these two items represented more than US $600 millions p.a., out of a total investment in fixed assets and stocks, averaging somewhat more than US $800 millions p.a. during 1955-1963, that is, about 75 percent of the total.

Entry of new foreign risk capital into the country reached an annual average of US $91 millions during the eight years 1954-1961. Practically all of this investment was in manufacturing. Net loan capital inflow averaged US $175 millions during this period. However, these last figures include capital for the public sector—in the main for activities other than manufacturing.

Provisionally, the total inflow of foreign resources for manufacturing (risk capital and loans) may be estimated at less than US $200 millions a year. The remainder of the estimated total of more than US $800 millions per year in industrial investments, must have been financed by credit, finance, and investment companies and by the National Bank of Economic Development.[7]

A third choice involved postponement of a program of social reform, particularly in the field of land ownership. Although he spoke of agrarian reform as an urgent necessity in his first message to Congress, little was heard from Juscelino on this subject during the rest of his term. The thinking of Kubitschek in this area was that in the late 1950s no Brazilian government was in a position to successfully undertake agrarian reform, because the existing balance of power in the society would not permit it. He felt that any government that attempted such a policy at that time would not be able to remain in office because the political power of the rural landlord class and its allies was too great. It was necessary, therefore, first to strengthen the economic, social, and political position of the urban sectors through industrialization. Kubitschek was not unaware of the eventual need for land redistribution, but thought the moment inopportune. He felt that his development policies would tend to engender disequilibriums and discontent with the status quo, and hence develop pressure for revolutionary changes in the society and economy which would facilitate such programs at a later time. In his campaign for reelection before the coup d'etat of 1964 he stressed both agricultural development an agrarian reform.[8]

Fourth, Kubitschek's strategy of development meant concentration of the government's industrialization efforts principally in the southern part of the country, already the most highly developed area. In other parts of the country, his program consisted largely of laying the groundwork for future development. The president's belief in the need for rapid development explains this emphasis. The São Paulo-Rio de Janeiro-Belo Horizonte triangle in the southeast already had more electricity, transport facilities, educational institutions and other elements which would be needed by the new industries fomented by his regime, than did any other part of the country. Furthermore, the largest part of the national market was located in that area. In the northeast, or other regions, on the contrary, it would have been necessary first to provide adequate infrastructure before manufacturing enterprises would have been established, and the major markets would have been a considerable distance from the new industries.

Kubitschek himself wrote about this aspect of his development strategy that

> it conformed originally to the precept of concentrating those investments in areas in which their return was greatest. That precept, to disobey which in the initial phase of the administration would have provoked the failure of any global plan of development, led to the choice of sectors of the economic infrastructure for the most concentrated investment in the regions which already had external economies linked to investments previously made. However, as quickly as possible, some of that effort was reoriented, towards less immediate economic gain and securing greater social justice in the distribution of resources. For this, SUDENE

166

[Superintendencia do Desenvolvimento Economico Nordeste] was created, the beneficent impact of which was fully felt in later years, to the point of providing the northeast with a rate of development compensatory to its backwardness, that is, more rapid than any other sector of the national economy.[9]

Dealing with the Northeast

Thus, although most of the efforts to expand infrastructure and encourage manufacturing were centered in the south and south-central regions, Kubitschek took important steps toward laying the basis for large-scale development programs in the northeast and Amazon regions. One of these was the strengthening of the Banco do Nordeste (BNB). Kubitschek named Raúl Barbosa, a former governor of Ceará, as head of the Banco do Nordeste (which had been established during the second Vargas administration), and gave him wide freedom to expand the bank's activities. Stefan Robock, the United Nations economic adviser and former chief economist of the Tennessee Valley Authority, in commenting on a period encompassing the Kubitschek administration, has noted that

from 1954 to 1960 the BNB increased its number of branches from 7 to 41, its number of employees from less than 200 to 1,500, and its resources from about 320 million to 6.5 billion cruzeiros, or from about U.S. $6 million to U.S. $33 million. . . . Of major significance, however, the BNB, in all of its operations, determinedly maintained a reputation, almost unprecedented for a government agency in the northeast, of nonpolitical and business like practices.[10]

Not only did the Banco do Nordeste expand its operations, it gave special attention during this period to building up a training and research organization essential to its own success and the future expansion of the economy of the region. With the help of Robock, the Escritorio Tecnico de Estudos Economicos do Nordeste was established to bring together the available research on the economic and social problems of the region, and institute studies of its own. As a result of its work, "this flow of economic and technical

167

research formed the foundation for policies and activities of public and private institutions in the region."[11] Robock added that

> from 1955 to 1960 the BNB sponsored twenty special training programs involving more than 700 trainees in economic analysis, economic development, statistics, industrial project evaluation, administration, rural credit including training for agronomists and veterinarians. About half of the participants were employees or potential employees of the bank. University professors brought into the programs as both teachers and students, and into contact with advanced training methods, stimulated great changes in the major regional universities. Businessmen, private consultants, army officers, and employees of other government agencies also enrolled in the courses.[12]

The second major move of the Kubitschek administration to aid the future development of the northeast was its establishment of the Superintendencia do Desenvolvimento Economico do Nordeste (SUDENE). In 1956 the president took the first step in this direction when he established the Working Group for Northeast Development (GTDN) which undertook a number of studies of the mineral reserves and transportation facilities in the area, and of the activities of various federal agencies operating there. However, at that point the president had no more extensive plans for dealing with the problems of the northeast. In the first two years of his administration, he merely carried on previous governments' programs for building reservoirs as defenses against drought.

It was not until the disastrous drought of 1958 that President Kubitschek's attention was centered on the northeast. He went to that part of the country to see the disaster for himself. He has described the situation as "too horrible to be believed." There were long lines of people fleeing the drought areas, stretching along the roads for as far as the eye could see. These people, Kubitschek noted, were merely looking for food and water, nothing else. The president talked with many of them, asked them about their problems, and when he left, he promised that a crisis such as this would never happen again.[13]

Upon returning to Rio de Janeiro, Kubitschek asked the National Bank of Economic Development (BNDE) to help him find new solutions to the problem of the northeast. The result of this request was the elaboration of a detailed report entitled "A Policy for the Economic Development of the Northeast," prepared by Celso Furtado, a director of the BNDE. After analyzing the problems of the area, Furtado suggested the establishment of an overall agency to have charge of planning and supervising the work of all government agencies operating in the region, as well as to undertake a coordinated regional effort placed in the context of Brazilian economic development. Kubitschek responded to Furtado's suggestion both by converting the GTDN into an interim Economic Development Council for the northeast, and by sending a bill to Congress for the establishment of an expanded and powerful development agency for the region, the Superintendencia do Desenvolvimento Economico do Nordeste. This law was passed on 15 December 1959, and the SUDENE began to function in March 1960 under the aegis of Furtado, whom Kubitschek named as its first director.[14]

The actions of the Kubitschek government in laying the basis for development were even more dramatic in their ultimate effect on the Amazon valley area. For forty years before the advent of Juscelino to the presidency, that region, including well over half of the area of the country, had been living on memories of the glories of the past, the period of the short-lived rubber boom between 1890 and World War I. A long and painful decline had followed the collapse of the rubber euphoria, and the people of the Amazon area had felt themselves the stepchildren of Brazil. Their communication links with the rest of Brazil, principally by sea, were long and tenuous and the residents of the area felt themselves all but cut off from contact with their fellow citizens farther south. Until the Kubitschek administration, a feeling of hopelessness characterized the region. It was the construction of roads through the interior of the country, resulting from the building of Brasilia, that changed the psychology and actual economic state of the Amazon region.

Other Aspects of Kubitschek's Development Strategy

The fifth element in Kubitschek's strategy of economic development involved his willingness to pay a considerable price for development in terms of inflation, foreign exchange difficulties, and corruption. The government ran a highly unbalanced budget to cover much of the cost of development and issued large amounts of currency to cover the deficit. This had the effect of intensifying an already existing situation of too much income looking for too few goods and services, and resulted in an increase in the rate of rise of the general price level (inflation). It is worth noting, however, that in Kubitschek's last year in office the rate of inflation declined substantially. We shall deal more extensively with the inflation issue in a later chapter.

The Kubitschek program also involved straining to its limits the country's ability to buy goods abroad—consisting of the foreign exchange it earned by selling goods overseas and the funds it was able to borrow or otherwise obtain in foreign currencies. The country's foreign debt increased substantially during this period, and Kubitschek's refusal to sacrifice his development program on the alter of fiscal responsibility brought him into conflict with the International Monetary Fund (IMF). Kubitschek had no regrets about increasing the Brazilian foreign debt. He commented to me on one occasion that the only reason he had not raised this debt to fifteen or twenty billion dollars instead of from two to three billion, was that he was not able to do so. He argued that the debt was not that important, that with the development of the national economy the country would be able to bear a debt many times larger than that with which he left it when he quit the presidency.[15]

The is no doubt that corruption was widespread during the Kubitschek administration. However, it certainly did not originate with the regime of Juscelino. At least since the first government of Vargas, beginning in 1930, the bribing of government officials and the misuse of influence by government officials, had been endemic in the Brazilian public administration. During the Kubitschek administration, corruption was at least in part a function of the pressure for very rapid economic development. If projects were to be concluded and factories built in record time, it was impossible that every single item of expenditure could be carefully scrutinized before, during, and after the projects' fulfillment. Undoubtedly, emphasis was more on speed than on financial honesty. However, there is no indication that Kubitschek himself was corrupt.

Finally, there is little doubt that Kubitschek's strategy between 1956 and 1961 involved the conviction that the period would be only the first installment of the Kubitschek program for development of Brazil. Juscelino was confident that after an intervening term he would return to the presidency. The Constitution of 1946 did not allow the reelection of a president until he had been out of office for at least one term. Kubitschek felt that in his second term he would be able to carry out another stage in the process of development as he conceived it. The program for his second term, which he developed in the period before the coup d'etat of 1 April 1964, involved a shift of emphasis from industrialization to the growth of agriculture and of those parts of the country which had been relatively untouched by achievements of his first period in office.[16]

Although Kubitschek was not an economist, and had little or no formal training in economic science, he had developed intuitively an appropriate program for the development of the Brazilian economy. He correctly saw that the first phase was the completion of the process of industrialization through which Brazil had been passing for a generation—that is, the completion of import substitution (although there is no evidence that Kubitschek thought of it in those terms). The succeeding phase was to be that of expanding the market, through encouraging agriculture, and concentration of development efforts in the less developed parts of the nation—that is fulfilling the requirements of the post-import substitution phase of Brazilian economic development.

Bureaucratic Problems

In order to be successful in achieving his goals, Kubitschek not only had to have a clear vision of what it was he was trying to achieve and of the most appropriate strategies to use in the economic field, he also had to have a political strategy to complement his economic one. Certainly one of the fundamental elements in Kubitschek's political strategy was his belief that in handling thorny political and administrative problems it was better to sidestep issues if possible, rather than to have serious confrontations. He showed this belief in his handling of the problem of the Brazilian state bureaucracy. It left a great deal to be desired in terms of efficiency, dynamism, and in some cases honesty. Most of the members of the bureaucracy had gotten their positions through patronage, known in Brazil as the *politica de clientela*. However,

171

although Kubitschek needed highly qualified people to man the agencies dealing with the Target Plan, he did not have the time or the desire to undertake fundamental reforms in the governmental bureaucracy. In this case, as in many others, he went around a problem rather than confronting it head-on.

Lafer has noted that two of the key agencies used in the Programa de Metas, that is, the Banco Nacional de Desenvolvimento Nacional and the Banco do Brasil, were exceptions to the general rule of the bureaucracy. Historically, they had tended to choose their personnel on the basis of competence rather than political influence. However, in addition, new personnel were needed by those two banks during the Kubitschek administration, and there were other people needed for various other organisms associated with the Target Plan. Lafer has noted that

> the use of borrowed personnel . . . was to become Kubitschek's main solution in overcoming, for his nuclei of plan implementation, the normal fragmentation of competence and expertise within the bureaucracy. The legal possibility of the 'requisicão,' through which personnel . . . from permanent and fixed positions of the federal service . . . can be assigned by the president to other agencies, was the device that made possible this best utilization of the system's most efficient members.[17]

Thus, Lafer concludes that "Kubitschek, through the use of borrowed personnel, reapportioned to his nuclei of plan implementation the personnel with competence and expertise from the rest of the bureaucracy." Lafer adds that this did not damage his relations with his political supporters, for whom this continuation of the *politica de clientela* was very important. The staff of the National Development Council was completely made up of "borrowed" civil servants. Other bodies dependent upon the Council, such as the executive groups and task forces, were also manned from the same source, as were the Council on Customs Policy, SUMOC, and various other agencies which were working on the Programa de Metas.[18]

Impact of Kubitschek's Optimism

Kubitschek was by temperament and conviction an ebullient optimist. He was convinced absolutely that Brazil was destined to be one of the great nations of the earth, and that it could become one in a relatively short period of time. He felt, too, that Brazil had an important role to play in hemispheric affairs, and should take the lead among the Latin American countries. Thomas Skidmore has noted that "the essence of Kubitschek's style was improvisation. Enthusiasm was his principal weapon, reflecting an infectious confidence in Brazil's future as a great power. His basic strategy was to press for rapid industrialization, attempting to convince each power group that they had something to gain or at least nothing to lose. This required a delicate political balancing act."[19] Philip Raine has also emphasized the importance of Kubitschek's optimism in facilitating economic development. He wrote that "Kubitschek stimulated internal investment by creating a development mystique that had other important consequences, not the least of which was to engage the people in an enthusiastic commitment to his plans . . . Kubitschek's charisma, however, coupled with the people's evident belief in and practice of democracy proved to be a substitute for weak political institutions."[20]

More important, perhaps, than Juscelino's own optimism was his ability to transmit it to the mass of the Brazilian citizenry. During the Kubitschek administration there was more solid pride in their country's accomplishments among the broad ranks of the population than during any other period of recent Brazilian history. During these five years the Brazilians lost once and for all the inferiority complex which had characterized them to a large degree theretofore. The economist and journalist Eduardo Matarazzo Suplicy has borne witness to the impact of Juscelino's optimism on those who were teenagers at the time of his administration. He commented that "the enthusiasm for development that JK stimulated in all the youth during his government was exceptional. During my secondary school I never could understand why so many of my teachers, twenty or thirty years older than I, did not believe in the possibilities of the country. For the youth, the enthusiasm appeared to be spontaneous and contagious."[21] Writing in 1976, Matarazzo Suplicy noted that for the youthful generation to which I belonged, furthermore during the period of JK, there was an enormous advantage when compared with those who attended school in the last decade. Just as we could become spontaneously enthusiastic about Brazilian development, we also felt fully free to discuss and learn the costs of that development, the advantages and disadvantages of the various paths to be taken, and we had the sensation that we could decide democratically which road to take.[22]

There was an almost universal feeling during the Kubitschek administration, particularly among the humbler folk, that in spite of present difficulties, the fabled riches of Brazil were finally being exploited, and the economy would soon be able to provide its citizens with the high level of living to which they increasingly were aspiring. But even beyond this, the exuberance of the Kubitschek period tended to turn the average Brazilian's attention to some of his nation's accomplishments to which he had hitherto given little heed—its contributions to modern architecture, to literature, and to other cultural fields. He began to take pride in these things as well as in the more mundane achievements which he saw taking place before his eyes.

Juscelino's dynamism had a very practical effect on the functioning of the Brazilian government. Leôncio Basbaum, no admirer of Kubitschek, commented that

demonstrating that he possessed tremendous energy and extraordinary capacity to work (he was the only president who never took a vacation during the period in which he directed the country) he succeeded in really mobilizing the ministries, institutes, bureaus, mobilizing the bureaucracy from its inertia. In his presidential airplane, he visited the whole country, never stopping more than three days in the presidential palace, so that he came to be called 'the flying president.'[23]

Kubitschek himself commented on the change in national psychology. He said that

174

this transformation carried out in the country had a highly salutary psychological effect: it dissipated the inferiority complex of the Brazilian. In those five years, thanks to the indoctrination which I engaged in and the works which I accomplished, he saw that he was perfectly capable of constructing ships, automobiles, gigantic dams, tractors, of attacking the Amazon jungle, and in three years and a half establishing a large city in an empty demographic area.[24]

Furthermore, the change which he brought about was permanent. Kubitschek commented that

in spite of all the vicissitudes through which the country passed in the decade of the 60s—resignation of Jânio Quadros, ideological agitation in the João Goulart government, and finally, the revolution of March 1964—it was never possible to abandon planning of the accelerated growth of the national economy. Still all the plans so far elaborated virtually consist of the expansion of the bases created by the Programa de Metas, in the sectors of energy, steel, auto industry, naval construction, railroads and roads, and above all, the implications of national integration, with Brasilia as the center of radiation.[25]

Upon coming into office at the end of January 1956, Kubitschek took immediate steps to make his promise of "fifty years progress in five" a reality. The day after his inauguration, he established the Conselho Nacional do Desenvolvimento (National Development Council), the task of which was to draw up the details and supervise the execution of a national economic development plan. By the end of February this plan had been elaborated in the form of the famous "Programa de Metas" (Target Plan), which became the hallmark of the Kubitschek administration. Based in large part on studies which had been made by the Banco Nacional de Desenvolvimento Economico, the programa set forth what the regime hoped to achieve in thirty different fields. Subsequently, a thirty-first goal, the construction of Brasilia, was added. The economist Gilberto Paim has suggested that the Programa de Metas

175

consisted really of aspirations rather than plans.[26] They were aspirations, however, that Kubitschek largely succeeded in converting into reality.

The National Development Council

The Conselho Nacional do Desenvolvimento played a key role in the development program of the Kubitschek administration. It consisted of the members of the cabinet plus certain other key officials. It was presided over by the president of the republic. Robert Daland noted of Juscelino that "he calls for meetings of the Council. Kubitschek, founder of the Council and deeply interested in its work, insured for it a key place in the pattern of top level decision-making."[27] Once the Programa de Metas had been announced, the Conselho broke down the various goals into specific projects and had general supervision of their execution.

The National Development Council was not without precedent in the task of drawing up development plans for the Brazilian economy. Celso Lafer has noted that there were at least five previous efforts to develop a broad gauge program for the country's economic development. Two of these were bi-national Brazilian-US study missions, the so-called Cooke Mission of 1942-1943, and the Abbink Mission of 1948, both of which made general studies of the economy and presented extensive suggestions for its development. The third was the report prepared for President Vargas in 1944 by his influential adviser, the industrialist Roberto Simonsen; the fourth was the so-called SALTE Plan, developed during the Dutra administration for expansion of five segments of the economy: health, education, housing, transport, and electricity, the most notable result of which had been the launching of the Paulo Affonso dam project on the São Francisco River. Finally, there had been the Joint US-Brazilian Economic Commission set up by President Vargas in his second administration to draw up specific projects following from the Abbink Report.

Not only did the National Development Council draw heavily on these reports for data and some ideas for the Programa de Metas, but the leading figures in the Council were to a large degree drawn from the Cooke, Abbink, Joint Commission, and SALTE groups. The major drafters of the technical aspects of the Target Plan were Lucas Lopes and Roberto Campos, both of whom had

176

been important members of the Joint Commission. Lopes was the first secretary general of the National Development Council and was succeeded by Campos who in July 1959 was himself succeeded by Lucio Meira, a one-time member of the presidential staff of President Vargas concerned with his economic programs. Both of the executive directors of the Council, Victor da Silva Alves Filho and Ottolmy Straugh, had been staff members of the Joint Commission. At least a dozen other key officials and executives in the National Development Council or working directly under its supervision, had also been associated with one or the other—and sometimes several—of the earlier efforts to begin to plan Brazil's economic development.[28]

General Nature of the Target Plan

The objective of the Programa de Metas was nothing less than the transformation of Brazil from a country which was still predominantly agricultural, and whose industries produced principally consumer goods, into one with an integrated industrial economy, capable of turning out virtually any kind of manufactured commodity. Carlos Lessa has said that the targets "represented in Latin America the most ample action oriented by the state for the purpose of establishing a vertically integrated structure." It sought, he added, "the qualitative transformation of the economy through the creation of industries producing basic products, of an important sector producing capital goods, and of the supporting public services."[29]

Although the administration boasted that "for the first time in Brazil, the government established a Global Plan of Economic Development in the form of a Programa de Metas in which the union, the states and the municipalities collaborate together with private initiative,"[30] the Target Plan was not in fact a national development plan in the generally accepted sense. Although it set development targets in a large number of fields, involving both the public and private sectors, it dealt with only about one fourth of the total economy. Furthermore, it did not provide any carefully worked out program for financing all of its components and the program as a whole. Neither did it attempt seriously to coordinate the various goals with one another. Although the National Development Council continued to function throughout the Kubitschek administration, it

177

did relatively little to change the metas in the light of actual performance, or to correct errors in judgment which might have been made in drawing them up, as a central planning agency might have done.

The introduction to a pamphlet entitled *As Metas Do Governo*, a document which was issued for popular distribution by the Office of the Presidency in 1958, contains a simple statement of how the various goals were determined. It explains that "this Global Plan, which received the name Programa de Metas, was elaborated by the coordination of new and existing projects on the federal, state, and municipal level, to which was added the weighty efforts of private initiative for carrying out projects beneficial to the Brazilian economy." Thus, there was relatively little overall planning of the whole economy in the execution and notification of the Kubitschek Programa de Metas. The Conselho Nacional de Desenvolvimento had relatively limited powers, and it was confined largely to drawing up the Target Plan and studying the results which had been so far achieved. Financing of the program was carried out on a particularly ad hoc basis, without any clear planning of the source of funding. Financial problems tended to be dealt with as they arose, without any overall coordination of monetary resources.

Lessa has summed up the planning approach of the Kubitschek administration in the following terms:

> The line of least political resistance was followed, sacrificing theoretical elegance and the exactitude of the instrument to its efficacy in the shorter run. With rare exceptions, in that period there was no preoccupation with instrumental reformulation and the redefinition of the role of the state. The old apparatus was mobilized and was used intensively, introducing into it only, as in the past, partial readjustments, but without any global definition of the task. However, due to the increasing complexity of the objectives imposed by the superior state of industrialization, certain refinement was given to some instruments (foreign exchange budget, financial funds, etc.) and there was also established an incipient harmonization of other instruments (executive groups coordinating the stimuli to private industrialization). In the same way, in this period there was established an

178

embryonic organism of central planning (the Conselho do Desenvolvimento), which had limited success. Such advances were strongly pragmatic and empirical. Advance in these matters was only that strictly necessary for the direct obtaining of the proposed objectives. No autonomous effort was made to get more adequate instruments, but rather there persisted and in some sense was accentuated the unharmonic and improvised character of the means of carrying out economic policy. However, because it was forged in the process, the modification of the system of governmental action resulting from the partial readjustments alongside of the old system proved very efficacious. In any case, what had been said is valid for the instruments of policy looked at in their totality; in contrast, undoubtedly a certain coherence was obtained in the means used concretely for the execution of the Plan.[31]

The situation described by Lessa reflects a basic fact which we have noted earlier, that Kubitschek did not conceive of his first administration as being one of reform. Rather, his whole concentration was on the problem of molding existing institutions to the central purpose of getting the most possible industrialization and development in the five short years which he had at his disposal. Innovations could be made to make existing institutions function more effectively. But any kind of basic reform would have to come later. Any attempt in his administration to alter fundamentally the existing economic devices would have consumed precious time, energies, and talents which, from Kubitschek's point of view, might better be used for the development objective.

There were several instruments used for coordinating various phases of the Programa de Metas. One of the most important of these was the Banco Nacional de Desenvolvimento Economico. It not only was instrumental in allocating financial resources to those segments of the economy in which the administration was most concerned, it also served as the intermediary through which both government enterprises and private firms received loans from abroad. A second instrumentality of primary importance was the Superintendencia de Moeda e Credito (SUMOC). This was the organization through which the government allocated the country's limited supplies of foreign exchange for the importation of capital goods and raw materials needed for fulfillment of the government's program. It also was the group which gave foreign firms permission to bring in capital goods without first making a deposit of an appropriate cover of foreign exchange, under Instruction 113, which we shall discuss in the following chapter.

Complementing the work of SUMOC was the Confederacão Nacional de Industria (CNI) and its affiliated federations and *sindicatos*, remnants of Vargas' Estado Novo. SUMOC submitted to the appropriate affiliates of the CNI requests it received for foreign exchange, and they gave their judgment as to whether the introduction of the new equipment which was being suggested was necessary or appropriate for the industry involved. Although the SUMOC was not legally bound to accept the recommendations of the sindicato concerned, these were usually honored by the Superintendencia.[32] Within each segment of the public sector, there were important instruments for the planning and execution of the Kubitschek administration's program. For instance, the highway phase was under control of the Departmento Nacional de Estradas de Rodagem; railway expansion and reequipment was in the charge of Rede Ferroviaria Federal, SA, the government railway firm. The government oil company, Petrobras, was in control of the program for the petroleum industry and the petrochemical part of the Target Plan. The Conselho Nacional de Aquas e Energia Electrica supervised the efforts of the government in the field of electric power.

The Government Budget Under Kubitschek

The budget of the federal government was drawn up as in the past principally by the Departamento Administrativo de Serviço Publico (DASP), which had first been set up under the Vargas regime in the 1930s. However, Lessa has commented that the DASP "is not equipped to formulate a proposal for financial policy nor to harmonize the various investment programs. In reality it only brings together and coordinates the financial requests, organizing them formally and from the accounting point of view." Lessa adds that "This conglomeration of requests has not been submitted previously to any financial discipline or to any global evaluation of their priorities." Lessa went on to explain the course of budget making after DASP had completed its work: "Once this group of requests has been completed and has been brought together on the executive level, it is sent to the legislative power, where once again it is aggregated, without any previous definition of financial policy or of general orienting principles, and there is added a large number of other appropriations which originate from unintegrated interests." Lessa concluded that "from such additions there results a budget difficult, when not impossible, to execute." However, he notes that the Ministry of Finance then further modified the budget and in addition "there exist legal dispositions which permit expenditures without a corresponding authorization of Congress."[33]

Lafer, however, has pointed out some of the reasons for this apparently chaotic way in which budgets were prepared during the Kubitschek period. He noted that the Plan by no means allotted all of the budget to its purposes. There was left "an ample margin of short-term investments . . . left to the Congress decision. . . ."[34] Lafer pointed out that this leeway in the budget was crucial to Juscelino's political maneuvering on behalf of the Programa de Metas. Speaking in terms of the elite-worker alliance which gave backing to the regime, Lafer noted that

> this margin of short-term investments was the safety-valve of the alliance, allowing the adjustments necessary for the maintenance of political support and it was the existence of this safety-valve which permitted Kubitschek to go one step further in his backing of the Target Plan. In fact, aware that the Plan could engineer consensus and knowing that eventual future political adjustments of this consensus could be made through the flexibility granted by this margin of short-term investments, Kubitschek adopted, via a vis the Target Plan an attitude of *commitment* or *prior decision.* . . . On 1 February 1956, one day after his inauguration, Kubitschek made his prior decision, and thus provided for the setting-up of the framework to which all the actors of the political system had to make adaptive adjustments.[35]

Some people closely associated with him during his presidency attested to this limited but definitive focus of Kubitschek's objectives as president. Antônio José Chediak, one of his principal speech writers, has noted that there were problems and issues on which Kubitschek did not have any position or even any particular knowledge. Upon occasion, Juscelino would in such circumstances, come to Chediak and ask him: "What in the world do I think about this problem?"[36]

The Goals and Their Relative Importance

In spite of whatever drawbacks there might have been from the point of view of central planning and budget-making, the Programa de Metas represented a major attempt by the Kubitschek administration to organize in a more rational way the process of industrialization of Brazil. Lafer has pointed out that the selection of parts of the economy to be included in the Target Plan was based on four basic concepts. Sectors involving these concepts were included, those which were conceived of as not fitting them were left out. The first concept which determined the Programa de Metas was that of bottlenecks. Lafer writes that "according to this concept there were critical sectors obstructing the full performance of the Brazilian economy. Government planning would thus have as its first aim the limitation of these bottlenecks. This was one of the basic assumptions of the Target Plan."[37] Lafer argues that the targets involving energy and transport were determined by the conviction of Kubitschek and his planners that those were two very constraining bottlenecks in the economy. Similarly, it determined the nature of the targets in the agricultural field, which dealt with such things as establishment of warehouses and silos, packing houses, and mechanization of agriculture.[38]

Another major idea involved in selection of targets for the Programa de Metas was that of growing points. Lafer defines this as involving projects which "could be approved and justified by the rationale that investment in social overhead capital would induce directly productive activities." The most notable target of this type was Brasilia, the new capital in the center of the country.[39] A third concept determining constituent parts of the Target Plan was that of import substitution projects which would reduce the "external bottleneck represented by the reduction of the capacity to import." Most notable in this area was the automobile industry target, since motor vehicles were one of the three largest components of Brazil's import bill when Kubitschek took power, and their production in the

182

country would save something in the nature of $200 million in foreign currency.[40]

Finally, the idea of linkages was a major determinant in deciding on targets to be included in the Programa de Metas. Lafer says that "the Target Plan . . . reached the concept of *linkages*, through which the potentialities of *derived demand* brought about by the existing and future internal production of goods was taken into consideration of targets" (emphasis in the original). This was the concept which led to the basic industry targets, since it was argued that the fulfillment of other targets would give rise to such derived demand for the products of these heavy industries. These targets included not only steel, but heavy machinery and equipment, as well as those of naval construction and cement.[41]

The List of Targets

The detailed statement of the targets filled several volumes. However, Lessa sums up their objectives thus:

> In the most simple form, the plan set forth the direct investment by the government in the transport and energy sectors and in some basic industrial activities, particularly steel and petroleum refining, for which private initiative was insufficient; as well as setting forth the most extensive concessions and stimuli to the expansion and diversification of those industries producing capital goods and other products, the production of which required a great density of capital . . . . In the face of the objectives, which provide for a vigorous transformation of the structure of the economy, such considerations as price equilibrium, the balance of payments, and "healthy" behavior in the monetary, fiscal and exchange sectors lost importance, and were relegated to a secondary plane, at the service of industrialization.[42]

As set forth in the pamphlet *As Metas do Governo*, the Target Plan encompassed programs in the following areas:

183

(1)	Electric Energy	(16)	Industrial Packing
(2)	Nuclear Energy		Houses
(3)	Coal	(17)	Mechanization of
(4)	Petroleum Production		Agriculture
(5)	Petroleum Refining	(18)	Fertilizers
(6)	Railroad Construction	(19)	Iron and Steel
(7)	Railroad Equipment	(20)	Aluminum
(8)	Highway Construction	(21)	Non-ferrous Metals
(9)	Highway Improve-	(22)	Cement
	ment and Paving	(23)	Alkalis
(10)	Ports and Dredging	(24)	Paper and Cellulose
(11)	Merchant Marine	(25)	Rubber
(12)	Air Transport	(26)	Iron Export
(13)	Agricultural	(27)	Automobile Industry
	Production	(28)	Shipbuilding
(14)	Warehouses and Silos	(29)	Heavy Electric &
(15)	Meat Warehouses		Mechanical Equipment
		(30)	Technical Education

In spite of this formidable array of sectors in which the Kubitschek government stated its intention of pushing forward development, the really significant impact of the Programa de Metas was considerably more restricted than is indicated by a mere recitation of the various targets. Lessa has commented that

> the various objectives followed can be classified in four large groups. In the first are the direct investments of the government in the transport system and the generation of energy; in the second are the amplification and installations of the intermediate productive sectors, and in this group that of most significance is the steel goal; the third refers to the industries producing capital goods; and finally comes the construction of the country's new capital. It is true that there are not included in this classification certain goals linked with the commercialization and warehousing of agricultural and grazing products, the expansion of export of iron and primary production, nor are certain investments of a social character included. However, the small magnitude of these goals permits us to mention them only marginally in presenting the Plan.[43]

Some idea of the relative importance given to the various aspects of the Kubitschek development program can be gotten from the investments which were foreseen in the Target Plan for the 1957-1961 period. These amounted to a total of 236.7 billion cruzeiros and 2.3 billion U.S. dollars. Of this, 46 percent of the cruzeiro expenditures and 37 percent of the dollars were to be spent on energy production; 32 percent of the cruzeiros and 25 percent of the dollars on transportation; and 15 percent of the cruzeiros and 32 percent of the dollars on basic industries. In contrast, education was to receive only 5 percent of the expenditures in cruzeiros, and no dollar funds; and food production was to involve 2 percent of the total cruzeiros and 6 percent of the dollars of the whole Programa de Metas.[44]

Conclusion

Kubitschek had a clear vision of what he wanted to accomplish in terms of economic development. He wanted to complete one phase of the evolution of the national economy, and lay the basis for a subsequent phase in this evolution. He also made several key strategic decisions concerning how to obtain his objective. He would seek to conciliate potentially conflicting interests; he would concentrate industrialization efforts in those parts of the country in which they could bring about the most rapid results; he would merely lay the groundwork for later development thrusts in sectors of the economy and parts of the country which would not be the main beneficiaries of the efforts of his first term in the presidency.

Most of all, Kubitschek was committed to raising the sights of his fellow countrymen. He was determined to convince them that they were capable of much more than they had hitherto achieved, if only they would put before themselves challenging targets and work together to achieve them. He made no effort to deny that such a program would entail sacrifices, but he sought to compensate for these sacrifices in terms of increasing national pride in their country's achievements in the short run, and the possibilities for material benefits deriving from them in the slightly longer run.[45]

Chapter 10

THE FULFILLMENT OF THE TARGET PLAN

Kubitschek's Programa de Metas was concerned with two broad types of economic development. One was the expansion of the country's infrastructure. This was largely the province of the national government, in cooperation frequently with the state and municipal governments. The other was the intensification of the rate of industrialization, particularly in the areas of heavy industry and machine building and (except for steel) was largely under control of the private sector duly aided and encouraged by the national government. The two parts of the Target Plan not only dealt with different segments of the economy, they also involved use of different techniques to stimulate rapid economic development.

The Energy Program

Juscelino concentrated his major attention on the installation and amplification of electric power resources. The federal administrations after World War II had paid relatively little attention to the problem, except for the establishment of the Paulo Affonso project in the state of Baia, for providing power for part of the northeast. As a result, there was by the middle 1950s a severe shortage of electricity, particularly in the central-south region, where most of the nation's industries were located, and where the Kubitschek administration was concentrating most of its own industrialization program.

Lessa has commented with regard to the extent and implications of the Kubitschek program in electricity that

> the objective of amplifying the installed capacity of electric energy with its corresponding system of distribution was fixed at 5 million kilowatts for 1960. There also was planned the beginning of works which

would increase the capacity by more than 60 percent by 1965. These objectives were practically achieved . . . as a result of which a deficiency of power was avoided throughout the Program. In view of the high capital/ output ratio of the largest projects, the effort to construct new hydroelectric installations was concentrated basically in large units. The immense resources required for such projects, the long periods of maturation and their low profitability, resulted in the public sector amplifying its participation in the production of energy.[1]

The installed capacity of electric power rose dramatically during the Kubitschek period. The total in 1955 was 3,149,000 kilowatts; by 1961 had risen to 5,205,000 kilowatts, an increase of 2,056,000.[2]

Expansion of hydroelectric power facilities was by no means the only target in the energy field. There was a modest goal for nuclear energy, and more significant ones for coal and petroleum. The nuclear program, for which the federal government had only marginal responsibility, consisted principally of the establishment at the University of São Paulo of the first nuclear reactor in Latin America, the training of personnel in the field, and the accumulation of a quantity of atomic materials under the aegis of the National Council of Atomic Energy. The coal target was substantially more ambitious. It sought at first to increase output by 2,500,000 tons by 1960, a goal which was subsequently raised to 3,000,000 tons. The second target was only about two-thirds reached, with output in 1960 being 2,199,000 tons of coal. One reason for the partial failure in this field was a reduction of the demand for coal during the 1955-1960 period, as a result of conversion of most of the railroads from coal to diesel fuel. However, Lafer points out that in building a number of pithead thermoelectric plants, the Kubitschek administration laid the basis for a considerable ultimate expansion in the demand for and use of coal.[3]

In the field of petroleum extraction, too, the target was changed. Starting with a production goal of 90,000 barrels a day, it was raised to 100,000 barrels. Actual production in 1960 was 75,500 barrels; in 1961 it had risen to 95,400 barrels. This resulted in a rise in the proportion of the domestic share of the petroleum consumed in the country from 5.5 percent in 1956 to 31.4 percent in 1960.

There was also a dramatic increase in the amount of petroleum refined in Brazil. The revised target for refined petroleum was 308,000 barrels a day by 1960, compared with only 108,300 barrels in 1955. Although in 1960 only 218,000 barrels were produced, in the following year the target was more than met, when output was 308,600 barrels a day.[4]

A significant institutional change was made in the energy field which was not originally contemplated in the Target Plan, but resulted directly from the expansion in activity which the Plan brought about. This was the establishment in July 1960 of the Ministry of Mines and Energy, which brought together virtually all branches of the government dealing with these matters, which formerly had been dispersed among many agencies.[5]

Transportation Network Targets

Great attention was also concentrated in the Programa de Metas on improving the national transportation network. Although considerable resources were expended on reequipping and extending the railroads, and on improving the ports, the objectives of the Target Program were not completely achieved in those fields. Much more dramatic was the success in the field of highway construction.

The Programa de Metas proposed both extensive reequipment of the railway system and a modest expansion of its mileage. The revised target for reequipment encompassed the purchase of 9 electric and 403 diesel engines, as well as of 1,006 passenger cars and 10,943 freight cars. It also proposed purchase of 781,600 tons of track. By 1960 the railroad target had only been about 76 percent achieved: the system had acquired the 9 electric engines contemplated, but only 380 diesel ones, 554 passenger cars and 6,498 cargo cars. Some 613,259 tons of track had been purchased and 14,931,505 dormants had been changed in the rights of way. Insofar as track expansion was concerned, the goal was only about half achieved, with 826.5 kilometers having been added, instead of the planned 1,626.4 kilometers. However, as Lafer points out, although the federal railroad system had only been expanded by 3.2 percent, cargo increased between 1955 and 1960 by 21.7 percent. The number of passengers carried grew by 19 percent.

In this sector, as in that of energy, there were institutional changes made during the Kubitschek administration. The major one was establishment in 1959 of a centralized company, known as the Rede Ferroviaria, to administer the 77 percent of the country's railways which belonged to the federal government.[6]

In the highway sector, not only was the Belem-Brasilia highway completed, and the Brasilia-Acre one begun, but important additions to the national road network were made in the areas closer to the coast. The net result of these improvements was a fundamental alteration in the means by which goods were shipped from one part of the country to the other, with a significant relative decline in the role of the railroads and maritime shipping in the transport of goods and passengers, and an increase in the part played by automotive transportation—a result much stimulated also by the establishment of a national automobile industry.

Lessa has sketched the achievements of the Kubitschek regime in the highway field as follows:

> Contrasting with the railroad sector, in which all objectives are not achieved, the highway sector grew very sharply in extension and quality, particular progress being made on the federal and state roads. In the 1955-1961 period the increase of these amounted to 47.7 percent, while the paved highway network rose by 351 percent. In the Plan were included only the federal roads; at the beginning the construction of 10,000 kilometres of new highway was foreseen, with the improvement of 3,800 kilometres and the paving of 3,000 kilometres. In 1957 these objectives were expanded to include the construction of 12,000 kilometres and the paving of 5,000 kilometres; at the end of 1958 the notable success of this program permitted the amplification of plans, to 5,800 kilometres.[7]

The road construction program was one of the aspects of the Target Plan which was dearest to Juscelino Kubitschek's heart. This was particularly the case with the roads which connected Brasilia with various parts of the country. We shall pay particular attention to them in connection with the discussion of the new capital.

Important investments were also made in the merchant marine. These included funds spent to provide Petrobras with a sizable fleet of oil tankers, as well as expenditures on the government-owned coastal and high seas shipping lines. Lessa has commented thus on the success of the Kubitschek program in this field:

> in 1955 the situation of the national merchant marine was the following insofar as ships of more than 100 tons were concerned: coastwise, 315 units with 600,000 tons; high seas, 20 with 150,000 tons; oil tankers, 31 with 217,000 tons; and river ships, 53 with 23,000. In the Plan special importance was conceded to the fleet of oil tankers and to coastwise shipping, with provision for the incorporation of them of 200,000 and 330,000 tons, respectively. Insofar as the high seas fleet was concerned, which handled only 11.2 percent of the country's total imports, the Plan provided only for the incorporation of 30,000 tons. However, the means adopted to obtain a better utilization of the disposable fleet made it possible for national participation in handling imports to rise to 18.7 percent in 1959. The success achieved in amplifying the merchant marine was practically total. Between 1956 and the end of 1960 there were incorporated vessels with a total of 550,000 tons, corresponding to 299,0000 for tankers, 179,000 for coastwise ships, 64,000 for high seas vessels and 8,000 for the river ships.[8]

Even these increases in the country's merchant marine were not sufficient to overcome the crisis in the country's maritime transport. A still inadequate proportion of the country's exports and imports were carried in Brazilian bottoms, the coastal shipping service continued to have too many pre-World War II vessels of dubious quality, and little was done by the Kubitschek administration to reorganize the handling of cargo so as to reduce the excessively large amount of damage and pilfering. Almost another decade was to pass before these problems had been resolved more or less satisfactorily. However, there is no question but that the Kubitschek administration took major steps to begin the expansion and improvement of the country's merchant marine.

190

The Kubitschek Steel Program

Steel production was the last of the major fields in which direct government expenditures played the principal role in the Target Plan. As governor of Minas Gerais, Kubitschek had understood the importance of the expansion of the steel industry to the overall development of the Brazilian economy. One of the accomplishments of his Minas administration had been the establishment of the Mannesmann plant in Belo Horizonte, with intensive help from the state administration. Lessa has noted that

> in 1955 the productive capacity of the industry had reached 1.2 million tons of raw steel, with which about 80 percent of the national market was covered. In the Plan it was proposed to expand to 2.3 million tons by 1960 and to begin construction of plants which would permit output to come to 3.5 million tons by 1965. The objective was not exactly self-sufficiency, but rather to guarantee the supply necessary to meet the increased needs of the economy without undue stress on the balance of payments. To such a degree was this the case that the absolute amount of imports even grew somewhat during the period.[9]

The production of steel ingots increased from 1,365,000 tons in 1955 to 2,485,000 tons in 1961. At the same time, imports of steel ingots rose from 339,000 tons in the former year to 433,000 in the latter. Production of laminated steel products rose from 1,074,000 tons in the first year of the Kubitschek administration to 1,928,000 tons in 1961, while imports of the same commodities were rising from 242,000 to 331,000 in the same period.[10]

During the Kubitschek administration construction was begun on two other major steel plants to complement Volta Redonda, and expansion of a number of private enterprises in the sector was encouraged. The two major plants were the Companhia Siderurgica Paulista (COSIPA) in the state of São Paulo, and the USIMINAS firm in the state of Minas Gerais. Werner Baer in his book *The Development of the Brazilian Steel Industry* has discussed the origins of COSIPA and USIMINAS. He noted that the idea for the former originated with private interests in 1951, and that the firm was formally established as early as 1953. However, by the middle of the decade it had become obvious that private entrepreneurs did not have sufficient resources to do the job. As a result, Baer notes that, "in 1956 the state of São Paulo supplied additional capital by becoming a shareholder in COSIPA, and a little later on the Brazilian National Economic Development Bank (BNDE) did likewise, gradually becoming the majority shareowner of the enterprise." Baer also notes that "it was not until the end of the fifties that construction in COSIPA began. The building of the steelworks took substantially longer than was initially planned and was considerably more expensive than originally estimated. . . . It was only in December 1963 that the rolling mill section began to operate."[11]

With regard to USIMINAS, Baer states that the idea originated with local private and local government interests. Finally, "Usiminas was created in 1956. Since it was obvious that the technical co-operation and resources of foreign capital were needed to build the project, negotiations were immediately started with Japanese, German, and even some East European groups. Finally, in 1957, an accord was reached with a Japanese group." The Japanese interests acquired 40 percent of the original capital and "undertook to plan and supervise the erection of the steel mill and to supply the equipment, most of it coming from Japan." The BNDE provided 24.64 percent of the capital for the firm, the government of Minas Gerais 23.95 percent, the federal government's Companhia do Valle do Rio Doce 9 percent, the Volta Redonda firm 1.52 percent and private Brazilian interests about 1 percent. Baer adds that "most of the sections of the mill were completed by the end of 1962, and in November of that year the blast furnace began to function. By late 1963 all the main sections of the mill were in operation."[12]

Instrumentalities Used in Private Sector

In addition to those sectors of the economy in which government direct investments were of primary importance, the Programa de Metas involved several major segments of manufacturing in which private enterprise was predominant. These included cement, the auto industry, shipbuilding, agricultural machinery, and electrical and mechanical machinery.

The Kubitschek administration used a variety of methods of encouraging and even coercing private entrepreneurs to go into those sectors of the economy in which the Target Plan allowed them to be predominant. Most of these methods did not originate with the government of Juscelino. Here too, for the most part, Kubitschek did not try to establish new institutions or uproot old ones. Rather, he tried to mold the institutional instrumentalities which were already at hand, to his purposes. These included the "law of similars," so-called "Instruction 113" of the SUMOC, the protective tariff system, foreign exchange controls, and the government banks. Perhaps the only significant innovation of the Kubitschek administration was the Executive Group, through which many or all of those other instrumentalities were brought to bear upon a single sector of the economy.

The Law of Similars

One of the most ingenious levers for bringing pressure on firms to expand and diversify their operations was the so-called law of similars. This was an old instrument of Brazilian foreign trade policy, originally established in the 1890s, during the first great government effort to encourage industrialization. According to this statute, industries in Brazil which could produce sufficient quality and quantity of a given product were able to obtain more or less automatic protection from foreign competition within the Brazilian market. A Register of Similar Products was established in 1911, and firms doing business in Brazil, whether of national or foreign origin, could apply for inclusion in this register. Such inclusion brought a firm various advantages. According to Gordon and Grommers, "administrative tariff exemptions or reductions were forbidden with respect to items thus registered." They add, writing soon after the Kubitschek administration, that "in recent years registration of a product as a 'similar' has become the basis, in practice if not always a matter of law, for broad tariff protection and also for classification in a high foreign exchange rate category under the multiple rate system."[13]

During the Kubitschek administration, the law of similars was a particularly strong inducement for foreign firms which had been importing goods into Brazil to establish in the country plants making these same kinds of products. Not infrequently such action was preventive, to forestall the establishment of such a plant by a competitor, and to get the benefits of the law of similars against any possible encroachment by rival firms. The law of similars also proved to be a powerful factor in encouraging vertical integration in Brazilian industries. Gordon and Grommers commented that

> usually the participating companies have moved—in order to protect an established market position and their pre-existing investments in distribution or assembly facilities. The more a company has invested in its physical importing and distribution apparatus, and in intangible assets such as goodwill, product acceptance, and knowledge of the market, the more determined it is to protect its position by initiating an assembly operation. Once this has been done, it becomes even more difficult to abandoned the investment when confronted with the choice between making the final step into manufacturing or being squeezed out of the market.[14]

The law of similars had obviously been on the books many decades before the advent of Kubitschek to the presidency. However, the Kubitschek administration differed from its predecessors in making deliberate and extensive use of the statute in effect to coerce firms either to begin manufacturing activities in the country, or to push these efforts into fields new to those firms. It enthusiastically applied the law of similars on behalf of an existing enterprise in the hope that that firms's rivals would establish operations in the same field, of only as a lesser evil to losing their Brazilian business completely. It was a powerful instrument for bringing into existence a widely integrated industrial system, extending from raw materials to finished products.

Tariff Policies of Kubitschek

As has been noted, one of the reasons for the effectiveness of the law of similars was that its application usually brought to a firm substantial tariff protection. Again, the protective tariff was not something which began with the Kubitschek regime. However, few

194

Brazilian administrations have used it with more effectiveness as an instrument for economic development.

During the period of the Brazilian Empire (1822-1889) most efforts to convert Brazil into a high tariff country were unsuccessful. However, during the early 1890s, the administration of the republic's second president, Floriano Peixoto, resorted to a high tariff system as a temporary measure. Throughout most of the years of the Old Republic, the issue of the protective tariff was hard and sometimes bitterly fought. It was not until 1922 that Brazil became definitely a protectionist country.[15] The existing tariffs were subsequently raised considerably during the first period of the rule of President Vargas in the 1930s. No substantial modification in this instrument of protective policy had been made between that time and the Kubitschek administration.

In the years preceding Juscelino's advent to power, the effectiveness of the tariff as a protective device had declined seriously. This was because the duties were generally "specific," that is, providing for a fixed tax on a quantity of a given commodity regardless of the monetary value of the unit of commodity in question. With mounting inflation, the tax had become increasingly small in relation to the value of the goods imported. So, the Tariff Law of 1957, passed under the auspices of the Kubitschek administration, changed this system. Gordon and Grommers have explained that

> the specific import duties, which had long since lost any real importance as a result of continuing price increases, were replaced by a schedule of ad valorem duties, which varied according to the essentiality of the imported goods and the availability of similar products from local sources. On producer goods typical rates ranged from 10 to 100 percent, and on consumer goods they were frequently between 100 and 150 percent.[16]

This effective increase in the general tariff law provisions was completed during the Kubitschek administration by giving exemptions to import duties on machinery and other equipment needed by industries which the government was encouraging to establish or expand their activities. Gordon and Grommers have noted that exemptions and reductions became more important. The new Ad Valorem duties on machinery range generally between 20 and 100 percent with most items falling between 35 and 60 percent. Reductions of up to half the duty can be granted by the Customs Policy Council on imported machinery provided no national equivalent has been registered as a similar. In addition, full exemptions have frequently been awarded by special law. Savings on imported machinery of 30 to 60 percent, and even more, have thus been realized by various companies in this period. In the more important cases, these savings usually combined with the advantages of Instruction 113.[17]

Exchange Control as a Protective Device

Instruction 113 was part of the mechanism of exchange control which the Kubitschek administration inherited. What exchange control meant was that the Banco do Brasil had a virtual monopoly on all dealings in foreign currency. All of those who earned dollars, pounds, francs, marks, or other kinds of foreign exchange had to sell them to the Banco do Brasil. Anyone who wanted to obtain any appreciable amount of foreign currency had to obtain it from the same source. This system had been established under Vargas during the Great Depression in the 1930s, when the country had been faced with a disastrous fall in its exports of coffee and other products, and therefore a sharp decline in the amount of foreign currency that Brazil earned. At first, exchange control was purely and simply a rationing mechanism, seeking to make sure that the essential import needs of the country were met. However, it was soon discovered that exchange control was a useful protective device for specific industries. Making importers pay a relatively high price for foreign currency needed to import a given product had the same effect as levying a tariff duty on that product. In one form or another, exchange control had been used since the late 1930s as an instrument for protection.

The exact exchange control system used during the Kubitschek period had been established in 1953 during the second administration of Vargas. It provided for a "foreign exchange budget." This involved an estimate of the total amount of foreign currency available in a given time period, and allotted that amount among the various needs: payment of contractual obligations, government and private projects which needed a license from the Superintendencia de Moeda e Credito (SUMOC) before they could seek foreign exchange, and those projects which did not need such a license. Insofar as the foreign currency which was available to private firms was concerned, SUMOC had a complicated list of priorities. Within each priority group it would establish the upward and downward limits within which it would make foreign currency available. The actual price of foreign exchange at any given time would then depend on an auction system, in which those wishing to purchase it would bid against one another.[18]

Within this system, Instruction 113 had been introduced during the administration of President Café Filho, by Minister of Finance Eugenio Gudin. Convinced that the economic development of the country depended largely on the steady inflow of sizable amounts of foreign capital, Gudin had sponsored issuance of Instruction 113 of SUMOC to greatly liberalize the conditions for entry of foreign capital. Gordon and Grommers wrote that

> under Instruction 113 a foreign investor was permitted to import machinery if he agreed to accept payment, not in the form of cash or deferred debt, but by assuming instead a cruzeiro capital participation in the enterprise by which the equipment was to be used. The Foreign Trade Department of the Bank of Brazil (CACEX) which . . . is responsible for the administration of Instruction 113, was to give approval only if the investment was desirable for the economy of the country. The criterion was met automatically if the equipment was to produce goods classified in Categories I to III of the import control system. For lower categories where in fact most goods fell, CACEX was to consult the Council of SUMOC and various interested agencies and outside bodies, generally including the National Confederation of Industries, were heard before approval was granted.[19]

Gordon and Grommers go on to indicate that "approval was normally to be given only for complete sets of manufacturing equipment, although in exceptional cases permission could be obtained to complete the modernization of existing industrial units." They also indicated that "the Brazilian company concerned also had to agree not to dispose of the machinery during its normal economic life and not to make any direct payment abroad corresponding to its value." Gordon and Grommers conclude that

> the treatment under Instruction 113 was clearly much more advantageous to foreign investors than the alternative of sending dollars into Brazil at the free market rate and using the cruzeiros thus obtained to repurchase dollars at a higher price in the auction market. The measure of the advantage was the difference between the cost of foreign exchange in the relevant auction category. . . and the free market rate. For dollar imports this differential has at most times been very substantial. . . . For machinery from nondollar sources the differential was generally smaller and occasionally negative. These differences among currencies largely disappeared with the achievement of currency convertibility by most major exporting countries at the end of 1958.[20]

The foreign exchange policies, and particularly the use of Instruction 113, aroused considerable opposition. The Nationalists in particular saw this as a means of giving unfair advantage to foreign enterprises, as compared with Brazilian ones.

Use of Government Banks

The Kubitschek administration also used the government banks extensively to encourage private participation in its development program. Most important were the Banco do Brasil, which at that time carried out most of the functions of a central bank, but also served as an important commercial and investment bank, and the Banco Nacional de Desenvolvimento Economico (BNDE). Neither of these institutions were established during the Kubitschek administration. The Banco do Brasil was one of the oldest banking institutions in the country. The BNDE had been established in the early 1950s, during the second Vargas government.

The operation of these institutions was of particular importance for two reasons. First, the Brazilian private banking system—with the possible exception of some of the banks of São Paulo—had never been particularly concerned with the long-term credit needs of their customers. They were basically commercial banks, interested in short-term operations, and to a considerable degree were still more attuned to the needs of a country principally concerned with financing its major exports, than to those of a nation which was rapidly industrializing. In addition, the constant, and sometimes very rapid, rise in the general price level had the result of making interest rates of private lending institutions exceedingly high, with the result that the private banks were even less prone than before to lend on a long-term basis. For the most part, they were quite content to have the public lending institutions take over the bulk of the financing of industrialization.

Lessa has underscored the significance of the increase in the private lending operations of the Banco do Basil. He has noted that

> there is clearly a transformation of the structure of credit operations. The participation of the public sector in the total loans at the end of the year rose from 15.3 percent in the three year period 1954-56, to 19.5 percent in the following three year period. During the same period the participation of the Banco do Brasil in the total of banking operations grew: at the end of the decade of the 1950s it provided approximately half of the total loans to the private sector. This amplification of the role played by the official bank did not exclude from these resources the private sector, since this also was favored in the expansion of the operations of that institution. With the accentuation of the dependence of firms on official loans, there increased, at least in theory, the role played by the state as orientor of economic activities.[21]

The Banco Nacional de Desenvolvimento Economico also played a very important role in financing industrialization during this period. Previous to that time, its activities had been largely centered on financing expansion of the infrastructure of transport and electricity, and in stimulating the growth of agriculture. However, under Kubitschek, it turned its attention heavily towards manufacturing. Lessa has noted that

> to these advantages offered to all activities the government wished to encourage, there was added sometimes the lower cost of financing of long-term credits given by the BNDE. . . . In the same way, entrepreneurs were assured access to financial resources by way of official guarantees given by the BNDE for credits obtained from abroad. These two procedures, which assured long term loans without financial readjustments, not only made investments possible, but under conditions of a rapid deterioration of the internal price level, represented an additional unforeseen subvention to private investment.[22]

Various industries were able to take advantage of the opportunities for credit provided by the BNDE. Among those which were most heavily financed in this way were the nonferrous metal, machine, electrical material, paper and cellulose, shipbuilding, and chemical industries.

The Use of Executive Groups

One instrumentality of development which, if it did not originate with the Kubitschek administration, was certainly used by it on a large scale for the first time, was the so-called Executive Group (Grupo Executivo). An Executive Group consisted of representatives of all government institutions the activities of which were relevant to the development of a particular industry. Each Executive Group was given powers to cut through red tape and bureaucracy, as well as to give preference within its own competence to the needs of the industry under consideration. The best-known of the Executive Groups of the Kubitschek period was the Executive Group for the Automotive Industry (GEIA). Others were established in the fields of shipbuilding, tractors, automatic telephone equipment, and several parts of the heavy machinery industry.

The Automotive Executive Group was typical of this kind of organization. It was established by a series of decrees between June and December 1956. It contained representatives of the exchange and foreign trade departments of the Banco do Brasil, the Tariff Policy Council, the BNDE, SUMOC, and the principal interested ministries.[23] Special incentives were established for the Automotive Executive Group to apply for the purpose of encouraging development of the auto industry. According to Gordon and Grommers,

> under the laws and decrees creating the GEIA program, which dated mostly from June to December of 1956, the following favors were extended to imports of manufacturing equipment for the automotive industry. In the first place, such equipment would automatically be awarded Instruction 113 treatment. Secondly, firms that were unable to bring in their entire industrial equipment as a foreign investment in kind, under Instruction 113, would be granted preferential cost-or-exchange treatment for debt financing with a minimum repayment period of five years. Finally, for a period of thirty months, subsequently extended to last until June 6, 1960 (and with a further retroactive extension still under consideration by the Brazilian Congress in mid-1960), such equipment would be exempted from import duties (and also consumption taxes).[24]

The Grupo Executivo was granted special amounts of foreign exchange. At the same time, special consideration was given the industry, in terms of giving it priority status, its components being placed in preferential exchange categories. The tasks of the Grupo Executivo pela Industria Automovilistica (GEIA) were varied. They included promoting the idea of establishing plants in Brazil among those firms which might participate in the program for development of the national auto industry; administering the foreign exchange allotments to the development of the auto industry; and keeping track of the degree to which the provisions for "nationalization" of the industry (increasing the percentage of components produced in Brazil) were being carried out.

The importance of the GEIA program in giving a sense of direction to the growth of the Brazilian auto industry has been stressed by Baer: "The guidance provided by GEIA not only led to rapid integration of automotive production within the country but it was also responsible for bringing about what was thought to be the correct mix of the types of vehicles produced. Thus, by the end of the Kubitschek administration, only half of the output consisted of passenger cars, while the rest consisted of utility vehicles and trucks."[25] The scope and nature of the activities of the executive groups established in other sectors of the economy during the Kubitschek period did not differ fundamentally from those of the GEIA. Their success in accomplishing the objective for which they were established is evidence of the utility of this rather unique instrumentality for economic development.

Development of the Auto Industry

As the success achieved in the fields of transportation, electrification, and steel was preeminent in the government controlled part of the Brazilian economy, so the accomplishments in autos, machinery, and shipbuilding were most noteworthy in the predominantly private area. Most famous was the establishment of an automobile manufacturing industry of major size.

For several decades Brazil had possessed some auto assembly plants, subsidiaries of North American and European automobile manufacturing firms. In 1956 there was also one small government firm assembling trucks of Alfa-Romeo design. However, the objective of the Kubitschek Target in this field was to convert the auto industry from one which merely assembled pieces brought in from abroad to one which was virtually all Brazilian, in terms of getting its raw materials within the country, and producing in Brazil virtually all of the parts which entered into assembly. To this end, a time schedule was worked out by the Grupo Executive pela Industria Automobilistica. This schedule underscored the determination of the Kubitschek administration to bring about within the time of one presidential administration really profound alterations in the structure of the economy. According to the schedule of the GEIA, the percentage of nationally made components of cars assembled in Brazil had to rise from 41.6 percent which it was at the end of 1956 to 50 percent in the following year, 67.6 percent on December 1, 1958, 80 percent on the same day of 1959, and finally 92.8 percent by the end of 1960. In addition to this "nationalization" of the components of autos made in Brazil, the Kubitschek Target provided for an augmentation of the number of finished vehicles turned out in the country. It foresaw the increase of the total number of automotive vehicles produced in Brazil from 30,700 in 1957 to 170,000 in 1960, by which time the country would be virtually self-sufficient insofar as the production of trucks, jeeps, and passenger cars was concerned.[26]

Although the goal of the Kubitschek administration in the automotive field was not completely met, spectacular progress was made and the auto industry was established on a solid basis. Ten foreign companies and the government's Fabrica Nacional de Motores (which had been established during World War II) entered into full-scale manufacturing during the program. The foreign firms were Ford Motor do Brasil (producing trucks, busses, and utility vehicles), General Motors do Brasil (turning out the same kinds of vehicles as Ford), International Harvester (making trucks), Mercedes do Brasil (trucks and passenger cars), Scania Vobis (producing only trucks and busses), Vemag S.A. (utility vehicles, jeeps, and passenger cars), Volkswagen do Brasil (utility and passenger cars), Willys-Overland do Brasil (making utility vehicles, jeeps, and Aero Wills and Dauphine passenger cars, the last arrangement with the French manufacturer), Toyota do Brasil (jeeps), and Romi Isetta and Simca do Brasil, both making passenger cars.[27]

The automobile industry development program of the Kubitschek administration was severely criticized at the time because of the large number of firms which were encouraged to establish production facilities under it. Critics pointed out that in each of the world's major auto producing countries an appreciably smaller number of firms was operating in the industry. It was also argued that the small size of the initial market for automotive vehicles in Brazil made this proliferation of companies particularly unwise.

However, Kubitschek apparently felt that the important thing was to get the auto industry well established. Hence, he would welcome the entry of any firms which might be willing to push forward this objective. The multiplicity of companies would also undoubtedly stimulate competition among them, and in any case there would be a period of settling down once the industry was firmly established, with an appropriate market structure emerging out of the industry's own experiences. That the Kubitschek administration was more nearly right than its critics is indicated by the fact that within a decade there did take place a process of consolidation and rationalization, with the result that there were only about half as many firms in the industry although its total output had increased substantially.

In 1960 the Brazilian auto industry turned out 134,371 vehicles, compared with 30,340 in 1957. Of the 1960 total, some 42,222 were trucks, 34,366 were utility vehicles, 19,524 were jeep-type vehicles, and only 38,259 were passenger cars.[28] In subsequent years, the proportion of output consisting of passenger cars rose considerably. By 1969 Brazil was the ninth largest producer of automotive vehicles, behind the United States, Japan, West Germany, Great Britain, the USSR, Spain, and Australia, turning out 349,519 vehicles in all, of which 234,928 were passenger cars, and 114,591 were trucks and busses.[29]

Brazil also benefitted from the "linkage" effect of an automobile industry, from the point of view of overall economic development. For instance, the development of the auto parts industry was an integral part of the Kubitschek administration's target for the automotive sector as a whole, and spectacular progress was made in this field. In 1955 there were only 700 factories in the country making automobile parts, but by 1960 this number had risen to 1,200.[30] An important aspect of the growth of this segment of the automotive industry was the fact that a large proportion of the parts producing firms were Brazilian owned, in contrast to the assembly plants which with one exception were all foreign owned.

There is little question but that the establishment of a sizable auto industry in Brazil by the Kubitschek administration was of great strategic importance for the development of other key parts of the country's manufacturing sector. It not only served to stimulate the growth of firms providing parts, but also acted to encourage investment in sectors of the economy producing raw materials—steel, rubber, glass, plastics, and so forth—which were consumed by the auto industry. Finally, it tended to provide for the first time a sufficiently large market to justify the establishment of important industrial machinery, electrical material, and allied products sectors in the national economy.

Growth of Machinery Industry

Kubitschek had as one of his major goals the implantation of a part of the economy which was capable of producing most of the industrial machinery, heavy construction equipment, and large-scale electrical material which was needed by the nation's manufacturing industries. With the installation of such a branch of production, Brazil's economy would have the capacity for thorough vertical integration, and hence the ability to grow in the future largely from its own resources.

The creation of the capacity for Brazil to provide its own machines, machine tools, construction equipment, machines to make other machines, had several long-range results of great importance. It created the possibility of Brazil in a relatively short time being able to produce most of these products for itself. Furthermore, the establishment of this type of industry raised new possibilities for diversification of Brazilian exports. With an integrated industry, ranging from the turning out of machine-making machines to plants making textiles and processed foods, the basis was laid for the future development of manufactured goods as an important element in the nation's exports, something which began to occur during the decade following Kubitschek's administration.

The actual progress that Kubitschek made in bringing about the establishment of this sector in Brazil was considerable. Lessa has commented that

> the Plan programmed the installation and amplification of industries of heavy mechanical construction, heavy electrical material, and of industrial machines, although without setting forth figures on the objectives to be attained. . . . According to the Development Council, in the 1955-60 period the production of machinery and equipment in general increased more than 100 percent and of heavy electrical material more than 200 percent, and the sector came to produce a large number of capital goods which were previously imported. According to the official estimates presented in the Plan Trienal, the effort expended had reduced to approximately one third, by the end of the decade, the foreign participation in the overall supply of capital goods.[31]

Lessa gives some estimates concerning the capacity of Brazilian industry to produce the economy's needs for specific kinds of machinery and equipment which shed considerable light on what had been achieved by the end of the Kubitschek period. For example, the nation's predicted need for electric turbines during the period 1961-1970 was some 48,860 tons, of which Brazilian industry would be able to supply 42,700 tons. Electric generators needed between 1961 and 1970 were estimated at 65,310 tons, with the national capacity exceeding this, being able to turn out 68,500 tons. In the field of electric transformers and boosters, too, Brazilian capacity in 1961 exceeded the estimated needs of the economy in the following decade.

By 1961 the country's own industries were physically able to provide a substantial proportion of the predictable equipment needs for expanding oil refining and petrochemicals. The 1961 capacity to produce oil storage tanks was 45,000 units, whereas the estimated need in the 1961-1970 period was 55,600. Heat exchangers were probably going to be required in the number of 100,700 and national output capacity stood at 35,300; but the nation was in 1961 already able to produce more than the number of steam generators which would be required by its oil industry, and almost five times as many specialized metallic structures as that industry would require in the 1961-1970 period. The country was almost self-sufficient in production of machinery for cement manufacture by 1962, it was able to produce more paper making equipment than was estimated to be needed at that time, although if it were to meet the needs of the 1961-1970 period, the industry was going to have to continue to expand.[32]

The importance of the efforts made by the Kubitschek administration in machine production has been underscored by a study of this industry in Brazil made in 1962 by the Economic Commission for Latin America (ECLA). It commented that

> with regard to the volume of fabrication, the data and information gathered demonstrates clearly the enormous effort achieved by the makers of machines after 1956. In only six years the annual tonnage produced increased by 260 percent, coming in that period to a total of more than 60,000 tons, equivalent to more than 62,000 machines. In 1961 this industry achieved a production of

15,517 units with a weight of 13,250 tons. This great increase in national production found its explanation in the strong increase in demand between 1956 and 1961 as a result of the establishment of the automobile industry and the expansion of various branches of the mechanical sector.[33]

The ECLA study went on to comment on the diverse nature of the new machinery industry brought into existence by the Kubitschek regime. It noted that "the industry now offers on the market 25 types of machines in about 150 principal models, which puts it in a quite respectable position. However, this line is somewhat incomplete in relation to the importance which the national industry achieved in number and in variety of types and models and shows some deficiencies in quality of some machines."[34] One factor which the ECLA study did not emphasize was the importance of the linkages of the establishment of a major machinery industry in Brazil. Not only did it result in considerably increasing the demand for such other elements of the development program as the steel industry, it also stimulated the training of large number of Brazilian workers in skills which were very scarce in the economy. In the future, such workers would not only be available for employment in the machinery industry but in other sectors of the economy as well. The depth of the country's store of skilled manpower was very considerably increased by creation of the large machinery sector.

No mention is made in the above discussion of the expansion of the machinery industry of the comparative costs of production of the new Brazilian industry and those in other countries. However, at the stage of development at which Brazil was during the Kubitschek administration, it was a matter of secondary importance, whether or not the new firms producing machinery and machine tools would be able to turn out these goods at prices which were competitive on an international basis. The important fact was that Brazil had acquired the physical equipment and had developed the trained manpower necessary to turn out the larger part of the capital equipment needed by the national economy. The mere fact that as of the early 1960s there existed a sector of the economy physically capable of producing two thirds of the country's capital goods requirements was of major significance, regardless of price considerations. It meant that the nation was able to obtain these capital goods without the expenditure of foreign currencies for them. They could be paid for in cruzeiros, and no longer represented a drain on the chronically short foreign exchange reserves of Brazil.

Furthermore, once these industries were established within the country, they could be expected to expand as the demand for capital goods continued to grow. To the degree, therefore, that their competitiveness on an international basis depended upon economies of scale, it could be expected that in time they would reach the size which would make it possible for them to compete, at least in the Brazilian market, without the kind of tariff and other protection which had been necessary to bring them into existence in the first place. Hopefully, they would in time be able to enter the international market, and begin to supply the requirements at least of other Latin American countries which, like Brazil, were also faced with long-run shortages of hard currencies.

Growth of Shipbuilding

The establishment of a sizeable modern shipbuilding industry was another major achievement of the Kubitschek Programa de Metas. Lessa has noted that

> an objective with a character similar to that in the automobile industry, although of more modest proportions within the Plan, was that with regard to shipbuilding. It was more modest to the degree that more importance was given to the program of road transport than to maritime or river transport; and it was similar in respect to the way in which its dynamism was transmitted to the rest of industrial activities, although there was no programming of "Nationalization" of the industry. Until 1957 the whole industry consisted of a few shipyards capable of producing small ships and making minor repairs.
>
> The Plan proposed the creation of two shipyards capable of producing large units and the renovation of fourteen existing yards, so as to endow the country with a total nominal capacity of 130,000 tons annually, a figure which was later increased to 160,000. It was also

208

proposed to construct three drydocks for ships of 35,000 and 10,000 and 5,000 tons. . . . By 1960 the Grupo Executivo de Construccão Naval . . . had approved 12 projects, two of which involved construction of large shipyards with a capacity of 60,000 and 40,000 tons a year. The total of projects approved by 1960 represented a nominal capacity of 158,000 tons a year, with exception of the production of dredges . . . and the repair of ships.[35]

In this industry, as in that making automobiles, foreign investment was relied on extensively. Among the firms participating on a major scale were a Japanese enterprise and a Dutch one.

By the end of the Kubitschek administration, Brazil had the largest shipbuilding industry in Latin America, and one of the important ones in the world at large. During the following decade the resources of the new industry were called upon to carry out a major effort to reequip both the Brazilian overseas merchant marine and the lines servicing the country's costal trade. In this connection, in 1965 Brazil produced the largest ship which had up until then been built anywhere in Latin America, the 18,110 deadweight ton *Mario d'Almeda*, some 168.9 meters long and capable of 16.4 knots per hour. This ship was the first of five similar vessels which had been ordered by a Brazilian consortium.[36] The shipbuilding industry also began in the decade after the Kubitschek period to be a source of foreign exchange, with ships being built in Brazilian yards for a number of foreign concerns.

Agricultural Equipment Industry

Of less immediate importance than the automobile, machinery, and shipbuilding programs, but of great potential significance, was the Kubitschek administration's effort in the field of tractors, principally for agricultural use. One of Juscelino's major reasons for concentrating upon the development of manufacturing instead of upon agriculture was his belief that in order to undertake a major effort to expand and improve Brazilian agriculture, it was first necessary to have a manufacturing sector which could supply most of the inputs which such an effort would require on a long-term basis.[37]

A significant beginning was made in this direction, insofar as tractors were concerned, although this program did not begin to bear fruit until the last year of Kubitschek's term of office. In that year, 1960, some 37 medium-sized tractors were turned out. In 1961, 25 light tractors, 1,573 medium ones, and 80 large, for a grand total of 1,678 tractors were constructed in the country, and in the following year, the total number was 7,586, divided among 1,984 light vehicles, 4,779 medium-sized ones and 823 large tractors.[38] As in the case of the automobile machinery, and shipbuilding industries, and major efforts in the tractor and agricultural equipment fields were made by private firms, most of them foreign.

Net Effect of Kubitschek Program

The accomplishments of the Kubitschek Administration in terms of economic development were fundamental. They transformed the nature of the nation's economy and closed an era in the country's history. Lessa has summed up the accomplishments of the Programa de Metas thus:

> The termination of the "Plan de Metas" coincides to a certain degree with the end of the long process of industrial diversification, through which the Brazilian economy passed in accordance with the model of development through import substitution. In the period 1957-1961 the internal net product increased at 7.9 percent per year, against 5.2 percent in the preceding five-year period. That result obeyed the concentrated effort of investment in the construction of a vertically integrated industrial system, in which there were present and were important the sectors producing capital goods and infrastructure. Although there still existed disconnections in this structure, the essential ends were achieved: from the qualitative point of view, Brazil entered the decade of the 1960s with the industrial structure of a mature economy.[39]

Celso Furtado has also emphasized the significance of the new directions in which the Kubitschek program took Brazilian industrialization. He has noted that "since the production of manufactured consumers goods grew at the same rate as the gross product, one deduces that the basic factor of growth was the rapid expansion of the capital goods industries. Thus, between 1955 and 1961, while industrial production as a whole grew about 80 percent, that of steel increased 100 percent, of mechanical industries, and of transport material about 600 percent."[40]

Lessa also has noted the significance of what had been accomplished by Kubitschek's industrialization for the future expansion of the economy:

> For the later evolution of the economy the most significant aspect was the accentuated process of substitution for the imports of capital goods. The coefficient of these imports in the internal supply of capital goods fell from 54 percent in 1949 to 33 percent in 1958. Given the flexibility of the already installed industry of machine production and the presence of certain unused capacity in that sector, one can think that, once certain problems (technological deficiencies, lack of internal financing of sales, etc.) are resolved, it will be sufficient to have reduced complementary investments for the substitution of capital goods imports, now potentially realized, to a point very superior to the coefficient indicated. In a recent study of the ECLA it is indicated that with the existing industrial installations, 80 percent of the needed capital goods for the expansion of basic sectors can be produced internally. Parallel to industrialization one can observe in that period the supremacy of the urban sector and the confirmation of its conquest of the mechanisms of political decision. From this conjunction of factors it results that for the first time there exists the possibility of defining the future trajectory of its evolution with great independence of the economy's relations with the rest of the world. There exist some of the necessary conditions for a process of self-sufficient and independent development.[41]

This quotation presents a somewhat optimistic view of the degree to which the industrialization effort had resulted in the transfer of political power to the urban groups.

Chapter 11

BRASILIA

Brasilia is Kubitschek's monument. While he was president, Brasilia was his most vaulting ambition; in ostracism, his greatest consolation; as he grew old, his greatest source of pride, his certainty of a secure place in the history of his country. Certainly, the construction of Brasilia is central to an understanding of Kubitschek's impact upon Brazil. It was his single most important contribution to the country's economic development. It was crucial to his successful effort to inspire in his fellow-countrymen a pride in their own accomplishments and in themselves. At the same time, it was the supreme example of his ability to harness his political talents and overpowering energy to the fulfillment of a vision, in part by getting others to share that vision.

While it was under way, the construction of Brasilia was also the most controversial aspect of Kubitschek's administration. It was a favorite target of his political opponents. Even many of his friends and allies were skeptical about, or hostile to, the idea. Kubitschek found it necessary to use at different times guile, arm-twisting, and devious political maneuvering to bring into line those political leaders who, not sharing his vision, sought at various times to subvert or destroy what he came to call his 31st Target, his "integrating target." At was the rank and file Brazilian who shared Juscelino's vision of the new capital most clearly. As Thomas Skidmore has pointed out, the building of Brasilia "gave the rest of Kubitschek's economic program, the details of which remained unknown to much of the public, an immediately understandable symbol."[1]

I became aware of the wide popular support for Brasilia in mid-1959, when I first visited the new capital, which was still only beginning to take shape. Upon my return to Rio and São Paulo, I frequently asked taxi drivers, hotel employees, and other folks whom

I met what they thought of Brasilia. In each case, the first reply was a recitation of the difficulties which its construction was imposing on the people in terms of higher prices, shortage of cement and other materials elsewhere in the country, and corruption. However, when I then asked these people whether they were therefore opposed to Brasilia, the reply was always: "Oh, no sir, it is wonderful! If we can do that, we can do anything!"

Historical Antecedents of Brasilia

The idea of moving the capital to the central part of Brazil did not originate with Kubitschek. As early as 1789, the Inconfidentes Mineiros rebels of Minas Gerais, precursors of independence, included in their demands the movement of the capital of the colony from Rio de Janeiro to the interior. José Bonafaçio de Andrada e Silva, the architect of Brazilian independence, on at least two occasions wrote official papers emphasizing the importance of establishing a new capital in the interior. One of the Brazilian deputies to the Portuguese parliament of 1821, the year before independence, presented a bill suggesting that a new capital be established "in the center of Brazil, between the headwaters of the rivers Paraguay and Amazonas," and that it should be called Brasilia or something else.

With the establishment of the republic, one of the decrees of its first provisional government provided that when the capital was moved to the interior, the existing federal district—the city of Rio de Janeiro and its environs—would be converted into a state. This was reiterated in the first republican constitution of 1891, when in it Article 3 provided for the acquisition by the federal government of an area of 14,400 square kilometers in the central highlands for the location of the future capital. On 17 May 1891, President Floriano Pexioto named the first of what were to be various commissions to lay out the contours of the region of the new capital, and in December it rendered its report, suggesting an area ninety kilometers wide and one hundred sixty kilometers long in the highlands of the state of Goias. Although nothing concrete was done in the following decades to make this the new center of the federal government, a small monument was raised in the center of the designated area on the first centenary of independence, 7 September 1922, as a "cornerstone" for the new capital.

214

The second and third republican constitutions of Brazil, those of 1934 and 1937, also proclaimed the ultimate intention to move the capital to the central highlands. So did the Transitory Article No. 4 of the Constitution of 1946, which read "the capital of the Union will be transferred to the Central Plain of the country." The first president under this new basic law, General Dutra, on 19 November 1946 established a Study Commission for the Localization of the New Capital of Brazil. It reported on 13 December 1947, suggesting the same region which had been staked out in the 1890s, but adding some additional territory to it.

Nothing further of a concrete nature was done until 5 January 1953, when Congress passed Law No. 1803 authorizing President Vargas to name yet another commission to make a definitive selection of the location of Brasilia. A year later, a United States firm, Donald J. Belcher Associates, was employed to make photoanalyses of the general area under consideration in the central highlands. In October, the Commission for the Localization of the New Capital, established under Law #1803, was reorganized. On 30 April 1955, after receiving the report from Donald J. Belcher Associates, the commission officially chose the area of the new federal district, between the Rio Prety to the east and the Rio Reseoberto on the west, and between latitudinal parallels 15 degrees 30 minutes and 17 degrees 3 minutes south. The area involved 5,850 square kilometers. Soon afterwards, the government of Goias, in which state and new federal district was to be located, forbade the alienation of any land within the area, and began buying up privately held lands in the region. It also established a Commission for Cooperation in Moving the Federal Capital.

Thus, the decision ultimately to move the Brazilian capital to the interior had been made many decades before Kubitschek became president. Also, by that time a site for the new city had formally been selected. However, in the light of his immediate predecessors' leisurely attitude about the matter and their insistence that "it was not yet the time" to establish Brasilia, few thought that Kubitschek would get the process of transfer underway, and hardly anyone dreamed that he would carry through the transfer in the short span of one administration.[2]

215

Kubitschek's Conversion to Brasilia

Kubitschek's assumption of the idea of building Brasilia seems to have been accidental. There is no indication that he had thought about the problem before launching his campaign for the presidency. However, early in his presidential campaign, he addressed a meeting in the town of Jataí in the state of Goias. During the meeting he stressed that he would fully carry out the constitution. In the question period he was asked whether he intended to carry out that article which called for construction of a new capital of the country in Goias. Juscelino later wrote that "the question was embarrassing. I already had my Target Plan, and nowhere in it was there any reference to that problem. I answered, however, as befitted the occasion: 'I have just promised that I shall carry out completely the Constitution and I do not see any reason why that part should be ignored. If I am elected, I shall construct a new capital and I shall carry out the change in the seat of government.'"[3]

Once he had publicly committed himself to building a new capital, the idea grew on Juscelino. He began to see its potentialities for opening up the great and almost unoccupied interior of the country. As he later wrote, he began to see Brasilia as "the factor which would unleash a new bandeirante cycle." So he added the construction of Brasilia to his Programa de Metas, as Target No. 31 (PQ.9). In time it was to dwarf all of the others in importance. However, it was not until he had been in office almost a year that Juscelino indicated, in his 1957 New Year's Message, that he seemed fully to understand the implications of the construction of Brasilia. Then he commented:

> I wish to deal now, my fellow citizens, with the problem of the moving of the capital to Brasilia. I know the criticisms of the work which has been undertaken by my government to transform into reality the provision of the Constitution to transfer the Capital to the interior of the country. I am not the inventor of Brasilia, but there has lodged in my spirit the conviction that the hour has come, in conformity with the orders of our Magna Carta to carry out an act of renovation, a political, creative act, an act which, forced by the national growth which

216

I have just discussed, will foster the beginning of a new era for our fatherland.

The foundation of Brasilia is a political act, the significance of which cannot be ignored by anyone. It is the march to the interior in all its amplitude. It is the complete consummation of the possession of the land. We are going to build in the heart of our country a powerful center for the spread of life and progress.

I know and have weighed all the consequences of this moving of the Capital. I am not unaware that I have added burdens and tiring tasks to the hard work which weighs on the shoulders of the Government. But it was necessary to take the decisive step. And the decisive step was taken. No one should have any illusions: the Constitution will be fulfilled, in benefit of the whole country, and of this Rio de Janeiro, which will suffer nothing with the change, quite to the contrary, because this city did not grow because it was the Capital of the Republic, today it has profound roots and will continue, stronger and more beautiful.[4]

The Planning of the New Capital

Once he had taken office, Juscelino moved to fulfill his campaign promise. He called in Santiago Dantas and asked him to prepare a bill to be submitted to Congress which "once approved would be a complete legal diploma, capable of taking care of all phases of the execution of the transfer, without my being obliged to return once again to Congress." This Dantas did, with one exception—the date of the transfer, according to the Constitution of 1946, had to be fixed by Congress (PQ.9). The bill, which ultimately became Law No. 2,874 of 19 September 1956, provided in its first article that the federal capital of Brazil would be located in the central plateau and defined the specific dimensions of the new federal district. Article 2 provided for establishment of the Companhia Urbanizadora da Nova Capital do Brasil (which came to be popularly known as Novacap). It was given full charge of construction of the new city (PQ.40).

Kubitschek submitted the bill on the new capital on 18 April 1956. However, it aroused immediate opposition, particularly from the União Democrática Nacional, which succeeded in bottling it up in the Justice Committee of the Chamber of Deputies, to which it had been referred. There it stayed, without any action being taken by the end of August. At that point, Kubitschek called together all of the members of Congress from the state of Goias, the opposition members as well as the government supporters. Public opinion in Goias was overwhelmingly in favor of the building of the new capital, and there, even the UDN congressmen supported the idea. However, Juscelino told the assembled deputies and senators that if the law was not passed by the first of October, he would give up the whole idea, since there would not be time to complete the new city and to transfer the capital there before the end of his term, unless action on the bill were taken immediately. A UDN deputy from Goias undertook, successfully, to get the bill reported out of committee, and it was passed finally by both houses, Kubitschek having little problem in the Senate, where the government had an ample majority (PQ.39-40).

However, once the bill became law, Kubitschek behaved with unaccustomed modesty. There was no public ceremony when he signed it. In his memoirs, he wrote that "in reality, it would have been counterproductive to make a fuss over the matter. If I had done so, that would have alerted the Opposition to the significance of the Act, and then endless interpolations of the Executive would have been made, creating difficulties for the beginning of the work on the central plateau" (PQ.40). Juscelino moved almost immediately to name the president and three-man board of directors of Novacap called for in the new law. For two members of the board he selected Ernesto Silva and Bernardo Sayão. The law had provided that the major opposition party should submit to a list of three names from which the president of the republic would choose the third member of the board. In this case, Kubitschek chose UDN deputy Iris Meinberg (PQ.41). The management of Novacap was put into the hands of Israel Pinheiro, a fellow native of Minas Gerais and a close friend of the president. He was a graduate of the Minas Gerais School of Mines in Ouro Preto, and had attained a considerable reputation as manager of the Rio Doce Railroad during World War II. His father had been a governor of Minas Gerais early in the century. Pinheiro as president of Novacap was offered all of the facilities in terms of money, materials, and other things in order to get the job done.

Thereafter, Juscelino exerted the utmost pressure to get the city built, so that the official transfer of the capital could be achieved before he left office. The fundamental objective was to have the basic buildings constructed which would be necessary for the moving of appreciable portions of the government. These included the presidential palace, the executive office building, the Supreme Court, the Congress, office buildings which would permit at least portions of the cabinet ministries to be installed there, as well as sufficient housing for the personnel who would work for the government in Brasilia.

The first step was to adopt a pilot plan for the construction of the new city. For this purpose a nationwide competition was announced. Although only Brazilians could submit plans, the jury which selected among those submitted had architects from Great Britain, France, and the United States as well as Brazil. Israel Pinheiro presided over the jury and Juscelino's old friend Oscar Niemeyer was one of its Brazilian members. Those wishing to participate were given 120 days in which to submit their designs. Twenty-six were finally presented, and of these, sixteen were quickly eliminated. Of the ten remaining designs, that submitted by Lucio Costa was finally accepted. Kubitschek wrote about Costa's project, that "it was presented without any preoccupation with being outstanding. It was on a sheet of common paper, designed by hand, with some sketches, and accompanied by an 'exposition' in defense of the project." Juscelino added that "The Constutec Co. spent 400 thousand cruzeiros to present their project, with models, colored graphs in aluminum frames. Lucio Costa, to do the same, spent 25 cruzeiros on common paper, pencils, ink, eraser, as well as 64 hours of work, and took the prize" (PQ.56).[5]

Kubitschek did not hold any contest to decide who should be in charge of setting the architectural tone of the buildings of the new city. He chose his old friend and collaborator Oscar Niemeyer for this task. As Costa put his imprint on the general layout of the city, Niemeyer set the pattern for the architectural style of Brasilia, a style which, with minor exceptions, still persists. Although Niemeyer undoubtedly thought in the terms of the functional nature of his building designs, in fact one of the principal criticisms which can be made of these plans is that many of his buildings were in fact not functional. This was notoriously the case with the row of ministerial buildings, running from the Place of the Three Powers to the transport and cultural center of the city. These edifices were entirely too small to carry out the functions for which they presumably were designed, and it became necessary to add sizable annexes to them before they could be adequately serve as the headquarters of the various executive departments. There has also been some criticism of the monotony of having all major edifices in the city of more or less the same style of architecture. I do not share this feelings. There is in fact considerable diversity within the general mold established by Niemeyer, and imaginative use has been made of forms, of color, and even of mosaics to differentiate the various public and office buildings of the new capital.

The Concept of Brasilia

Costa, creator of the pilot plan for the city, has himself summed up his conception of Brasilia. He has said that

> it should be conceived of not as a simple organism capable of carrying out satisfactorily and without difficulty the vital functions of just any modern city, not just as *urbs* but as *civitas*, possessing the attributes of a capital. And, therefore, the first condition is to have an urbanist imbued with a certain dignity and nobility of intention because from this fundamental attitude came the ordering and sense of convenience and balance capable of conferring on the projected total the desired monumental character. Monumental not in the sense of ostentation, but in the sense of palpable expression, that is to say, consciousness of what is worth while and significant. A city planned for orderly efficiency, but at the same time a lively city to be appreciated, appropriate to intellectual speculation capable of becoming in time, in addition to a center of government and administration, the most lucid and sensitive focus of culture.[6]

Costa recapitulated the city plan which he created in the following terms:

Summing up, the solution presented is easy to understand, since it is characterized by simplicity and clarity of original design, which doesn't exclude, as can be seen, variety in the treatment of the parts, each of which is conceived in accordance to the peculiar nature of its original function, resulting in harmony from apparent contradictions. Thus, being monumental, it is also comfortable, efficient, and intimate. It is at the same time extended and concise, bucolic and urban, lyric and functional. Automobile traffic proceeds without crossings, and the pedestrian is given his just place. And because the plan is so clearly defined it is easy to carry out: two axes, two terraplanes, one platform, two long streets in one direction, a main automobile road in the other, a road which can be constructed in parts—first the central portions with a cloverleaf on each side, afterwards the lateral streets, which can advance with the normal development of the city. The installations will always have free space in the green areas contiguous to the streets. The blocks will be barely levelled and landscaped, with the areas alongside planted in grass and later with trees, but without sidewalks of any kind. On the one hand, streets, on the other hand landscaping of parks and gardens. . . . Brasilia, air and motor capital: city-park. The ages long architectural dream of the Patriarch.[7]

Betty Wilson has written that Costa's project conceived of the city as having the form of a giant airplane, in which

the shorter Monumental Axis is Brasilia's main stem—the (to return to the airplane simile) body of the plane. The Residential Axis, which overpasses it, is the swept-back wings. The juncture of those arteries, typical of Brasilia in that there are to be no level crossings in the principal parts of the city, is to be capped by a huge traffic-free concrete platform set aside for theaters and restaurants and flanked by the business district. The "cockpit" of the Monumental Axis will be a vast triangular embankment, the Plaza of the Three Powers, with the Govern-

221

ment Palace, the Supreme Court, and the Congress buildings at its corners; behind this are the ministries and cathedral; at the "tail" is the railroad station. Parks, gardens, a university a diplomatic quarter, and various cultural and sports facilities, are all neatly fitted in, but no industry; the business of Brasilia's half million people will be government.[8]

In practice, in the two decades or more after the capital was transferred to Brasilia the city had not continued entirely to conform to the mold which Costa set for it, in spite of vigorous efforts on his part to prevent deviation. For one thing, in the "right wing" of his airplane design there developed a kind of shopping center along the main lateral road—Avenida 3, which was originally intended only to be a delivery route—leading to the east which was not contemplated at all in Costa's design, which saw commercial and service enterprises being an integral part of each of the huge housing blocks. In addition, there developed a certain sprawling of commercial and government buildings near the "cockpit," which certainly was not contemplated by Costa. However, fundamentally, Brasilia remains "the city that Costa built."

The Construction of Brasilia

Some construction work was begun in Brasilia even before the pilot plan had been adopted. Workers began to pour in from all over Brazil, but particularly from the northeast. These were the famous *candongos*. Outside the bounds of the planned city there quickly grew up what was for a time known as "Wild West," but is now referred to as the Cidade Livre (Free City). During the years of the construction of Brasilia, it was reminiscent of the frontier towns of the American Wild West of a century ago, with wooden sidewalks, jerry-built wooden houses, a multiplicity of saloons, houses of prostitution, and gambling centers. This was "home" for tens of thousands of workers employed in constructing the new capital. Although it was theoretically to be torn down once Brasilia was a reality, it has become a permanent suburb of the city—now with paved streets and sidewalks, with more solidly built houses supplied with electricity, plumbing, and other appurtenances of modern living. It still represents one of the anomalies in Brasilia, contrasting architecturally as it does with the modern buildings of the center of the capital.

Kubitschek himself commented on the transformation of the Cidade Livre. He said that

> it was in my plans to order to demolition of that urban excrescence as soon as Brasilia was inaugurated. However . . . I saw the impossibility of carrying out that intention. The Cidade Livre was an autonomous force. It lived by itself, as a subproduct of the new Capital. Furthermore, I had a debt of gratitude to that population. It was they, to begin with, who listened to my call to promote, without waiting, the populating of the vacant plateau. They came, without setting conditions They raised their wooden houses and opened their businesses. And, during the three years of the construction of Brasilia, they contributed in a decisive manner to seeing that nothing was lacking that the candangos needed. (PQ.310)

The first building to be constructed within the confines of the city of Brasilia itself was a provisional residence for President Kubitschek, to use during his frequent visits. Juscelino had made his first trip to the area on 2 October 1956, about two weeks after signing the bill authorizing the construction of the new capital. He was accompanied by Israel Pinheiro, Niemeyer, and Minister of War Henrique Teixeira Lott, among others. On the spot he conferred with a number of the engineers and technicians who were already in the process of organizing the work for building the city. Many years later he commented that "seeing, from above, the immensity of the plateau, I was convinced that in trying to bring about the transfer of the capital I was facing the most dangerous challenge which a chief of state could confront. I understood, then, the craftiness of some opposition deputies who had voted for transferring the capital. They had said, in doing so, that they acted because 'Brasilia will be my political tomb'" (PQ.47).

After this first visit, he continued to go back to the site of Brasilia a couple times each week. However, the flying time there and back from Rio de Janeiro was eight hours, and he had all too little time to talk with the people who were beginning to stream in and were undertaking the first tasks in the construction of the city. So the idea was born that the president needed a place where he could stay overnight. A group of ten of Juscelino's friends, including Niemeyer and Kubitschek's personal pilot, João Milton Prates, not only undertook to raise the money for the construction of this building, but saw to it that the edifice was constructed in ten days between 22 October and 31 October 1956.

The miniature presidential palace, which was dubbed the "Catetinho," the little Catete, consisted of a one-story "palace of planks," built up on wooden pillars, to keep it out of the reach of the snakes and other creatures which proliferated in the vicinity. It had only four rooms, and was less than 100 feet long. However, it was sufficient for Juscelino to have a place to sleep, maintain a study, have meals served, and be able to put up a few friends who might be accompanying him on his visits to the new capital. The Catetinho was inaugurated in a formal ceremony on 10 November 1956, on the occasion of which the first electric light was turned on it Brasilia provided by a small diesel engineer generator to serve the new presidential palace (PQ.49-54).

The Rhythm of Brasilia

For the first year or more of the construction of the new capital virtually everything which went into it had either to be flown in by air, or be brought in over trails across the plateau, because until early in 1958 there were no paved or all-weather roads reaching it. Once means of transport had been opened from Anapolis, 130 kilometers to the south, and from Belo Horizonte (which road was not completely finished until 1959), work went on night and day the areas under construction being lighted up in an eerie fashion with giant searchlights so that the workers could see what they were doing. Once started the rhythm of work on the new city never ceased until it was in such shape that Brasilia could be declared the capital of the republic. The phrase to do something "with the rhythm of Brasilia" came to mean to do it with the utmost rapidity and intensity.

The first buildings of major significance to be completed were the beautiful presidential residence of Alvorada (Dawn), the nearby Brasilia Palace Hotel, which put up the businessmen, politicians, artists and architects and the curious who streamed into Brasilia during its construction, and the residence of the chief executive of Novacap, Pinheiro. This last included not only a beautiful house, but also delightfully landscaped gardens.

By the middle of 1959 work was going ahead full steam on the Square of the Three Powers and the row of ministerial buildings, and the first housing blocks had been completed. By the time the capital was officially transferred nine months later, the administrative heart of the new capital had been completed, housing for tens of thousands of government employees had been constructed, as had the first group of houses on the Peninsula of the Ministers, meant as residence for members of the cabinet and the Supreme Court justices.

The Transfer of the Capital

The final step was taken on 21 April 1960, when Brasilia formally succeeded Rio de Janeiro as the capital of Brazil. For Kubitschek this was probably the happiest day of his presidency and one of the happiest in his life. The occasion was one of both solemn ceremonies and outbursts of enthusiasm, particularly by the people in the streets of the new capital. The ceremonies began with the inauguration by Kubitschek of a joint session of the two houses of Congress, the first meeting of the legislature in the new capital. It was presided over by Vice President Goulart and speeches were delivered by Senator Felinto Muller and Deputy Ranieri Mazzili. The latter, in his peroration said that Brasilia was "the dream of many men, the remote ideal which would slowly have passed into action, hampered always by some momentous headache, since it would have been difficult to have found the right or adequate time to bring us here without the dynamo of faith which found its interpreter and its focus of radiation in President Juscelino Kubitschek" (PQ.296).

The ceremonies in Congress were followed by the solemn installation of the Supreme Court in its building on the Praça dos Tres Poderes. Then this part of the ceremony was completed with the inauguration of the monument dedicated to the birth of Brasilia as the capital, which as Kubitschek wrote "was a block of concrete covered with marble, with in its interior a model of the city, as well as a repository of opinions of the most diverse personalities concerning Brasilia." Juscelino continued: "Added to the

225

monument, on the initiative and generosity of my friends, was a sculpture in granite of my head, and alongside, an inscription" (PQ.296-97). (It is remarkable that this monument, dedicated as it was to Kubitschek, was never removed or desecrated by the military men who ruled Brazil after 1964, in spite of the great hatred which many of them had for Kubitschek.)

In the afternoon, there was a military parade, followed by a parade of the candangos. Headed by Pinheiro, Niemeyer, Costa, and uniformed students, it consisted principally of "hundreds of trucks, filled with candangos, who carried their work tools like real weapons. Finally, there paraded all of the machinery used for levelling, excavation, dirt removal and construction." Kubitschek said that "this was one of the most vibrant moments of a glorious afternoon" (PQ.299).

However, in spite of the undoubted symbolic importance of this legal transfer of the capital of the country to Brasilia, it was many years before the task of fully moving the center of government to the central plateau was completed. Neither of Kubitschek's two immediate successors, Quadros and Goulart, liked Brasilia, and they were not particularly interested in intensifying the job of moving the machinery of government there. Thus, for many years, although the Congress and the Supreme Court regularly conducted their business in Brasilia, the executive branch of government did not move there. Neither did the foreign embassies of the innumerable private organizations move their headquarters to the new capital. They were very much involved with the work of the government and had to have their headquarters near the effective seat of government.

A visitor was able to see what was happening. I visited Brasilia several times in 1965-66, and it was then clear that most of the government's business was still being conducted in Rio de Janeiro, not in Brasilia. The buildings available to the executive departments in Brasilia were utterly inadequate to handle more than a small portion of those organizations' activities. The foreign embassies, at best, had symbolic branches in Brasilia, but continued to conduct most of their business in Rio de Janeiro, where the Itamaraty (foreign office) was still functioning.

However, a decade later, by 1975, this had all changed. The ministries were really functioning along Brasilia's Monumental Axis. The strikingly beautiful cathedral, which in 1966 had been a hole in the ground, had been completed and was functioning as the principal church in the capital. If one wanted to talk with the country's leading labor leaders, officials of the major organizations of industrialists, merchants, agriculturalists and the like, one had to go to Brasilia. By that time, Brasilia had really become the capital of Brazil.

Pros and Cons of Brasilia

In the beginning, Kubitschek encountered relatively little opposition to the idea of Brasilia. He succeeded in getting the basic laws needed for the project through Congress with comparative ease, because no one really took the idea of Brasilia seriously. However, as it became clear that he really did intend to build the new capital, the opposition intensified, and continued throughout the rest of his administration.[9] Upon occasion, it required all of Kubitschek's resources as a politician to block efforts by opposition leaders to hamper the construction of the city or to kill the idea entirely. The project was criticized from a great variety of angles. There were those who argued that the modern style of architecture made Brasilia an unpleasant city in which to live. Others argued that the whole idea of the new capital was premature, that Brazil should wait for another generation or two, by which time the virtually uninhabited areas lying between Brasilia and the centers of population nearer the coast would have been filled in to some degree.

Kubitschek himself has described the long-run impact of the construction of Brasilia by citing the American economist Albert Hirschman's argument that sometimes a shock to the economy of a developing country may have the result of creating such disequilibriums that a variety of efforts are needed to bring it back into equilibrium, and that these may bring about development. Brasilia, Juscelino argued, created the kind of disequilibrium which Hirschman describes, and the building of roads and the development of a range of other activities were necessary to reestablish equilibrium.[10]

Thomas Skidmore has suggested another effect of the construction of Brasilia. He has commented that

> the building of Brasilia . . . diverted attention from many difficult social and economic problems, such as reform

227

of the agrarian system and the universities. In both cases, optimists in the Kubitschek regime argued that the mere construction of the new capital would have side effects leading to the solution of the problems in question. . . . [Thus, the roads to Brasilia] would open up previously uncultivated lands and ease the burden on the inefficient system of food distribution. . . . The radically new university there would serve as a model for educational reform throughout the country.[11]

Three Criticisms of Brasilia

Perhaps the three most serious criticisms of the project were that it was a misuse of resources, that it was built too rapidly, and that too much corruption was involved in its construction. Each of these complaints is worthy of notice. Many economists and others have argued that the tremendous sums of money and resources which Kubitschek invested in Brasilia could better have been spent in building roads, schools, and other projects in the parts of Brazil which already had a sizeable population.[12] The answer to this is that the Brazilian people would in all likelihood not have submitted to the discomfiture and hardships which were part of the cost of Brasilia for anything as mundane as school building or ordinary road construction. Only a project which caught the popular imagination as did Brasilia would have been sufficient justification for people to submit to the increased tempo of inflation, the shortages of construction materials, and other consequences which flowed from this effort.

The argument that Brasilia was built too rapidly at first might appear to have some justification. It was certainly extraordinary to construct a city in the wilderness in the short span of time involved in the building of Brasilia. Within three and a half years after passage of the law establishing Novacap, the capital was officially moved to Brasilia. The cost of construction, both in terms of finances and of deprivations for the rest of the economy, certainly was increased considerably by the rapidity with which the city was built. However, there was clearly a political need for having the capital transferred before Kubitschek left office. He did not know who his successor would be or what attitude that successor would have towards Brasilia. It was therefore necessary to present his successor, whoever he might be, with a *fait accompli*. Once the capital was officially in Brasilia, it would be very difficult to move it back to Rio de Janeiro, but it would by no means be difficult for the next president to fail to move it at all. Should this occur, all of the vast expenditure on Brasilia would have been in vain.[13]

Juscelino's decision to build a major city within a single presidential term caused controversy even before the law authorizing the construction of the new capital had been passed. Marshal José Pessoa, who was head of the predecessor to Novacap, the Planning Commission for the Construction and Transfer of the Federal Capital (which had existed for several years before Kubitschek became president) advised the president to undertake the building of Brasilia in stages. Kubitschek noted that "I reminded him of the traditional lack of administrative continuity which was one characteristic of Brazil. Almost all governments, upon taking office, show the preoccupation either to stop or to alter the initiatives taken by their predecessors. Brasilia was too serious a matter to remain subject to the oscillations of personalist tendencies. That being true, I would construct the new capital and inaugurate it, leaving to whoever came afterwards, only the job or enlarging it and improving its services." The marshall was not convinced. He told Kubitschek, "your excellency will not succeed in that endeavor," to which the president replied: "I shall succeed, my dear marshal, and I shall be sure to send you an invitation to the inauguration ceremonies." The marshal resigned as a result of this disagreement (PQ.41-42).

The need for rapid construction of Brasilia was indicated by the owner of the Paris newspaper *Le Monde*, who visited Brasilia in 1958, when its construction had just begun. He noted that he had been informed that Brasilia was likely to become "the most important ruin of the twentieth century." This might well have been the case, had Kubitschek not transferred the official seat of the national government there before leaving office.[14]

It will probably never be known how much it cost to build Brasilia. Greatly varying estimates have been offered concerning the amount spent during the Kubitschek period. Perhaps the lowest of these was made by the Banco do Brasil, in answer to a request by a parliamentary commission of inquiry which was investigating the accounts of the Kubitschek administration, and specifically those of Novacap. It suggested that the cost had been the equivalent of approximately US $324 million. However, Ernesto Street, the chief economist of the National Confederation of Industry estimated in 1965 that somewhere between $500 and $600 million had been spent on constructing the new capital.[15] Philip Raine cites a study of the Getúlio Vargas Foundation that said that "by 1962 a billion dollars had been spent on it."[16] In any case, in retrospect, in view of the profound effect which the building of Brasilia had in terms of bringing about the expansion of the whole Brazilian economy, the cost of its construction was relatively modest. Corruption undoubtedly added to the cost of building the city; it was closely linked to the rapidity of construction of the new capital. If the city was to be built within less than four years, it would be physically and bureaucratically impossible to keep minute track of every cruzeiro spent on the project. As a result, it is probably true that illicit fortunes were made out of the construction of Brasilia.

A final comment on the pros and cons of Brasilia may be that of Mario Pedrosa, the country's leading art critic in the post World War II period, and a political opponent of the Kubitschek administration. He argued in 1959 that Brasilia was being built too fast, because Juscelino feared that his successor would drop the idea and because he wanted to be known as the one who had transferred the capital. However, Pedrosa said that architecturally Brasilia was a marvel, that it was wonderfully laid out and was the greatest experiment in a planned city to be found anywhere in the world. Finally, he said, Brasilia was a wonderful site for the exercise of the talents of Brazilian architects.[17]

The Roads to Brasilia

The basic thinking of Kubitschek in pushing through the construction of Brasilia was that it was necessary as a means of assuring the rapid development of the vast interior of the country, particularly the states of Goias and Mato Grosso. This area is a great plain, roughly comparable to that lying in the center of the United States. The opening up of the region would provide vast areas for new land settlement, for agriculture, and grazing. It was also widely believed that the area contained large mineral resources—although knowledge was scanty. In any case, it was certain that until people began to move into the region in considerable numbers it was unlikely that whatever mineral resources there were would be discovered and their exploitation begun. Therefore, as important as the construction of the city of Brasilia was, the building of roads linking it with various parts of the country was possibly even more important. When I asked President Kubitschek on one occasion what the fundamental purposes of constructing the new capital was in his estimation, he replied: "To have someplace to build roads to."[18]

Four of the roads from Brasilia are of particular importance. These are the ones linking it to Belo Horizonte in Minas Gerais and thence with Rio de Janeiro; that linking the city with São Paulo, via the Goias capital of Goiania and the so-called Minas Triangle; the Belem-Brasilia Highway; and the Brasilia-Acre Highway. By the end of 1965 the first two of these highways were paved. They acted as a major stimulus to agriculture in the areas they traversed, providing readily available markets for crops and livestock of the area in the cities and towns of Minas Gerais, in Rio de Janeiro, and in São Paulo, as well as in Brasilia with its quarter of a million people.

Of even more importance were the Belem-Brasilia and Brasilia-Acre roads. Kubitschek was proudest of the Belem-Brasilia link. General Vernon Walters and his colleagues have noted that

> unbelievers had scoffed at the idea of a road which would have to cut through the empty heart of Brazil and the hostile Amazon jungle. Juscelino Kubitschek found a man who shared his dream in Bernardo Sayao—an engineer who undertook to build the road. A special government corporation known as RODOBRAS was set up to build the road and maintain it. Without aerial surveys, in many cases using only a compass, the road was built with construction starting at both ends. In the south it crossed the highlands of Goias and in the north it cut across the Tocantins River, the bridge at Estreito was built with cement and steel flown in by C-47's. Inch by inch, mile by mile, the road crept towards a meeting of the north and south sections.[19]

The other road into the deep interior of the country, the Brasilia-Acre Highway, was a kind of afterthought, when the Belem-Brasilia was approaching conclusion. It was constructed in record time, running from the new capital to the town of Porto Velho, not very far from the Bolivian frontier, on one of the tributaries of the Amazon. Kubitschek wrote about it that

> everything in the construction of the Brasilia-Acre was adjusted to the exigencies of a record time. Between the decision to carry out the work and its inauguration, there was an astonishing succession of tabus which were broken. What had been until then taken to be impossible was converted into routine in the opening up of the great roadway.
>
> In January the construction was decided upon. In March, the technicians of the DNER arrived at Vilhena. And on July 4, I would preside at the meeting of the two groups which had been advancing towards one another, linking the two parts of the work. The four thousand workers . . . along 1700 kilometers of forest, establish a true record, since the activities of penetrating the forest and road building, started on the 4th of March were completed on the 29th of June, that is, in a minimum period of three months and two weeks. (PQ.315)

Both of these roads served the purposes for which they were created. Hundreds of thousands of people moved in along the highways by the early 1960s, to provide for the needs of the truck drivers, bus passengers and occasional private car owners who were traversing them, as well as to open up farms and cattle ranches along them. Within half a decade of Kubitschek's exit from the presidency, the part of the Belem-Brasilia highways nearest Brasilia was providing increasing quantities of goods for southern Brazil, particularly the state of São Paulo. The northern half was oriented economically towards Belem and the Amazon region. The effect of the Belem-Brasilia road on Belem and the Lower Amazon as truly revolutionary. It freed this area from dependence on the exceedingly unreliable and expensive system of maritime transportation for important goods which it needed from the south. By 1965 about 80 percent of the goods coming from the south were reported to be arriving up the highway.

Equally important was the psychological effect of the road on Belem and its environs. Ever since the collapse of the rubber boom at the end of World War I, Belem had been in the economic doldrums, and its people had the feeling that they were at the end of the world, virtually out of contact not only with the rest of Brazil, but with the rest of the globe as well. There as a feeling of hopelessness in the city, a feeling that nothing could be done about its problems. The Belem-Brasilia Highway gave the people of Belem the possibility of getting overland to São Paulo or Rio in five days. It turned the attention increasingly of Paulista and other southern businessmen towards the exploitation of the market and the economic potentialities of the Lower Amazon basin. Instead of looking nostalgically to the past, the businessmen, political leaders, and rank and file citizens began to look optimistically to the future development of that part of the country.

The Brasilia-Acre road was of equal importance to the Upper Amazon. It became possible to ship goods from São Paulo to Manaus, the capital of the state of Amazonas, via the road in about ten days—six days from São Paulo to the river port of Porto Velho on one of the branches of the Upper Amazon, and thence four days by ship down to Manaus. Previously, it had been necessary to wait for a minimum of two months for goods sent by ship from the south, with the great likelihood that the goods would arrive in damaged condition, or would not arrive at all, having been lost or stolen en route.[20]

It has been argued that these roads and others in the central-west area of Brazil could have been built without the tremendous expense of constructing Brasilia. However, Kubitschek and those around him were convinced that without a terminus in the central plateau area, out from which the various highways could extend, it would have been politically and psychologically impossible for a very long time to build roads from the Amazon area to the heavily populated center-south (Belem-São Paulo or Belem-Rio, for instance). Alkmin, Kubitschek's lifelong friend, for instance insisted to me that no such highways had ever been discussed seriously before the establishment of Brasilia. There seemed no reason before the construction of Brasilia to build such roads; Brasilia was a reason to do so.[21] It seems to me highly unlikely that these highways would have been built much before the end of the twentieth century, if then, if the new capital had not been present to function as a terminus for them.

John Dos Passos has dramatically described the difficulties of Sayão, who spent almost a lifetime pushing forward the idea of a road to tie the delta of the Amazon to the south of Brazil. For years he had had to fight to obtain even the most minimum official backing from the state of Goias for his project, and before the Kubitschek administration had been able to inch the road only a bit more than one hundred miles north of the Goias town of Anapolis.[22] However, under Juscelino, who made Sayão a member of the Board of Directors of Novacap in addition to putting him in charge of finishing the Belem-Brasilia Highway (until Sayão's death in a construction accident), a passable road was completed the rest of the 1430 mile distance in only three and a half years.

One can understand the problem best, perhaps, by making a comparison with the economic history of the United States. After the Civil War, the railroads served much the same purpose in the United States that highways serve today in Brazil, of linking together various parts of the country, and providing a means of getting goods to market and people from one part of the nation to the other. But the American railroads were built to go from one place to another. At very least, they went from St. Louis or Chicago to the Pacific Ocean. They were not built out into the middle of nowhere without any palpable destination.

In Brazil, before Brasilia, there was nowhere in the central west area for roads from Belem or Porto Velho, or even from Rio or São Paulo to go. Centers of population were all but nonexistent in this two thirds of the national territory. But Brasilia provided a destination for the highways, a reason for their construction. The new capital had to have overland connection with other parts of the country, it could not be left with only airlines as its means of commerce with the outside world. Hence, the highways were an economic as well as a psychological necessity. That Kubitschek himself was aware of the historical parallel with the United States is indicated in an interview he had with Dos Passos, who wrote that

> he turned to look me full in the face. 'During your pioneer days,' he said, 'you North Americans always had the Pacific Ocean for a goal to lure you on across the mountains. That's why you populated your part of the continent so quickly. Our way west has been barred by impenetrable forests and by the Andes. Brasilia will

continue a goal, a place to head for on the high plateau. Building Brasilia means roads. A movement of population into fine farmlands of the interior is already going on.[23]

Conclusion

Perhaps Milton Eisenhower has summed up both the short-term objections to the construction of Brasilia and its long-range advantages as well as anyone. In his book *The Wine is Bitter* he wrote that

> while at present the construction of this remote city (financed . . . with worthless money) appears to have been an act of folly, it may be that in the long future the creation of Brasilia will be hailed as the beginning of a better era. If the opening of the interior induced large numbers to move to it from the coastal area . . . especially from ruined farms and from overpopulated cities . . . if settlers develop family-sized economic units and produce food and fiber which will eliminate the need of imports and enrich the diets of the Brazilian people . . . then Brazil will have made giant strides toward permanent prosperity and political stability.[24]

Kubitschek himself summed up his vision in building the new capital. He first wrote this in the so-called Gold Book of Brasilia, a notebook which all distinguished visitors who come to Brasilia when it was under construction were asked to sign. Subsequently, what he wrote there was put in golden letters on the wall of the Alvorada Palace in Brasilia: "Here on this high central plateau—in the midst of this loneliness—that tomorrow will be the center of the great decision of our national life—I have cast my eyes once again towards the tomorrow of my country and I face that oncoming dawn with unbreakable faith and a confidence that knows no bounds in its great destiny" (PQ.47).

Chapter 12

INFLATION AND THE KUBITSCHEK REGIME

One of the principal attacks which has been made on the administration of Kubitschek both in Brazil and abroad has been that his policies were largely responsible for the spiralling inflation which plagued Brazil in the years immediately following his retirement from the presidency. Inflation had been a problem in Brazil long before he assumed the presidency. Although the rhythm of price increases rose considerably during part of the Kubitschek administration, he was aware of the problem, and during the last year of his government, the rate of increase declined. There is considerable doubt that inflation hampered the economic development of Brazil in the 1930-1961 period, as some of the critics of Kubitschek have argued. It certainly did not do so during his administration.

History of Brazilian Inflation

Inflation—a general rise in the price level—is nothing new in Brazilian economic history. It has been occurring at least since the early days of independence. Although figures on the subject are unreliable until the time of World War I, there was certainly a general trend towards increased prices throughout the nineteenth century. Oliver Onody has calculated that with prices of 1829 as an index number of 100, the general price level had risen to 149 by 1860, to 177 by 1874, to 231 by 1887, and 464 by the outbreak of World War I. Prices continued upward for the following fifteen years, and the index number stood at 1094 by 1929. During the early years of the great depression prices declined slightly, but by 1932 they had begun an upward march which has not yet ceased.[1]

Inflation assumed much greater importance during the post-1939 period. Its rhythm increased dramatically, while at the same time Brazil had a rate of economic growth which was one of the highest in the world. Table 1 indicates the rise in the cost of living in the cities of Rio de Janeiro and São Paulo between 1939 and 1960, according to the figures of the Getúlio Vargas Foundation:[2]

Table 1

COST OF LIVING IN RIO DE JANEIRO AND SÃO PAULO
1939 TO 1960

Year	Index	Rio Percentage Annual Variation	Index	São Paulo Percentage Annual Variation
1939	21.6	---.-	14	---.-
1940	22.2	4.2	15	8.3
1941	24.6	10.8	17	7.7
1942	27.4	11.4	19	14.3
1943	30.3	16.6	22	15.6
1944	34.1	12.5	30	31.5
1945	39.7	16.4	37	24.0
1946	46.3	16.6	42	14.5
1947	56.4	21.8	54	29.6
1948	58.3	3.4	59	8.7
1949	60.9	4.5	58	2.0
1950	66.5	9.2	62	6.1
1951	74.5	12.0	67	8.7
1952	87.4	17.3	82	23.0
1953	100.0	14.4	100	21.6
1954	122.4	22.4	118	18.3
1955	150.7	23.1	141	19.5
1956	182.2	20.9	173	22.2
1957	211.9	16.3	206	19.2
1958	242.9	14.6	237	15.2
1959	338.0	39.1	325	37.2
1960	437.4	29.4	329	24.9

As these figures for Brazil's two largest cities indicate, the rate of inflation during the period from the beginning of World War II until the end of the Kubitschek administration increased markedly. With the exception of the immediate post-war years, when the

237

sudden influx of foreign goods, purchased with large foreign exchange reserves which Brazil had accumulated during the conflict, slowed down the inflationary spiral very dramatically, the increase in prices was strong and tended to become constantly greater.

Inflation and Brazilian Economic Development

According to most orthodox economic theory, such a rapid increase in the general price level should have had deleterious effects on the rate of the country's development. However, the fact is that these years of intense inflation were also years of rapid economic growth. Mario Simonsen, a Brazilian economist not particularly favorably disposed towards inflation, has commented thus on this situation:

> For the orthodox observer the most surprising aspect of the Brazilian inflation in the post-war period consists of its capacity of coexisting, at least until 1961, with a high rate of economic growth. Thus, between 1947 and 1961, in spite of the chronic increase in prices, the real product of the country increased at an average rate of 5.8% a year—one of the most rapid rates anywhere in the world in the post-war period. The real product per capita expanded on the average of 3.0% a year—which undoubtedly represents a rhythm of economic development which is quite satisfactory.
>
> Even more surprising is the fact that until 1961 the intensification of inflation is not associated with any weakening of the rate of economic development. On the contrary, between 1957 and 1961, in spite of the acceleration of the general increase in prices, the total real product succeeded in increasing at the rate of 6.9% a year. Although this last figure had been somewhat influenced by the overproduction of coffee (which was responsible for about half a percentage point in the rate under discussion) this is a result which is quite an aberration for the orthodox observers.
>
> Interesting also is the fact that statistics reveal the coexistence of an inflationary process with an excellent capital/output ratio. In accordance with the estimates of

238

the Getúlio Vargas Foundation . . . the average gross rate of capital formation in the 1947/60 period would correspond to 16.6% of the Gross National Product. Deducting five percentage points, which correspond to the estimate of depreciation of fixed capital, which would give a liquid rate of investment of 11.6% of the GNP. Comparing that rate with the 5.8% annual average increase of real product, one concludes that the incremental capital/output relationship would be, on average, equal to 2.0—which corresponds to an elevated index of average productivity of investments.[3]

The problem of the country's inflation has long been the subject of controversy in Brazil. Two schools of thought developed around the issue, the so-called orthodox or monetarist group and the structuralists. They disagreed about both the causes and cure for inflation. The orthodox school of economists saw the main causes of Brazilian inflation in the government's unbalanced budget and in excessively liberal credit, and in the tendency towards too frequent general increases in the wage level as a major contributing factor. Their prescription for dealing with the problem consisted of standard procedures for budget balancing, credit limitation, and wage freezing. The structuralists blamed inflation on bottlenecks in certain key sectors of the economy, such as agriculture, transport, and public utilities. Their theoretical formula for ending inflation was to wipe out these bottlenecks, although as Ignacio Rangel has pointed out, when the structuralists were given responsibility for establishing and carrying out government policy, they tended to adopt orthodox measures.

Neither the orthodox nor the structuralist economists felt that inflation was positively linked to Brazil's rapid economic development between 1930 and 1961. The most either camp has been willing to admit has been that the two phenomena had been coincidental, and to leave open the question of whether Brazil's relatively high rate of inflation had in fact contributed to the speed of the development of the nation's economy. Rangel, head of the Council of Economic Development during the Kubitschek administration, was one of the few economists who positively asserted that inflation made an important contribution to development.[4]

Long Run Factors Tending Towards Inflation

In trying to ascertain the factors which gave rise to inflation in Brazil in the 1930-1961 period, it is useful to separate the factors into two groups. The first consists of those elements in the structure of the Brazilian economy which provided a bias towards a rising price level. The second is composed of those elements which reinforced this basic trend once substantial inflation became accepted as a more or less permanent characteristic of the Brazilian economy.

Certainly one of the fundamental elements in the Brazilian economic picture which created a tendency towards rising prices was the Vargas System. One aspect of this system was the decision to leave the rural sectors of the economy alone, to not interfere with the system of large landholdings, or with the social and political conditions arising from the landholding system. Between 1937 and 1945, particularly, the system also provided a labor movement which, though widespread, was almost powerless to influence the wages of the urban workers. As a result of these aspects of the Vargas System, a large part of the population was kept out of the market. Most agricultural laborers, tenants, and share-croppers received incomes too small to allow them to purchase any significant quantity of manufactured goods. This limitation of the market meant that the new industries which were growing up in the post-1930 period could not in many cases enjoy the economies of large-scale production. They were always faced with the problem of having more productive capacity available than the market could use. Thus, there was a constant tendency for unit costs of production to be considerably higher than would have been the case if the market could have expanded at a rate to keep pace with the ability of the country's industries to produce.

In spite of the limitations on the expansion of the market which were imposed by the Vargas System, the industrialization process went forward. This was because during the period 1930 to 1961 Brazilian industrialization was based on import substitution. The new industries created during this period were producing goods which the country had theretofore been importing. This meant that there was some market in existence when an industry was set up, even though that market was not large enough in many instances to provide a basis for the economies of large-scale production.

Import substitution went forward in three waves. Between 1930 and 1945 it consisted largely of the establishment of industries producing light consumer goods—textiles, clothing, processed foodstuffs. Between 1945 and 1955 the emphasis was on setting up plants to produce consumer durables. Finally, during the Kubitschek period, the process concentrated largely on establishing heavy industries and machine production enterprises.

Each wave of industrialization tended to provide some amplification of the market. The incomes of the workers and entrepreneurs engaged in the light consumer goods industries constituted a demand for some of the products of the industries in which they were employed. The same was true of those engaged in the consumer durable lines of production. These two earlier phases of industrialization likewise provided a potential market for the industries established during the Kubitschek phase of Brazilian industrialization. However, even at the end of the Kubitschek period it was still true that about half of the population could be considered out of the market.[5]

In addition to long-term deficiency of demand which led to a tendency for higher prices of some manufactured goods, there were various factors on the supply side of the picture which had the same result. After 1945 the labor movement in the main manufacturing centers of Rio de Janeiro, São Paulo, Minas Gerais, Porto Alegre, and Recife were sufficiently strong economically and politically to exercise a certain pressure on the rates of money wages. Through labor court *dissidios colectivos* and collective bargaining agreements they were able to obtain wage increases and fringe benefits which considerably increased their money wages and the wage costs of the industrial employers. In addition, periodic increases in the legal minimum wage levels between 1945 and 1961 had the effect of bringing general readjustments of wages to maintain differentials between the minimum—paid mainly to unskilled workers—and the wages paid to those with more skill and training.

There were additional factors which increased the real cost of labor to the urban employers. The expense of training new factory workers fell largely on the employers, while another part was paid for by a tax imposed on the employers for that purpose. The social security system was extended during this period. It tended to be excessively expensive and bureaucratic. Even more significant was the institution of *estabilidade* or tenure. According to Article 492 of the Consolidation of Labor Laws, no employee could be dismissed without grievous cause if he had been employed for ten years. In practice, the law came to be applied to dismissals in any period after nine year's employment. In addition, an employer had to grant considerable dismissal pay to laid off workers who did not have tenure.

The tenure law added to labor costs in several ways. It tended towards considerably more labor turnover than would otherwise have existed, since many employers adopted the rule of not keeping any worker more than seven or eight years, no matter how good he was. Also, it was necessary for employers to keep on hand sizable funds out of which to pay dismissal allowances for workers without tenure and to pay the very large indemnities required if a worker with tenure was released from employment.

Another important factor giving an upward bias to the prices of goods produced by Brazilian manufacturers was the lack of external economies faced by many of the new industrialists. It often was not possible in Brazil merely to go out into the market and purchase the factors of production which the entrepreneur needed. Skilled labor, managerial talent, and an adequate capital market, were not readily available. For those who built their plants outside of the major cities, there often did not exist sufficient electricity, sewage facilities, water, transportation, communications services or housing for their workers, and the industrialist would have to provide these things for himself. Even those establishing their factories in the major cities frequently were faced with shortages of electricity which resulted in rationing and hence slowing down of production, with maddeningly inadequate telephone service and with other kinds or problems which added to costs.

Closely associated with this problem of lack of external economies for the country's industries was the uneven growth of the economy. Serious bottlenecks developed which influenced both the demand for industrial products and the costs of producing them. Manufacturing grew much more rapidly during most of the 1930-1961 period than did the public utilities or agriculture. The agricultural bottleneck was of particular importance in exerting an upward pressure on the general price level. Although agricultural output did increase during the three decades 1930-1961, its growth did not keep pace with that of industry or with urbanization of the country. In part, this was a problem of land tenure, the large landholding system in some of the older agricultural areas keeping large amounts of land out of cultivation or in the wrong kinds of crops. In part, it was a function of inadequate capital devoted to agriculture, with the result that there was a serious shortage of storage capacity, and of farm-to-highway local roads.

Another agricultural problem which exerted an upward pressure on prices was the long-run government coffee policy. Although government coffee subsidization helped to get Brazil out of the great depression in the early 1930s, after the middle of that decade that same policy tended to be inflationary. It pumped large amounts of income into the economy without there being any offsetting goods and services made available to the economy. In the depression period of the 1930s, when the basic problem was a fall in aggregate demand, this had a salutary effect on the general economy; by the 1950s its effect was not so healthy.

Self Re-enforcing Factors of Inflation

In addition to these long-term factors which created a bias towards inflation in the Brazilian economy between 1930 and 1961, there were other elements which tended to make the country's inflation self-perpetuating. Long continued and generally predictable increases in prices made for a low liquidity preference on the part of key segments of the population. Since the purchasing power of money was constantly failing, there was a tendency to buy goods and services rather than to hold cash. In the case of consumers, there was particularly a tendency to buy durable consumers goods, and among the better-off groups to buy apartments, not because they could get much income from the latter or because they needed them to live in, but because they would appreciate in value with the inflation. With the entrepreneurs, the tendency was to invest in expanding capacity, even though this was seen in advance to be excess capacity.

Still an additional effect of prolonged inflation was to make the situation of public utility enterprises increasingly precarious. It was politically very difficult—especially with regard to those public utilities in the hands of foreign investors—to permit them to raise their rates with sufficient rapidity to keep abreast of general price increases. As a result, their ability to replace worn out equipment, let alone their ability to expand, was very much limited, thus creating another bottleneck and generating additional inflationary pressure.

Finally, the long-continued existence of inflation tended to make a government budget deficit endemic, and thus to reenforce the inflation. It was always easier to finance new expenditures by borrowing from the Banco do Brasil or by issuing new currency than it was to impose new taxes. Furthermore, given the nature of the Brazilian tax system, with its heavy emphasis on indirect taxes, new imposts were more likely directly to intensify inflation than to reduce it, since they would immediately result in increases in the prices of the goods or services which were additionally taxed.

Offsets to Adverse Effects of Inflation

Until after 1961, the Brazilian inflation did not have many of the bad effects which orthodox economic theory indicated it would. This was because there existed various protective mechanisms. For instance, there was not the degree of flight to real estate as a result of the inflation which might have been expected. This was probably due to three factors. First, the country's tax laws imposed sizable capital gains taxes on profits coming about as the result of appreciation of real property.[6] Also, as Mario Simonsen has noted, "there was an atrophy of mortgage credit due to the combination of inflation and usury laws."[7] In the third place, rent control laws continued in operation throughout the period and were reasonably well enforced. As a result, buildings as a source of income were not as profitable as they otherwise might have been. Although some people did buy apartments for their appreciation in value, the tendency to speculate in real estate was much less than might have otherwise been the case, and the inducement to invest in some productive enterprise was relatively more attractive.

The scarcity of long-term capital funds, which might also have been expected from the continued inflationary situation was also avoided. Here, the government played a major part. Through the Banco Nacional de Desenvolvimento Economico and the Banco do Brasil, the government provided the funds for much long-term investment. Simonsen commented that although

> the statistical indices on the growing participation of
> the government in investments, although somewhat

244

incomplete, are very suggestive. In accordance with the estimates of the Getúlio Vargas Foundation, this participation, without counting the Mixed Companies, increased from 25.9 percent in the 1947/50 period, to 37.1 percent in the four-year period 1957/60.

Even more important, however, was the growth of Mixed Companies. In the four-year period 1957/60, these companies were responsible for no less than 10.8 percent, on the average, of gross fixed capital formation in the country. Including these companies, the governmental sector would have covered 47.9 percent of the fixed investments in Brazil.[8]

In addition to these effects of the government to offset possible adverse effects of inflation on the accumulation of fixed capital, there was also a considerable contribution made by foreign investors. Whatever hindrance inflation may have presented to the decision of foreign firms to invest in Brazil between 1945 and 1961 seems to have been offset by the potential size of the Brazilian market and government policies. Gordon and Grommers have noted that "the chronic inflation as such has not generally discouraged the participating companies from making additional investments, whether in expansion of existing facilities or in new lines of businesses."[9]

Simonsen has suggested another factor which tended to offset the negative effects of long-continued inflation on Brazilian economic development. This was the periodic attempts by various ministers of finance to stop or slow down the rate of inflation. On this point, he wrote that

> to use a very simple image, no administration until now has shown itself totally uninhibited in emitting paper-money, although they systematically lacked the courage to take the road to austerity. There always appeared some minister of finance preoccupied with combatting the inflation in the correct way and even if he did not last for long in his party, he did succeed in arousing some consciousness of the problem. Various monetary stabilization programs were announced and initiated.[10]

Favorable Aspects of Inflation for Economic Development

However, Brazil between 1930 and 1961 not only presents a situation in which the negative effects of inflation on economic development were offset by countervailing factors, but one in which the steady rise in prices actually favored the process of development. Ignacio Rangel has noted that because the process of import substitution came in waves—light consumers goods from 1930 to 1945, consumer durables 1945-1955, and heavy machine industries from 1955-1961—there existed a built-in tendency for aggregate demand to weaken periodically at the end of each wave. When each phase of import substitution was drawing to a close, the more obvious profitable areas of investment began to become more and more restricted. Thus, other things being equal, investment would have declined, with a consequent adverse effect on the national income and a slowing down if not halting of the economic development process.[11]

At the end of each phase of import substitution, adjustments were needed. There was the danger of a depression, since consumption was in any case at relatively low levels and the incentives to investment threatened not to be enough to offset the low rate of consumption. It was in this phase that inflation played its most significant role, by creating a very low liquidity preference, inducing people to buy goods rather than to keep cash or bank accounts. Thus, by encouraging consumers to spend and investors to invest at times when there would otherwise have been a marked tendency for investment to drop sharply, thus preventing recessions or depressions, inflation made a very positive contribution to the economic development of Brazil. For almost three decades it helped to prevent alternation between rapid development and cessation of development, which if they had occurred would have certainly meant a much slower overall rate of growth and diversification of the economy. The excess capacity created during the period between development spurts was available to be used during the succeeding phase of import substitution.

Rangel argues that the creation of so much excess capacity tended to lower the marginal productivity of capital, because much of the new investment was admittedly not going to produce a profit for some time. It was entered into in order to avoid the effects of depreciation of the value of the currency. Since the marginal productivity of capital was declining—and in fact, he argues, in many cases reached a minus quantity, and was accepted as such for considerable periods by entrepreneurs who nonetheless continued to invest even when they knew that there would be no immediate profit forthcoming—the real interest rate also had to fall. He argues that for a considerable period of time Brazil had a negative real rate of interest, that is, the rate of interest was less than the rate of inflation.[12] Rangel sums up his view of the favorable impact of inflation on economic development thus: "The activity of the Brazilian economy and, as an expression of this, the Brazilian national income, are intimately dependent on the existing rate of inflation in the economic system. Inflation is necessary to depress the liquidity preference of the system, which in turn will induce both investment and consumption, as well as a supply of capital funds at negative rates of real interest."[13]

Another effect of inflation was to force firms to become largely dependent upon the banking system for their working capital. This was because of the tendency of firms to put any funds which they get into something tangible to avoid the effects of a rapid rate of currency depreciation. Since the money value of the capital equipment and other goods which firms tended to purchase continued to increase, their expanding net worth continued to justify continuing short-term loans from the banks. This willingness of the banks to meet the short-term credit needs of industrialists was a spur to Brazilian economic development. Certainly before the period under discussion, the Brazilian commercial banking system had not been designed to serve a modern industrial economy; it had been developed principally to finance the country's exports and imports on a short-term basis. The inflation contributed to developing a banking system which could meet some of the demands of a diversified economy.

Another favorable effect of inflation on Brazilian economic development was its role in redistributing income. Inflation had the effect of limiting severely the participation of wage earners in the benefits arising from the increase in their own productivity. There do not exist sufficient data to adequately analyze this problem of income transference. However, there are some indications of what has happened. On the one hand, in the major manufacturing centers the real income of industrial workers tended to increase between World War II and the end of the Kubitschek administration. This was particularly true of workers with some degree of skill, which gave them a relatively good bargaining position in an economy in which skilled workers were scarce.

Some other groups aside from industrial workers also enjoyed increases in their real incomes. Millions of peasants left the rural areas, where their money incomes had been all but non-existent and their real incomes had been exceedingly low. They moved to the urban parts of the country, particularly into the expanding areas of the center-south. Many of those who did not obtain jobs in industry but went to work in service trades or domestic employment and many who could only find part-time work obtained real incomes considerably higher than they had had before they had migrated. On the other hand, there were certainly large elements among the wage-earning population whose real wages declined. This was probably true of many unskilled workers in the cities and was certainly the case with agricultural workers in general. Workers in more remote parts of the country, such as the cities of the Amazon valley and the northeast suffered particularly from the unequal race between their wages and the price level.

Furthermore, even in the case of workers whose real wages rose, there was in all likelihood a relative transfer of real income to their employers. Workers who migrated from rural areas to the cities to work in industry undoubtedly increased their productivity. The technological level of most of Brazilian agriculture was still very low, and after moving to the industrial sector these workers turned out products of much greater value than they had done on the farms and plantations. However, inflation served to prevent the workers from obtaining more than a limited part of the increase in their own productivity. Even when their real wages increased, they seldom rose to such an extent as to account for anywhere near the whole increase in their productivity.

The entrepreneurial groups were the largest beneficiaries of inflation. They were heterogeneous. Many of the mercantile elements, particularly large numbers of intermediaries in the handling of agricultural products, undoubtedly profited while contributing little new to the process of economic development. Industrial entrepreneurs were also important beneficiaries of inflation and they were a major contributing factor in the expansion and diversification of the economy. The importance of the ability of industrialists to plough back inflationary profits into their

248

enterprises was particularly great in Brazil. Most industrialists had developed their manufacturing enterprises from workshops, or from small commercial firms which had at first established factories as auxiliaries to mercantile operations. Even in the late 1950s most Brazilian manufacturing firms were still closely held family enterprises, which did not sell their stock in public markets. Until several years after the Kubitschek period these markets were very weak, badly organized, and unreliable. Thus, they raised most of their capital from internal sources and ploughed back profits.

Negative Effects of Inflation

Of course, all effects of long-run Brazilian inflation were not positive. The most unfortunate effects of inflation were undoubtedly social and political. The constant increase in prices led to wide social discontent, provoking strikes and other movements of protest after the end of the Vargas dictatorship in 1945. The major factor which prevented social and political discontent from having more serious repercussions than it did in the years before 1961 was undoubtedly the Vargas System. The persistence of the social and economic arrangements established during the Estado Novo resulted in the trade union movement being weaker and less militant than might otherwise have been the case. The loyalty of most workers to Vargas even after his suicide tended to weaken the appeal of other political groups which but for Getúlio might have been able to mobilize a stronger protest against the price increases.

Kubitschek and Inflation

Inflation certainly continued during the Kubitschek administration. However, contrary to charges made then and later by many critics of Juscelino's regime, it did not constitute an uncontrolled or uncontrollable increase in the price level. In fact, during the first three years that Kubitschek was in power, the rate of increase in prices fell. In 1955, the year before he came to power, prices rose 23.1 percent, whereas in his first year in office they rose by 20.9 percent. In the following year the rate fell to 16.3 percent and in the third year of the Kubitschek government, 1958, it was down to 14.5 percent. However, during 1959, the year in which the greatest emphasis was put on the building of Brasilia, the price level rose by 39.1 percent, the largest increase in more than two decades. In the last year of the Kubitschek government, the rate of inflation was reduced to 29.4 percent.[14] Kubitschek was by no means oblivious to the problem of inflation. However, he felt that the best way to combat it in the long run was by developing a more diversified and a stronger Brazilian economy. He was not willing to sacrifice development in order to reduce the rate of inflation in the short run, feeling that that would be self-defeating in terms of controlling price increases on a more long-run basis. This attitude was at the root of Juscelino's famous quarrel with the International Monetary Fund, with which we deal in another chapter.

In 1958 and 1959, the Kubitschek administration did take steps to deal with the inflation problem. In June 1958, Alkmin was succeeded by Lucas Lopes as minister of finance. Lopes and Roberto Campos, the director of the National Bank for Economic Development, drew up a price stabilization program. Skidmore has noted that "Campos and Lopes, well aware of the danger of stagnation, hoped to achieve stabilization gradually rather than by the shock treatment often urged by the International Monetary Fund."[15] The measures proposed by Lopes and Campos were more or less orthodox, involving attempts to cut the government's budget deficit, limit credit and wage increases, and reduce the balance of trade deficit. The government did reduce subsidies to the coffee industry, which were a major contributor to the budget deficit. It also reduced subsidies to wheat and oil imports, although not to the degree demanded by the IMF. For a short while, it also resisted demands for wage increases. However, as Skidmore noted, "public expenditure was the area where the president was most reluctant to sanction any attempts at real austerity measures. He would not compromise his Target Program. Deeply committed to his goal of accelerating industrialization and overcoming structural bottlenecks, he continued to declare that it would be compatible with stabilization."[16]

The showdown came in June 1959, when President Kubitschek ordered negotiations with the International Monetary Fund broken off. Two months later, Lopes resigned as minister of finance and was replaced by Sebastião Pais de Almeida, who as president of the Banco do Brasil had refused to limit credits to industrialists, a practice which Kubitschek supported.[17] Although considerably modifying the original stabilization program announced in 1958, the

Kubitschek regime did succeed in its last year in substantially reducing the rate of inflation.

Kubitschek's Arguments About Inflation

Juscelino argued that it was not his Target Plan, even with the addition of Target No. 31, Brasilia, which was the principal cause of inflation during his administration, or even its intensification in 1959-1960. In his memoirs, he pointed out that expenditures on the Programa de Metas oscillated between 4 percent and 6 percent of the gross national product. Furthermore, even during the years of most intensive expenditures on the development plan, only about 40 percent of the investments for the Plan came from the government, "and more than half of this expenditure came from special funds, made up of specially designated taxes," which did not therefore increase the government deficit, according to his calculations.[18]

Kubitschek pointed to other factors which, in his judgment, were more important in stimulating inflation than the expenditures on the Target Plan. One of these was a general salary increase for all military and civilian employees enacted by the Café Filho government, which increased government salary expenditures by 70 percent. This salary increase also forced him, he argued, to enact a 60 percent minimum wage increase in June 1956, only about five months after taking office. Furthermore, he pointed out that 1957 was

> a year in which, as never before, in the total of goods and services of the country there was a much greater proportion of machines, vehicles, public works, and construction, a year in which the physical volume of imports of equipment increased by 87 percent and in which the great projects of Furnas and Tres Marias were begun, a year in which the construction of Brasilia was intensified and the automobile industry began its expansion—the cost of living, according to the data of the Getúlio Vargas Foundation, cited in *Desenvolvimento e Conjuntura*, rose at a rate of less than 1 percent a month, which had not occurred in twenty years.[19]

Another major factor which Kubitschek pointed out as contributing to inflation in his period, and which had nothing to do with his Programa de Metas, was the overproduction of coffee, which automatically resulted in large additional government expenditures on buying up large quantities to keep them off world markets.[20]

Juscelino summed up his comments on the problem of inflation during his administration as follows:

> One has to consider with regard to it a series of factors: (1) inflation is not today an illness peculiar to Brazil; (2) inflation in my government, in contrast to what occurred before, did not keep the country from undergoing a period of rapid and profound industrialization; (3) the government's investments, as I have said, did not represent more than a part of the investments undertaken and a small part of the expenses of the government; (4) the emissions of paper money were only the last link in a chain of the inflationary process, being in most cases emissions imposed by readjustments associated with causes established in previous governments and, in other cases, by the necessity to deal with deficits in a budget which was badly constructed from a technical point of view, and which were voted by the Legislature, without any clear notion of their impact on the general economy of the country; and (5) it is worth noting that during my government, the level of real consumption of the population, overall, increased, although modestly, since the successive changes in the minimum wage were generally superior to the increase in the cost of living in the previous period.[21]

Conclusion

Some of those people who have criticized the record of the Kubitschek government with regard to inflation have not referred so much to the actual situation while Juscelino was president as to what occurred after he left office. These post-1961 developments are blamed on the policies of his administration. There is no question that inflation during the early years of the 1960s reached unequalled proportions, with the rate of price increases hitting the annual rate of more than 100 percent during the first three months of 1964. It is hardly reasonable, however, to charge Kubitschek with the sins of his successors. He can hardly be held responsible for the sudden decision of Quadros to resign from the presidency in August 1961 or for the utterly irresponsible behavior of Goulart during his three and a half years in power. Kubitschek can only be held responsible for what he did during his own period in the presidency. During those five years, inflation declined for 60 percent of the time, increased dramatically during one year, and then declined again during the last year of his term.

It is clear that inflation in Brazil was not a problem invented by Kubitschek. A substantial rate of price increases had been a fact of life in the country for most of the quarter of a century before he took office. It had deep and complicated causes. In retrospect, it is clear that the record of the Kubitschek administration with regard to inflation was a very credible one when compared with other Brazilian administrations before and after his. It is clear, however, that Kubitschek did not regard the reduction of the rate of inflation as his highest priority. He was clearly willing to pay a considerable price in terms of inflation in order to push forward his economic development program. Given what he accomplished and in terms of the changes in the price level during those five years, one can hardly argue that Kubitschek's policy with regard to inflation was irresponsible.

Chapter 13

THE KUBITSCHEK REGIME AND THE BRAZILIAN CULTURAL RENAISSANCE

The impact of the Kubitschek regime was not confined to the country's economic and political life. The rapid economic expansion of the period, the enthusiasm and optimism it generated, and the freedom which the government provided during the five-year period, all tended to stimulate a cultural renaissance. The flowering of talent and performance in a wide variety of the literary and plastic arts had its antecedents before the inauguration of Kubitschek, and continued for at least half a decade after he left the presidency. However, it was during the five years 1956-1961, when Kubitschek was president of Brazil, that this blossoming of Brazilian cultural activity received its major impetus. Much of its suffered severe curtailment in the years after he left the presidency because of the catastrophic political events of that period.

Beginnings of Cultural Renaissance Before Kubitschek

Brazilian accomplishments in various cultural fields did not appear suddenly, any more than Italian achievements in art, literature, music, and architecture began with the High Renaissance. The flowering of Brazilian cultural activities had its roots in developments extending over many decades, and in some cases encompassing several centuries. Three hundred years ago Brazil produced poets of some note. A century has passed, however, since its most accomplished novelist, Machado de Assis, began to write. In the nineteenth century some Brazilian composers at least were minor figures in world music; more than two hundred years ago the country produced Aleijadinho, a great baroque sculptor.

However, with few exceptions the fame of these individual artists or writers during their lifetime, did not extend beyond the frontiers of their own country, or even of their own province. In some instances, they have been rediscovered only recently, when the general attention of the artistic and literary world had begun to include ever so modestly Brazil. Because of the general lack of importance of Brazil in world affairs, and perhaps too because of the impediment of the Portuguese language, the cultural accomplishments of individual Brazilians for long received little attention elsewhere.

Gilberto Freyre has been one of the most enthusiastic expositors of the Brazilian cultural renaissance. In his book *New World in the Tropics*, which is devoted in large part to the origins of this phenomenon, he claimed that

> it is as a new and modern type of civilization in the tropics—a predominantly European, but not sub-European, type of civilization carried on and developed in the tropics by a population in whose ethnic composition the number of non-Europeans is considerable and the amount of race mixture still more considerable—that Brazil is most significant. And it is as a modern tropical civilization that its creative originality is most conspicuous, in architecture as well as in music, in cookery as well as in landscape gardening.[1]

Impact of Kubitschek Regime on Cultural Development

The developments in the cultural field under Juscelino can be attributed to two basic causes. First was the strong economic upsurge during the Kubitschek administration. Economic prosperity provided the basis for financing a wide range of cultural activities. As a result, university teaching, literature, as well as the dramatic and plastic arts began to become full-time professions instead of hobbies or avocations. At the same time, many more people had the leisure and education to enjoy the arts and incomes sufficient to patronize them than formerly had been the case.

A second cause of the cultural expansion was that in many lines of cultural endeavor, Brazilians had ceased merely to copy foreigners. Although continuing to be interested in techniques and themes used abroad, and even to borrow heavily from them, they began to incorporate into them specifically Brazilian elements. This

255

trend was intensified greatly as a result of the Kubitschek era, because of the feeling of optimism, pride, and even adventure which the rapid economic development of the era encouraged. Large numbers of Brazilians became convinced that their nation and they themselves could do things of which they had never dreamed before. This new national self-confidence encouraged many people to try their hands at one or another kind of intellectual or artistic activity for the first time. The economic and psychological events of the Kubitschek period made possible a rapid broadening and acceleration of developments in the arts and related fields which had been under way for a long time. The construction of Brasilia was of particularly great importance in drawing the Brazilians' attention to their own cultural achievements.

Publishing

One of the factors which undoubtedly fostered the Brazilian literary renaissance was the growth of the publishing industry. Although books have been published in Brazil since João VI brought the country's first printing press with him from Portugal in 1808, it was not until the middle 1950s that the country began to have a major publishing industry. This was undoubtedly a result of the general economic development of the country which came after the inauguration of Kubitschek early in 1956.

A number of the nation's most important publishing houses antedate this period. These include the traditional O Globo firm of Porto Alegre and Rio de Janeiro, the Companhia Editora Nacional (which specialized in textbooks for many years), as well as Editora Martins of São Paulo and Editora Civilizacão Brasileira and Editora José Olympio both of Rio de Janeiro. Some of these, particularly Editora Martins and Editora José Olympio, had taken a very important part in launching such authors of the 1930s as Jorge Amado, Raquel de Queiróz, Graciliano Ramos, and José Lins do Rego.

However, the number of publishers and the range of books which they have put out proliferated spectacularly after 1955. A decade later, the largest of the Rio de Janeiro publishers was issuing about two hundred titles a year. Various others were putting out several scores of different books a year. The variety of books published was very great. There were publishers who specialized in

256

textbooks, and others who concentrated on encyclopedias and collections of various kinds—complete histories of the world, the complete works of famous authors, and the like. There were others which emphasized "serious" current works including novels and poetry, as well as works in the social sciences. There were also pulp publishers.

By the late 1950s the Brazilian publishers were putting out both books translated from other languages and original works in Portuguese. It became possible to purchase in Brazil good Portuguese translations of the classics of virtually every Western language. The most important current works published in the United States and Western Europe soon appeared in a Portuguese translation in Rio or São Paulo. Almost all technical and scientific books (which were numerous), as well as "how-to-do-it" volumes appearing in Brazil were translations. In this work of translating foreign titles the Brazilian publishers had a certain advantage in the relative isolation of their language. Unlike publishers in Spanish-speaking countries, they did not have to face competition from firms in other nations for the rights to a book in their language. The only other countries speaking Portuguese were Portugal, Mozambique, and Angola. The Salazar dictatorships prevented Portuguese publishers from bringing out most of the foreign works which Brazilian houses were translating and publishing.

Wilson Martins, writing in *O Estado de São Paulo*, on 20 November 1965, cited a study which indicated that in 1960 there were published in Brazil some 464 books translated from foreign languages, placing the country as number 23 in the 44 countries studied. This same survey showed that 45 percent of the translations in that year were from English, 26 percent from French, 8 percent from German, 4 percent from Russian, and 17 percent from other languages. However, the growth of the publishing industry also gave a much wider market to Brazilian writers. Poets, novelists, playwrights, and non-fictional prose authors all found their places in the lists of the many Brazilian publishing firms.

By the late 1950s, most Brazilian publishing houses functioned on a commercial basis. They had to be as concerned with the salability of a book as with its literary or scholarly value. However, there was a growing number of noncommercial publishers as well. Several of the more important universities, such as those of São Paulo, Ceará, and Pernambuco began putting out works of high scholarly value which probably would not have been able to obtain commercial publication. In addition, a few state governments also entered the publishing business, tending to specialize in books about their particular states, or fictional or poetic works by local writers who had not as yet attained national recognition. The number of copies of an edition of any given volume was still likely to be small. Five thousand copies became more or less normal for a commercial publisher, except in the case of the country's most popular writers, or a few outstanding foreign translations. The noncommercial publishers issued editions in even smaller numbers, and in many cases gave away a sizable part of the edition of a book.

In view of this situation, there were very few writers in Brazil who were able to live only on their royalties. Although all respectable publishers paid royalties which were comparable in percentage terms to those of United States firms, the volume of sales was not yet enough to provide an adequate income to even many of the best known literary figures. By the middle 1960s the only two fiction writers in Brazil who were reported to live from their literary income were Jorge Amado and Erico Verissimo. Other writers tended to hold jobs as government employees, journalists, teachers, or businessmen, and to write in their spare time.

Several factors explained the relatively small editions put out by Brazilian publishing houses. One major factor was mass illiteracy, which affected about half of Brazil's eighty million people. A second was the very small number of people who had a university or even a secondary education, and who therefore logically constituted the bulk of the market for books. Although the rapid spread of universities after 1955 was one of the major factors spurring the growth of the publishing industry, the number of university graduates was still not large enough to provide a truly mass market.

Another major problem of Brazilian publishers was that of distribution. Brazil was a huge country with a very inadequate means of transportation. Thus it was difficult to get books to their destination in any but the largest cities. In addition, the number of outlets for books still remained surprisingly small. There were many sizable cities in the country which had only one or two bookstores, and quite a few which did not have any such enterprise really worthy of the name. Still another problem facing the publishers was the relative lack of libraries in Brazil. The public library was an institution confined almost exclusively to the larger cities. The

258

private lending library of the type once common in the United States was all but unknown. University libraries remained for the most part woefully inadequate and their funds for buying new books stringently limited. There were relatively few private organizations or business enterprises which had libraries of any appreciable size.

Hence, the great majority of books were bought by private individuals. This raised still another problem, that of price. Because of their relatively small editions and high transportation costs, Brazilian publishers had to charge relatively high prices for their books. The average paperback book—and most Brazilian publications are paperback—sold in the middle 1960s for at least the equivalent of U.S. $1. Although in the United States terms that was not expensive, in terms of the income of the average Brazilian student, government employee, housewife, or professional man who might want to build up his or her private book collection, the price was high.

The Development of Literature

The growth of the publishing industry acted as a great stimulus to the creative efforts of Brazilians with a literary bent, whether they were novelists, nonfiction writers, or poets. With the proliferation of publishing houses and the assurance of a more or less respectable market for their works, in the 1950s a growing number of people with literary ambitions and some degree of talent were putting their pens to paper and beginning to write and to turn out increasingly large numbers of works. As might have been expected, these varied greatly in style and quality.

The Brazilian nonfiction writers tended to concentrate very largely on their own country and its problems. The studies of one or another aspect of the economic development grew in number with astonishing rapidity. Probes into the nation's sociological problems, such as race, education, sex, and crime, appeared in increasing numbers. Histories of Brazil or studies of one or another period or aspect of its history were numerous. So were biographies of the country's leading statesmen and literary figures, as well as autobiographies of politicians, military men, and literati. The only other country in which Brazilian writers and publishers showed major interest in this period was the United States. Innumerable books by Americans about the United States appeared in translation

259

in Brazil, and an increasing number of Brazilians were writing books about the USA and Brazil's relations with it. However, equally striking as the subjects covered by Brazilian writing and publishing were the gaps which they showed. There was astoundingly little written or even translated dealing with Latin American countries other than Brazil. There was little or nothing written or translated about contemporary Europe or Asia and only a scattering of books about Africa.

Virtually no Brazilian scholars and writers in that period were interested in problems considerably removed in time and space from contemporary Brazil. Thus one looked in vain for Brazilian studies of Medieval Europe (such as those found coming from some Argentine writers), biographies of foreign statesmen of past or present, books by Brazilians on archeology, non-Christian religions, or on philology, psychology, or psychiatry (except for textbooks)— although Brazilian publishers brought out various translations of volumes written in other countries on these and other subjects. Brazilian scholars and writers paid little attention to the development of art and architecture outside of Brazil, a notable exception being a three-volume study which came out in the middle 1960s of the plastic arts from the time of the Renaissance to our own days by Carlos Fleixa Ribeiro, a professor of Art History in the University of Brazil, who served for several years as Secretary of Education in the State of Guanabara.

Brazilian Novelists

The novel is by no means of recent origin in Brazil. There had been some experiments with this form of literature even in the colonial period, and during the empire several novelists were of first-rate importance. These included the great romantic writer José de Alencar, Bernardo de Guimarães, and Aluisio Azevedo who was particularly concerned with the problems and results of slavery. In the early years of the republic there appeared Machado de Assis, the novelist who is still widely regarded as the greatest literary figure that Brazil has produced. A mulatto of Rio de Janeiro with little formal education who made his living as a relatively minor government employee, Machado de Assis was widely acquainted with the major currents of literature not only in his own country, but in Europe as well, in spite of the fact that he never left the shores of his native country. He wrote Portuguese with a clarity and precision of style which is still the envy of those who have come after him in the Brazilian literary community. Worthy of mention also is Lima Barreto, a novelist who for his period was over-shadowed only by Machado de Assis. Like him, Barreto was a mulatto, lived in Rio and wrote about that city in universalist terms which make his works very readable even by those who never visited Brazil. In the fields of history and sociology, Oliveira Viana is perhaps the best known figure.

Famous also was the prose writer Euclides da Cunha, whose descriptions of the War of Canudos in his book *Os Sertões* (*Rebellion in the Backlands*) is one of the great masterpieces of Brazilian literature. Samuel Putnam, who translated Euclides da Cunha into English, has commented that *Os Sertões*

> is one of the most remarkable books ever written. In the place it holds in the esteem and affections of an entire people, it can only be compared to the *Divine Comedy* or *Don Quixote*. Like these great classics it is the expression of the very soul of a race in all its strength and all its concealed weakness. In search of a comparison one thinks especially of Cervante's masterpiece, which in all probability no one but a Spaniard can ever fully comprehend. . . . In *Os Sertões*, but far more grimly, the Brazilian beholds his own national neurasthenia, a deep soul agony that attained to peak at the turn of the century and found embodiment in a literary production that defies all classifications. . . . Perhaps when all is said, no other book ever laid hold of a nation in the same way and to the same degree as this one. It has been termed "the Bible of Brazilian nationality," and it comes near to being just that.[2]

The Modernist movement of the 1920s culminated in an outburst of literary activity in the 1930s. However, even at the end of the 1930s conditions were not yet favorable to the development of literature, both fiction and non-fiction, on a more ample scale. In spite of some impetus given to the publishing industry by World War II, the dictatorship of Vargas did not encourage a too great intellectual curiosity; the serious publishing houses remained relatively few in number and could handle only a limited group of authors. The reading public was still small.

The curse of the literary world still remained the phenomenon of amateurism. There were few people who could devote much of their time to creative efforts and research. Most of the people who wrote novels or poetry as well as most of those who dabbled in sociology, economics, or political science had very little time available for these efforts. The feeling of frustration which this situation generated among people with literary or research ambitions was well described by the literary critic Afranio Coutinho. Writing as late as 1953 specifically about university professors with a desire to do creative work or research, he noted that

> our intellectual level does not demand much of the professor, who at first excited, ends up feeling that nothing is worth doing, because what he does will not be noticed. Soon he tends to become disheartened, and tries to get through his work as rapidly as possible. They have no stimulus outside of the classroom; furthermore, research is not stimulated, there is nowhere to publish serious works, nor do these pay him anything, either, materially or intellectually, because no one pays any attention to them. . . . Among us, what point is there in deeply studying romantic lyricism, or the origins of tragedy? Never will one be able to apply one's knowledge. He will end up number one in his city in the subject, but will end up speaking to himself in a language no one else can understand. It will be said that he is crazy. . . .[3]

Coutinho also emphasizes another problem of the literary world down to the middle 1950s, the so-called *vida literaria* (literary life). By this, he and other writers refer to the literary bohemia patronized generally not by those who really were writers, but by those who wanted to appear to be writers. They met in small groups and over coffee cups or alcoholic drinks, exchanged ideas, discussed reputation of their peers and of the really serious writers. This vida literaria was characterized by rival cliques, which sought to eulogize their own members, whether or not they had really produced any literary works, good or bad, and to denigrate rival groups. To this end they sought to gain control of literary magazines and the literary supplements of the large newspapers, where they assiduously praised their own and either damned or ignored their rivals. The vida literaria did great damage to Brazilian literature. Aside from the vituperation to which it often submitted serious writers, it meant that many people who really might have become writers of some worth wasted their time and their talents in sterile literary discussions and intrigues.

Two things began to change this situation in the latter half of the 1950s: the spread of the universities and the growth of the publishing industry. The first meant that increasingly large numbers of people could earn their living with teaching activities at least corollary to either literary or scientific interests, and that a growing number of people were interested in serious literature and the results of research in the social sciences. The second meant that if they had something to say, they were likely to be able to get their work before an expanding public.

This change was reflected in the growing number of writers in both the fiction and non-fiction fields. In the Northeastern genre new figures such as Adonias Filho and some of lesser importance arose. A school of regionalists of Minas Gerais, of whom João Guimarães Rosa and Mario Palmerio were the outstanding representatives, appeared. Novels on the Amazonia area were published by Paulo Jacob and Virginio Santa Rosa, among others. A growing school of novelists using Rio de Janeiro as the locale of their stories made its appearance; among them Carlos Heitor Cony was the most popular if not necessarily the best from a literary point of view, and the names of Esdras de Nasimento (who also write Northeastern novels about his native sate of Piauí) and Alina Paim might be mentioned.

One literary goldmine which was not seriously exploited during this period between roughly 1955 and 1965 was that of the transformation of São Paulo. That state had yet to produce the novelist who could describe the epoch of the mass migration of Europeans, Japanese, and Northeasterners into the area, and the conversion of São Paulo into one of the most modern industrial centers to be found anywhere on earth. There were Paulista novelists, such as José Geraldo Vieira and his wife Maria de Lourdes Teixeira, but they did not deal particularly with these themes. Many of the newer writers abandoned the social

263

consciousness themes made famous by the Northeastern group. Thus José Montello, from the Northeastern state of Maranhão, chose to write about more intimate personal problems. Clarice Lispector, though choosing Rio as the scene of her novels, wrote in introspective psychological terms rather than in terms of social problems.

Other Aspects of Literature

One interesting sidelight on the literary renaissance which took place beginning in middle 1950s was the heightened popular interest in the activities of the Academia Brasileira de Letras. This organization of the supposed immortals of Brazilian literary life was founded in the 1890s by Joaquim Nabuco and Machado de Assis. For many decades its membership and activities were of interest almost exclusively to those who were or thought themselves to be literati. The quality of members elected to the group was by no means always immortal.

After the middle 1950s the interest of the general public in the Academia grew by leaps and bounds. The election of new members became the subject of considerable debate in the press and discussion among laymen. For instance, the election of Jorge Amado stirred up considerable controversy. Furthermore, the prizes given by the Academy tended to be taken much more seriously than in the past, and an author who received one of those fairly numerous prizes could be assured of a considerable interest in his books among the reading public. Shortly before his death, Kubitschek sought (unsuccessfully) to be elected to the Academy.

The novel was by no means the only literary form which prospered after 1955. The short story, or conto, had for long been a favorite vehicle for Brazilian writers. A number of novelists of note were also short story writers of some importance, such as João Guimarães Rosa and Raquel de Queiróz. The poet Carlos Drummond de Andrade also published books of contos as did Monteiro Lobato, famous for his tales for children. Volumes of short stories sold widely throughout the country from the mid-1950s.

The *cronica*, a kind of essay, was particularly popular with Brazilian writers. Cronicas can be of many sorts. Some are reminiscences of the past, some are sharp commentaries on contemporary affairs, some are satirical comments on general human foibles or on those of particular individuals. Although the cronica frequently dealt with political themes, it was always done in terms of commentary rather than analysis. The reader was usually left to draw his own conclusions about the matter being discussed. Cronicas had long been popular in the daily press. Most major daily papers came to carry a cronica in almost every issue. Some of the earliest writings of Machado de Assis were newspaper contributions in this genre. Novelists such as Raquel de Queiróz and Carlos Hector Cony wrote cronicas more or less regularly and writers such as Fernando Sabino and Rubem Braga were known principally for them. Even writers principally famous for their poetry, such as Cecilia Meirelles and Carlos Drummond de Andrade, also published cronicas.

Poetry is the oldest literary form in Brazil. It is still exceedingly popular. A foreigner is struck by the very sizable number of books of poetry which are offered for sale—and prominently displayed—in the average Brazilian bookstore. Cecilia Meirelles, Manuel Bandeira, and Carlos Drummond de Andrade generally are considered to be the country's most important poets of the middle decades of this century. Andrade was nominated along with Jorge de Amado as a possible recipient of the Nobel Prize in literature. However, perhaps the most widely sold poet was J.G. Araujo Jorge.

One frustration from which Brazilian writers of all kinds suffered until recent decades was the handicap of writing in Portuguese, a language spoken only in Brazil, Portugal, and a handful of African countries. Since Portuguese is not a language widely learned by foreigners, works written in the language often did not come to the attention of people outside of the Portuguese-speaking areas. The result was that few books written in Brazil were translated and published abroad. This situation began to change in the mid-1950s. Many of the works of Jorge Amado and Erico Verissimo began to be published in the United States. The same was true of some of the novels of João Guimarães Rosa and José Lins do Rego. Elizabeth Bishop, an American poet long resident in Brazil, translated and published a number of works of her Brazilian counterparts. European publishers, particularly those of France and Germany, also began to take an interest in bringing out Brazilian works; even some of the younger and as yet less well-known authors began appearing there. The chances became reasonably good for a Brazilian novelist who became known in his own country also to

265

have his books read in a foreign language, a recognition abroad of the growing importance of Brazilian literature.

Legitimate Theater and Motion Pictures

The cultural renaissance of Brazil which was largely stimulated by the atmosphere of the Kubitschek period was by no means confined to literature. It was also manifest on the stage and screen, in the plastic arts and architecture, and in other fields of cultural endeavor. The cultural awakening of Brazil was perhaps most dramatic in the 1955-1965 period in the fields of the legitimate theater and the movies. Although Brazil has had playwrights since colonial days, until recent decades few of these were ever able to see their works produced. And when this did prove possible, it was only for a few showings by an amateur group.

Stefan Zweig commenting on the sad state of the theater at the beginning of World War II, wrote the following:

> I have not heard of a really remarkable play; and in public and social life the art of the theater has hardly any importance. This fact is not astonishing, as the theater is a typical product of a unified, organized society, a form of art which can appear solely within a definite layer of society. And this form of society had not had time to develop in Brazil. Brazil has not lived through an Elizabethan period, never experienced a Court of Louis XIV, nor possessed a middle class group of theater-lovers as in Spain or Austria. . . . Today, when there would be a receptive audience in the cities of millions, it is possibly too late to make a start.[4]

The German writer's gloomy prognostication proved to be unfounded. Although both the legitimate theater and the motion picture industry were still in their formative period in Brazil during and immediately after the Kubitschek period, they were by the early 1960s important parts of the country's cultural life.

The first serious attempt to establish a permanent legitimate theater had been taken in São Paulo in 1945 right after World War II by a Polish entrepreneur named Zeminiski. He established a group known as "Os Comediantes." This venture did not prove financially feasible and it had collapsed by the end of the decade. However, in 1953 there was established in São Paulo the Teatro Brasileiro de Comedia (TBC). Composed of young actors and technicians, it was an attempt to establish in Brazil a European-type theater on a permanent basis. It presented largely Portuguese language translations of European plays done in a European manner. It was begun largely due to the efforts of a group of Italians who had had experience with the theater in their home country. They included Jani Ratto, Luciano Salce, Adolfo Celli, and Ruggeiro Jacobi. These people were joined in their efforts by Zeminiski whose earlier theater by that time had gone out of existence. By the end of the Kubitschek regime, the TBC had given rise to a number of other theater companies. Like the group from which they had sprung, these specialized in European plays and to a lesser degree in American ones. Another theatrical entrepreneur, at first associated with the TBC, Oscar Ornstein, followed United States models rather than European ones. Among his very successful productions were "My Fair Lady," "Barefoot in the Park," and "Sound of Music," all of course rendered in Portuguese.

In addition to the Teatro Brasileiro de Comedia, the other principal source of the modern Brazilian theater was the Teatro de Arena, also originating in São Paulo. It consisted of people who were somewhat younger than those in the TBC. It was inspired with a different point of view. Instead of wanting to copy foreign models, they aspired to develop a purely Brazilian theater, to use new techniques, to use strictly Brazilian language, and when possible to present plays by Brazilian writers. Their first big success was a presentation of John Steinbeck's "Of Mice and Men" which was followed by a play by Gianfrancesco Guarnieri, a young man born in Italy but brought up in Brazil, entitled "Eles no Usan Black Tie" dealing with a Brazilian strike. In general, this group which started in 1958 tried to present plays which they thought would appeal to Brazilian audiences in terms of problems which they themselves felt.

Like the TBC, the Teatro de Arena de São Paulo spawned offspring. One of these was the Centro Popular de Cultura in Rio de Janeiro. The Centro was an attempt to expand the audience of the theater from the more or less fifty thousand regular theater goers in São Paulo and an equal number in Rio, to include workers and lower middle class people who could not afford to go to the regular theater. It showed plays at factory gates and other places

267

where workers congregated. However, this effort degenerated into almost purely political propaganda during the Goulart administration (1961-1964), presenting plays which had a political message but which were not necessarily of very high quality. Another theater group deriving from the Teatro de Arena de São Paulo was the Rio de Janeiro Teatro Repertorio, which had somewhat the same idea as its parent group of trying to present plays which would be attractive to a wider audience. Among their presentations were a play by Sartre translated by the novelist Jorge Amado and works by Bertold Brecht as well as works by new playwrights, both Brazilian and foreign. A third group with origins in the Teatro de Arena was the Grupo de Opinião. It tended to present topical pieces, involving political satire and to experiment with offbeat techniques.

By the end of the Kubitschek period, there were about twenty legitimate theaters in Rio de Janeiro and approximately the same number in São Paulo. Outside of these two cities, there were one or two permanent theaters in Porto Alegre, Curitiba, Salvador, and Recife. These faced very grave difficulties, both in terms of financing and in maintaining a sufficiently large interested public to justify a full-time theater. The writer encountered this latter problem in Salvador early in 1966 when a showing of "The Portrait of Dorian Gray," which he sought to attend, was cancelled because only three people turned up to see it.

Most of the actors engaged in legitimate theater worked full time in the acting profession by the early 1960s. However, they tended to divide their time among stage plays, movies, and television. For the most part, producers, directors, and stage technicians worked in the theater only in their spare time, earning most of their living from other jobs. During this decade Brazil still suffered from a considerable dearth of adequately trained theater people. This applied less to actors, perhaps, then to people in other parts of the industry. Although by the middle 1960s there were two schools for training professional theater people of all sorts being maintained by the Federal Government and four or five others financed privately, it was still a constant complaint by actors, critics, and others in a position to know that there was too much improvisation and amateurishness and too little professional competence on the Brazilian stage.[5]

The Motion Picture Industry

The Brazilian motion picture industry also got its real start during the Kubitschek period. A decade later Brazil produced about forty pictures a year. They included grade "B" and "C" productions as well as first-class ones. Themes ranged widely consisting of light comedies, semi-historical pieces, socially conscious dramas, and adaptations of some of the country's great novels, as well as whodunits and westerns (usually with their locale in the Northeast.)

Most interesting was the so-called Cinema Novo (New Cinema) which appeared in the late 1950s and early 1960s. Undertaken principally by young men in their twenties, it sought to deal specifically with Brazilian material, to specialize in excellence of photography, and to experiment with new techniques. Perhaps the first movie in this genre was *Rio 40 Graus*, directed by Nelson Pereira de Santos. Santos subsequently turned out two other outstanding films *Rio Zona Norte* and *Vidas Secas*, the latter based on a novel of Graciliano Ramos. Another young director, Glaubert Rocha, directed and largely wrote the movie *Deus e Diabo na Terra de Sol*, which won several international prizes, and appeared also as a book. The other important directors of the Cinema Novo were Carlos Diegues, who gained fame with a movie *Ganga Zuma*, and Roberto Farias, who in 1960 turned out *Asalto ao Trem Pagador*, based on a train robbery. The film traced what happened to each of the robbers when he returned home to his favela. Still another, Walter Lima, directing the enchanting *Menino de Engenho*, in 1965, a movie based on a novel by José Lins do Rego. This film was billed at the time as the first of several motion pictures to be adapted from the works of leading Brazilian novelists.

By the middle 1960s the Brazilian movie industry was well established but still faced serious difficulties. It had not yet proved possible to maintain regular production companies similar to those operating in the United States or Western Europe. Rather, companies tended to be organized for the purpose of producing individual films. Those concerned with each film had first to seek the funds to make production possible, and usually such funds were forthcoming from private banks, whose directors were interested in seeing the motion picture produced either for financial or artistic reasons. The movie critics of the country's major dailies encouraged their country's motion picture industry by dealing more kindly with

Brazilian films than they did with comparable productions from abroad. The Brazilian Government assured the national movie industry a certain market by making it mandatory for every movie house in the country to have a certain percentage of Brazilian films among those which it exhibited.

Neither the Brazilian theater nor the Brazilian movies received the attention abroad which they deserved. Although a number of Brazilian films—particularly those of the Cinema Novo—won prizes at foreign films festivals, few Brazilian actors, directors, or playwrights had as yet been sought after by either the legitimate stage or the motion picture industry of other countries.

There is no doubt about the fact that the environment of the Kubitschek period served greatly to stimulate the development of both stage and screen. The rapid economic development helped to provide both resources to produce plays and movies and an audience with incomes large enough to patronize the theater. At the same time, the sense of optimism and self assurance of the period gave writers, directors, producers, and others associated with the theater arts a new confidence in their own ability to turn out things worthy of their audiences' attention. Finally, the atmosphere of cultural and political freedom encouraged experimentation with both ideas and techniques.

The Kubitschek Administration and Architecture

The Kubitschek administration had a gigantic impact on architecture. Here, as in most other aspects of Brazilian culture, Juscelino's regime gave great impetus to something which was already under way, rather than starting *de novo*. As early as 1925, architect Rino Levi published a kind of manifesto in *O Estado de São Paulo* in which he endorsed for use in his country the modern architectural trends then a rising in Europe and the United States. He wrote that "the movement which is manifested today in the arts and principally in architecture is worthy of note. Everything makes us believe that a new era is developing. . . . Architecture, as a mother art, is the one which feels most the modern influences due to the new materials at the disposition of the artist and to the great progress made in recent years in techniques of construction."[6]

By the late 1950s the dean of modern Brazilian architects was Lucio Costa, the man chosen by Kubitschek to develop the plans for

Brasilia. By the early 1950s he had already obtained a reputation which went far beyond his country's frontiers. John Dos Passos has sketched the importance and the early career and training of Lucio Costa as follows:

> It was through Lucio Costa that this whole generation of Brazilian architects was brought into contact with the stimulating European work of the twenties. Coming from a family prominent in the government and in the armed services, he had the European upbringing of the wealthy Brazilians of the period before the wars. His father was a naval officer and eventually an admiral. Born in Toulon, Costa learned to read in London and attended a Swiss boarding school. The Europe he was brought up in teemed with revolutionary ideas in the arts.
>
> Costa's attitude is that of the gifted amateur. As a boy he developed a taste for painting watercolors. In his teens he turned up in Rio to study design at the School of Fine Arts. There his interest in colonial architecture earned him the friendship of another talented and self-effacing Brazilian, the Melo Franco de Andrade who devoted his life to the protection and restoration of Brazil's rich heritage of baroque architectural work. His early house plans were in the neocolonial style.
>
> When Le Corbusier, the French theorist of glass and steel construction, first visited Brazil in 1929, Lucio Costa had prepared the way for him. He had already been telling the young architects about his work and the work of Gropius and Frank Lloyd Wright and of the Italian futurists. They streamed out from the Frenchman's lectures dizzy with the 'functional' use of the new materials: concrete and steel and tile and glass. Already a Polish settler named Warschavchik had been designing dwellings in 'functional' concrete for wealthy businessmen in São Paulo. The new architecture took root.[7]

In a study of the life and work of Le Corbusier, Peter Blake records the circumstances of the construction of the Ministry of

Education building in Rio de Janeiro by a group of young architects led by Costa:

After his visit to the U.S., Corbu made a trip to Rio, where a group of architects under the 'grand old man' of Brazilian architecture, Lucio Costa, had banded together for the design of the new building for the Ministry of Education and Health. The group asked Corbu to come in as a consultant—possibly a rather reckless gesture on its part, as Corbu has a way of dominating any situation in which he finds himself. At Rio he was soon the dominant influence, designed first a long slab building rather like his centrosoyus in Moscow, and later, after the site preferred by him turned out to be unavailable, a taller slab for the more confined lot. The Ministry sketched by Corbu was built substantially as proposed by him, and completed in 1945. By that time Costa, an extremely modest and self-effacing man, had virtually withdrawn from active participation in the group's work as he realized that Corbu was obviously going to be the dominant spirit— whether he was physically present or not. During the development of the project a young Brazilian, Oscar Niemeyer who had been rather a quiet and reticent participant in the planning of the building prior to Corbu's arrival, suddenly blossomed forth, under the influence of Corbu's stimulating presence, as a brilliant designer in his own right. Today the Ministry of Education building is often referred to as the work, primarily, of this remarkable young Brazilian; indeed, with its completion, Niemeyer suddenly became the outstanding young architect in South America . . . Costa . . . with the magnanimity of true greatness, celebrated the completion of the Ministry building by writing a letter to Corbu which acknowledged, in effect, that Corbu's work on that structure had dramatically changed the direction of Brazilian architecture.[8]

However, that Lucio Costa was not merely a disciple of the great Le Corbusier but also drew on Brazilian roots is indicated by Gilberto Freyre, who commented that

> Costa's achievements seem to be the result of the fact that he is a man who has carefully studied the social past of Brazil and Portugal as reflected in their traditional architecture. He even has shown in his most recent work a tendency to use color boldly on the exterior of his buildings, so associating his modernism with the Moorish, Portuguese Brazilian tradition of freely using tropical, vivid colors, and not only the conventional blues and greens of tiles (azulejos) with religious motifs in the outside decoration of these buildings. Even large apartment buildings where this use of vivid colors asks for a particular care in the combination of blues with reds, are now being built in Rio; a victory for Brazilian writers who have clamored for this since the beginning of the present modernist movement in architecture in Brazil.[9]

Kubitschek had early shown an interest in the talents of Oscar Niemeyer and other young Brazilian architects. We have noted that both as mayor of Belo Horizonte and governor of the State of Minas Gerais he had given commissions to Niemeyer for a number of public buildings. However, it was the building of the new capital of Brasilia under Kubitschek's auspices which really established the importance of Brazil in the architectural field. There is little doubt that Brasilia is the most ambitious single architectural plan so far carried out anywhere in the world during the twentieth century. In its conception and its execution, it surpasses both Canberra (Australia) and New Delhi (India), its nearest rivals; and it is almost completely Brazilian in its design and implementation.

Kubitschek undoubtedly intended that among other things Brasilia be a vast surface on which Brazil's architects could demonstrate their talents to the full. Only Brazilians were allowed to submit pilot plans for the city as a whole; only Brazilians—Oscar Niemeyer and others—were commissioned to lay out the individual public buildings which are the heart of the city. Many other Brazilian architects were able to use their talents to plan the nongovernmental buildings, private homes, embassies and other edifices which over the years since the founding of the city have filled in the original plan of Lucio Costa, and have created a vibrant modern metropolis. The Brazilian architectural community was thus not only able to show their fellow citizens the range of their abilities, inventiveness and skill, but gained international attention from around the world. After Brasilia, there could be little question about the country's architects being in the vanguard of their profession in the twentieth century.

Another form of architecture in which Brazilian accomplishments have gained world-wide attention is that of landscape architecture. Here the outstanding figure has been Roberto Burle Marx. He virtually got his start with Kubitschek, making his reputation in the 1940s when Mayor Kubitschek commissioned him to plan the landscaping of Pampulha, as well as of smaller parks in Belo Horizonte. Subsequently, he received a commission to develop the large area of land fill along the Praia do Flamengo in Rio de Janeiro. He had various other commissions, not only in Brazil but abroad. Outstanding among the latter was his work in laying out the Parque del Este in Caracas, Venezuela. Writing in the Italian weekly newspaper *L'Espresso* of 6 September 1964, Bruno Zevi commented that

> Roberto Burle Marx has three sources of inspiration: the flora of the Brazilian forest, which constitutes the perpetual renovating stimulus; modern painting, in which the components are more naturalistic than geometrical; and the dialectical rapport with the forms of contemporary architecture. . . . From a variable combination of these three motifs is born the unique poetic timbre of Brule Marx who is judged to be the greatest landscape architect in the world.

Futebol and Other Sports

Sports are not a cultural manifestation. However, interest in them is often coincident with the general development of a nation. In Brazil starting in the late 1950s, interest in sports was evidence of the growing self-assuredness of the people, and coincided with the burst of economic development which took place during the

274

administration of Kubitschek. There are Brazilians who rate their country's winning the World Football Cup for the first time in 1958 as one of the outstanding accomplishments of the Kubitschek regime.

Futebol, or soccer as it is generally known in the United States, was fostered in Brazil by a group of social clubs in Rio de Janeiro and other major cities. British subjects played a major part. It was the Britishers who introduced soccer as a major activity in these clubs. For many years, the soccer games sponsored by these organizations were run on a strictly amateur basis. Stefan Zweig attested that the sport had not aroused the popular imagination in the early 1950s in the way that it did subsequently. At the beginning of World War II, he wrote in his book *Brazil: Land of the Future* that

> it is not by chance that sport, which after all means a passion for competition, never was received in this climate with that ridiculous overestimation it is elsewhere—which is partly the reason for the brutaliza-tion of, and the lack of intellectual power in, European youth . . . These frenzied scenes and insane ecstasies of hero-worship occurring every day in our so-called civilized countries simply do not exist here.[10]

However, by the end of World War II, Zweig's comment was no longer true. Futebol had become a more serious business. The competition among the various leading clubs was intense. Clubs began to employ people to play on their teams. Within a few years, futebol had become a highly commercialized and extremely popular sport. This change presented the clubs which had sponsored futebol with problems. Many of the best soccer players in Brazil were Negroes or mulattoes and some of the clubs were unwilling at first to accept such people as members. As a result, different clubs adopted different methods of resolving their dilemma. Some decided to give up the game as part of their regular activities rather than accept people of color among their membership. Others adopted the strategem of frankly employing the futebol players, without pretending that they thereby became members of the organization. Still others adopted the practice of having two headquarters, one to which the futebol players of color had access, and the other from which they were excluded. Finally, some went all the way and decided that men who were good enough to carry the organizations' colors in soccer were good enough to frequent their club rooms. Those in the last group were in the decided minority.

Futebol was very popular with the Brazilian public. Not only did games in the major cities draw scores of thousands of patrons, but even the smaller cities began to develop professional and semi-professional teams. Soccer became the sport of every schoolboy, and the most famous players, whether black or white, became national heroes.[11] Freyre has sought to explain Brazilian fondness for futebol in ethnic and cultural terms. In his book *Brazil: An Interpretation* he commented that "the Brazilians play it as if it were a dance. This is probably the result of the influence of those Brazilians who have African blood, or who are predominantly African in their culture, for such Brazilians tend to reduce everything to dance—work and play alike—this tendency is apparently becoming more and more general in Brazil and is not solely the characteristic of an ethnic or regional group."[12]

The various major professional teams were kept busy the year round playing one another, the smaller professional and semi-professional organizations in the provinces, and occasionally foreign teams either in their own countries or in Brazil. A kind of national championship, played between the major teams of Rio de Janeiro and São Paulo became the most important sports event of the nation. At the same time, in 1950 Brazil began to field all-star teams in the World Football Cup competition.

In 1958 Brazil won the international cup contest for the first time. This immensely increased the popularity of soccer and converted it into a kind of national passion. Brazilian success in futebol provided yet another source of pride in the nation's accomplishments, along with Brasilia and the new national automobile industry. Brazil won again in 1962, lost four years later, and then retired the cup by winning it a third time in 1970. Just as the original winning of the Cup in 1958 had had the somewhat strange result of enhancing the popularity of President Kubitschek, the recapturing of the World Cup in 1970 considerably increased the popularity of President Emilion Guistazu Medici, who gave an official reception for the victorious team.

Longtime *afficionados* of Brazilian football noted another subtle change taking place in the crowds that flocked to the games. Previously, Brazilians had been notable as poor sports, with a

276

tendency to become riotous if their favorite "time" (team) lost. However, as the accomplishments of Brazil in this field became more widely recognized, the average Brazilian futebol fan began to become more reasonable. He started to recognize and admire the good technique and the ability of the players whether or not they were on the team which he supported. Good sportsmanship seemed to come along with the heightened passion for the sport, and greater self-confidence.

As a result of this increased interest in futebol, popular attention tended to become more and more concentrated on the activities of the leading players. There was avid public interest every four years in the selections for the Brazilian team for the World Cup contest and newspaper readers followed with critical concern the process of training for the competition. The love affairs of the leading futebol stars became material for discussion in the daily press. Leading soccer stars began to be asked to endorse all kinds of products. Little boys started to make collections of the pictures of their futebol heroes. The greatest player of them all, "Pele" (Edson Esdras do Nascimento) became a real national hero. If by nothing else, this fact is attested to by a plaque between the two elevators on the ground floor of the Hotel Novo Mundo in Rio de Janeiro, which records the "historic" fact that Pele spent the night there just before he played his one thousandth game.

It was not only in soccer that Brazilian excellence in sports began to be evidenced. Maria Bueno became a leading contestant in international tennis matches. Eder Joffre became the first Brazilian of note in international boxing, winning the world bantamweight competition. Brazilians even began to evidence some interest in baseball, although it continued to be played mainly among the Brazilians of Japanese descent, particularly in the state of São Paulo.

The Fate of the Cultural Renaissance After Kubitschek

The flowering of Brazilian literature and other cultural activities which had become so evident and received so much stimulation under Kubitschek, continued for some time after Juscelino left office. However, it was greatly imperiled after a coup d'etat in 1964 established a military dictatorship. Under General Humberto Castelo Branco, whose dictatorship was relatively mild in the beginning, there was some censorship over the theater and the movies, and even over publishing. Probably the most serious danger in that period was a kind of self-censorship among book publishers and theater and movie producers, whereby they generally did not offer works which they might otherwise have sponsored, so as to avoid coercive action by the government. Also, some writers and publishers were *cassado* by the Castelo Branco regime, which is to say that they were deprived of their civil rights, and were officially banned from pursuing their professions.

By the end of the 1960s, the stream of inventiveness and originality which in considerable degree had been responsible for the flourishing of all of the arts during the Kubitschek period and immediately thereafter had been largely dried up. A number of novelists and other writers had been driven into exile or silence; the same thing had occurred with dramatists, movie script writers, and producers. The New Cinema had been largely destroyed. Very few new novels of value were being published, the studies of the country's social and economic problems which had been so numerous a few years before had been greatly curtailed. Symbolic of what was occurring was the debacle of the 1969 São Paulo Bienal. In contrast to what had occurred during the previous decade and a half, this great art exhibit did not attract the kind of participation of artists from all over the world which had become customary. In protest against what had been happening to their counterparts in Brazil, artists from many other countries refused to allow their works to be exhibited in São Paulo.

It may well be that the most disastrous result of the dictatorship which Brazil suffered during the late 1960s and early 1970s was the stunting of the growth of Brazilian cultural life. Although somewhat more favorable conditions under Presidents Geisel and Figueiredo after 1974 saw a modest revival of the streams of inspiration and innovation which were so notable during the 1955-1965 decade, it is by no means certain when or if they will fully recover. Meanwhile, the historical standing of Kubitschek, under whose aegis the flowering of Brazilian literature, dramatic arts and other cultural activities gained such momentum, was that much more enhanced in the light of what occurred afterwards.

Chapter 14

THE FOREIGN POLICY OF THE KUBITSCHEK ADMINISTRATION

Kubitschek's foreign policy, like his domestic one, centered principally on issues of economic development. The two major questions which arose in Brazilian foreign relations during the Kubitschek years—Juscelino's initiative to suggest a planned and multilateral program of Latin American development—under the name Operation Pan America, and the controversy with the International Monetary Fund and the United States Treasury over a suggested program for stabilizing prices in Brazil—both dealt with issues of economic development. In each case, Kubitschek stressed both the need for Brazil and other Latin America countries to direct their own development process, and the obligation of the already industrialized countries, and particularly the United States, to provide ample resources to aid this process.

Impact of "Developmentalism" on Kubitschek's Foreign Policy

At least since the days of the country's great foreign minister, the Visconde de Rio Branco at the turn of the century, the traditional Brazilian foreign policy generally had been to disassociate Brazil from Spanish America. Differences of language and culture as well as a tendency to concentrate largely on internal problems helped to explain this attitude. The great distances separating the country's populated coastal strip from most of its neighbors undoubtedly contributed to this attitude.

Foreign affairs had to a marked degree been in the hands of the expert professional diplomats of Itamaraty, the Brazilian Foreign Office, who had seen their country as being different from both the relatively small and frequently highly unstable Spanish American states, and the huge Anglo Saxon neighbor to the North. They tended to pose Brazil in somewhat the role of buffer and good neighbor vis-a-vis Spanish America and the United States. Brazilian good offices were offered on various occasions to resolve or smooth over conflicts between the United States and the Spanish-speaking countries of Latin America. Rarely were there issues of major importance between Brazil and other Latin American countries, or between it and the United States. Rio Branco had succeeded during the first decade of the twentieth century in bringing about the liquidation of all border disputes with Brazil's ten neighbors.[1]

However, a very significant process of change in the vision of Brazil's role in hemispheric and world affairs began to take place during the Kubitschek administration, a change which was to be intensified later. Vladimir Reisky de Dubnic noted the nature of this alteration when he said that

> the psychological foundations for a more dynamic foreign policy were laid during Kubitschek's presidency. His policy of *desenvolvimentismo* (rapid economic development) mobilized the national consciousness and contributed to a wave of optimism and a desire for a greater role in world affairs for Brazil. The mood of the public caught up with the spirit of the Brazilian Foreign Office, whose high esprit de corps was partially the result of the professional foreign office members' long-standing confidence in the future global role of Brazil. While rapid economic development contributed to a spirit of optimism in the great future of Brazil, it also brought about great economic stresses that increased the need to modify Brazil's foreign policy and to diversify its international economic ties.[2]

During the Kubitschek administration the country began to abandon its stance of semi-isolationism. Juscelino pushed Brazil forward as the spokesman for all of the Latin American countries, in their insistence on the responsibility of the United States to give substantial and decisive help to the economic development of the other American countries. He also gave an example of the need for the Latin American countries to establish their own terms for the conditions under which their development would take place.

Kubitschek and the Cold War

Kubitschek's foreign policy placed Brazil definitely on the side of the West in the Cold War. He did not put forward the kind of general association of the country with the so-called Third World which was suggested by his successor, President Jânio Quadros. Nor did he ever present his resistance of United States pressures and his own suggestions that the United States had a greater responsibility in hemispheric affairs than it had recognized or undertaken, in terms of threats to go over to the other side, so to speak, if his position was not accepted by the United States.

Juscelino put forth the basic framework of his foreign policy in a speech to the Brazilian Superior War College on 26 November 1958. He commented: "We are not forcing friendly peoples and allies to make dolorous choices, or conditioning our support—which is unrestricted and spontaneous—for the West. We present a problem which is preeminately to the conscience of America, using the voice of frankness and loyalty."[3] In this same speech, Kubitschek elaborated further on this attitude. He noted that "the Soviet menace was, until a few years ago, considered a menace of purely military type, localized in Western Europe. Now it is seen clearly that the cold war is changing very much its character, with an attenuation of its purely military aspects, and with daily increasing emphasis on the economic, industrial, and technological aspects." He went on to note that right after World War II all efforts of the West in the Cold War were concentrated on bringing about the recovery of the war-torn countries, and suggested that perhaps this had been justified at the time.

However, Kubitschek commented:

We cannot maintain in 1958 the same kind of action which was considered indispensable in 1945. Today, Latin America is in a situation much more precarious than the reconstructed countries of Europe, and constitutes the weakest part of the Western coalition. And because of that fact we shall not cease to point this out to our friends of the United States of America, with frankness, loyalty, and even hard and realistic words.[4]

281

It was his objective, he said, "to place Latin America, by means of a process of total development, in a position to participate more efficaciously in the defense of the Occident."[5]

In another speech which he gave to the Faculty of Law of the Catholic University of Rio de Janeiro on 29 October 1958, Juscelino summed up his position by saying that "we desire to take our place on the side of the Occident, but we do not desire to constitute its 'proletariat.' We wish to participate in the present world, with all of its dangers and uncertainties, but also with all of its promises and hopes."[6]

Operation Pan America

Kubitschek apparently had in mind the Operation Pan America program a long time before he made it public. Milton Eisenhower records that when Juscelino as president-elect came to the United States to talk with President Eisenhower, he broached the subject. In 1963, Milton wrote: "He talked of a program to be called 'Operation Pan America,' which was the formation of a massive development fund with the United States putting up the bulk of the capital. He made no suggestion of reform or the need for it."[7] He took advantage of another meeting with Eisenhower at a gathering of all the American presidents in Panama in the summer of 1956. Here he indicated his unhappiness with the United States' policy toward Latin America. As he recorded in his memoirs:

At that time, I gave a warning. I pointed out errors. I demanded a change of attitudes on the part of the United States in relation to its brothers of the South. All, however, had been done in accord with protocol. That was a casual encounter, promoted by the North American president himself, and, in those conditions, there was no opportunity for political debate. Eisenhower listened to everything with great interest and promised to take into consideration my warnings.[8]

However, almost two years later Juscelino saw his chance to take a much more decisive step. This opportunity came with the fateful trip of United States Vice President Richard Nixon to Latin America in April-May 1958. Nixon went to South America on a supposed good-will tour. However, he encountered a markedly hostile reception in several of the countries which he visited. He had problems with student groups in Uruguay, and failed in efforts to engage in a dialogue with demonstrating students at the University of San Marcos in Lima, Peru. His bad reception culminated in Caracas, Venezuela, where hostile demonstrators at the airport were only kept away from him by strong military contingents; his car was stopped by hostile crowds on the way to the capital city, and he had to cancel most of his projected program there because of the violence of reaction to his visit.

Shortly after Nixon's return to the United States, President Kubitschek sent a letter dated 6 June 1958 to President Eisenhower which opened the public discussion of the idea of Operation Pan America. Although this letter did not go into the specifics of Juscelino's ideas, it did lay stress on the need for a thorough reappraisal of Inter-American relations. As published in the *New York Times* on 7 June 1958, the text of the letter was as follows:

> I want to convey to Your Excellency on behalf of the Brazilian people as well as for myself, an expression of the sentiments of solidarity and esteem, the affirmation of which has become necessary in view of the aggressions and vexations undergone by Vice President Nixon during his recent visit to countries in Latin America.
>
> The widespread reaction of aversion on the part of the governments and of public opinion in the very nations in which occurred those reprovable acts against the serene and courageous person of the Vice President, constitutes a proof that such demonstrations proceeded from a factious minority.
>
> Nonetheless, it would be hardly feasible to conceal the fact that, before world public opinion, the ideal of Pan American unity has suffered serious impairment. These disagreeable events, which we deplore so much, have nevertheless, imparted an inescapable impression that we misunderstood each other on this continent. The propaganda disseminated by the tools of anti-Americanism is apparently now directed toward presenting such supposed misunderstandings as actual incompatibility and even enmity between the free

283

countries of the American community. Fortunately, this is far from being the truth.

It appears to me, Mr. President, that it would be utterly inconvenient and unfair to allow this false impression to prevail, naturally weakening the cause of democracy to the defense of which we are pledged.

In addressing these words to Your Excellency, my sole purpose is to acquaint you with my deep-seated conviction that something must be done to restore composure to the continental unity. I have no definite and detailed plans to that effect, but rather ideas and thoughts which I could confide to Your Excellency should an early opportunity to do so arise.

I might venture at this juncture, however, that the hour has come for us to undertake jointly a thorough review of the policy of mutual understanding on this hemisphere and to conduct a comprehensive reappraisal of the proceedings already in motion for the furtherance of Pan American ideals in all of their aspects and implications. The time has come for us to ask ourselves the pertinent question as to whether or not all of us are doing our utmost to weld the indestructible union of sentiments, aspirations and interests called for by the graveness of the world situation.

As a soldier who led democracy to victory, as an experienced statesman, and above all, as a man sensitive to the ways of truth, Your Excellency is in an unique position to evaluate the seriousness of the question which I postulate with the exclusive purpose of defining and subsequently eliminating an entire range of misunderstandings that are easily capable of being removed at this moment but which may perhaps suffer a malignant growth should we fail to give it proper and timely attention.

It is hoped that the unpleasant memory of the ordeal undergone by Vice President Nixon will be affected by the results of earnest efforts, toward creating something deeper and more durable for the defense and preservation of our common destiny.

As I have already said to Your Excellency, it is advisable that we correct the false impression that we are not behaving in a fraternal way in the Americas, but besides that corrective effort, and in order that it be durable and perfect, we must search our consciences to find out if we are following the right path in regard to Pan Americanism.

It is my earnest hope that Your Excellency will feel that this letter was written under the impulse of a desire to reaffirm the warm and sincere fraternal sentiments which have always bound my country to the United States of America, in perfect attunement with the ideas outlined by Your Excellency on the occasion of the meeting of the chief executives of the American nations in Panama.

Kubitschek himself said of his letter that it "did not constitute a program of action or a project for revision of the Pan American political system. It was only an invitation to debate, having in view the interests of the peoples of the continent" (PQ.153). However, Tad Szulc has noted that

Dr. Kubitschek's 'Operation Pan America' contained all the political, psychological, and economic concepts required to make it a success. Handled imaginatively, it could have become anything the United States wanted it to be, for the idea met with great receptivity. But General Eisenhower knew little about Latin America, and Mr. Dulles' interest in the potentialities of the imaginative policies there was limited, to say the least. Mr. Nixon had vanished from the Latin American scene as quickly as he had entered it.[9]

Brazilian-U.S. Negotiations

President Eisenhower replied immediately to Kubitschek's letter by sending Roy Richard Rubottom, the assistant secretary of state for Latin American Affairs, to Juscelino with a letter. This letter agreed with Kubitschek that the state of relations between the United States and Latin America was very bad and agreed with the need for a wide discussion between the United States and Brazilian leaders. It added that the basic purpose of Rubottom's trip was to prepare the way for a subsequent visit by Secretary of State John Foster Dulles.

Although Kubitschek was pleased with Eisenhower's letter, he was not so happy about his conversations with Roy Rubottom who "disagreed entirely with my point of view. For him, the problems of Latin America were of a purely police nature. The masses were exploited by the communists, and they promoted the disturbances" (PQ.156). In reply to Rubottom, Kubitschek asked why the communists were able to exploit the Latin American masses, and answered his own question as follows:

> Exactly because the appeal of that minority finds the masses psychologically hostile to the United States. The evil was not Communism, which was incipient in the hemisphere, but was in the social deterioration, which was typical of all the Latin American nations. What was necessary to do, I declared with vehemence, would be to promote an approach of the United States to Latin America through execution of a multilateral program of development, on a long-term basis. I suggested then that this be called Operation Pan America, to reflect the global character of its implications involving all of the peoples of the Western Hemisphere. (PQ.157)

After Rubottom's departure, in order to emphasize both the urgency of the issue and the nature of what it was that he was proposing, Kubitschek summoned all of his cabinet members, the vice president and all of the heads of diplomatic delegations accredited to Brazil, to the Catete palace. There he expounded at length on the Operation Pan America proposal. He argued that

> there must be intensified pioneer investment in the economically backward areas of the continent, to counterbalance the lack of internal financial resources and the scarcity of private capital. Simultaneously, to improve productivity, and consequently, the returns on this investment, programs of technical assistance must be greatly increased. Of equal significance and of great

urgency will be the adoption of methods to protect the price of the basic products from excessive and dangerous fluctuations which characterize them. Finally, we must augment the international financial organizations, through amplification of their resources and liberalization of their statutes, with the objective of giving them greater breadth of action. These things, and others which should be proposed, must find their own forum in a meeting at the highest political level of the continent, in which, in contrast to what has occurred, there are practical efficacious and positive solutions. (PO.158-59)

Secretary of State John Foster Dulles was scheduled to arrive in Brazil early in August 1958. However, just before the date set for Dulles' visit, the Lebanon crisis broke and so Eisenhower sent a message to Kubitschek suggesting that Dulles' visit be postponed, and asking whether that would be acceptable. Kubitschek replied that he understood the gravity of the Lebanon crisis, but that he thought that a postponement of Dulles' trip would make a very bad impression not only in Brazil, but throughout Latin America and that he thought that Dulles ought to come as scheduled. As a result, Dulles did come at the time originally agreed upon.[10]

Dulles conferred for three days with officials at Itamaraty, specifically Foreign Minister Francisco Negrão de Lima, Roberto Campos, Lucas Lopes, and Sabastião Pais de Almeida. In these discussions, "Foster Dulles showed himself a tenacious arguer, intransigent, almost incapable of reaching agreement. He put forth his points of view, and from them there was no way out" (PQ.161). The disagreement was such that Dulles and the Brazilian negotiators could reach no accord on a common communique, and Dulles asked to discuss the matter with Kubitschek himself. After Dulles and Juscelino had each drawn up his own communique, they were able to merge the two into a single document. Dulles then insisted that both men sign it, but Kubitschek demurred, insisting that on the Brazilian side it was appropriate that it be signed by Dulles' counterpart, Foreign Minister Negrão de Lima. Thereafter, Dulles and Kubitschek took off for Brasilia, where a farewell dinner was given for the secretary of state. Kubitschek wrote that "at this dinner, taking advantage of the atmosphere of cordiality which was established between us, I succeeded in completing the *weaving* of the plan which would be Operation Pan America." He added that "after exhaustive labor, I felt comforted. There had been established the basic points which would support the new policy" (PQ.162).

Kubitschek maintained that one concrete thing which came from his meeting with Dulles was the decision to set up the Inter American Development Bank. Kubitschek kept insisting with Dulles that Latin America was not looking for charity, was not looking for a Marshall Plan, which he realized that the United States voters would not accept. However, he insisted Latin America did not need financing for its development projects and urged the establishment of a new special institution for this purpose.[11]

The United States also supported the proposal by Kubitschek to summon a meeting of Foreign Ministers of the Americas in Washington, D.C. on 23 September 1958, to consider the proposals for a new multilateral program for the economic development of Latin America. This meeting established a "Committee of Twenty-One," consisting of one representative from each of the foreign ministries. It charge was to draw up recommendations to be submitted to the various governments and to a meeting of the Inter American Economic and Social Council. A major basis for elaborating these recommendations would be provided by the *Aide Memoire*, which the Brazilians had submitted to the foreign ministers.

The Brazilian Aide Memoire

This Aide Memoire contained of a number of major points. The first was a definition of "development," which it described as "obtaining a level of living per capita which permits the beginning of a process of a cumulative and autonomous growth with local resources, to a satisfactory level, without brusque or grave institutional alternations." The second major point of the document called for "the fixing of continental consensus of a rate of cumulative development for the gross national product of the Latin American countries as a group, sufficient to surpass the increase in population, and bring about the beginning of the autonomous process of development at a satisfactory rate." The third point was "the determination of the sources and magnitudes of international public or private resources required to complement national savings." The Brazilians argued that "this study must include, for

288

the period covered, a rational plan for the increase of imports needed for maintaining the progress of development, which implies a corresponding expansion of the Latin American capacity to export."[12]

Although no specific amount of money from foreign sources was suggested in the Aide Memoire or at the Foreign Ministers Conference in Washington, Juscelino did make a specific estimate of the need of his speech to the Superior War School on 26 November 1958. He commented there that

> the economic studies being made by Itamaraty, indicate $3.5 billion as the minimum needs for external credits which Brazil alone will need to finance the difference between the amounts received from exports and the imports indispensable for the growth of its gross national product in the period between 1959 and 1980. For all of Latin America, the same calculations suggest a total of ten billion dollars.[13]

The estimate of Kubitschek and his Foreign Office concerning the needs for outside financing of Latin American development turned out to be relatively modest. Three years later, at the Punta del Este Conference which launched the Alliance for Progress, the figure of $20 billion for the period 1961-1970 was agreed upon, and United States Representative Douglas Dillon promised that the United States would, in one way or another, provide half of this amount.[14]

The fourth point in the Brazilian Aide Memoire argued that there should be "identification of the principal centers of strangulation of the Latin American economies which must be removed by individual or collective action," an approach similar to that being used domestically in Kubitschek's own Programa de Metas. It went on to suggest that the most important economic sectors in this category were energy and power, transport and communications, foodstuffs and agriculture, basic industries, and education. The fifth point dealt with the need for a "statement of the alternatives of action open to Latin America to assure its obtaining the rates of development which can be adopted as the goals of 'Operation Pan America.'" The document ended with the statement that "the Truth, however, is that, in the long run, for

Operation Pan America to be completely successful, it must bring together the Governments and peoples of the Hemisphere behind a rational program, with specific dates and predetermined quantities, which will reverse the present tendency towards increasing impoverishment of Latin America compared to the great economic powers."[15]

President Kubitschek made energetic efforts to align support for the ideas of Operation Pan America as set forth in the Aide Memoire among other Latin American leaders. He sent personal letters to all of the Latin American presidents, as well as dispatching emissaries to talk with them. They expressed wide support for his proposals. Three presidents, Arturo Frondizi of Argentina, Alfredo Stroessner of Paraguay, and Ramón Villeda Morales of Honduras, who visited Brazil in this period, personally expressed to Kubitschek their backing for his ideas (PQ.195). One of the most interesting replies to Kubitschek's letters came from President Alberto Lleras Camargo of Colombia. Lleras wrote that this was the first time in fifty years that a president of Brazil had written to any other Latin American president, and that the rest of the countries had begun to think that Brazil was part of Europe.[16]

The Committee of 21, established by the Meeting of Foreign Ministers of the Americas in Washington in September 1958, made extensive studies during the next few months of the economic development needs of the Latin American countries. The first practical result of Operation Pan America and the work of the Committee of 21 was the formal acceptance by the United States of the idea of establishing the Inter American Development Bank. For more than a decade the Latin American countries had been insisting at every Inter American meeting on the setting up of such an institution, to be largely financed by the United States. The USA with equal consistency had rejected it. Vice President Nixon's experiences in South America in 1958 as well as the Operation Pan American proposals of Juscelino Kubitschek had served to begin to change the minds of the United States policy makers.

Juscelino's Unhappiness at Washington's Response

However, Kubitschek was convinced that deliberate efforts were being made in the United States to sabotage the idea of Operation Pan America. Concerning the Washington meeting, he

290

wrote later that "this coolness, however, was artificial, or rather, deliberate. From the beginning of the meeting it was clear that there was something going on behind the scenes, tending to frustrate Operation Pan America. And, incredible as it appears, that was supported exactly by elements of the Department of State." Kubitschek believed that the reason for such an attitude on the part of State Department officials was their feeling that the United States had enough problems without taking on those implied in Operation Pan America (PQ.197).

The next international meeting of consequence on Operation Pan America was that of the Committee of 21 in Buenos Aires in April 1959, which was attended by Fidel Castro. Kubitschek was by no means happy with the results of that conference. In his memoirs he noted that

> the movement begun by me and which in a short time had been converted into a real crusade, bringing together and inspiring all of the Latin American nations, was displeasing to the defenders of the traditional policy of conserving Latin America only as the 'backyard of the United States,' according to the expression of Kennedy. What was lacking to torpedo the OPA was a motive. A pretext. A reason which justified itself, leaving no need for explanation. (PQ.207-8)

According to Juscelino, that reason was found in the Buenos Aires conference in the person of Fidel Castro. The immediate result, in spite of twenty-four resolutions passed at the Buenos Aires meeting, was the postponement until September 1960 of a further meeting, a time long enough it was thought by those seeking to block Operation Pan America "to destroy the spirit of the Latin Americas, the preoccupation for their well being, and above all the anxiety for their development" (PQ.207-8).

The Visit of Eisenhower

Kubitschek continued to urge the need for the broad-gauge program of Operation Pan America when he was host to President Eisenhower in March 1960. Juscelino welcomed Eisenhower to Brasilia, the first stop on the American president's visit to several

Latin American countries. They went from there to São Paulo and Rio de Janeiro. Although the two men had met twice before, Kubitschek got a much greater chance during the several days that Eisenhower was in Brazil than he had had before to expound upon his ideas concerning the restructuring of Inter American relations.

Kubitschek was convinced that the nature of the popular reception which Eisenhower received in Brazil helped to drive home the message which he was trying to impart to his North American counterpart. He wrote that

> in Brazil, the acclamations that he received were very great. However, it was clear that they were tributes to the war hero, to the Supreme Commander of the Allied Forces, and not to the president of the United States. The resentment against the government of Washington— both in Brazil and in the other Latin American nations— had clearly become aggressive, and this could not be hidden. . . . I could feel how preoccupied he was with the evident—and for him incomprehensible—sentiment of hostility towards his country. (PQ.250)

To Kubitschek's great delight, Eisenhower was very much impressed with Brasilia. He said the city exceeded all of his expectations and that it was an inspiration. Juscelino said that Eisenhower was surprised, that he looked at everything and asked questions. In the new Brazilian capital-to-be, the two men signed the "Joint Declaration of Brasilia." This statement "reaffirmed the determination of the two nations to defend democratic liberties, to foster harmony in the Inter American community, to maintain the principles of political and economic solidarity contained in the Charter of the OAS, and to struggle to give concrete content to the ideas contained in Operation Pan America" (PQ.252-53).

Kubitschek found out from his discussions with Eisenhower that the US president was not sufficiently informed concerning the idea of Operation Pan America. Kubitschek wrote that "he had decidedly supported the movement, but he did not know that the Department of State, reviving the errors of the past, was attempting to transform the question into a simple pretext for international conferences, without having the basic idea of the movement examined with the objectivity and speed which was necessary"

(PQ.253). Finally, Eisenhower promised that upon his return to Washington, he would insist that the State Department move more rapidly on the question of Operation Pan America (PQ.255).

However, Kubitschek was not satisfied with Eisenhower's attitude towards Operation Pan America after the United States president returned home. In a letter to Juscelino dated 8 July 1960, Eisenhower wrote that "we can count on subsequent concrete results in Bogota, especially in the following sectors: (a) financing of economic development; (b) the role of technical assistance to obtain increased industrial and agricultural production; and (c) later consideration of the problems of basic products" (PQ.335).

Very much disappointed with this letter, Kubitschek noted that it "was limited to generalities, without fixing a direction, an objective which could be achieved, which was contrary to my habitual political attitude, which was that of, first of all establishing a goal and, only then studying the means of making it feasible within a given period of time" (PQ.336).

In his reply to President Eisenhower, which was published as a paid advertisement in the *New York Times* of 2 August 1960, Juscelino reiterated once again his point of view. Part of the letter reads as follows:

> Permit me to reaffirm to Your Excellency what already has been said concerning Operation Pan America. It is not a question of an appeal to generosity, but to reason. Reason dictates the necessity of fighting in the only efficacious manner against the cold war which insinuates itself and seeks to involve our Continent. The fight which all of us must undertake together for the common ideals of the Americas will be valid only if we combat the causes of unrest and discontent, without seeking merely to correct and diminish their effects and consequences.
>
> We ought, therefore, to have the courage to draw the conclusions which reality presents to us. The truth is that, despite all previous efforts, not enough has been done and an adequate rate of development for the Latin American peoples has not been achieved. To wish to attribute the present unrest of these people to mere propaganda or agitations by extra-continental agents

would be to ignore the fact that poverty and the frustration of economically stagnant peoples have a much greater capacity for agitation. The problem therefore consists in giving a new dimension to the work to be accomplished.

Rightly or wrongly, Kubitschek felt that his letter was influential in bringing a marked change in the attitude and policy of the United States government at the Bogota conference.

The Bogota Conference

The proposed plenary meeting of the Committee of 21 took place finally in Bogotá, Columbia, in September 1960. The major decision of the conference was the establishment of the Social Projects Fund. Initially this fund was to have some $500 million which would be made available to the Latin American nations in the form of grants, rather than loans particularly for social projects, that is, efforts in such field as education, public health, housing and the like.

The acceptance of the Social Projects Fund idea, like the establishment of the Inter American Development Bank, represented a major shift in United States policy. Ever since the days of the Marshall Plan, the United States had steadfastly rejected the idea that its financial help to the economic development of Latin America should be in the form of grants. Although the Latin Americans continued to point out that most of the Marshall Plan aid had been in that form, although the Europeans were potentially much more able than the Latin Americans to repay loans, the United States authorities had remained unconvinced. At Bogotá, the first step was taken to change this long-term position of the United States Government.

Obviously, some basic aspects of Operation Pan America were not accepted. There did not emerge, as the Brazilian delegation to the Washington meeting of September 1958 had urged, any joining "of the Governments and people of the Hemisphere behind a rational program." Nor was there any specific United States commitment to finance on a long-range basis an integrated and planned Latin American development program. Efforts in that direction had to await a new administration in Washington and the launching of the Alliance of Progress by President John F. Kennedy. However, in retrospect at least, Kubitschek felt that the Bogotá meeting and the so-called Act of Bogotá which summed up its results was a victory for Operation Pan America. In his memoirs he wrote that "in fact, everything was different in Bogota. There was greater cordiality between the North Americans and Latin Americans. The discussions, although marked by great vivacity, reflected a desire, secret but perceptible to any good observer, to deal with the revindications which had given origin to Operation Pan America" (PQ.336). Kubitschek cited a statement of Augusto Frederico Schmidt, the head of the Brazilian delegation to Bogotá, upon his return home. Schmidt commented that "for the first time in the history of Pan Americanism, the United States has agreed to sign a document which commits them to a policy of social and economic development of Latin America" (PQ.338).

Kubitschek felt that the major points of significance agreed to at Bogotá were as follows:

1. Quantification of the goals of Latin American development
2. Promise of adequate external assistance, determined in the light of that quantification
3. Abandonment by the United States of the thesis that 'the house must be put in order' before assistance could be granted, commonly known as the thesis of the International Monetary Fund
4. Abandonment of the thesis that external aid should only cover imported goods
5. Abandonment of the thesis that the Latin American countries could not accelerate their development because of technological inability to absorb resources rapidly
6. Abandonment of the ideological thesis of development through foreign private capital (PQ.337-38)

The Significance of Operation Pan America

In putting forth Operation Pan America, President Kubitschek had dramatically underscored the need for all of the countries of the hemisphere to work together to elaborate and put into effect an

295

overall development program in the Latin American countries, mobilizing much more extensive resources from outside than previously had been made available, as well as mobilizing much more fully the indigenous resources for development available within Latin America itself. Also, by his proposal, Kubitschek had put Brazil into a position of leadership of the Latin American nations such as it had never had before. In effect, he rallied them behind a joint insistence to the United States that it give practical expression to the often asserted desire of the United States to see the Latin American countries develop their economies. The first step towards United States acquiescence to the Latin American demands expressed by Kubitschek was taken at Bogotá.

Kubitschek went out of office and John Kennedy became president of the United States at almost the same time. However, the proposals put forward for hemispheric cooperation by the new American administration followed to a marked degree the suggestions which the Brazilian ex-president had urged three years earlier. The original proposal for the Alliance for Progress was basically for the kind of multilateral effort to develop and diversify the Latin American economies with extensive aid from the United States to which Juscelino had given the title Operation Pan America. The kinship between the two was recognized in the documents establishing the Alliance for Progress which were signed in Punta del Este in August 1961.

However, Kubitschek was unhappy with the fact that Kennedy adopted a new name for his program, instead of calling it Operation Pan America. The author heard Juscelino comment in a lecture in New York City that Kennedy for some reason which he did not know had rechristened his proposal Inter American program for development.[17] A decade later, Kubitschek told me that he thought that Kennedy had erred in not accepting the title Operation Pan America, which had originated in Latin America, instead of adopting a completely new name which was thought up in the United States.[18]

The Controversy With the International Monetary Fund

A year after the launching of Operation Pan America, President Kubitschek gave clear indication that he did not believe that because the Latin American countries needed outside financial and technical assistance to help their economic development that those countries, and Brazil in particular, should allow the donor institutions to determine national development policy. This was the nub of the issue between the Kubitschek administration and the International Monetary Fund (IMF) in 1959-1960.

The controversy between the IMF and the Kubitschek administration centered around the perennial problem of Brazil's balance of payments deficit. The International Monetary Fund, which existed largely for the purpose of meeting short-run foreign exchange difficulties of its member countries, had extended a credit of $300 million to Brazil in 1958 to help out the balance of payments crisis of that year. However, in 1959 the IMF informed the Brazilian government that it would extend no further credit to that country until drastic steps were taken to stabilize the national currency and curb the deficit in the balance of payments. It demanded that inflation be brought down to the rate of 6 percent a year. However, Kubitschek absolutely rejected this idea, saying that his objective would be to keep inflation at 20 percent a year or somewhat less and that he put first priority on development; rapid economic development made necessary sacrifices by the people in the form of inflation.[19]

The Fund completely rejected Kubitschek's point of view. It submitted a list of prerequisites which it insisted would have to be met before any further financial aid would be forthcoming. The most important of these demands was an insistence on the elimination of the multiple exchange rate system, and a drastic reduction of the federal budget deficit. The effect of both of these measures would have been to slow down, if not halt, the Kubitschek government's development program. As we have noted, the administration made extensive use of multiple exchange rates to encourage the growth of those sectors of the economy in which it was most interested. The budget deficit was intimately connected with the building of Brasilia and other development projects of the administration, as well as the patronage expenditures which made the administration's development program politically feasible. As a result, there was understandable reticence upon the part of Kubitschek to accept the demands of the International Monetary Fund.

During the early months of 1959 Minister of Finance Lucas Lopes conferred extensively with the IMF and drew up an extensive program for achieving monetary stability. He also had considerable contact with the United States Government, since it was the policy of the United States not to provide economic aid to a country which was not in good standing with the International Monetary Fund. The contacts with the US included a visit by Thomas Mann, then assistant secretary of state for Latin American affairs, to Brazil in May 1959 during which he conferred at length both with Kubitschek and Lopes. In May, Lopes was forced to resign as minister of finance "for reasons of health." That Lopes' illness may have been more diplomatic than real was indicated in June, when President Kubitschek rejected the International Monetary Fund's demands and broke off any further negotiations with the IMF.

In his memoirs, Juscelino commented on the last phase of his negotiations with the IMF that

> at the time, the Fund was presided over by Mr. Jacobson, representative of Sweden and intransigent defender of monetarist ideas. He visited me on a certain occasion. In the conversation which we had, he condemned everything I was doing in favor of development of the country, saying that the direction I must follow would be the direction of reducing inflation to 6 percent, to obtain which I should stop all of the projected works, including the construction of Brasilia. My arguments were to no avail, which obliged me to break with the International Monetary Fund. (PQ.360)

Kubitschek chose a meeting of the Partido Social Democrático members of the Federal Senate as the place to make the announcement of the rupture with the IMF. He insisted that the demands of the Fund were politically unacceptable, would demand changes in the government's overall policy which he could not and would not make. He specifically announced that the government would continue to use the multiple exchange rate system as a tool in the development campaign.[20] Kubitschek said that he was unwilling to go along with the recommendations of the IMF because they would mean a curtailment of the economic development which was the essence of his government program. He maintained that carrying out the measures urged by the IMF would mean political difficulties for the administration which he was not willing to accept.

Kubitschek stuck to his position on this issue for the rest of his administration. However, although relations with the IMF remained bad through the rest of 1959, they did improve somewhat the following year. Kubitschek was convinced that his discussion of the issue with President Eisenhower, during the latter's visit to Brazil, was of key importance in bringing about a change of attitude on the part of the IMF. Kubitschek wrote that

> I still remember that Eisenhower asked me, in referring to the International Monetary Fund, if I was disposed to reconcile myself with that important international institution. I replied that I would do it with pleasure, as soon as its directors ended the demands which they had formulated, and which, if adhered to, would curb all of the development of Brazil.
>
> The North American president listened to me with attention and remained quiet. A month later, my ambassador in Washington, Walter Moreira Salles, came to Rio to tell me that the International Monetary Fund was disposed to renew relations with my government, depending only on a letter proposing this from the Embassy of Brazil. I refused to send the letter and told the ambassador that he should make only personal overtures, without leaving behind any written document. That's the way it was done. Weeks later, Brazil could obtain the quota to which it was entitled from the IMF. (PQ.255-56)

On 20 May 1960 the International Monetary Fund allowed Brazil to draw $47.7 million for six months as "a goodwill gesture that the IMF hoped would result in Brazil's taking the stabilization steps it had recommended." The Fund was still urging Brazil "to cut its budget deficit, curb inflationary credit expansion, eliminate subsidies on imports, and adopt a single exchange rate in place of the multiple rate system currently in existence."[21] The only difference was that its exhortations were no longer accompanied by a refusal to lend at least some of the funds which Brazil needed.

Relations with Castro

One hemispheric problem which became increasingly difficult for Kubitschek during the last two years of his administration was that of his relations with Cuba. Right after the Castro revolution, the Brazilian government, like most of those in the hemisphere, greeted the new regime with considerable enthusiasm. In conformity with this popularity of the Castro regime, Kubitschek invited Fidel to visit Brazil, which he did in May 1959. The Brazilian president played host to the Cuban prime minister at lunch, but upon this occasion, Castro completely dominated the conversation. He spoke virtually without interruption for six hours, recounting the whole history of his revolution, leaving little time for Kubitschek to say anything (PQ.206).[22]

Kubitschek believed that the United States' attitude towards Castro was to a large degree responsible for the direction in which the Cuban leader took his revolution. Juscelino recorded that after the conference in Buenos Aires, where Fidel had urged a $30 billion US aid program for Latin America, "I concluded that what was involved was an embittered idealist, who suffered personally the consequences of support given by the United States to military dictators in Latin America. At that time, Fidel Castro had not yet revealed his adoption of the Marxist-Leninist creed. He was living a drama of self-definition between democracy and totalitarianism." Kubitschek said further that

> the USA, persevering in its lack of tact, ended up losing not only its sugar mills, but the good business of sugar exportation. And, insofar as its traditional area of influence was concerned, it provoked the fragmentation of the political unity of the continent. Lenin used to say that the North Americans, in the face of a problem, only thought about the profits in seeding cord, forgetting that it was going to be used to hang them. (PQ.205-6)

By the middle of 1960 relations between the Brazilian regime and that of Castro were still comparatively good. President Dorticós of Cuba made an official visit to Brazil on the invitation of Kubitschek at the end of May 1960.[23] At the San José, Costa Rica

Inter American Conference a few weeks later, which dealt particularly with the problem of Cuba. Kubitschek wrote that

> the policy adopted by Brazil was to attempt conciliation. At that time I believed that Fidel Castro, reflecting the discontent which was general in Latin America, was still recuperable for democracy. What I had in view in attempting a reconciliation was to impede Cuba from separating from the American community—while maintaining its hostile attitude towards the United States, which was its right—so that the unity of the Latin American bloc could be maintained. (PQ.334)

Kubitschek added that "to this end, I gave instructions to Foreign Minister Horacio Lafer, chief of the Delegation of Brazil, and he did everything in the initial phase of the conversations to attain this objective. Unfortunately, Cuba was already compromised excessively with Moscow, and the aggressiveness of Fidel Castro rose in tone with each day, making any compromise solution impossible." The Brazilian delegation signed the so-called Declaration of San José which condemned "energetically the intervention or menace of intervention of extracontinental powers in the affairs of the American Republics." The Declaration also proclaimed that acceptance of any intervention of this type put "in danger the solidarity and security of the hemisphere" (PQ.334).

Relations with Portugal

One of the most widely criticized aspects of Kubitschek's foreign policy was his maintenance of close relations with the Portugal of Dr. Salazar. His attitude on this issue seems to have been motivated largely by a personal feeling of solidarity with Portugal as Brazil's one-time mother country, and a personal friendship with Salazar, rather than by any sympathy for the dictatorship over which Salazar presided.

The policy of the Kubitschek administration was particularly reflected in the attitude which the Brazilian government took in the United Nations and elsewhere towards the struggle of Portugal's African colonies for their independence. José Honorio Rodriguez has written that whether in its own field of action or in the United Nations, Juscelino Kubitschek's government ignored African progress toward freedom and, after the African states had achieved independence limited itself to *de jure* recognition. Nothing more; no encouraging message, no solidarity, no gesture, not to mention cooperation, as though we were ashamed of the springtime of African power, as though we were humiliated by our alter ego.[24]

Rodriguez attributed this attitude to Juscelino's concentration on hemispheric affairs. He wrote that "the failure of Juscelino Kubitschek's foreign policy was due to the one-sidedness of its regionalistic vision." Wayne A. Selcher has said of the Brazilian attitude on the question of Portugal's African colonies that "the Brazilian delegation to the United Nations aided Portugal by subscribing to and defending the thesis of 'overseas provinces' and by maintaining the discretionary and voluntary right of any administering power to yield or withhold information on the territories within its jurisdiction, under Article 73(c) of the charter."[25]

In 1957, when the anti-colonialist group in the UN General Assembly insisted that Portugal had to report on affairs in its African colonies, "Brazil defended Portugal as ably and in the same manner as did Portugal's own representative." It generally maintained that administrative powers in general had the right to determine if and what they would report and

in the specific instance of Portugal, additional, unique factors were marshalled to show that ever since 'Portugal took her civilization overseas,' Portuguese territory had been a 'cultural and psychological whole, a single unit' without discrimination as to race, color, religion, or social condition. The Brazilian representative concluded that his delegation could not find "any concrete reason for disagreeing with the Portuguese Government when it states that Portugal does not administer Non-Self-Governing Territories."[26]

In August 1960 Kubitschek made an official state visit to Portugal. According to his own account, his reception was very warm. The occasion for this visit was the celebration of the five hundredth anniversary of the death of Prince Henry the Navigator. During his stay, Kubitschek signed six treaties with Portugal to regulate tourist exchange, passport visas, juridical assistance, diplomatic and consular representation, extradition, and questions pertaining to individuals holding citizenship in both states.[27] On this visit, Juscelino again expressed on this visit his feeling of a special relationship between Brazil and Portugal, telling Portuguese President Américo Tomas that "we have not merely diplomatic or cordial relations, but family ties. We are a unique case in the world." He added that there was a "solidarity which transcends material interests, which is even independent of our volition, which is stronger than our will—the solidarity of kinship, the solidarity of the cradle, of the first hours of development."[28]

Admittedly there was a certain incongruity between President Kubitschek's close relationship with the Salazar dictatorship in Portugal and his professed belief in democracy. Subsequently, he maintained that he sought to keep this relationship from appearing to be an endorsement of the Portuguese dictatorship. He noted that in his 1960 trip, for instance, he laid a wreath on the statue of Antonio José de Almeida, a one-time Portuguese president who he said was a symbol of the opposition to the Salazar regime.[29] Kubitschek claimed that he sought privately to get Salazar to modify his position on the African colonies. At one point, he suggested the organization of a Portuguese-speaking "Commonwealth," consisting of Portugal, Brazil, and the African territories (as independent members). At first, Salazar seemed interested in the idea, Juscelino claimed, so he (Kubitschek) made the suggestion public. Subsequently, however, Salazar repudiated the suggestion.[30] Finally, the Kubitschek administration certainly did take one step which indicated that emphasis on old ties with Portugal did not necessarily mean endorsement of the dictatorship there. In September 1960 it granted personal political asylum to General Humberto Delgado, one of the most important and colorful leaders of the anti-Salazar opposition.[31]

303

Other Aspects of Kubitschek's Foreign Policy

In spite of his friendly attitude towards Portugal, Kubitschek maintained cordial contacts with black African countries. He invited Haile Selassie, Emperor of Ethiopia, to visit Brazil, which he did in December 1960. Among other places, Haile Selassie visited Brasilia, where he commented that "the city was worth twenty years on his throne." While Haile Selassie was in Brazil, he was temporarily overthrown by rebel elements in Addis Ababa. He had brought with him a check for ten thousand dollars to use on his trip, but after his ouster from power, no bank in Brazil would honor the check. Although the Brazilian government also would not cash it, Kubitschek arranged with Horacio Lafer, his foreign minister and a very rich man, to honor the document on a personal basis. Upon his return home the Ethiopian Emperor was restored to his throne. The check was covered.[32]

Another distinguished foreign visitor during the Kubitschek administration was President Giovanni Gronchi of Italy, the first Italian chief of state ever to visit the country. The two presidents signed the "Declaration of São Paulo," on 10 September 1958 in which they "pledged to work for new agricultural and industrial collaboration between the two countries. . . . Military, cultural and technical cooperation agreements were also signed."[33]

Late in 1959 Kubitschek announced that a trade mission would be sent to the Soviet Union, in an attempt to widen Brazil's markets for its major exports, particularly coffee. This resulted in the signing of a trade agreement in December 1959, which provided for an exchange of $25 million each way between Brazil and the USSR during 1960, and a slow increase in this amount subsequently, to reach $42 million in 1962. Brazil was principally to purchase oil and wheat and sell coffee.[34] However, in spite of this trade accord. Juscelino refused to reestablish diplomatic relations with the Soviet Union "for fear that that act might have unfavorable repercussions in religious circles, which constitute the spiritual majority of the Nation," as he himself explained it. Some difficulties arose over the importation of Soviet oil. Petrobras, the government firm controlling most of the Brazilian oil refineries, announced in May 1960 that it would not bring in Soviet crude oil because it was too salty to be processed by Brazilian refineries. However, it was agreed instead that Brazil would import quantities of Soviet diesel fuel.[35]

Kubitschek had other foreign interests. On 25 June 1960, he signed a five-year trade treaty with Czechoslovakia, providing for the total exchange of some $70 million worth of goods each way. Earlier in the year somewhat similar agreements had also been made with Poland and East Germany.[36] Finally, Kubitschek made a somewhat tentative step toward involvement in the Middle East dispute which had preceded the landing of US troops in Lebanon. On 26 July 1958, he wrote a letter to President Eisenhower suggesting that a summit conference on the Middle East be called within the United Nations Security council. Eisenhower, in a somewhat equivocal reply, endorsed the idea of dealing with the issue through the Security Council but rejected the notion of a summit conference.[37]

Conclusion

The Kubitschek foreign policy was closely linked with domestic policy, particularly in connection with those issues which were relevant to the problem of economic development which were the main preoccupation of Juscelino in the presidency. The efforts of the Kubitschek administration to create an integrated industrial sector in the Brazilian economy had a direct effect in changing the way in which the Brazilians looked at the role of their country in the world. This changed view found reflection in the attempt of President Kubitschek to assume a position of leadership in Latin American relations with the United States, through the Operation Pan America proposal, and through the beginning of diversification of Brazil's foreign economic relations.

Chapter 15

THE POLITICS OF THE
KUBITSCHEK REGIME

Upon his taking office, Kubitschek's hold on power seemed exceedingly tenuous. He had won only a narrow plurality in an election the results of which were challenged by at least some of the opposition. Between election day and Juscelino's inauguration, two coups d'etat had been executed, presumably to make it possible for him to become president. His dependence upon the goodwill of General Henrique Teixeira Lott seemed absolute. It is an indication of the political talent of Juscelino that he overcame these formidable handicaps. Not only did he serve out his full five years in office, but he was in full command of his administration during most of the period. He left the presidency a great deal more popular than he had been when he entered it.

Kubitschek and General Lott

To a very large degree Kubitschek owed his chance to become president to General Lott. The general had made it possible for him to become chief executive, and in the beginning he seemed to have had the power to remove him from the presidency.

During the first year or so of his administration, President Kubitschek had certain problems with his minister of war. One of the most serious of these involved a group, the Clube de Novembro, of which Lott was the honorary president. This was a group organized and controlled by the communists, although Lott did not realize this, because it went out of its way to laud him. President Kubitschek decided that the group would have to be legally dissolved in conformity with the law passed a decade before outlawing the Communist party. He told General Lott of his intention. Lott did not like it and subsequently sent the president a letter of

306

resignation as minister of war. Juscelino called in a mutual friend, a civilian, told him what had happened, and asked him to see Lott, explain the situation surrounding the Clube de Novembro to him, and tell the general that if he insisted on his resignation, Kubitschek would accept it, but that he would prefer that the minister withdraw his letter. The friend succeeded in dissuading Lott.[1]

Although at the beginning Kubitschek was exceedingly dependent upon Lott, he was less so the longer he remained in office. By the end of his first year in office, Juscelino felt himself to be fully in control of the armed forces, and sure that he could deal with any challenge coming from that quarter.[2] Skidmore has noted that "throughout his term, President Kubitschek courted the military with a variety of wiles. He was attentive to their demands for pay increases and modern equipment. In December 1956 he purchased for the Navy's amusement a cast-off British aircraft carrier which was refitted at considerable expense. The Navy, which, along with the Air Force, harbored more conservative political views than the Army, was delighted to receive the new ship." Skidmore added that "throughout his term, until Lott's resignation to run for President himself, Kubitschek was aided in his efforts to maintain support within the armed forces by his strong-minded 'pro-legality' war minister."[3]

Several times the president had occasion to test his control over the military. One of these was when a magazine allied with Carlos Lacerda launched a strong attack on the leadership of the army, and particularly on General Odylio Denys. Immediately a delegation of twenty military men approached Kubitschek and insisted that the publication be closed. Kubitschek refused their demand, and told General Lott that he would be held responsible if anything happened to the periodical. When the chief of police, an Army general, took it upon himself on his own initiative to suspend publication of the journal in question, the President immediately dismissed him, replacing him with another general. Kubitschek insisted to me that this was the last time he had to deal with that kind of challenge.[4]

Interservice rivalries within the military may well have strengthened Juscelino's hand in dealing with them. It was reported that Kubitschek told one of his military advisers that the competition between the Air Force and the Navy had helped him because it reduced the time which their leaders had to conspire against him.[5] For his part, General Lott loyally supported Kubitschek throughout Juscelino's administration. He remained minister of war throughout most of the period, resigning only in time to become a candidate in the 1960 election.

Maria Victoria de Mesquita Benevides has emphasized the importance of the continued presence of General Lott in the Ministry of War throughout most of the Kubitschek administration. She noted that "the firmness and stability of General Lott in command of the Ministry of War must be underscored because of the intense ministerial change during that period and the violent attacks of the opposition on his person and his methods."[6] She added that

> the continuance of General Lott in the Ministry of War proved to be highly functional: the unity of the Army, the leading branch, around the sentiment of discipline and military unity exemplified by the General was a fundamental factor in maintenance of order and the relative political stability of the period, in spite of absence of unity among the three arms. This sentiment of military discipline and unity is reinforced by the same permanence of General Lott in the Ministry, since this continuity, that *unity of leadership* is an indispensable condition for the stability of the period.[7]

It is also certainly true that the dynamism, record of achievement, and optimistic view which Kubitschek had of the future of Brazil won over numbers of military officers who might otherwise have been skeptical towards him. They strongly approved of his efforts to strengthen the industrial base of the Brazilian economy. They shared his vision of Brazil as the most important of the Latin American countries, and as a nation which was soon to be one of the world's great powers.

Furthermore, Juscelino integrated into civilian positions in his development program a large number of officers. They sat on the National Development Council, SUDENE, the National Bank of Economic Development, and the National Petroleum Council, and held posts as president of such institutions as the National Steel Company, the National Motor Factory, the National Petroleum Fleet and served as members of many of the Working Groups set up to

308

organize development of specific parts of the Plan of Goals. Officers of all three forces were undoubtedly deeply involved in the Kubitschek government's economic development program. Juscelino deliberately sought to meet many of the "military" needs of the armed forces. Benevides has noted that "it is clear that Kubitschek 'courted' the military during the whole period, taking care of their requests: equipment in general, salary increases, promotions (even of enemies), training of personnel, etc. . . ."[8]

The Politics of the Pro Government Forces

Kubitschek had risen to national prominence as a member of the famous PSD de Minas. The leadership of the Partido Social Democratico of the state of Minas Gerais had the well-earned reputation of being one of the most capable and crafty group of politicians in Brazil. They had strongly supported one of their own, Kubitschek, in the 1955 presidential race, and they continued to be his closest political associates during his tenure in the presidency. Members of the PSD de Minas held important posts during the Kubitschek administration. It was Israel Pinheiro, son of the former governor of Minas Gerais, and himself an important member of the state political machine, whom Juscelino had entrusted with the presidency of NOVACAP, with the task of building Brasilia in four short years. Jose Maria Alkmin, another member of the PSD de Minas and a boyhood friend of Juscelino, was both minister of finance and leader of the government forces in Congress. Lucas Lopes succeeded Alkmin as minister of finance.

Apart from his particularly close associates in the Partido Social Democratico in his native state, Kubitschek made ample use of the well-organized machine which the PSD had throughout most of Brazil. Patronage was a very important part of the bonds which held the party together. The president had many jobs at his disposal, which provided both power and a chance to prosper economically. Kubitschek was enough of a machine politician to know how to use this patronage in order to strengthen the loyalty of his own followers. Nor did he have any particular prejudices against doing so.

Lawrence Graham, student of the Brazilian civil service, emphasized the significance of Kubitschek's use of patronage in the following passage:

The one available unifying factor able to bring these diverse interests and groups together was the use of public office to provide jobs and favors as rewards to those assisting in amassing the necessary votes and resources required for election. After election the same technique was necessary to pass legislation. It was a highly pragmatic system and it functioned most effectively during the government of Juscelino Kubitschek, for even more than Vargas he understood how and why the system functioned and in most cases was able to obtain a majority in the congress to pass the bills he favored. A product of the existing party system, he was a political leader who understood the bargaining aspects of politics in the sense that neither Quadros nor Goulart seemed to grasp.[9]

Graham, in elaborating on Kubitschek's political techniques, noted that "the course of Brazilian political development has been hindered by a failure to develop two crucial mechanisms: a built-in structure capable of dealing with reform and a style of politics in which bargaining and compromise became possible." He added that "for all the imperfections of the Kubitschek government, it still stands as the government which made the greatest progress in developing these mechanisms."[10] One feature of this aspect of Juscelino's style of government was his preference for conciliation over confrontation, and his refusal to hold a grudge or nurse a grievance. This was demonstrated even in his relationship with João Cafe Filho of whom he certainly had no reason to be fond. At one point, he offered to guarantee the ex-president's election to the Senate by assuring that the government parties would not oppose his candidacy in his native state. However, Cafe Filho turned down the offer.[11]

Some observers of recent Brazilian history and politics have pictured Kubitschek's governing technique in rather less positive terms. Vladimir Reisky de Dubnic has described it as a process of trying "to escape the contradiction of an outdated paternalism by sharing power with unscrupulous elites on the one hand, and conforming to the surviving popular image of the omnipotent president on the other. He concentrated on building a monument to himself, the new capital of Brasilia."[12]

310

The opposition frequently complained about the use of patronage. During the first months of the administration, when my wife and I were in Brazil, we heard many wry comments by opposition figures about the *tiburões grandes* and the *tiburões pequenos* (little sharks). It was alleged that the former (big sharks), were the members of the Partido Social Democratico who received the potentially most lucrative positions. The latter were identified as the members of the PSD's partner, the Partido Trabalhista Brazileiro, who received less desirable positions, principally in the social security system.

The PSD was at the time still the country's largest party. It had strength in virtually every state except São Paulo, where none of the largest parties (PSD, UDN, PTB) had very big followings. Unlike most of the country's other significant parties, it had relatively little factionalism. Lacking any particular ideology about which few of its leaders worried, those who formed the PSD machine in the states and on the national level, were interested primarily in obtaining and holding public office. With one of their own in power in the federal capital, they were disinclined to quarrel over much with the man who could spread a considerable number of the rewards of power among loyal party members. There is no question but that the well-organized PSD was the backbone of the civilian support of the Kubitschek administration.

A much smaller party which was closely associated with the Kubitschek regime, and gave the president very little if any trouble, was the Partido Republicano. It was a party which had its principal strength in Minas Gerais and had been associated with Juscelino's administration as governor. It had members of his cabinet throughout his presidency and formed part of the government majority in Congress.

Troubles with the PTB

Relations between the president and the second major party in his coalition, the Partido Trabalhista Brasileiro, were a great deal more difficult than those with his own party or the PR. For one thing, the PTB had within it several warring factions, with all of whom Kubitschek had to try to maintain contact. For another, the most notable figure in the PTB, Kubitschek's vice president, João Goulart, was a person who was distrusted by much of the military

311

leadership, even by some who were generally supporters of the administration, and so he constituted something of an embarrassment to the president.

Goulart was widely regarded as the political successor of Vargas. As such, he had emerged as the principal national leader of the PTB. He and his party had a strong base among members of the organized labor movement. However, it is interesting to note that at the first post-Vargas congress of the Partido Trabalhista Brasileiro, virtually all old-line trade unionists—many dating from the Estado Novo period—who had made up the bulk of the leadership of the party, were removed, and were replaced by middle-class politicians with little or no roots in the labor movement.[13]

Since the Kubitschek-Goulart ticket had been created in 1955 as the means for unifying most of the forces which had supported President Vargas, the PTB was definitely a partner in that coalition. However, it was the junior partner. It was still only the third largest party in the country, and although its appetite for patronage was large, its legitimate claims were somewhat more modest.

Relations between Kubitschek and Goulart were described by the former as "formally friendly."[14] However, Jango had little understanding of Juscelino's vision for Brazil and what it was that the president was trying to achieve. Even many years later, he described Kubitschek to me as being merely a conservative politician without any ideology, who had tried to convert "developmentalism" into an ideology but had failed in his effort to do so.[15] Goulart and his faction of the PTB were assigned the social security system as their particular province. At that time, the Brazilian social security system was unbelievably complex, consisting of thirty or more separate institutes and funds, covering workers in different parts of the economy. Each had its own personnel, the top echelons of which usually consisted of political appointees. There were thus many jobs available to Goulart, but they were neither as numerous nor as prestigious as those reserved for the PSD.

However, Goulart was not the only leader of prominence in the Partido Trabalhista. There were elements which controlled the party in some states which were very strongly opposed to Goulart and his leadership of the national PTB. Kubitschek had to keep their claims in mind, and he was particularly willing to do so, since he had no special desire to make João Goulart more powerful than was absolutely necessary.

One way of limiting Goulart's influence was to keep the ministry of labor outside his personal control, although conforming to the original electoral agreement whereby it would be headed by a member of the PTB. Juscelino's first choice for minister of labor, as we have noted, was Parsifal Barroso from the Northeastern state of Ceará, who continued in the position until the congressional and gubernatorial elections of 1958 when, at the president's request, he resigned to run for governor of his state. He was successful, defeating the UDN nominee, Juarez Távora's nephew, Virgilio Távora.[16] Even after Barroso's resignation, the Ministry of Labor continued to remain in the hands of a PTB leader not closely allied with João Goulart.

The Kubitschek Regime and Organized Labor

As a result of not controlling the Ministry of Labor, Goulart was not in a position to impose people of his choosing on those unions which might resist his influence. As a matter of fact, during the Kubitschek regime the Ministry of Labor intervened—that is, removed the elected leadership—in virtually no unions. The labor movement probably had less government interference and had more freedom to control its own affairs during those five years than it had had since the advent of the Estado Novo in 1937, or than it ever had after Juscelino went out of office until the end of the military dictatorship in 1985.

Among the other changes in government handling of the labor movement brought about by the Kubitschek administration was removal of the requirement that all elected union officials had to obtain police approval before being allowed to take office.[17] Partly as a result of this, and partly because of the general strengthening of the Nationalist elements during the Kubitschek administration, more radical union leaders began to appear. Some of these were communists, including such on old-time veteran communist as Roberto Morena, who became an important figure in the National Confederation of Industrial Workers, and others who gained control of the Bank Workers Federation, and some were Nationalist PTB elements, more or less closely associated with João Goulart.

Even political opponents of Kubitschek recognized the relaxation of government controls over the unions by his administration. For example, Bayard Boiteux, a socialist and

313

president of the Teachers Union of the Federal District, told me in 1959 that during the twenty years that he had been active in the labor movement the unions had never been so free as they were under Juscelino.[18] The freedom of the labor movement under the Kubitschek regime was due to his generally democratic policies, rather than from any enchantment with the labor movement and its leaders. Juscelino said to Edward Riedinger that although telling the union leaders that he agreed with them on several labor issues, "I warned them that I would never have anything to do with them politically. I was afraid of their communist leadership, which would have been a deadly embrace." He added that he had "never met a good labor union leader. They are all either submissive to the president or threatening to him."[19]

Although politically serious labor disputes were relatively few during the Kubitschek administration, there was a conflict of considerable significance shortly after the 1960 presidential election. The railroad, port, and maritime workers went out on strike in protest against the failure of Congress a few months earlier to raise their wages when it had raised the salaries of the military. These three categories of workers were government employees, paid according to civil service scales. This strike provoked the resignation of Minister of Labor Batista Ramos, and his successor Alirio de Salles Coelho threatened strong reprisals against the strikers. However, at the insistence of the three military ministers, Juscelino came to Rio from Brasilia and at the cabinet meeting decided to ask Congress for the declaration of a state of siege, which would have permitted him to enact the wage changes by decree. However, instead of granting this, Congress quickly passed a law raising the wages and salaries of civil servants.[20]

As was true in other fields, Kubitschek brought few major reforms in the labor sector, other than relaxing government controls. He refused requests of various workers groups to allow formation of an overall national labor confederation comparable to the AFL-CIO in the United States. He also resisted their suggestions that a system of automatic wage increases to keep up with inflation be established instead of the existing system of periodic but episodic augmentation of the minimum wage which had existed since 1942.

There were, however, two changes in the labor area which the Kubitschek government did undertake. The first was to separate the Ministry of Labor, Industry and Commerce which had been

314

established by Vargas in 1930, into two separate ministries, those of Labor and Social Security, and of Industry and Commerce.[21] The second was the Social Security Law of 1960, which reorganized the management of the country's multiple social security institutes and funds, providing that each of them henceforward would be governed by a tri-partite board, consisting of representatives of the appropriate workers unions, employer groups, and the government. This change, although not having any impact during the remaining few months of Juscelino's government, was of great importance subsequently, particularly during the administration of João Goulart. It gave key trade union leaders control over a substantial degree of patronage in the social security institutions which greatly increased their power.[22]

Ronald Chilcote has summed up the trends within the labor movement during the Kubitschek administration:

> Control over the trade unions relaxed somewhat; thus the administration adopted a cautious policy of generous wage settlements, and Goulart restored his links with the Labor Ministry. Meanwhile nationalist issues, like the defense of Petrobras, unified the worker with student, intellectual, and other social elements. Likewise, such issues as the right to strike and increased social welfare encouraged radicalization of the labor masses. Toward the end of Kubitschek's term a new leadership, in general anti-Communist and less concerned with nationalism than with wage demands, challenged the hegemony of the PCB and communist labor leaders.[23]

The various labor tendencies juggled for position in the Third National Trade Union Congress in 1960. The new leadership was confronted, on the one hand, with a communist-nationalist alliance; and on the other with the old-line *pelegos*, that is, leaders dating from the Estado Novo who had maintained their positions largely through working closely with the Ministry of Labor.[24]

During the Kubitschek administration there arose two leaders within the PTB who sought to revolt against Goulart's control of the national party. Seemingly, Kubitschek did little to encourage either of these efforts, but also did nothing in particular to discourage them. The first attempt was led by Senator Alberto Pasqualini of the state of Rio Grande do Sul. Both men sought to give the PTB a more ideological orientation, using as their model the British Labor party. Fernando Ferrari finally broke away from the PTB, setting up his own Movimiento de Renovacão Trabalhista. Another new figure to arise in the PTB during Kubitschek period did not challenge Goulart, but sometimes embarrassed him. This was Jango's brother-in-law, Leonel Brizola. He was elected governor of the state of Rio Grande do Sul in 1958, was strongly aligned with the extreme Nationalists, and became a force of some importance during this period. On several occasions, he complicated relations between President Kubitschek and the vice president.

The Communists During the Kubitschek Regime

The illegal Communist party had supported Kubitschek in the 1955 election. It might well have claimed that its backing gave Juscelino his margin of victory. Juscelino never formally reestablished the legality of the Communist party. However, the generally democratic atmosphere of the Kubitschek period allowed the reemergence of the party on a semi-legal basis. Its leaders were allowed to come out into the open for the first time in a dozen years, and to function more or less normally, except that they could not run candidates under the party's own name.

When the Communist party had been outlawed in 1947 serious charges had been brought in the courts against its principal leaders. Thus, to avoid certain incarceration should they allow themselves to be brought to trial, Luis Carlos Prestes, the party's secretary general, and other major figures in the party had remained in hiding for the following decade. It was not until 1957 that first Prestes and subsequently other leading elements in the party came out in the open, and presented themselves before the courts to face the charges made against them. Since Kubitschek had no desire to make martyrs of the communist leaders, the result of these appearances was that they were declared innocent and were allowed to walk away free. From then on, they conducted their activities largely in the open.[25]

Moisés Vinhas has described this process of emergence of the communists into legality, in virtually every sense except formal registration of the party with the Electoral Tribunal and participation in elections under their own name. He has said that

> the Communists came out of clandestinity and passed to open and de facto legal political activity. Even in 1958 they began a theoretical review *Estudos Sociais*, edited by Astrojildo Pereira, and a weekly *Novos Rumos*, publications that fulfilled an important role in the process of renovation. Their organization came into the light of day, from Luis Carlos Prestes and the Central Committee to state, municipal and even district committees, which were installed in their own offices. Plenary meetings of the Central Committee and of many state committees met in their own headquarters. At the same time, the Communists succeeded in establishing the most diverse social and party alliances for the elections of 1958, in which they participated under the names of the PTB and other parties.[26]

However, in spite of the tolerance of the Kubitschek government for their return to de facto legal status, the communists were nonetheless very critical of the Kubitschek regime. Although they did not launch any major campaigns against Juscelino, they did ally themselves with the nationalist critics of the administration. They were particularly opposed to the major role in the industrialization process which was being taken by foreign enterprises. However, Tad Szulc has noted that at the time of Kubitschek's quarrel with the International Monetary Fund, "Luis Carlos Prestes stood next to him during a round of speeches in the gardens of the Presidential Palace in Rio de Janeiro."[27]

The Nationalist Critics of Kubitschek

Some of the severest critics of the Kubitschek administration were the so-called Nationalists. They were found particularly in the ranks of the PTB, but also included some elements from the Socialist and Christian Democratic parties, the small splinter groups of the PTB, and even a few members of the PSD. They formed a bloc in Congress, the Frente Parlamentar Nacionalista, which energetically criticized many of the policies of the Kubitschek regime, and made suggestions and introduced bills of their own. The constant criticism of the Nationalist group was a significant aspect of the politics of the period.

The Nationalists were particularly critical of the willingness of Kubitschek to allow foreign enterprises to come into the country to establish new industries. They took special exception to Instruction 113 of the Superintendency of Money and Credit, originally enacted in the Café Filho government but much used by the Kubitschek regime. It permitted foreign enterprises which brought in new machinery and equipment to do so without placing on deposit beforehand the foreign currency necessary to pay for the imported machinery. The Nationalists argued that this constituted a special advantage of foreign firms over their Brazilian competitors who had to make such a deposit.

One of the leading Nationalist spokesmen both in and out of Congress was Sergio Magalhães, a PTB deputy. In a book published during the last year of the Kubitschek administration, Magalhães set forth in schematic form his principal criticism of the way in which the Kubitschek government's development effort was being conducted. His statement reflects pretty faithfully the line which was being taken by the other left-wing Nationalist critics of Juscelino. He wrote as follows:

1. The process of industrialization under a regime of privileges for foreign investments aggravates the dependence of the country on foreign capital.
2. The continuation of the process of economic denationalization will increase the dependency of our country with relation to the great foreign powers, particularly the United States.
3. The increase of the economic development of the country in the face of foreign capital will bring about the exaggerated growth of the process of differentiation of social classes in our country; it will signify, notably, an absence of reinforcement and subsequent weakening of the Brazilian industrial bourgeoisie. It is no secret that even now, in the industrialists' associations there exists a dominant influence of the representatives of foreign companies, bringing about the

318

disappearance of a climate of frank discussion of ways to liberate national investments from the pressure of the foreign sector.

4. The increase of colonial dependence will bring about in consequence the perpetuation of the phenomena related to the instability of power—the instability of the representative regime, the degeneration of the political parties, the deformation of the class organizations, etc.

Within this framework it is our duty, as spokesmen for the nationalist sectors, to discover ways of avoiding the process of denationalization and restructuring increasingly the sphere of influence of the patrons of the foreign cause.[28]

It is interesting to note that in retrospect, half a decade after Kubitschek had left office, Magalhães told me that he was sorry that he had so strongly attacked Juscelino's policies. He commented that he now recognized that the very significant advances in industrialization made by the Kubitschek administration had strengthened Brazil, and concluded that the historical record of that administration was a good one.[29]

Paulo Singer has insisted that "the nationalist and leftist currents never conducted closed opposition against the government of Juscelino, in part because they saw it as a lesser evil to the Udenista opposition, in part because the financial policy practiced by the government created an inflationary euphoria, in the process of which the economic difficulties of the petty bourgeoisie were attenuated to some degree."[30]

However, the Frente Parlamentar Nacionalista and elements associated with it sometimes caused embarrassment to the Kubitschek government, and even constituted a certain danger for it. Thus, in mid 1959, when Juscelino reorganized his cabinet, he met opposition from the Frente. About this, Kubitschek wrote: "The Frente Parlamentar Nacionalista showed itself opposed to the choices of Sabastião Paes de Almeida for the Ministry of Finance, and Horacio Lafer for the portfolio of Foreign Affairs. The frentistas thought that both were linked—not politically, but by commercial interests, since they were industrialists in São Paulo—to the political future of Jânio Quadros."[31] However, they were not able in Congress to interfere with Kubitschek's appointments.

Juscelino saw the activities of Governor Leonel Brizola of Rio Grande do Sul, the brother-in-law of Vice President Goulart, and an ally of the Frente, as much more dangerous than those of the Frente itself. He not only "expounded the nationalist thesis with his habitual vehemence, and then went on to create disagreeable political issues," but "there came to me information that he had undertaken to conspire against the established order, attempting to develop with General Osvino Alves, commander of the III Army, a coup d'etat."[32]

What Brizola had in mind, according to Juscelino, was a movement worked out with the ad hoc nationalist labor group, the so-called Pact of Inter Union Unity, in September 1959, when many collective bargaining contracts would be up for renewal.

> At that time, exorbitant demands would be made on the government. Numerous and successive strikes would be provoked. And, when the social tension reached a peak, some troops, worked upon by the Rio Grande governor, would come into the streets presenting an alternative: alignment of the government with the Trabalhista demands, with the retirement of the candidacy of General Lott, and presentation of a 'popular and nationalist' candidate, in favor of whose victory at the polls all government organs would be used. It would be a pre-determined 'election,' with a candidate imposed on the country . . . otherwise, 'trade union demonstrations' would erupt in the streets, convulsing Brazil.

Kubitschek heard of these plans when Vice President Goulart, head of Brizola's party, the PTB, was out of the country. He therefore waited until Jango had returned before acting. When he consulted with the vice president on the matter, and Goulart was evasive, reticent, amd uncommunicative, Juscelino called a meeting of the military ministers, the commander of the First Army (headquartered in Rio), the heads of the security services, and the chiefs of the civil and military households of the president. After the meeting, a communique was issued saying that the meeting had been held "to examine the movement organized and oriented by known agitators, in order to create conditions which would menace order and the peace of the Brazilian people, through provoking illegal strikes, and at the same time, inspired by marginal groups, planning a general strike."[33]

This communique provoked a hornet's nest in Congress and the press. Opposition members demanded to know who the known agitators were, while the press publicly identified them as being Vice President Goulart and Governor Brizola. This frightened João Goulart, who immediately sought out the president

> to explain that he had nothing to do with what the Pact of Interunion Unity was planning. He indicated the support of the PTB for the Lott candidacy and asked me finally, to issue another communique, exempting him from those accusations, and that in exchange, he would make vehement declarations with respect to legality and the preservation of the institutions. João Goulart fulfilled what he had promised.[34]

The ISEB

The principal intellectual center of the Nationalist opponents of Kubitschek came to be the Instituto Superior de Estudos Brasileiros (ISEB). Established in 1955, before Juscelino came to power, ISEB consisted of a group of economists, sociologists, political scientists, and other scholars who had the avowed objective of trying to work out some kind of developmentalist ideology. Kubitschek strongly encouraged them. The ISEB undertook translation and publication of a number of works by various foreign scholars in the economic development field. It also arranged seminars and other meetings on a wide range of Brazilian economic and social development problems, and published various books and pamphlets by Brazilian sociologists and economists on aspects of the nation's economic and social problems. During the Kubitschek administration, the ISEB did not by any means come up with any definitive statement of a developmentalist ideology. In fact, it became increasingly critical of the administration. In 1958-1959, a serious split developed within the Instituto, as a result of which Helio Jaguaribe, Candido Mendes, and others closely associated with the Kubitschek regime, resigned from the organization. Control was then taken by left Nationalist elements who used it as a platform to attack various of the policies of Juscelino's government.[35]

The Problem of Mutinous Elements in the Military

Although the support of General Lott assured the Kubitschek administration of the backing of most of the country's armed forces, there were military elements which were more or less violently opposed to the regime. These were found particularly in the Navy and the Air Force. On two occasions during the Kubitschek period, Air Force opponents mutinied unsuccessfully.

The first and most serious of these insurrections, which took place in February 1956, only a few weeks after Kubitschek's inauguration, was led by Major Haroldo Coimbra Veloso of the Air Force. He had for several years been in charge of opening up military airfields in the deep interior of the Amazon region, and had built up a corps of supporters among Air Force personnel stationed on those bases, and civilians associated with them and living near them. He took advantage of this following to try to launch an uprising in the interior, which he hoped would provoke a wider movement among the Armed Forces. He first seized the base of Jacareacanga. When he heard that the Amazon port city of Santarem was only very lightly garrisoned, he seized that town, holding it for several days. However, he received very little support from other branches of the Armed Forces. Veloso himself was finally captured; several of his supporters sought refuge in Bolivia.[36]

The Jacareacanga revolt lasted in all about two weeks. Coming so early in his administration, it made even the naturally optimistic Juscelino wonder whether his government would be able to survive the mutiny. He faced widespread insubordination among the ranking officers of the Air Force, and many years later Kubitschek told Edward Riedinger that during the period the revolt was in progress he ordered the arrest of several hundred officers. Kubitschek told Riedinger that "I personally had to call sergeants, waking them up, to activate retaliation. The Air Force would not supply planes and so I ordered those of Panair to carry parachute troops from the Army to the region. To bomb the airfield of Jacareacanga I finally found a loyal officer."

For two weeks during this crisis, Kubitschek remained in the Catete Palace, "sleeping in chairs, not returning to Laranjeiras." Juscelino said that he "could depend on none of [his] military ministers, least of all the Air Force. [He] kept them with [him] in the Catete at all times, to guarantee their not talking with contrary influences." He told Riedinger that he "told the ministers that [he] would broadcast from the Catete to the nation exactly what they were doing to [him]. [He] told them that [he] would leave the palace only with victory or death." Once the revolt was suppressed, Juscelino went to visit Jacareacanga, where it had been centered. Years later, he told Riedinger that "it was a place infested with mosquitos, snakes, and maddening remoteness. I think the situation made the rebels crazy."[37]

The second uprising took place in December 1959, and also involved principally officers of the Air Force. Its leader was Lt. Col. João Paulo Moreira Burnier, and among the conspirators was Veloso, by now pardoned by the president for his earlier revolt and promoted to Lieutenant Colonel. The plan of the rebels was to seize airplanes from the Galeão airport in Rio, bomb two of the presidential palaces in Rio in the hope of killing Kubitschek and Goulart, and then to proceed to the Amazonian airbase at Aragarças, where they would be joined by other Air Force rebels from bases at Belo Horizonte and Campo Grande (Mato Grosso). At the last moment, they abandoned the idea of bombing the presidential residences, thinking that they had an assurance from Admiral Silvio Heck that if they desisted, the Navy would support their revolt.

Three planes took off from Galeão, and another from Belo Horizonte, but the conspirators of Campo Grande backed out of the enterprise. Also, a Panair do Brasil civilian Constellation was hijacked on the way from Rio to Belem, and was also landed at Aragarças. However, from then on, the whole "revolt" became a fiasco. One of the first to hear about it was Carlos Lacerda, who the rebels undoubtedly thought would be sympathetic to their movement but was not, and he notified General Lott, who in turn informed President Kubitschek. By the time a hurried cabinet meeting was called, it was clear that the insurrection was very localized. Within seventy-two hours it was all over, the principal figures in it having taken refuge in Argentina and Bolivia.[38]

323

Kubitschek was surprisingly tolerant with these military rebels. Although they were court martialed and given prison sentences for their mutinous activities, most were pardoned by the president within a short while. This is demonstrated by the case of Veloso, who after being captured in early 1956, was free, back in uniform and promoted in time to participate in the second uprising in December 1959. Some of these officers were never willing to forgive Juscelino for being so lenient with them, the refusing to provide them with the martyrdom which they were seeking.

The Extremist Civilian Opposition

Most of the leaders of the civilian opposition, including the União Democrática Nacional, did not try to plot or conspire against the Kubitschek regime. However, it was widely rumored that some of these politicians did participate in subversive activities against the administration. Carlos Lacerda was one of those most frequently rumored to be conspiring. He had been a member of the Communist Youth in the 1930s. However, he became disillusioned with the communists as a result of the great Stalin purges and of the attempts of the Soviet Union and the Comintern to seize control of the Spanish Republic during the Civil War.[39] Thereafter, he retired from politics for some years. He emerged again early in 1945, when as a journalist he wrote articles which helped to break the censorship of the Estado Novo. Thereafter, he seemed to be motivated in his political activity by two passions: enmity towards the Communist party and opposition to Vargas and anyone who had been or was associated with him. His career of crusading journalism found principal expression in the newspaper *Tribuna da Imprensa*, which he founded soon after the end of the Estado Novo.

Lacerda was a founding member of União Democrática Nacional and belonged to its most violently anti-Vargas wing. An unsuccessful attempt to assassinate him provoked the military movement in August 1954 which led to Getúlio's suicide. Fifteen months later, Lacerda was among those who boarded the cruiser *Tamandaré* in an unsuccessful effort to arouse military and civilian opposition in São Paulo to the coups of General Lott.

Lacerda was particularly vituperative in his opposition to Kubitschek. When Juscelino was only a candidate for president, Lacerda drew up a several hundred page dossier on him, full of outrageous accusations about his having millions of dollars in Swiss bank accounts, of having been a partner in companies which did business with the State of Minas while he was governor and of his having gotten graft in many other ways. Lacerda sent copies of this to every military garrison in Brazil.[40] This was probably one of the sources of long-standing opposition to Kubitschek by many military officers.

As early as 1954 Lacerda had established an organization known as the Clube da Linterna (Lantern Club), which in the early months of the Kubitschek administration was charged with subversion, and was finally dissolved by the government. The writer attended a meeting of this group in March 1956. It was held in the Brazilian Press Association. Many proposed programs were discussed: establishment of a legal department to give advice and help to workers; a program of recreation, particularly available to workers' children; a social welfare scheme, and an employment agency. The avowed purpose of establishing these programs was to win workers from their loyalty to the Partido Trabalhista Brasileiro and the tradition of Getúlio Vargas. Nothing in this gave any indication of subversive intent. Perhaps another project might be deemed as being more designed in that direction. It was announced at the meeting that the Clube was going to have a group of people who traveled on business regularly in the interior to carry messages and instructions from the Rio headquarters to branches which they hoped to set up all over Brazil.

Whether or not the Clube da Linterna had subversive purposes, I knew from personal experience that there were conspiracies against the Kubitschek regime, at least during its early months. Inadvertently, I was present at the founding meeting of such a conspiracy in the apartment of a friend, attended by several intellectuals of his acquaintance, as well as some military officers in mufti. Abut two weeks later, a professional man who was the principal figure in the group was arrested on charges of subversion. He was released soon afterwards, and so far as I know was never brought to trial. This particular conspiracy went no further.

Aside from whatever conspiratorial action he may have engaged in against Kubitschek, Lacerda used his journalism to attack Juscelino and his regime with special vehemence. For instance, on one occasion, a magazine owned by Lacerda appeared with a large picture of the president, with the legend stamped on his

325

forehead "Chefe de um Governo de ladrões" (Chief of a Government of Thieves). Juscelino's first reaction to this was to sue Lacerda's magazine for libel. However, when he consulted his chief legal adviser, this man told him that although it was all right for ministers to sue for something like this, it was not good for the president to do so. He said that the libel laws were so written as almost always to favor the newspapermen, and in all probability, the president would lose such a suit, which would leave him in the embarrassing position of having an assumption left that the charge made in Lacerda's magazine was true. The president decided to take no action.[41]

The Parliamentary Opposition

The bulk of the opposition to the Kubitschek regime was not found either among the conspirators in the Armed Forces or among those civilians who were trying to organize the overthrow of the administration by subversive means. It was made up of the anti-administration forces in congress and the parties which they represented throughout the nation. The pro government forces held a majority in Congress consisting of the Partido Social Democrático, Partido Trabalhista Brasileiro, Partido Republicano, and a number of other small parties which usually aligned themselves with the regime. However, the really substantial opposition was led by the União Democrático Nacional, the second largest party behind the PSD, which since 1944 had been most consistently opposed to the Vargas tradition. Aligned with the UDN on most issues were the Partido Liberador, and on many occasions the Partido Socialista Brasileiro and Partido Democrata Cristão.

In spite of the UDN's role as the core of the opposition, some elements in it were influenced by Juscelino's optimistic message. There appeared within the party the so-called "Bossa Nova" faction which had some influence particularly in the Northeastern and Amazonian states. Its supporters were attracted by Kubitschek's developmentalism and felt that development and reform ought to be part of the UDN program, so that the party could adequately confront the PSD and PTB coalition.[42] The opposition concentrated its attack on a number of issues. Inflation, which gained momentum particularly during the middle years of the Kubitschek period, was a frequent source of criticism. On several occasions

326

there were more or less serious riots provoked by this issue. Perhaps the effect of such criticism was reflected in the considerable efforts of the government to reduce the inflation during the last year and a half of the administration.

A major charge against the Kubitschek regime by the parliamentary opposition was that it was corrupt. The president and other leading administration members were charged with using their positions to build up substantial private fortunes. These charges centered particularly around construction of Brasilia and the administration of the foreign exchange control system by the Banco do Brasil. It was the impression of the writer during several visits to Brazil during the Kubitschek period that the charges of corruption were widely believed by the general public. In the case of those who had traditionally supported Vargas and now were behind Kubitschek, corruption was more or less accepted as a natural part of the political process, and regarded as rather an unimportant basis upon which to judge an administration. Charges of corruption continued to be levelled at Kubitschek after he left office. Following the military coup of 1964, anti-Kubitschek military men engaged in the most exhaustive search of his career, for the purpose of drawing up criminal charges against him. They were unable to come up with anything which would serve even as the basis for an indictment to be tried *in camera* by a court marital under a military dictatorship. This record would seem to speak for itself.

There were various other lines of attack on Kubitschek. It was alleged that he was pro-Communist. It was claimed that he was loading the Brazilian economy down with a burden of foreign debt which it could not possibly repay. The government was frequently accused of fiscal irresponsibility, a charge which found echo abroad, particularly in the United States and in the international lending agencies. Elements of the Left attacked Kubitschek for his unwillingness to undertake major social, economic, and political reforms.

Parliamentary Struggles Over Brasilia

The construction of Brasilia was a major source of conflict in the press and in Congress between the administration and its opponents. One of the most vigorous and consistent journalistic critics of the new capital was the columnist David Nasser. He "adopted the term that seemed most adequate for ridicule . . . To express the firmness and obstinacy of the President in pushing forward the task, he used a term which appeared to him to caricature and demean Juscelino. This term was brasilino."[43]

Many arguments were used against Brasilia. The opposition at first claimed that construction of the new capital was inopportune, should be undertaken sometime in the more or less distant future, but not in the late 1950s. It was frequently argued that it would in fact be impossible to finish building the city in time to transfer the capital there before the end of the Kubitschek term. The opposition also centered attack on the roads being built to Brasilia, and which were an integral part of Kubitschek's concept of the nature of the new capital. Carlos Lacerda was particularly violent in attacking the Belem-Brasilia highway, which he christened "the highway of the jaguars," and which he claimed was a tremendous waste of money which would never serve any economic purpose. The vituperativeness of the opposition's attacks on Brasilia was shown by a denunciation by Octavio Mangabeira, leader of the Opposition in the Chamber of Deputies. He said: "I see Brasilia, at this moment, only as the symbol of the regime of subversion—if this is in fact a regime—in which we live. . . ."[44]

However, as construction of Brasilia progressed, and Juscelino's promise that the capital would be officially transferred there seemed likely to be fulfilled, attention among opponents in Congress came to be centered particularly on the question of moving the capital to Brasilia on 21 April 1960. Two major attempts were made in Congress to frustrate this, attempts which came near to success because of the fragility of the parliamentary alliance between the PSD and the PTB. The first of these efforts came early in 1959. The UDN leaders decided to shift their attack from Brasilia itself to the way it was being constructed. For this purpose, they proposed that there be special Parliamentary Commission of Inquiry (CPI) into the finances and particularly the alleged corruption of NOVACAP. Kubitschek indicated the purpose of this maneuver:

> The procedure is well known: witnesses are called in succession, debate being prolonged indefinitely on details of no importance; account books are subpoenaed; and the presence of as many functionaries as conceived to be necessary is required. And, while this is occurring in Rio, all would be paralyzed in Brasilia—

328

the directors of NOVACAP absent; the treasurers without authorization to make payments; the contractors not knowing how to proceed with the jobs given to them.[45]

Kubitschek had no fear that such a CPI would be established, given the government's supposed majority in Congress. However, to his consternation he found out that the PTB was supporting the motion for a CPI on Brasilia. He immediately went into action, contacting the PTB leaders in Congress, and was told by them that this was a party decision, and he should contact Goulart. Upon reaching Goulart, Juscelino found that Jango seemed more or less determined to go ahead with the idea. However, when Kubitschek threatened an open break with the PTB if it continued in this policy—which would deprive it, and Goulart, of very much desired patronage—the real reason for the PTB's move was disclosed: Jango and his associates were unhappy about Kubitschek's inviting Santiago Dantas to be minister of agriculture. Although he was a leader of the PTB, Dantas was not an ally of Goulart. This problem was finally resolved when Dantas refused Juscelino's invitation to join the cabinet, as a consequence of which, with most PTB deputies not signing the petition for the CPI, it failed by one name to receive the number necessary to launch the investigation.[46]

The final effort by the opposition in Congress to block the establishment of Brasilia as the new capital came only a few days before that event was scheduled to take place. With organization of a new Federal district including Brasilia, the old Federal district, the city of Rio de Janeiro, would become the new state of Guanabara. However, two weeks before the date for transferring the capital, a necessary organic law providing for organization of the new state had not yet been passed, and without it, the capital could not constitutionally be transferred.

The opposition did its utmost to procrastinate on the issue. Again, it found an ally in the PTB, which threatened to have its deputies join those of the UDN in leaving the Chamber of Deputies, thus depriving the body of a quorum. Kubitschek wrote that, "although they would not confess it publicly, the PTB, in its majority, was always contrary to the transfer of the capital. They judged that the establishment of the government in a city still under construction would be a disaster for their group, since it would not

329

have, as it did in Rio, a large mass of workers it could mobilize to pressure the authorities and Congress."[47] The opposition used the excuse that the new law provided for appointment of an interventor to administer the new state until the first gubernatorial election. They preferred the phrase "provisional governor." Their real fear was that Kubitschek would appoint someone to that position who was hostile to them. However, when Juscelino gave them assurances on the point, they finally joined with other groups supporting the government, to push through the Guanabara law in time to make the transfer of the capital constitutionally possible.[48]

A last effort of some Udenistas to defy the reality of Brasilia turned out to be ridiculous rather than dangerous. This was what Kubitschek himself called "the rebellion of the 19 senators." He described the rebellion thus:

> In the inconveniences of moving, nineteen senators, who had gone to Brasilia, decided that everything was awful there and decided to return to Rio. In that, there was nothing extraordinary. The important thing, according to some newspapers, was that those senators were disposed to 'symbolically reopen the Senate in Rio, until Brasilia can guarantee the real functioning of Congress.' From that 'rebellion' of the senators—pontificated the oppositionist press—there arose the menace of a 'duality of the legislative power.'[49]

The rebellion, however, came to naught. A meeting of the national directorate of the UDN repudiated it, giving "a categorical manifestation of support for the transfer of the capital." The national president of the UDN, deputy Magalhães Pinto (of Minas Gerais), announced that "where the Government is, there must be the Opposition."

Democratic Atmosphere of the Kubitschek Regime

Sometimes Kubitschek replied to the attacks of his opponents, but more frequently he did not. However, he seldom tried to end or even to limit the right of the opposition to oppose. We have already noted his tolerance even with military elements which rose in arms against his regime, and the freedom of action which he gave organized labor, which under previous administrations had been subject to close government control. But it is worthwhile to emphasize once again that political freedom and strict observation of the rules of democracy were an essential and outstanding aspect of the politics during the Kubitschek administration. Leôncio Basbaum, one-time communist leader, who on most economic and social issues was very critical of Juscelino, summed up well the political atmosphere which characterized the regime. He noted that "even more, the governmental period of Juscelino was one really of absolute political freedom. For the first time in history there were no political prisoners in the country, and even the Communists moved about with complete liberty."[50]

Juscelino set the tone for the democratic nature of his regime at its inception. In his memoirs he noted that when he took office "the newspapers were under censorship. There were political prisoners. There existed in the country a climate of terror and apprehension." However, he took immediate steps to change this situation. As soon as the diplomatic reception at Itamaraty for his inauguration was over, he met with the minister of justice, and the heads of the military ministries, and told them that he would "not govern under a state of siege," adding that he was going to cancel immediately the state of siege established by President Neuru Ramos. Since such a move would have to be ratified by Congress, he told his ministers that he was in the meanwhile immediately ending all press censorship. An official communique was issued which said: "By order of the president of the Republic, as of today censorship of organs of news and publicity (newspapers, magazines, radio, and television stations) is suspended."[51]

Very rarely during his five years as president did Kubitschek modify this democratic position. Skidmore has noted two such cases very early in his administration, which are virtually the exceptions that prove the rule: in June 1958, he temporarily closed the Dock Workers Union of Rio de Janeiro and the National Emancipation League, both of which were dominated by the Communist party, and in August 1956 he had one issue of *Tribuna da Imprensa* seized.[52] In contrast to Vargas before him, and Jânio Quadros after him, Kubitschek as president found that he could work quite congenially within the confines of the democratic system. There is little evidence that he chafed under whatever restrictions it imposed upon him, and

331

he at no time sought to establish any kind of dictatorial regime instead of the constitutional democratic one.

On 3 October 1958, President Kubitschek presided over congressional elections for the whole 326 member Chamber of Deputies and half of the Senate of 63 members. As a result of that election, the PSD had 115 deputies and 22 senators; while its ally the PTB had 66 deputies and 18 senators, giving the government parties strong majorities in both houses. The UDN was still the second largest party in Congress with 70 deputies and 17 senators. The only other parties with substantial parliamentary representation were the Progressive Social party of Adhemar de Barros, with 26 deputies and one senator; the Republican party with 17 deputies and one senator, and the Brazilian Socialist party (PSB) with ten deputies. The rest of the Congress seats belonged to six other parties with one senator being independent.[53]

Juscelino the Missionary

Kubitschek's willingness and ability to work within the democratic system obviously did not mean that he remained quiescent, more or less satisfied with carrying on a routine administration within the boundaries marked by the institutions and his responsibility under them. He gave dynamic leadership to his government and to the country during his presidency. Nevertheless, he proved himself quite capable of getting most of the things which he wanted within the limits of the institutional framework he inherited, through a combination of persuasion, inspiration, and the skillful use of favors, patronage and other instrumentalities available to a democratic chief executive.

Aside from his determination to do so, one major reason that Kubitschek was able to accomplish so much while remaining within the democratic framework and the constitution was his ability to get out among the people and explain what he was doing. As he had been as mayor and governor, Juscelino was exceedingly peripatetic. He spent a great deal of his time travelling around the country inspecting the many projects which his administration was pushing forward. He made particularly frequent visits to Brasilia, but also constantly inspected road projects, hydroelectric installations, and new factories under construction. On these visits, he talked extensively with the people who were building the various undertakings, encouraging them, praising them, explaining to them how their particular enterprises fitted into his vast program for making "50 years progress in 5."

He used the beginning and completion of projects as a means of reaching a somewhat wider audience. There were always ceremonies on such occasions, with invited politicians, business leaders, clergymen, and other citizens, invited to come to see what it was that the government was undertaking and accomplishing. As time went on, more and more of these ceremonies were for the opening of a highway, the inauguration of a hydroelectric dam, the turning on of the power for some new industrial enterprise. With each of these occasions, the ability of the government to accomplish what it had promised became increasingly evident.

In addition to his missionary work, Juscelino frequently went on radio and television to explain his government's policies. His most striking use of the mass media was on 5 February 1960 when he held forth for three and a half hours on nationwide television. In this marathon appearance he went over in detail all of the original thirty goals which he had set for his administration, reporting on the progress achieved in each of them. Naturally, he also expounded expansively on the building of Brasilia. Likewise he dealt with other elements of his government's activities, giving particular attention to his foreign policy, and especially Operation Pan America.

Eduardo Matarazzo Suplicy has commented on the didactic nature of these radio and television talks of Juscelino. He wrote that

> from 1955 to 1960, when I was fourteen to nineteen, I began to become interested in politics and economics. I think that my first teacher of economic development, as well as that of many of my generation, was President Juscelino Kubitschek. His prolonged expositions of economic problems, about the Programa de Metas, and about Brazilian geography, on television were the best classes that I had had up to that time.[54]

In all of his travelling and his expositions on the mass media, Kubitschek was trying to do much more than just advertise himself and his administration. He was trying to change the way of thinking of the Brazilian people. In his memoirs he summed up his objective thus:

333

The activity which I carried out as chief of government had a revolutionary meaning, but oriented in the direction of making the country understand its own capacities and how to use them to achieve economic development. The action which I undertook had, then, motives of a psychological character. It was a titanic struggle against taboos—the taboo of the inability of the Brazilian to accomplish things, the taboo of the impossibility of establishing heavy industry, the taboo of the unattainability of any plan of national integration, the taboo of the unrecuperability of the devastated areas of the Northeast.[55]

Antônio José Chediak, who was one of Juscelino's speech writers during his presidency, suggested another reason why the president was able to change the outlook of the people of Brazil. He said that Kubitschek succeeded in raising the individual levels of aspiration of many Brazilians. He convinced many of his fellow citizens of their ability to improve their own situation, and aroused their ambitions.[56]

From my own observations of Brazil over more than a third of a century, it is clear that one of the most important and lasting achievements of Juscelino Kubitschek was exactly his success in overcoming these taboos of which he talked. Prior to the Kubitschek administration, the characteristic attitude of the average Brazilian towards his country was one of hopelessness, that for whatever reason the individual chose—the people's "laziness," there being "too much African" in the Brazilian racial mixture, the tropical climate of most of the country, among others—Brazil would never be other than "the land of tomorrow" in which "tomorrow" never arrived. By the end of the Kubitschek period, the typical Brazilian attitude had changed. This alteration survived all of the trials and tribulations through which the country passed in the decades after he left office at least until the 1980s. Brazilians in general became convinced that the future of their nation was one with unlimited horizons. They developed a pride in what their country had achieved—its burgeoning steel industry, its expanding agriculture, its thriving auto industry, its innovations in art and architecture, and above all, Brasilia—such as they had never had before. Brazil was destined, in the eyes of its citizens, to become a Great Power. The only question which remained was how long it would take.

This assessment of the change in Brazilian national psychology is borne out by the *New York Times* journalist who represented his paper in Brazil during the Kubitschek period. Tad Szulc subsequently wrote that

> perhaps a man more versed in economics and less endowed with imagination would not have even attempted to carry out this program that Dr. Kubitschek drew up for himself. But Brazil needed a visionary, and there was no stopping Dr. Kubitschek and his dreams. So, for five years, Brazil lived through an amazing and exciting era of contagious enthusiasm that propelled the nation from its erstwhile inferiority complex directly to a new sense of manifest destiny.[57]

The Jânio Quadros Phenomenon

By the end of the Kubitschek administration most elements of the opposition to the regime and to the tradition of Vargas had gathered around Quadros, the ex-governor of São Paulo. He was a unique figure in Brazilian politics of the 1950s. He had not become active politically until after the end of the Estado Novo. He had begun his career by running for city councilman on the Christian Democratic party ticket in São Paulo. In that post, he campaigned vigorously against the corruption which he alleged (correctly) characterized the administration of Mayor (and ex-governor) Adhemar de Barros. Quadros ran successfully for Mayor of the City of São Paulo in 1953, and only one year later was elected with a strong majority as governor of the state. In this race, he defeated ex-governor Adhemar de Barros.

Quadros was a picturesque character. Short, with a somewhat bushy mustache and prominent spectacles (he looked rather like Jerry Colona), he spoke with a high tone of voice which often rose to the point of shrillness. However, he was capable of arousing his audiences to a high point of enthusiasm. His major arguments, repeated over and over again, were a distrust of party politicians, condemnation of corruption in local, state, and federal politics, and calls for administrative efficiency. Perhaps Quadros' principal asset, however, was that he had no political antecedents dating back to the Estado Novo period. He was the only major national political figure of the 1950s who was not either very decisively a representative of the Vargas tradition or a strong opponent of that tradition. In his local and state campaigns, as a result, he had been able to draw backing from both groups.

His aversion to political parties and his fear of being tainted by corruption go far to explain a major handicap which Jânio suffered when he moved from being a state politicians to becoming a national one. This was his almost complete lack of acquaintance with the national political fraternity. He remained basically a provincial politician. He had few or no friends among the national political leaders, the members of Congress, the ministers, the major state governors, and certainly was intimate with none of them. Even when elected to Congress in 1958, he did not use this opportunity to cultivate such acquaintances and to become familiar with how political life at the national level functioned. He virtually never attended sessions of the Chamber of Deputies, and in fact was out of the country much of the time that he was nominally a member of the Chamber.[58]

The 1960 Presidential Campaign

In conformity with the democratic tenor of his administration, in 1960 Kubitschek presided over one of the freest elections ever held in Brazil. No more testimony is needed to this, perhaps, then the facts that the election was won by the candidate of the opposition, and no effort was made by anyone to challenge the results of the poll.

The presidential nominee of the pro-government forces seemed virtually a foregone conclusion. It was General Lott. He had figured as the probable successor of Kubitschek, insofar as the forces supporting Juscelino's government were concerned, from the very early days of the administration. I and my wife attended a meeting in one of the main plazas of Rio de Janeiro in February 1956, less than a month after the inauguration of Kubitschek, in which the virtues of the general were eulogized, and it was plainly evident that the intention of those who had organized the meeting was that he should be their next national standard bearer. However, there were those in the leadership of the Partido Social

Democrático who were not entirely happy with the idea of Lott's candidacy. Kubitschek noted that the PSD leadership in the states of Rio Grande do Sul, Mato Grosso, Para and Santa Catarina were among those opposed to the general's being the party candidate.

Some PSD leaders were even willing to entertain the notion that the PSD should support Quadros, perhaps on the thesis that since Jânio was unbeatable the old adage that "if you can't beat them, join them" applied. Carlos Castilho Cabral, organizer of the Movimento Popular Quadros, who was very interested in rallying PSD support for Jânio, indicated that a number of leading figures in that party were willing to meet with Jânio early in 1958, right after he had left the governorship, to discuss with him the question of his candidacy. These included Felinto Muller, vice president of the Senate, Ernani Amaral Peixoto, national chairman of the PSD, Victor Nunes Leal, Chief of the Civil Cabinet of President Kubitschek, and various others. However, as Cabral relates, Quadros failed to turn up at a luncheon which had been arranged between him and these and other PSD leaders, although he had agreed to be there.[59] Thereafter, there was little chance of Jânio receiving the backing of the pro-government forces. In any case, Kubitschek was never numbered among the PSD leaders willing to back Quadros.[60]

One tendency within the pro-government parties which developed early in the discussion of a government candidate for the 1960 election, was a movement for the reelection of Kubitschek himself, even though the constitution did not permit immediate reelection of a president. The argument was that the work he had undertaken was not yet completed, and he should have the time to carry it all to fruition.

The proposal that Juscelino should be reelected was first put forward early in 1959 by Tancredo Neves, a leader of the PSD in Minas Gerais. Subsequently, in March of the same year, Goulart, who apparently feared for his own position in the face of the probable weakness of Lott as a candidate, proposed to Kubitschek that he should seek reelection. By early 1960 the idea was "converted almost into a political movement." However, Juscelino himself would have nothing to do with this movement. As he explained the situation and his attitude towards it in his memoirs: "My reelection, according to the plans of the continuists, would be carried out through a constitutional reform. I repelled with vehemence the suggestion, since to accept it would be to give the lie

337

to all of the work of democratic consolidation, carried out by me with so many sacrifices."

Although Kubitschek made it clear to politicians who suggested his reelection that he wanted nothing of the kind, he sought for an opportunity to make this fact eminently clear to the people at large. This chance was given him in an interview with Carlos Castelo Branco, a political columnist for the Rio newspaper *O Jornal do Brasil*. In reply to a question by Branco, Juscelino replied:

> People opposed to Brasilia have sought to sow a lack of confidence in my objectives. They want, with this, to attack the president of the Republic and through suspicion to make difficult the transfer of the capital. I am going to leave here with the Constitution virgin. I have carried out all of its provisions, including those that were simple dead letters, such as the one referring to the movement of the seat of government to the Central Plateau.[61]

Kubitschek noted that this interview put an end to any further speculation concerning his reelection.

Another possible challenger to Lott in the ranks of the parties supporting the Kubitschek government might have been Goulart, vice president of the republic and chief of the Partido Trabalhista Brasileiro. A PTB national convention in May 1959 nominated him for the post.[62] However, had he continued as the presidential standard bearer of the PTB, this would virtually have assured the victory of the opposition. As it was, the position of the pro-government forces, faced with the candidacy of Quadros, was difficult enough. Furthermore, there still existed serious resistance in the military to any presidential candidacy of Goulart. As a result, Jango demurred, and settled for running once again as candidate for vice president. Goulart himself cited Kubitschek's support for Lott as a major factor in discouraging him from making his own bid for the presidency in 1960.[63]

Kubitschek, meanwhile, had sought to obtain another candidate from the PTB ranks to be Lott's running mate. Approaches were made in January 1960 to Osvaldo Aranha to accept the nomination for vice president on the ticket of the Partido

Social Democrático. Aranha, long-time close associate of Vargas, former minister of finance, minister of foreign affairs, and ambassador to Washington, was a member of the PTB and came from the state of Rio Grande do Sul, the same base as Goulart and Leonel Brizola. Finally, on 27 February, Aranha agreed to run with Lott as candidate for vice president. However, three hours after agreeing to this, he died of a heart attack. After that, there was no alternative to Goulart as the vice presidential candidate in the Lott-Goulart combination, no matter how reticent Goulart might be about having his name associated with that of the general, and no matter how much he sought to dissociate himself from the presumed head of his ticket.

The Candidacy of General Lott

From many points of view General Lott was not a very strong candidate. He was utterly lacking in charisma, which was a serious weakness indeed in someone who had to compete with Quadros. In addition, his ideas certainly were not in conformity with those of many of his supporters. During the campaign he made it clear that he would not curtail the entry of foreign capital, as the nationalists and the communists were demanding. At one point, he expressed serious reservations concerning the unlimited right of workers to strike, which certainly did not sit particularly well with his trade union and PTB supporters. He also expressed opposition to agrarian reform.[64] Finally, there was certain prejudice among many in the pro-government camp against the candidacy of a military man.

Juscelino himself was not enthusiastic about General Lott as the government candidate. His first choice for his successor was Juracy Magalhães, the president of the União Democrática Nacional. He thought that Juracy was a very good man, and would make a good president, in spite of his membership in UDN. He thought, too, that it would be good for the country to have Juracy, of the UDN, as president, since that party had failed to elect their candidates against Dutra, Vargas, and Juscelino himself, and that it would be a good idea to have some coalition of parties in office.[65] Osvaldo Orico has suggested another reason why Kubitschek favored Magalhães, when he said that "through the wear and tear which the UDN would suffer in five years of government . . . he would have preferred the successor to be an element of the party opposed to his."[66] Such wear and tear would help Juscelino in his own campaign for reelection in 1965.

Kubitschek at first sought to work out a grand alliance of the three major parties, the PSD, UDN, and PTB, to support Juracy, on the basis of a previously agreed-to governmental program. He was making progress with this when somehow Lacerda got wind of the maneuvers, went to São Paulo, and made a speech there in which he said that he would not back any candidate supported by Kubitschek, and declared for Quadros. This ruined the chance for the grand alliance in the 1960 campaign.[67]

Some political observers sensed Kubitschek's reservations about the Lott candidacy throughout the campaign. Leôncio Basbaum, for instance, noted that the president "failed to sign before the election what would have been a great political triumph— a new minimum wage law, so as *not to aid* the Lott candidacy. Keeping himself above the electoral struggle as 'chief magistrate,' he in fact aided Jânio" (Emphasis Basbaum's).[68]

This interpretation is more or less supported by Vladimir Reisky de Dubnic. He has commented that Kubitschek refused to campaign on behalf of the PSD candidate and instead "assumed a non-party position when the party needed him most." Dubnic adds that "his popularity was great and his active participation in the campaign would have kept many people in the government camp but his aloofness became a signal for many civil servants to desert the government."[69]

General Lott in any case became the candidate of the PSD-PTB coalition, and of the Communist party. The communists could not have been too happy about many of the pronouncements of the general, but they had long been committed to his candidacy. Luís Carlos Prestes, speaking to a group of port workers in Santos, expressed his party's backing for Lott in the following terms: "The Communist party of Brazil supports Marshal Teixeira Lott because he represents the thinking of our group and, in this way, the thinking of all Brazilian communists."[70] The communists' major contribution to the campaign, if that is what it was, was an attempt to picture the general's opponent as a reactionary or even a fascist.

Vladimir Reisky de Dubnic has commented that

> besides being clumsy, Lott's political campaign was also
> a series of contradictions. Standing for legality, he

340

predicted a revolution if his opponent should win; he was a conservative anti-communist who did not consider the communists an internal threat, but he allowed his campaign to be corroded by communist double-talk. He was for education yet insulted the intelligentsia; he proclaimed himself for social change but did not believe in agrarian reform. On rare occasions he professed to be the government candidate, but did not find it necessary to defend the record of the government's administration. He was concerned with the possibility of Soviet invasion of the Northeast of Brazil in case of war, but did not pay any attention to communist infiltration in the same area.[71]

The Quadros Candidacy

Meanwhile, Quadros had emerged as the nominee of a united opposition. This nomination did not necessarily represent great enthusiasm for him among all of the political leaders opposed to the Kubitschek regime. Rather, it reflected the widespread conviction that Quadros was going to win whether or not the opposition parties supported him, and their desire to support anyone who could defeat the forces which they associated with the memory of Vargas. The Partido Trabalhista Nacional, on the ticket of which Jânio had been elected to Congress in 1968, was the first party officially to put him forward as candidate for president. Several other smaller parties also endorsed him, and a UDN deputy, Cabral organized the Jânio Quadros Popular Movement (MPJQ).[72]

It was more difficult to win Quadros the endorsement of the União Democrática Nacional, the largest of the opposition parties. For one thing, the party had its own logical candidate in the person of Magalhães. A Tenente in the 1920s he had resigned from the Army after the Revolution of 1930, when Vargas named him interventor in the state of Baia. He was elected governor in 1934, and had been one of the only two governors to refuse to endorse Vargas' coup d'etat of 10 November 1937 which had established the Estado Novo dictatorship. Magalhães had been one of the organizers of the União Democrática Nacional. By 1960 he was governor of Baia again and was national president of the UDN. There had been a wide understanding that he would be the party's

341

1960 candidate when he was passed over in favor of Távora in the 1955 election.

In addition, there was wide skepticism about Quadros in the ranks of the UDN. Lacerda and various other leading party figures at first felt that Quadros was a demagogue and quite unreliable. They were particularly dubious of his disdain for political parties. Lacerda and others unwilling to work with Kubitschek in support of Magalhães were thus faced with a three-cornered race among Lott, Quadros, and Magalhães. Under these circumstances, it was clear to them that Jânio would win. The anti-Vargas element who had been fighting first against him and then against his shadow since 1945 would once again be deprived of the victory which they were convinced they deserved.

As a result, Lacerda, José Magalhães Pinto, and other younger UDN leaders switched to support of Quadros and began a decided campaign to get him the party's nomination. However, Magalhães was not willing to give up without a fight, and it was only after a major struggle that the pro-Jânio forces within the UDN finally in June 1959 won him the party's nomination.[73] Quadros had not been an easy candidate for anyone to support. At one point, he made demands on the managers of his campaign which still remain somewhat of a mystery, but when they were unwilling to concede what he wanted, he resigned his candidacy. It was only after much pleading, and the apparent concession of everything which Jânio wanted, that he again became the opposition's nominee.[74]

There still remained a problem concerning the opposition's candidate for vice president. After much negotiation and maneuvering, there remained two men running for that post while claiming to be Jânio's running mate. These were UDN leader in Minas Gerais Milton Campos, supported by the UDN, and Fernando Ferrari, nominated by the Christian Democrats. The latter was still technically a member of the PTB, but was leading a struggle against Goulart's control of that party. The many efforts to get Ferrari to retire his candidacy failed.

Quadros took no part in the efforts to get a single opposition vice presidential nominee. It has been suggested that he was in fact in favor of splitting the forces of the opposition in the contest for that post, hoping that this would result in the reelection of Goulart. Those who argued that way maintained that Jânio would feel more secure in the presidency knowing that he had a vice president whose

342

ascent to power would arouse violent objections among the military.[75] Quadros has denied this to the author.[76]

Vladimir Reisky de Dubnic has noted that

> the campaign of the opposition candidate, Quadros, was
> ostensibly not sharply critical of the government even
> though there was a basically different economic policy
> between him and Kubitschek. Despite Quadros' aggres-
> sive political temperament, he made it a point to appear
> to have fewer differences with the President than he
> had in fact, and he stressed their points in common.
> This was for a good reason; candidate Quadros did not
> want to antagonize President Kubitschek, whose
> neutrality during the elections was important because of
> his great influence over public opinion.[77]

Indeed, "the only candidate who mercilessly attacked the Kubitschek administration was the dark horse candidate, Adhemar de Barros."[78]

After an arduous campaign, Quadros, candidate of the opposition, won the 1960 election. He received 5,636,623 votes to 3,846,825 received by General Lott. At the same time, Goulart was chosen vice president once again, with 4,547,010 votes, against 4,237,719 for Campos, Goulart's nearest rival.[79] Thus on 31 January 1960 Kubitschek fulfilled his last duty as constitutional president, by turning his office over to his duly-elected successor, although he certainly could not have been happy about the man who took his place.

Chapter 16

EX-PRESIDENT JUSCELINO KUBITSCHEK

Kubitschek began running for reelection the moment he left the presidency late in January 1961. He made no secret about his ambition. I remember hearing Juscelino address an audience in New York City in March 1962 and smilingly admit that he hoped to return to the presidency in the 1965 election. He underscored his intention by describing his wide popularity with the rank and file Brazilian citizens and telling of the organization of "J.K. for '65" clubs throughout the country. He quipped that "you have your J.K. in the United States, and the Brazilians have their J.K. too." Juscelino toured the country extensively in the year or two following his exit from the presidency. By early 1962 he had visited ninety Brazilian cities and reported that he had received a tumultuous reception in all of them.[1]

Even before leaving the presidency, Kubitschek had decided upon the kind of program he would seek to carry out in his second administration. It would again be one which stressed economic development. However, feeling that his first period had resulted in Brazil having an integrated industrial economy, he believed that the country's next requirement was a large-scale effort to develop its agriculture. The industrialization efforts of his first administration had provided the nation with the capacity to produce the inputs—agricultural machinery, fertilizers, pesticides, and a variety of other products—necessary in a massive and sustained program to increase production and productivity of the rural sector of the economy. As an integral part of a program of agricultural development, Kubitschek foresaw the possibility of changes in land ownership and other reforms needed in some parts of the country.

One of his more interesting campaign suggestions was for establishment of a series of agrotowns, small towns in developing rural areas. He argued that it was impossible to expect farmers to settle in complete wilderness. The function of the agrotowns would be to provide schools, health care, technical assistance, credit, and other requirements for the farmers. He had particular plans for building such towns along the highways leading out of Brasilia.[2] However, in the best of circumstances, Kubitschek would have had to wait five years before he could return to the presidency since in the normal course of events, the next presidential election would have taken place in October 1965. In the meantime, the turbulent events of the years immediately following his presidency required considerable skill and maneuvering on the ex-chief executive's part. Soon after leaving the presidency, Kubitschek took an extended vacation of some four months in Europe. Upon his return, he received a boisterous welcome from large crowds in Rio de Janeiro, which led the leftist weekly *O Semanario* to comment that "Jânio is not popular; the popular one is Juscelino."[3]

Kubitschek returned to the political wars in a special election for senator from the state of Goias, where he ran as a candidate of the Partido Social Democrático. Juscelino was particularly popular in Goias. The new federal district in which Brasilia was constructed had been carved out of Goias and Kubitschek's efforts to develop the central part of the country, in which both Goias and Brasilia were located, were particularly appreciated in the state. Furthermore, he had the support in his campaign of the political machine of Pedro Ludovico, who had dominated Goias most of the time since the Revolution of 1930. Kubitschek was victorious in the election held on 4 June 1961.[4]

Quadros' Attacks on Juscelino

Meanwhile, Kubitschek had been subjected to very stringent criticism from the administration of his successor, President Quadros. In his inaugural address, in the presence of Kubitschek himself, Jânio had alleged that "the financial situation of Brazil is terrible. During the last five years, the circulating medium rose from 57 billions to 206 billions of cruzeiros . . . we owe abroad 3 billions and 802 millions of dollars, which means that just in this past period the debt increased 1 billion and 435 millions of dollars."[5]

Juscelino's successor had then gone on to a more general attack on the Kubitschek administration. He commented that

I see favoritism, nepotism strangling the nation and blocking the advancement of those with the most ability. In public life it is hard to distinguish the sacred from the profane. The state of dissolution to which we have come arises in part from the crisis of authority and of austerity of Power, compromised as its prestige is with official scandals carried out with greatest impunity. My government, be it noted, represents the end of this, definitive and final.[6]

The new chief executive began immediately to set up a series of more than thirty investigating commissions, most of which were headed by military men, to look into alleged corruption and other misdeeds of the Kubitschek administration. A few of the commissions had made their reports before the resignation of Quadros, and these reports made extensive charges of corruption and waste in various sectors of the government during the Kubitschek period. None directly accused Kubitschek of having been involved, although one commission did level charges against ex-vice president Goulart. With the resignation of President Quadros late in August 1961, this particular incident was closed, since Quadros' successor, Goulart, had little interest in going on with the investigations which Jânio had launched.

Kubitschek and the August 1961 Crisis

From his seat in the Senate, Juscelino served as virtual leader of the opposition during the last two months of the Quadros regime. Jânio suddenly resigned late in August 1961, giving rise to a major constitutional crisis, when the ministers of Army, Navy, and Air Force sought to prevent Vice President Goulart from assuming the presidency. Ex-president Kubitschek strongly opposed the maneuver of the military leaders. The day after Jânio's resignation, Juscelino issued a press release which was published in every state except Rio de Janeiro where it was held up by the censor. This statement stated: "To admit the possibility that the constitutional Vice President, Sr. João Goulart, cannot take office, is to deny my whole past, to destroy the results of a patient and constructive effort undertaken with great difficulty during five years of government on behalf of peace, concord, obedience to the law and rule of the

Constitution, on behalf of Brazilian civilization. All measures which take us outside the law would be extremely dangerous." He called upon the Armed Forces and all the parties to support the normal constitutional processes and allow Goulart to take office.[7]

Three days later in a speech in the Senate he said as follows:

> What brings me to this tribune is the imperious necessity of directing an appeal to the illustrious military chiefs that they not act contrary to national opinion, which asks, demands, insists on the ascension of the Vice President, Sr. João Goulart, successor, by the wish of the people in the last election, to the President who has resigned. It is not only the partisans and friends of Sr. João Goulart who insist on his taking office, but also his adversaries, including some who were until yesterday his most bitter opponents, who do not hesitate to express the opinion that the law must be obeyed, so that the nation's life can go on. It is not only the politicians, but all classes who demand the fulfillment of the law. And the law must be complied with, because it is not just a dead letter, but an expression of the life and will of our people.[8]

In the face of the threat of civil war, a compromise was suggested whereby a constitutional amendment would be passed that would strip the president of most of his powers, which would devolve upon a prime minister, whose tenure in office would depend upon the wishes of Congress; after the enactment of this, Goulart would be allowed to assume the presidency. In spite of one of the authors being José Maria Alkmin, Kubitschek's old and close friend, Juscelino opposed the proposed constitutional amendment—no doubt with his own hopes for a second administration in mind.

During the debate on the proposed amendment in the Senate, Kubitschek expressed his opposition in the following terms:

> It is not because we are all convinced that the new regime will be better for the country that it is being advocated, but rather to resolve a momentary crisis, only to aggravate this crisis tomorrow perhaps in an irreparable way. Only the people can decide on their own

347

destiny. To change the regime, to adopt new institutions, without consulting the people is an error. They are the only ones, in a democratic regime, capable of establishing the new norms of political life. The people have not been heard, the people do not know what has been decided under great pressure in the votes of the last 24 hours. The change is the fruit of a kind of pressure which is unacceptable in the regime which we have. This is the fundamental reason why I shall vote in the negative. I remain loyal to the people, to its mandates, its votes, which were given for presidentialism.[9]

Juscelino in the Goulart Period

In spite of Kubitschek's opposition, the constitutional amendment was passed, and Goulart took office. During the next fifteen months the president used all his influence to get the constitution changed once again to restore the presidential system of government, an effort with which Kubitschek undoubtedly sympathized. Goulart was successful in achieving this in a plebiscite in January 1963, in which 9,437,448 voted in favor of presidentialism and 2,073,582 for the maintenance of the parliamentary system.[10]

During all this period, Kubitschek had strongly supported the return to presidentialism. Upon coming back from a two-month trip abroad in November 1961, he issued a statement urging the reestablishment of full powers for the president, arguing that economic development would not be possible under the parliamentary system. A month later he denounced the parliamentary system as a three headed monster, involving a conflict of power among the president, prime minister and the other ministers, and called for an immediate plebiscite on the issue.[11]

Vladimir Reisky de Dubnic has explained the reasons for and results of Juscelino's opposition to the parliamentary system:

Kubitschek, one of the staunchest advocates of the return to the presidential system, believed that the Brazilian parliamentary system with its equal division of power among the President, the Prime Minster and the Congress, led only to a static, short-lived regime. Because Kubitschek planned to run again in the

348

presidential election of 1965, he feared that his chances to be re-elected would be slimmer if the parliamentary regime were to last, since the Congress would then elect the President. . . . Thus he was instrumental in influencing his party, the Partido Social Democrático (PSD), to support Goulart in his drive to terminate the parliamentary regime.[12]

At one point, early in June 1962, when even President Goulart was playing coy about calling a plebiscite on the issue, Kubitschek met at length with him and tried to convince him of the necessity of submitting the question to a popular vote. Juscelino annoyed some of his own party followers by his insistence on the subject. He provoked an official statement from the PSD that some of Kubitschek's remarks about the parliamentary system were uncalled for.[13]

The reestablishment of the presidential system did not increase the stability of the Goulart regime. During the fifteen months that followed, Goulart engaged in furious but futile maneuvering, playing a veritable game of musical chairs with his ministers, winning the distrust of virtually every element in national politics. During the early months of 1964 he engaged in a number of acts which seemed designed to create conditions for his overthrow, either from the Left or from the Right. These included enactment of a number of fundamental laws by decree, immediate pardoning of enlisted men and non-commissioned officers who had mutinied, and fiery speeches of virtual defiance of the hierarchy of the Armed Forces.

In the face of this situation, the position of Kubitschek appeared equivocal. His party, the PSD, had for almost two decades been allied with Goulart's Partido Trabalhista Brasileiro, and Juscelino wanted the backing of the PTB for his presidential aspirations in 1965. Furthermore, Kubitschek was very anxious to see the constitutional system preserved and the elections of October 1965 held on schedule. However, as Juscelino told Edward Reidinger many years later, on 5 September 1973, he regarded Goulart as a weak and ineffective president.

At one point, in October 1963, Kubitschek was reported to have had a meeting with President Goulart in which he promised to throw his support behind the president in return for a promise by

Goulart to back him in 1965. In the following month he seemed to be conforming with this agreement when he rebutted accusations by his own former minister of justice, Armando Falcão, that Goulart while serving as Kubitschek's vice president had helped organize a general strike against the administration.[14] Goulart himself stated to me that Kubitschek supported him throughout his regime.[15]

On one key issue raised by Goulart, Kubitschek offered less than complete support for Goulart: agrarian reform. Juscelino announced his support for agrarian reform, but opposition to the way in which Goulart proposed to carry it out. Thus, in November 1963, he declared his opposition to a constitutional amendment on the subject, and sometime later he was reported as opposing the government's decision that unused land within ten kilometers of all federal highways be set aside for agrarian reform purposes.[16] Certainly, as in the early months of 1964 Goulart veered increasingly to the Left, Kubitschek became increasingly worried about Jango's policies. Not only did he disagree with the positions assumed by Goulart, but he also feared that they would bring an end to the democratic regime, and thus end his chances for reelection.

Shortly after the March/April 1964 coup and the resulting cancellation of his civil rights, Juscelino was interviewed in Paris by a Brazilian newspaperman who asked him, "Your omission or benevolence in the face of the errors and crimes by which ex-President Goulart was taking the country to a subversive regime is much criticized. Can you defend yourself from the accusations against you with regard to this?" In answering this, Kubitschek said:

> I know that I am criticized for this; however, my pronouncements and my conduct in the period before the 31st of March don't entitle anyone to judge me as being in solidarity with the direction which things were taking in the government deposed by the Revolution. If I didn't publicly assume a combative attitude towards the doctrines which were gaining strength in the administration of my successor, I never gave those my support. I contributed, as was my task, with words of counsel and warning.[17]

350

Candidate for Reelection

Throughout the Goulart period, Kubitschek was an active candidate for the presidency. Upon his return home from Europe in November 1962, the *Hispanic American Report* noted that Juscelino was giving "every indication of being an active candidate for a second term as president," and added that "many moderates, including those who had opposed the inflationary policies of his first term, felt that his leadership was necessary to rescue Brazil from its present dilemma."[18]

In the congressional and state elections of 1962, Kubitschek used his influence to get the PSD in the state of São Paulo to oppose the efforts of Quadros to return to the governorship, and instead to support ex-governor Adhemar de Barros. There was speculation that in return Kubitschek had received promises of support from the Partido Social Progresista of Adhemar de Barros to back him in the presidential elections. If such was the case, Adhemar did not live up to his promise; in February 1964, a national convention of the PSP unanimously chose de Barros as its presidential candidate for the October 1964 election.[19]

In March 1964, about ten days before the coup against Goulart, a convention of the Partido Social Democrático nominated Kubitschek as its candidate for the presidency in the election scheduled for October 1965. He received 2,826 votes, to one for ex-president Dutra and thirty-nine abstentions. However, this time it was clear that he would not have the support of the Partido Trabalhista Brasileiro, which he had had in the 1955 election. Goulart and other PTB leaders had stated that Juscelino would be the last candidate of their party.[20]

The attitude of the PTB leaders towards Juscelino was representative of that of many of the leftists who played a major role in the last part of the Goulart regime. One of these was Francisco Julião, who gained fame in the early 1960s as a leader of the peasants in the Northeast. He claimed that "Juscelino was the leader who betrayed Brazil the most. He was most insensitive to the problems of the man in the fields. He impoverished them violently during his five years in office. He killed them. Brasilia was built over the corpses of hundreds of thousands of peasants." However, James Page has noted that Julião's attitude towards Kubitschek "threatened to isolate Julião."[21]

Foreign Travel

During the Goulart regime, Kubitschek did not spend all of this time in Brazil. He left the country on two short trips to Europe during 1961. For several months in the first half of 1962 he went on an extensive and lucrative lecture tour in the United States, during which he addressed a wide variety of university and other audiences throughout the country. His favorable reception in the United States reflected Kubitschek's prestige as the author of Operation Pan America, the predecessor of the Alliance for Progress, and as the man who had given great impetus to the economic development of United States' largest hemispheric neighbor, and who had built the imaginative new national capital, Brasilia.

Before reaching the United States, Kubitschek had traveled around the world. One of his first stops was in Portugal, where he again gave vent to his warm feelings for that country, and his support of Portugal's position on international issues. He is reported to have commented that "personally I feel that Brazil can have only one foreign policy: whatever best suits Portuguese interests," and he added that "The distinctions between Brazil and Portugal will eventually be wiped out." When Juscelino returned home, he commented that these statements were the result of "moments of gallantry when, more Oliveira than Kubitschek, he felt himself glow in sympathy with Portugal." José Honorio Rodriguez has commented that "it would have been preferable to have spoken seriously."[22]

In the process of this voyage around the world, Juscelino became somewhat involved in the crisis over the problem of Goa, between Portugal and the Republic of India. When he was in Portugal, he had been asked by Prime Minister Salazar to say something to Indian Prime Minister Jawarhalal Nehru about the issue of Goa, the Portuguese colony on the West Coast of India. When he got to India and had an interview with Nehru, he was assured by the Indian leader that India would not use force to absorb Goa, that elections were scheduled there, and that India would absorb Goa as a result of those elections. However, before Kubitschek had an opportunity to communicate this to Salazar, the invasion of Goa by Indian troops took place. Juscelino sent Nehru a telegram, saying that he lamented what had happened, and most of all lamented that he could not trust Nehru's word.[23]

Kubitschek and the Alliance for Progress

Kubitschek's prestige in the Americas in this period was reflected in the role he played in connection with the Alliance for Progress. The very concept of the Alliance, as put forth by President John Kennedy in April 1961, was an adaptation of the Operation Pan America which President Kubitschek had presented less than three years earlier. This fact was recognized in the charter of Punta del Este, signed by the representatives of the American Republics to launch the Alliance in August 1961. The last sentence of its Preamble read, "Inspired by these principles, and by the principles of Operation Pan America and the Act of Bogotá, the American Republics hereby resolve to adopt the following program of action to establish and carry forward an Alliance for Progress."[24]

In 1963 ex-president Kubitschek was called upon to become directly involved in the Alliance through suggestions which he set forth for its refurbishing and reorganization. As the Alliance had originally been set up at Punta del Este in August 1961, each Latin American country was to draw up both a short-term and a long-term (ten year) development program, and these were to be submitted for review to the so-called Committee of Nine, more popularly known as the nine wise men, for review and approval. The nine wise men were economists, all but one of whom was a Latin American. However, their effective power was limited, and by the time that the Alliance was two years old, a good deal of discontent had arisen in both parts of the hemisphere concerning their role.

As a result, Raúl Sáez, the chairman of the Committee of Nine, requested that Kubitschek, as author of the Operation Pan America, and Alberto Lleras Camargo, former president of Colombia and the first Latin American to serve as Secretary General of the Organization of American States, draw up suggestions for modification of the structure of the Alliance for Progress. Kubitschek and Camargo submitted separate reports to the meeting of the Inter American Economic and Social Council which met in São Paulo in September 1963.

Jerome Levinson and Juan de Onis have summed up the recommendations made by the two Latin American statesmen thus: "(1) that a new Inter American committee be established to give political direction to the Alliance for Progress and to emphasize its Latin character; (2) that the countries of Latin America agree

353

among themselves on the allocation of funds; and (3) that some operative agencies of the Alliance, such as the Inter American Development Bank, be physically located in Latin America."[25]

Out of the debate at the São Paulo meeting, centering on the reports of Kubitschek and Camargo, substantial changes were made in the organization of the Alliance, although the two presidents' recommendations were by no means fully accepted. Levinson and de Onis have summarized the agreements reached at the São Paulo meeting in the following terms:

> It established a special permanent committee of the Inter American Economic and Social Council, the *Comité Interamericana de la Alianza para el Progreso* (CIAP) in which seven permanent members (six elected by Latin American countries and one by the United States) and a large technical secretariat would carry out a continuing review of national and regional development plans, the availability of domestic resources in each country, and the availability and distribution among the several countries of external funds under the Alliance for Progress. CIAP was also to cooperate with the Inter American Development Bank and help to coordinate negotiations between the individual countries and potential sources of external aid. In a provision that applied primarily to the United States, the member states agreed to give 'special consideration' to the recommendations of CIAP in the allocation of public external funds under the Alliance for Progress, when providing financial and technical assistance through their own agencies and when instructing their representatives in the various international organizations that provide such assistance.[26]

Juscelino Kubitschek and John Kennedy

During this period Kubitschek maintained friendly relations with President John Kennedy. It was Kennedy who originally asked Kubitschek if he would be willing to undertake a study of the Alliance for Progress. Kubitschek saw Kennedy for the last time only three or four months before the United States president was murdered. At that point, Kennedy showed great concern for what was happening in Brazil. He commented to Kubitschek that if things went on as they were, Brazil would have 50 percent per year or more inflation, and that in any country in which that happened, there would certainly be revolution. Juscelino agreed with Kennedy, because he too felt that the situation was becoming impossible.

Kubitschek believed that Kennedy had a real concern for Latin America. He was convinced that the United States president sincerely wanted to help to do something about the situation in that area. Juscelino felt that Kennedy, of all the leading men of the time whom he met—and he was acquainted with virtually all leading figures except Churchill—was the greatest and most human, the most concerned, of all.[27]

Chapter 17

THE YEARS IN THE WILDERNESS

Kubitschek's ambitions to return to the presidency were smashed beyond repair by the coup d'etat of 1964 which overthrew President Goulart, and the events immediately succeeding it. The Army, Navy, and Air Force officers who assumed control enacted a so-called Institutional Act, which in effect was an amendment to the Constitution of 1946. Ex-president Kubitschek, as it turned out, was to be one of the major victims of this constitutional innovation.

Kubitschek and the 1964 "Revolution"

As the final crisis of the Goulart regime was developing, Juscelino did what he could to prevent a catastrophe. After a meeting, a few days before the coup, at which Jango gave a rabble-rousing speech to a group of sergeants in the Metal Workers Union of Rio de Janeiro, Juscelino was deputed by a majority of the members of the Senate to go to Rio to speak with Goulart and try to get him to change his position. After some delay, he got in to see the president.

Several months later Kubitschek recounted to a Brazilian journalist what happened in that interview. He said:

> I showed him the dangerous repercussions of his words to the Marine sergeants, particularly in the higher echelons of the Armed Forces, and made an appeal to him to reflect, to reconsider the terms of his statement, to avoid consequences which might be irreparably damaging to the tranquility of his government, and disastrous to the democratic regime, which it was the duty of all to preserve.

356

Goulart was not impressed by Juscelino's arguments. Kubitschek noted that "blindly confident in the force of his military backing, President Goulart thanked me for my good intentions in alerting him, but he underestimated the importance of the news which I offered him, showing unrestricted assurance in the group which sustained him."[1] Kubitschek seems to have been one of the first to inform President Goulart that the Armed Forces movement against him was under way. He telephoned the president to tell him that General Morão Filho, head of the Federal Army garrison in Minas Gerais was ordering his troops to march on Rio de Janeiro to overthrow the regime. Kubitschek himself had been informed of this by his friend, José Maria Alkmin.[2]

During this telephone conversation, the president asked Juscelino for help and for advice as to what to do to save his situation. Juscelino reported that he told Goulart that he could still dominate the rebellion if he would issue two proclamations. One of these had to be to the Armed Forces, to assure them that the hierarchy of the military would immediately be restored—it had been seriously undermined when Goulart had sided with Navy enlisted men when they had rebelled against their officers. The second proclamation, said Kubitschek, would have to be addressed to the Brazilian people, and be an absolute and unequivocal repudiation of the communists and communism. However, Goulart replied that he could not do what Kubitschek requested, that this would appear to be surrender, and that the President of Brazil could not surrender. Juscelino replied, citing a rule which he said he had always followed in his own career, that "he had no agreements with error," stressing that Goulart had erred very much, and that he should admit it, something which Kubitschek said that he himself had always tried to do when he came to the conclusion that he had made a mistake. Goulart still insisted that he could not act as Kubitschek suggested. Later on the same day, Kubitschek met with General Peri Bevilacqua, member of a high military court, and a considerable force in the army. Goulart had telephoned him, and when Kubitschek and Bevilacqua compared notes, it turned out that they had told Goulart virtually the same thing.[3]

Overthrow of Goulart

After General Amaury Kruel, commander of the army in the São Paulo region joined the revolt, Goulart became convinced that further resistance in the Rio-São Paulo area was hopeless. He then flew to Brasilia, hoping that he could mobilize military support there, but found out very quickly that that was not possible. Thereupon, he flew to Porto Alegre, in his native Rio Grande do Sul. There his brother-in-law, ex-governor Leonel Brizola, wanted to organize resistance. The army commander in the region was also willing to do so, according to Goulart. However, the general had only recently been appointed to the post, and did not feel that he had full control of the Third Army. As a result, after a short stop at his fazenda in São Borja, President Goulart fled into exile in Uruguay.[4]

Once the military movement had triumphed, the president of the Chamber of Deputies, Ranieri Mazzili, was sworn in as president. However, the revolutionary junta, the so-called Revolutionary Command, composed of the heads of the three armed forces, had no intention, this time, of allowing the civilian who was next in line constitutionally, to stay in the presidency. Rather, they decided to have a leading military man accede to the post. They enacted the Institutional Act (which turned out to be only the first of five such "Acts"). The Act had a number of provisions. It declared that Congress should elect a successor to fill out the unexpired term of President Goulart. It temporarily suspended the tenure of civil servants, it provided that the new president could cancel the mandates of members of Congress, state legislatures and municipal councils and remove state governors. Finally, it had an article which authorized the president for two months to cancel the civil rights of individual Brazilian citizens for as long as ten years.

Kubitschek and the Election of Castelo Branco

During the few days that elapsed between the overthrow of Goulart and the selection of his military successor by Congress, there was considerable maneuvering among the leading political figures. The São Paulo daily *O Estado de São Paulo*, long hostile to Kubitschek, reported that he and other PSD leaders were working to try to secure the election of the president of the PSD, Ernani

Amaral Peixoto, son-in-law of the late President Vargas, as the successor to João Goulart. The objective of the PSD leaders, according to *O Estado de São Paulo*, was to facilitate the campaign plans of Kubitschek for the 1965 election.[5]

There were some who suggested that the question of who should be the permanent successor of Goulart should be postponed for at least a month. However, Carlos Lacerda, the Governor of Guanabara (the city of Rio de Janeiro), spoke out most strongly against this idea. He claimed that this suggestion was being made particularly by supporters of Kubitschek's campaign for reelection. He argued that "we do not want Sr. Juscelino Kubitschek to become a Brazilian Frondizi and rob us of this revolution, as he has robbed the country."[6]

The military men who made up the Revolutionary Command after the fall of Goulart favored the election of General Humberto Castelo Branco, whose support from his post of Chief of the General Staff of the Army had been crucial in the success of the movement to overthrow Goulart. Reportedly, Governor Mauro Borges of the state of Goias was authorized to make their preference known to the leaders of the Partido Social Democrático, who had the largest bloc of members of the Congress which had to choose Goulart's successor.[7]

A meeting between Branco and the principal PSD leaders took place at the apartment of Deputy Joaquim Ramos in Copacabana. J.W.F. Dulles has commented that "despite the overwhelming political movement for Castelo . . . Kubitschek believed that Castelo's election depended on whether or not Kubitschek and his friends decided to work for it. Castelo, in accepting the invitation given him in Ramos' apartment on 6 April, had no such idea."[8]

Kubitschek was one of those who attended this meeting. When he arrived, somewhat late, General Castelo Branco greeted him as "Presidente."[9] Kubitschek himself subsequently recounted the essence of his conversation with Branco:

> I was frank and loyal with this military chief. I told him that the PSD already has a candidate for the elections of 65. I don't ask anything else from the new government but behavior above the parties, free elections, and inauguration of the winner. The answer of General

Castelo Branco was 'My past responds for me.' Stimulated by that reply, which appeared to be in conformity with the candidate's quality as it had been described to me by mutual friends, I decided to express my reservations, beyond what prudence recommended under the circumstances.

Juscelino went on to tell Branco

'I believe in the strength of your democratic convictions, General. Belonging, however, to the nucleus of the Superior War School, of which you are one of the most capable and representative elements, will your future action not be influenced by the ideological currents of that group of officers, where, I have been informed, there are elements of great intellectual value with great desire to put in practice a long maturing government program?'[10]

The General, certainly understanding the implications of the question, cut off other questions with the curt, incisive phrase: "I will not be at the service of anyone in the government, except to obey the law." In spite of his dogmatic tone, the declarations of General Castelo Branco seemed reassuring. They indicated a Chief of State in whom one could have confidence. Kubitschek left this meeting as soon as he had talked with Branco. Dulles has noted that "whatever was said, Kubitschek had soon heard enough; eager to be on his way, he asked permission to leave. The men, who rose to say goodbye to him, kept on conversing after he departed."[11]

Several other candidacies were under discussion. These included ex-president Eurico Gaspar Dutra and General Amaury Kruel, Commander of the Second Army based in São Paulo, whose last minute decision to throw his support behind the ouster of Goulart had been decisive for the success of the enterprise. General Kruel's candidacy was being pushed particularly by the Partido Trabalhista Brasileiro, and Kubitschek was approached on his behalf by Deputy Hugo Borghi. But Juscelino "made clear to him the impossibility of modifying a decision which, at that point, was a decision of my Party."[12]

At one point, Branco himself was apparently worried by the campaign in favor of General Kruel, and Juscelino was asked to reassure him by telephone. Juscelino commented later that he "took the phone and saw that the candidate was apprehensive about the news which had come to his attention about work on behalf of other candidates. [He] calmed his fears, showing him the groundlessness of the rumors around the name of General Kruel . . . [his] clear and positive words succeeded in removing a cloud from the spirit of the General."[13]

On 9 April, Senator Kubitschek issued a statement in which he said the following:

> with the responsibility of a candidate for the Presidency of the Republic, I declare that I am in agreement with the honored and worthy name of General Humberto de Alencar Castelo Branco for filling the unexpired presidential term of 1961-1966, certain that the conduct and past history of this illustrious military man will assure the complete respect for democratic norms, guarantee the functioning of the regime, and the respect for the wishes of the people, which will be expressed in the ballot boxes in October 1965.[14]

On the same day, almost every party represented in Congress indicated its support for the naming of Branco to succeed Goulart. Two days later, on 11 April, Branco, who had been promoted to Marshal, was elected president by 361 votes against 3 for Marshal Távora and 2 for Marshal Dutra.[15] Shortly after his election, Marshal Branco was inaugurated as president in a joint session of Congress. It was reported that the supporters of Juscelino applauded heartily when Branco said in his inaugural speech that he would turn over his post to his elected successor on 31 January 1966 as the constitution prescribed.[16]

Antecedents of Kubitschek's "Cassação"

In the meanwhile, the Revolutionary Command had issued several lists of citizens who were subject to cassação, the deprivation of civil rights. (One so treated was called a *cassado*). These included ex-presidents Goulart and Quadros and leading figures in virtually

361

all of the political parties. They also included leading intellectuals, such as Celso Furtado, the country's most outstanding economist, and author of the Kubitschek government's plan for reconstructing the economy of the Northeast, and first head of the Super-intendencia do Desenvolvimento do Nordeste (SUDENE). Soon after taking office, President Branco issued several additional lists. According to the Institutional Act, power to issue such decrees would expire two months after Branco took office—that is, on 15 June 1964. One cassado was Governor Mauro Borges de Teixeira of Goias, the state which Juscelino represented in the senate. Borges was a PSD governor. He had been one of those who supported the coup and backed the election of Branco. In spite of these actions, enemies within the military regime succeeded in getting him removed on vague grounds of corruption.[17]

Dulles noted that

> in mid-May, Juscelino Kubitschek decided that, as a PSD senator from Goias, he should speak in the Senate in defense of Mauro Borges. He was more than ready to express himself. For a man of his temperament it had been difficult to adhere to his month-old policy of maintaining a low profile; besides, that policy seemed to do nothing to deter the appearance of press reports about his so-called past corruption and subversion . . . [However,] Kubitschek's advisors, such as Francisco Negrão de Lima, argued that a defense of Mauro Borges would only irritate the military and increase the chances of Kubitschek joining Goulart and Quadros as a former president without political rights. With regret Kubitschek canceled his Senate speech at the last moment.[18]

The situation of Kubitschek in these circumstances was indeed very precarious. The military men who controlled the new regime were dedicated according to their own proclamations to eliminating all those guilty of corruption and subversion from public life. Many of them were convinced that Kubitschek had been corrupt, and that he had been exceedingly tolerant towards those whom the hard-line military conceived of as being subversive. On the other hand, Kubitschek had his supporters in the new administration. There was an element, admittedly a minority, among the leading armed forces officers who admired Kubitschek and what he had accomplished. In addition, Alkmin, probably Juscelino's closest political friend, was chosen by Congress to be Branco's vice president.

Juscelino also had a strong core of support among the civilian politicians who were for the Revolution more for reasons of convenience than of conviction. De Dubnic commented that

> the fact that the revolutionary leaders moved against ex-president Kubitschek made it difficult for many PSD members to support the regime wholeheartedly. Kubitschek had made little effort to share his own prestige with his PSD during the peak years of his popularity as President, but many in the PSD did not show the same aloofness towards him. He was still the national symbol of *desenvolvimentismo*, the "man who awakened Brazil" who skillfully played on the optimistic streak in Brazil. He was moreover the strongest political personality the party had.[19]

Kubitschek's name was not on the first lists of people to be cassado. However, by the end of May, rumors were rife that he would soon become a victim of the Institutional Act. There was open discussion of the matter in the press, and it was a frequent subject of conversation in public places and private homes. "Countless military officers expressed surprise that Kubitschek's candidacy still existed—in view of his 'well-known unpatriotic activities.'"

On 25 May Kubitschek replied to this insidious campaign against him and particularly against attempts to force him to withdraw from the 1965 presidential race. After recounting the achievements of his administration, he ended by saying that "the people have already made their judgment of me and I am sure that they want to do so again at the first opportunity. Only for this reason my detractors move against me. They seek to strike down not only a candidate but also the democratic regime itself."[20]

General Arthur Costa e Silva, the minister of war in the new administration of President Branco, publicly implied on several occasions that he thought that the ex-president ought to be cassado. One of times was after Juscelino's May 25 speech. Talking in São

Paulo the next day, Costa e Silva commented that "The pronouncement of Sr. Kubitschek—due to its violent language and also, in a
certain sense, its defiance—appears to me much like the speech of
Sr. Jango Goulart on March 30." A bit later, flying back to Brasilia
from São Paulo, Costa e Silva told reporters that Branco "must
decide *now* about the *cassação* of Kubitschek."[21] Costa e Silva may
well already have had his eye on the presidency and did not relish
Kubitschek's competition. A few days after the São Paulo incident,
he drew up a petition asking that Kubitschek be deprived of his
political rights. He said that the fate of the revolution depended
upon this and said that it was needed "to prevent future political
maneuvers, already quite well planned, for interrupting the process
of restoring moral and political principles."[22]

Kubitschek himself felt that the political atmosphere was
closing in on him. He was being shadowed by unidentified
individuals. He was informed that his records as a doctor in the São
Lucas Hospital in Belo Horizonte had been investigated and that
personal friends had been interrogated about his financial status.
Thus, "it was that atmosphere of animosity and suspicion that forced
me to react, and publish an energetic note of protest against the use
of such procedures."[23]

A delegation of the PSD executive committee headed by its
president, Ernani Amaral Peixoto, waited upon Branco to try to find
out whether he intended to cassar Juscelino. Branco replied to
Peixoto: "If I have to cancel the political rights of anyone, the
reasons will be so evident that you yourself will be in agreement."
Later Juscelino commented that "that pronouncement . . . could
calm the impatience of fear of anyone, because of the promise and
assurance it contained." But, Kubitschek added that, "at that point,
however, promises and words weighed little on my spirit and I
sensed that my mandate hung by a thread."[24] After a second
meeting with Branco on 3 June, Peixoto become convinced that he
intended to cassar Kubitschek. He so informed Juscelino. As a
result, on 4 June 1964 Juscelino Kubitschek flew to Brasilia,
appeared in the Senate, and gave there a speech which proved to be
his swansong.

Kubitschek's Last Speech in the Senate

Kubitschek's Senate speech of 4 June 1964 was not only a defense of himself but of the democratic system. At one point, he said:

> Before God, before the people, before this House, I can affirm that, as President of the Republic during five years, I strove for the peace of Brazil, not authorizing, not permitting, not agreeing to any attack on the liberty of anyone, no matter who he was, and acting always with administrative dignity. [In contrast,] by the mechanism of the Institutional Act, those who are accused are not given access to the accusations against them. Thus the revolutionaries of Brazil have turned against the most sacred conquests of the law. I do not know exactly of what I am accused. I only hear rumors and murmurs about old stories, already disproven and discredited by irrefutable answers. Now the Nation lives under the effects of terror, and I here express my solidarity with those who have been suffering the process of inquisition which reminds one of the most dramatic moments through which humanity has passed.

Referring directly to the new president, Juscelino commented: "My vote here helped to elect the present president of the republic, in whose democratic spirit I had believed, but my sacrifice, demanded by hate and by incomprehension, will serve to aid a new struggle in favor of the peace and dignity of the Brazilian people." Appealing beyond the confines of the Senate chamber, Kubitschek commented that

> I know that in this Brazilian land, tyrannies do not last. That we are a humane nation, imbued with the spirit of justice. Many of the people, brought to power always by the will of the people, I have before me the suffering which the people are going to confront in this hour of trial, which is falling upon us. We are to be sure going through a difficult hour, but this is a democratic country. . . . I repeat: the blow which they want to rain

365

down upon my person as ex-Chief of State, will damage democratic life, the free will of the people. They are not hurting me personally, but rather all of those who believe they have the right to choose, who want to choose those who are to preside over their destinies. This act is an act of punishment. Much more than cancelling my rights, they are cancelling the political rights of Brazil![25]

Considerable popular pressure had been mobilized against the cassação of Kubitschek. A petition bearing half a million signatures was presented to President Branco urging that he not take action against his predecessor.[26] These signatures were to no avail. The members of the National Security Council, the body which advised President Castelo Branco as to who should be deprived of their political rights, voted unanimously, with one exception (Roberto Campos), in favor of the cassação of Juscelino.[27]

Kubitschek Cassado

On 8 June 1964, President Branco signed the decree removing Kubitschek from the Senate and canceling his civil rights for ten years.[28] This action meant that not only could Kubitschek not hold public office during this period, but could not vote, could not publicly utter or publish any material dealing with political issues, or in any other way take part in political activities.

The French writer Georges-André Frechter argued that the cassação of Juscelino

> had become unavoidable both because the former president was a focus for the opposition and also because the hard liners, supported by the War Minister, General Costa e Silva, who was possibly preparing to offer himself as a candidate for the presidency, were demanding Kubitschek's head. In their view he epitomized all the excesses of populism and the symbol had to be struck down. . . . However, there appears to be every indication that Castelo Branco would have preferred to avoid taking this step against a man whose popularity was indisputable.[29]

366

Frechter also maintained that Branco got a quid-pro-quo for cancelling Kubitschek's rights. He wrote that "he obtained in exchange observance of the provisions of Article 10 of Institutional Act No. 1, which abolished with effect from 15 June the power conferred on the president of annulling any elective mandate, notwithstanding pressure by the hard liners who publicly demanded its prolongation."[30]

A few weeks later, Juscelino himself commented bitterly about his cassação that "the Marshal, in his reserved and prudent manner, did not disclose the arguments on which it was based, forgetting his promise to Admiral Amaral Peixoto that if he had to do it, his reasons would be agreed to by all. Later, the chief of his Civil Household was instructed to say that the deed had exclusively political causes."[31]

It was widely reported that Lacerda had played a major role in getting Kubitschek cassado. With the elimination of Juscelino as a possible presidential candidate, Lacerda remained as the civilian leader with most popular support. Subsequently, when Lacerda and Kubitschek formed an alliance against the military regime, President Branco is supposed to have commented that he hoped that Lacerda would show Juscelino the letter which he (Lacerda) had sent to Branco insisting on the need to have Kubitschek cassado.[32] It is clear that Lacerda supported the cassação of Kubitschek. On a trip to New York in June 1964, he commented that the deprivation of Kubitschek's political rights was "a courageous step by Castelo Branco."[33] Soon afterwards, however, when a movement developed to extend Branco's term of office by a year, thus imperilling Lacerda's own bid for the presidency, he apparently changed his mind about the way in which Juscelino had been treated. He remarked that the cassação of Juscelino had been an injustice because Kubitschek had not had the right of self-defense.[34]

Juscelino's Exile

After his speech in the Senate, life became increasingly difficult for Juscelino. His every move was followed by the police, and rumors began to circulate about his coming arrest. For several days he followed the practice of sleeping each night in a different place, but then decided to stay in his apartment in Copacabana. The Spanish Ambassador's residence was located on the ground floor of the apartment house and the ambassador offered Kubitschek diplomatic asylum which Juscelino at first refused. The entrance to his apartment was hindered by "the presence of ugly types, who placed themselves at the corner or in the hallway of the building." The government said that the vigilance on the building was for Kubitschek's protection. Later, Juscelino commented that "that was not, however, the impression given to me, my family and friends by that constant movement of groups moving in suspicious ways, as if they just awaited the moment to pounce on the hoped-for prisoner. If the objective was not that, it would be even crueler. Because it was designed to drive me to desperation or a heart attack."[35]

Because of his illness and that of his wife, Juscelino decided to accept the offer of asylum of the Spanish Ambassador. That diplomat informed the Brazilian Foreign Office that he had extended political asylum to Kubitschek and asked for a safe-conduct for him to leave the country. However, Itamaraty refused to grant this. Kubitschek later wrote that "with great surprise I heard from the Foreign Minister that his Ministry could not recognize the right of asylum, since nothing impeded my freedom of movement, and that if, in spite of the guarantees offered me, I desire to leave, I must use the passport which I had, exchanging it afterwards for a common passport in the diplomatic representation of Brazil in Madrid."[36]

Upon leaving the country, Kubitschek issued a final statement to the people of his country, in which he said:

I leave Brazil because this is the best form of expressing my protest against the violence of which I have been a victim, and because there do not exist the most minimal conditions in the country which would permit me to continue the struggle which I have never deserted to preserve democratic institutions, for the economic development and emancipation of the country. Our love of liberty will overcome the desperation, the hate, the iniquity, the tyranny, and under its banner the great historic destiny of Brazil will be fulfilled. Loyal defender of democracy, I prepare myself to face better the struggle and I shall shortly return for the civil battle in which the Brazilian people is engaged.[37]

As a matter of fact, Kubitschek stayed abroad, spending part of his time in Europe and part of it in the United States, until October 1965. While in the United States, he lectured and had two conversations with Vice President Hubert Humphrey. While in Europe, he was received by, among other people, French President Charles De Gaulle. He also had several long conversations with the novelist and Gaullist politician André Malraux. Both of these leaders had visited Brasilia while Kubitschek was president.[38]

During this period, participation by the Brazilian military in the occupation of the Dominican Republic took place, first by United States Armed Forces and then by an inter American force presided over by a Brazilian general. Kubitschek commented that the United States "always arrogates to itself the right to tutor in the hemisphere," and that it is "inclined to see a leftist regime in every reformist movement." He added that in no Latin American country could the communists come to power by free elections.[39]

Prosecution of Kubitschek

Kubitschek returned home for the first time in October 1965. The day before his return the first state elections under the military regime had been held and it soon became clear that they had been a defeat for the dictatorship, with its opponents generally winning the governorships in the largest states, including Guanabara and Minas Gerais. Juscelino's return was thus particularly dramatic. There were conflicting interpretations concerning the reason. The well-known novelist, José Montello, who had served in Juscelino's "civil household," wrote in the Rio newspaper *Jornal do Brasil* of 14 October 1965 that in Lisbon on 17 September he had received a long distance telephone call from Juscelino, then in Paris, in which Kubitschek had informed him that he was planning to return home to clear his name of charges made against him by the military. Montello said that he had sought to dissuade the ex-president from returning or at least to get him to postpone his trip home until Christmas time, when, Montello reasoned, the general atmosphere would be better and Kubitschek would run less risk.

There were those who were sure that Kubitschek went back under the impression that his sudden appearance in Brazil, on the heels of victories of his personal friends Israel Pinheiro and Francisco Negrão de Lima in the governorship races in Minas

369

Gerais and Guanabara respectively, would help to bring an end to the military control of the country. Kubitschek himself has said that he returned home on the morning after the election of 3 October 1965 because to have done so earlier would have looked as if he were trying to influence the election in which his two friends were candidates. The Kubitscheks arrived in Rio de Janeiro early in the morning before the results of the ballots had been counted but after they had been cast.[40] He and his wife were met at Galeão airport by their two daughters and a group of supporters who hoisted them on their shoulders. He told reporters that he did not intend to leave the country again.[41]

Whatever Juscelino's line of reasoning, it was clear to the author who was in Brazil at the time that Juscelino's sudden return home tended to strengthen very much the hard-line element among the military who wanted to convert the Branco regime into a much more rigid and repressive dictatorship. If the president was not willing to permit this, they would remove him and put in another military man. The result of the situation created by electoral defeat and Juscelino's return was that Branco was forced to enact the Second Institutional Act late in October which among other things dissolved all existing political parties, authorized packing of the Supreme Court, and reinstated the right of the president to remove elected officials and to cancel individuals' civil rights.

The hard-line military treated Kubitschek very badly. He was arrested on the afternoon of the day he arrived back in Brazil.[42] For the next thirty days, he was interrogated day after day, from ten in the morning until ten in the evening. This questioning centered on the charge of subversion against the ex-president. He was astounded to find out that virtually every one of his 1955 campaign meetings had been recorded. These recordings were played back him by the hour. He was very bored by this, and sometimes dozed off. But at the end of each recording the interrogating officer would ask him how he explained that on the same campaign platform, and talking at the same meeting in some interior part of the state of Pernambuco, for instance, was so-and-so, the local communist leader. Juscelino had spoken at hundreds of meetings, and he had not known, and sometimes had not even met, many of the people who spoke at these meetings.

Although his military persecutors did not ask him about his supposed corruption, the Political-Military Inquiry bodies which were investigating Juscelino, did scour the country to find proof of his alleged corruption. Virtually every branch of every bank in Brazil had its records scoured by the military investigators to try to find deposits by him. Banks in the United States and Europe, including Switzerland, were asked for the same kind of evidence. In addition, every company of any size in Brazil was investigated to find if Kubitschek had investments in it. The investigators were unable to come up with any evidence which could be used to bring Kubitschek to trial for corruption.[43]

Not only were the charges of Kubitschek's supposed corruption while in the presidency unsustainable, it is almost certain that the allegations of corruption in the Kubitschek regime had been greatly exaggerated. A leading Brazilian economist, Cleantho de Paive Leite, who served as Chefe do Gabinete in the Ministry of Transport and Works under Juscelino, assured me in 1966 that he had seen no evidence of corruption in that ministry. He had never been told to give contracts to anyone in particular. Although there might have been collusion among contractors in bidding on the ministry's projects, he said he saw no evidence of such behavior which in any case would be very difficult to prove.[44]

Protests and Release of Kubitschek

The cavalier treatment of an ex-president of the republic brought protests from the press which remained relatively uncensored. Typical was an editorial in *Correio da Manha* of Rio de Janeiro, which appeared on 14 October 1965. It commented:

President Castelo Branco should reflect a great deal on the case of ex-president Juscelino Kubitschek. This man who is at the present time being submitted to long hours of interrogation, by officers who do not hide their support of a subversive political line, is a former chief of state, who has popular support in our country and with reason has great prestige abroad. He and Marshal Eurico Dutra are the only Brazilian chiefs of state who, after the redemocratization in 1945, completed their terms to the end, turning power over to their successors, in order and legality.

371

Furthermore, returning to Brazil after visiting various countries, where he was received by political personalities of first rank, including chiefs of state, and where he gave lectures on the invitation of educational and cultural institutions, Sr. Juscelino Kubitschek is turned over by President Castelo Branco to colonels and majors thirsting for notoriety and power, who are disposed to use whatever means to acquire these. Is this the protection due an ex-president who returns to his country after free elections, when everyone imagined that Brazilian political life was returning to normal?

The editorial went on to offer a word of warning to Branco:

This establishes a dangerous precedent, which might affect other chiefs of state—including the present one. Disrespect of authority goes hand in hand with disrespect of the human person. President Castelo Branco should pay attention to what is happening, because there are two victims in all of this: the ex-president who had confidence in him in whom he should have had confidence; and the president who permits his subordinates to reduce the stature and majesty of the post which he is himself occupying at the present time.

After thirty days of interrogation, Kubitschek was kept under house arrest in his apartment on Avenida Atlantica in Copacabana. One evening when he was talking with some friends, Vice President Alkmin arrived and told him that Magalhães, who was the minister of justice, feared that the hard-line military men were going to incarcerate Juscelino in the Central Military Hospital, and have him tried for subversion in a military court made up of captains and majors and that he would more or less automatically be sentenced to five to ten years in jail. Alkmin transmitted Magalhães' advice to Juscelino that he leave the country immediately. Upon Alkmin's urging, Kubitschek finally agreed to go into exile once again.

Alkmin then went to the Foreign Ministry and got Kubitschek's passport duly processed so that he could leave. He went with several friends in a car to the Galeão airport but as they

372

were driving up there they were stopped by two officers who told Kubitschek to get out and into their jeep. They then drove him back and put him into a room, where he remained alone for about an hour. The officers then came back, told him to follow them, got into a jeep, and drove him right to the stairs of the airplane.[45] He did not know where the plane was going until it reached Miami.[46]

Kubitschek returned again at the end of May 1966 when his sister died. His wife, Sarah, called him and told him that his sister was dying. When he arrived in Rio, Alkmin met him at the plane and informed him that she had died. He wept and was greatly depressed emotionally for some time after that. He and his sister had been particularly close.[47] Juscelino was not allowed to stay in Brazil for the seventh day regular mass being forced by the authorities to go again into exile before that time.[48]

Juscelino was abroad when the successor to President Branco was finally chosen. Instead of being elected by the people, Marshal Arthur da Costa e Silva was named president by Congress on 3 October 1966. This was in accordance with the Second Institutional Act, which Branco had been forced to enact a year earlier. Although most senators and deputies voted for Costa e Silva as they knew that the military wanted them to do, one person, Senator João Alrão of Goias, was brave enough to lodge a protest on behalf of Kubitschek. He said that the election was a shameful farce, and that "the only choice recognized by the people was that of Juscelino Kubitschek."[49]

Return Home to Further Persecution

Although Juscelino's enemies would have liked him to stay abroad indefinitely, he refused to do so. To have remained in exile would have been implicitly to admit to some kind of guilt. So he returned home once again after the end of the Branco administration early in 1967.

When President Costa e Silva made a further coup on 13 December 1968, proclaiming the Fifth (and most oppressive) Institutional Act, Kubitschek was arrested—as were Lacerda and ex-president Quadros—and was subjected again to intense military interrogation. He was kept prisoner for forty-five days before being allowed to go abroad once again. When he was released from his most extensive session of interrogation, Kubitschek was told by the

373

general who had been in charge what the real reason for his persecution was: "This is a war. You are our strongest enemy, so we are not going to leave you alone."[50] Juscelino returned to Brazil once more in March 1969. During the next six months, he was kept under very close police and military surveillance; he was required to report all of his movements outside of Rio to the commander of the First Army, General Sizeno Sarmiento.[51]

In August 1969, Kubitschek was told that a further police investigation of his finances was being undertaken, and that he would have to produce evidence of his financial dealings throughout his whole lifetime. He was given eight days to provide this information. The police particularly wanted to know what he had earned in his lecture tours in the United States after his presidency, on the supposition that he had not paid his income tax on those honoraria. Since he did not have those records, he had to wire each of the schools at which he had lectured, to inquire of them what they had paid him. By the end of the eight days, he and his secretary had compiled a four-hundred-page document, covering his financial transactions throughout virtually his whole life.[52] Needless to day, his persecutors still had no evidence which could be used even in a kangaroo military court to convict him of corruption.

At the time of President Costa e Silva's mortal stroke in September 1969, Kubitschek was once again subjected to house arrest for a few days. However, with the inauguration of President Emilio Garrastazú Medici after the death of Costa e Silva, the persecution of Kubitschek was ended. He was no longer required to report his movements, and he was given back his passport, which the military had previously withheld. It was probably still the case, however, that his mail and telephone calls were censored.[53]

Reassessment of Kubitschek

After Kubitschek was cassado, although he was unable to take an active part in politics, his popularity and political influence did not end. Kubitschek tended to gain in prestige as the years passed, particularly in the light of the difficulties the country faced in the 1960s—the sudden resignation of President Jânio Quadros after only seven months in office, the chaos of the regime of President João Goulart and his final overthrow, and the three military-controlled administrations which succeeded Goulart.

The people remembered the economic prosperity of the Kubitschek administration. The installation of a major auto industry, the construction of Brasilia, the expansion of the electric power and road networks, and the many other economic advances accomplished under Juscelino continued to be sources of pride to the people and stood in stark contrast to the economic crisis of the Goulart, Branco and Costa e Silva periods. People also remembered with nostalgia the democratic atmosphere which had characterized Kubitschek's regime. Everyone remembered his warm personality, his tolerance, his extensive contacts with the people, and his unbounded optimism with increasing fondness particularly when they compared him with the idiosyncratic vengefulness of Jânio, the austere reserve of Branco, and the playboy reputations and incompetence of Goulart and Costa e Silva.

When I was in Brazil for almost a year in 1965-1966, I was informed by the widest range of people—including both those who had been friendly to Kubitschek and those who had been opposed to him—that if free elections were held in which Juscelino could have been a candidate, he would have won without question. I agree with the assessment of the *New York Times* in its editorial on Kubitschek's death, which appeared on 25 August 1976, that "in any free elections, he would probably have regained the presidency."

Kubitschek was very pleased at his continuing public popularity. Wherever he went around the country, people came up to shake his hand and wish him well. With some pride, he commented to me in 1974 that public opinion polls continued to show him to be the most popular public figure in Brazil. He added that only once, after the Brazilian soccer team had gotten permanent possession of the World Cup, and President Medici had given a public reception for the team, did someone—President Medici—surpass him in the popularity polls. Once the euphoria of that event had passed, Medici no longer even appeared on the list; Juscelino, renewed his position as the most popular figure in the country.[54] A number of Kubitschek's former bitter enemies changed their point of view concerning the achievements which Juscelino had had to his credit during his period in office. Politicians who had opposed him from a more or less left-wing nationalist position, tended to reassess his achievements.

375

Similarly, Lacerda changed his mind about Kubitschek. He had been one of the most violent right-wing opponents of Kubitschek when he was president, had been one of the principal civilian architects of the overthrow of President Goulart, and bore a major share of the responsibility for Juscelino's having been cassado. In 1967, when he was in New York, Lacerda commented that Kubitschek had made two fundamental contributions to Brazil. One was his democratic regime, ending in his turning the government over constitutionally to a member of the opposition. The other was his instilling in the people a feeling of optimism, a conviction that they could solve their own problems.[55]

Juscelino did not hold a grudge against Lacerda for the mistreatment which he had received from Lacerda. In November 1966, Kubitschek told me about the plans he and Lacerda had for launching a new political group to oppose the dictatorship. He commented that although it might seem strange to some that he and Lacerda should get together, he thought that if they did not have the courage to forget their past personal differences and work together for the redemocratization of the country, they would be wrong. He did not know whether Lacerda would have the patience necessary to build a party, since he was an impetuous man. However, Lacerda was the principal person who still had his civil rights and who was putting up opposition to the military dictatorship.[56]

Lacerda provided the initiative for the establishment of the Kubitschek-Lacerda alliance, the Frente Ampla (Broad Front). After announcing the formation of the Front in Rio de Janeiro, Lacerda visited Kubitschek in the house in which he was living in Lisbon, Portugal, to discuss the details. Lacerda suggested an alliance among himself, Kubitschek and ex-president Goulart, to pool forces to organize a new party to oppose the military dictatorship. Kubitschek was not particularly enthusiastic about including Goulart in the alliance. However, the association with Lacerda had great value for him, since Lacerda had been the most bitter of Juscelino's opponents, perhaps more responsible than anyone else for circulating rumors about his supposed corruption. Kubitschek felt that Lacerda's seeking out an alliance with him was the best public proof which could be offered of the falsity of Lacerda's long-standing charges.[57] It proved impossible, however, under the rules established by the military dictatorship to establish an effective political party along the lines of the proposed Frente Ampla. It was outlawed officially in May 1958. All possibility of such an alliance collapsed completely in December 1968, when Lacerda was cassado by President Costa e Silva, and joined Kubitschek as a political leader without civil rights.

The Medici regime which came to power after the death of Costa e Silva took the final step to make impossible any future effort of Juscelino to return to the presidency. Other things being equal, Kubitschek would have been eligible for election at the end of Medici's term in 1974, since his ten-year period of being cassado would have expired by that time. However, the Medici government enacted a new law providing that at the expiration of a period of being cassado, although one who had had his civil rights suspended would be able to vote and speak forth on public issues, he would never again be allowed to hold public office.

Juscelino the Banker

Unable to continue in politics, Kubitschek turned his attention to business activities. A group of Mineiro friends organized a private development bank, the Banco Denasa, with its headquarters in Rio de Janeiro. Kubitschek was made chairman of the board of directors of the new bank. For some time it was unclear whether such a role was legal for one who had been cassado. However, the Central Bank finally decided that Juscelino was eligible for the post. In his new role, Kubitschek continued his lifelong interest in economic development. The Banco Denasa specialized in giving loans to industries and other enterprises, for a minimum of one year, and at different interest rates from those of the commercial banks. He felt that his work in the bank was in a way like that which he had had as president of the republic in that he had to pass on various proposals for establishing industries. He said that he was a kind of president of a republic on a miniature scale.[58]

Farmer Kubitschek

Another activity of the retired Kubitschek was that of being a farmer. It was located near Lusiania, about fifty kilometers south of Brasilia, in the state of Goias. Kubitschek threw himself into farming with his customary enthusiasm. A reporter of the magazine *Manchete* who visited the farm not long before Juscelino's death commented that "only with excessive good will could one two years ago have called these 310 alqueires of Goias fallow land between the Corumba and São Bartolemeu rivers a fazenda. However, two years of fertilizer and irrigation, and the work of a small tractor were enough for the miracle to be realized."[59]

On this farm Kubitschek began to cultivate coffee and bananas and to raise cattle. By the time of his death, he had some 4,00 coffee trees and was preparing plans for expanding the number to 50,000. He got great pleasure playing the gentleman farmer, supervising the operations, and sometimes helping in the care of the livestock. On the farm he and Sarah had constructed a small house designed by Oscar Niemeyer. Its center was a very large living room-library with the two parts of the room separated by a large copper fireplace. His library on the farm contained particularly works of various Brazilian authors, so that Juscelino was able to continue there his lifelong habit of voracious reading.[60]

For Kubitschek, the establishment of his farm had more than personal significance. It was designed to underscore his conviction of the need to push the development of Brazilian agriculture particularly in the region centering on his beloved Brasilia. With it he sought to bear out his claim that "treated as they should be, the lands of this area can be as fertile as any others. Everything can be planted in them with success. Even wheat."[61]

Juscelino the Family Man

In terms of relations with his family, undoubtedly the most difficult period of Kubitschek's life, were the five years of persecution between 1964 and 1969. Much of the time that he was in voluntary or forced exile, his wife Sarah did not accompany him abroad, staying in Brazil to keep house for their two daughters, Marcia and Maristela, who were still living at home. However, after 1969, the Kubitscheks were able to maintain a more stable family life. They tended to divide their time between their home in Belo Horizonte and their apartment in Rio de Janeiro. During the very last years of his life, they also spent considerable periods at their farm. Juscelino still continued to travel frequently around Brazil, and occasionally abroad. Sarah sometimes accompanied him, particularly on longer trips. As had been true since the early days of their marriage, the Kubitschek's had an active social life. Evenings were often given over to festive occasions, either at home, at the houses or apartments of friends, or in more public places. Among other things, Juscelino was famous for his enjoyment of dancing. He and Sarah often found occasions for giving vent to this passion.

During the years after his presidency, the last fifteen years of his life, Juscelino lost several people who were particularly dear to him. One of these was his mother, Julia Kubitschek de Oliveira, She and her son had been particularly close, and he had never forgotten the sacrifices which she had made to give both him and his sister a chance to make the best use of their capacities and talents. During his political career, his mother had always been willing to offer encouragement, advice, and even chastisement, as any of these seemed to her to be appropriate, and he seems to have taken them with the spirit in which they were intended. Juscelino's sister Maria da Conceicão (Nona) also died suddenly, as previously noted, in 1966, when he was in exile. Her loss, too, must have affected him with severity.

However, there were also additions to the family which gave Juscelino and Sarah great joy. Their daughter Maristela was married to Rodrigo Lucas Lopes, son of Juscelino's old political friend Lucas Lopes, and Juscelino took great pride and pleasure in his role as the father giving away the bride. The Lopes' had several children, and the Kubitscheks had the usual grandparents' prerogatives of enjoying, giving advice about, but not having to be responsible for, their grandchildren. The birthdays of Marcia and Maristela were friendly excuses for a party for family and friends at which dancing was certain to be one of the main features. The birthdays of the small children were more intimate family affairs.

As he grew older, Juscelino tended to display a kind of personal vanity which sometimes provoked amusement among his friends and acquaintances, as well as the general public. It was widely rumored that he had use of the services of a plastic surgeon to make the impact of age less noticeable on his face, and it was certainly the case that his black hair showed absolutely no tendency to turn grey.

Candidate Once Again

By 1973, Kubitschek had finally become convinced that the military would never again allow him to run for office, let alone become president of the republic for a second time.[62] However, during the last couple of years of his life, he did once again become a candidate—for membership in the Academia Brasileira de Letras, the Brazilian Academy. In recent decades, the Academy had acquired a position of substantial prestige in Brazilian society. It had within its ranks many of the country's leading literary and public figures. The idea of a president or ex-president of the republic becoming a member of the body, even without any substantial record of literary publication, was by no means a new one. President Vargas, among others, had been elected a member and had taken part in its activities.

During his presidency, Kubitschek had refused to try to become a member of the Academy. This was not because of any lack of regard for the institution, a fact borne out by a story about Josué Montello, a well-known novelist, who was vice chief of Kubitschek's Civil Household. Montello approached the president at one point, and suggested that he could "link his name to an institution of capital importance . . . conceding it an area on which it could construct the headquarters of the future Cultural Center of the country," in Brasilia. Juscelino took two pieces of stamped paper and wrote his name on the second one. He passed the pages to Montello, and replied: "Agreed, but with one condition. You will have to choose the most convenient area for the project which you have suggested. Because the concession for it has already been signed."[63]

In 1975, Kubitschek finally became a candidate for membership in the Academy. This candidacy aroused his old instincts as a politician. He gave substantial thought to planning his campaign to get a majority of the thirty-nine current members of the body to choose him as one of the Brazilian "immortals." When I visited him in July 1975, he told me about the progress of his efforts. He confided to me that he naturally was able to line up the four members from Minas Gerais for his candidacy and had also won the backing of the four from São Paulo. Three of the members from Baia were likewise supporting him, but the fourth Baiano was very

380

much against him. Juscelino was his usual optimistic self about his possibilities for success in this new "political" contest.[64]

This time Kubitschek's campaign did not succeed. There was a rival candidate for the vacant position in the Academy, and at least some of the opposition to Juscelino had political motivation. It was reported that opponents of the ex-president suggested to the undecided members of the Academy that Kubitschek's election would be a disaster for the Academy. The government was watching the vote of each of the "immortals," and would suspend its payments to the organization were he elected.[65] Although there is no evidence that the government actually had such an intention, the rumor that it did may well have influenced the votes of some of the Academy members. Juscelino did not resent his defeat. He was at the home of his daughter Maristela when he heard the news that he had not been elected. Instead of being thrown into despair—he invited his wife to dance to the tune of "Peixe Vivo," which had been his theme song virtually since the beginning of his political career.[66]

Nor did Kubitschek lose hope that he would be chosen a member of the Academia Brasileira de Letras. When I wrote him to ask about it, not knowing whether or not he had won, he replied:

> Unfortunately my candidacy for election to the Academy of Letter [sic] was unsuccessful. I lost the election by one vote. Factors beyond my control outside of the Academy prevented my occupation of the chair which so many thought I would surely receive. Circumstances have now changed considerably so that I believe that on the occasion of the next vacancy, I will finally be admitted to the distinguished company of the Academy. I was recently honored with the distinction of "Intellectual of the Year" which compensated for the disappointment of my defeat and has encouraged me to believe that I will be successful in soon entering the Academy.[67]

Kubitschek was not to live long enough to get his second chance for election to the Academia Brasileira de Letras. However, the Academy paid a special tribute to him after his death. Osvaldo Orico wrote that "like the saying that 'after her death she was

381

queen,' for the ex-president and writer it was 'after death he took his chair in the Academy,' in the longest memorial session, longer than any of the deceased members had ever before merited."[68]

Chapter 18

DEATH AND COMMEMORATION

In the late afternoon of 22 August 1976, Kubitschek was killed in an automobile accident on the General Dutra Highway between São Paulo and Rio de Janeiro. The published account of the accident said that a bus veered out in front of the car in which Kubitschek was travelling, resulting in Juscelino's car jumping the divider and ploughing headlong into a station wagon coming in the opposite direction. Both Kubitschek and his long-time chauffeur and friend, Geraldo Ribeiro, were killed instantly, and their car was demolished. Ribeiro was one of Juscelino's closest and long-time friends. He had started to work for Kubitschek when the latter became Mayor of Belo Horizonte in 1940. Although the first time that Ribeiro picked up the mayor he was a little late, Juscelino noted in his memoirs that "he never again made me wait a second. Furthermore, during this long period, the nature of vehicles in which Geraldo Ribeiro transported me changed. Sitting at my side, in the front seat of the car, the motorist was, after a while, disappearing, substituted by the fraternal friend."[1]

After their death, there circulated a story, which may or may not be apocryphal, according to which Kubitschek had said to his friend, "Geraldo, if you die before me, I will take care of your funeral." The chauffeur was said to have responded, "And if you go before me, I shall do the same." Then, it was said, Kubitschek "thought for a little and came out with this: 'No, we are brothers, we shall die together.'"[2] Whether or not this occurred, it certainly reflected the feeling of the two men towards one another.

The People's Tribute

The bodies of Juscelino and Geraldo were taken by the police to the Medical-Legal Institute and then at the request of the families were transferred to the courtyard of the Manchete Building in Rio de Janeiro, where Kubitschek had had his last office. The two bodies lay there the night of 22 August and until 11 A.M. the following day. When news spread that the ex-president had been killed, thousands of people streamed through the courtyard, including both rank and file citizens and political and cultural leaders, to pay tribute to Juscelino and to express their shock and sorrow at his unexpected death.

At 11 in the morning of 23 August, Juscelino's body was taken from the Manchete Building to the Santos Dumont Airport. Spontaneously, rank and file citizens undertook to carry the ex-president's coffin. On the way, the large crowd of mourners began to sing what had been Kubitschek's theme song, "Peixe Vivo." They repeated over and over its chorus, "How can I live, How can I live, Without you, Without you, Without your company?"[3] At four o'clock in the afternoon, the Varig plane carrying Kubitschek's body arrived in Brasilia, where a three-day period of mourning had been decreed by Federal District Governor Elmo Serejo. For three hours thousands of people had been awaiting the arrival of the plane at the Brasilia airport. A procession was formed to accompany the casket from the airport to the Cathedral of Brasilia. This cortège, said to consist of at least 4,000 cars, continued to drive around the city for two hours. Again, rank and file citizens carried Juscelino's casket into the Cathedral.[4]

After the funeral mass in the Cathedral, celebrated by Brasilia Archbishop José Newton, during which the large crowd gathered outside the church chanted "J.K.," his body was transferred to the Campo de Esperança (Field of Hope). There he was buried alongside the grave of Bernardo Sayão, the builder of the Belem-Brasilia Highway, as Kubitschek had requested. These two graves were located 150 meters from the Tomb of the Unknown Candango, where unidentified workers who had died during the building of Brasilia are interred.[5]

Exactly a year after the death of Kubitschek, another ceremony was held at his gravesite to dedicate the memorial which Oscar Niemeyer had constructed over his tomb. The dedication day was declared a holiday for the school children of the capital city, thousands of whom attended, along with many distinguished political and cultural leaders. Sarah Kubitschek and Josué Montello, the novelist who had been a member of the civil household of President Kubitschek, were the principal speakers on this occasion.[6]

Juscelino's Last Controversy

Four years later, Juscelino's body was moved to a new resting place, the Memorial JK, constructed close to the place where the first mass had been said in Brasilia, and almost in front of the headquarters of the General Staff of the Armed Forces.[7] However, perhaps in true Kubitschek tradition, Juscelino's body was not transferred to its final tomb until there had been a considerable controversy. The money for the new ninety-foot high memorial had been raised by Juscelino's widow, Sarah, in a nationwide campaign. Among the many thousands of contributors was the then current president, General João Baptista Figueiredo. The architect for the new monument to the founder of Brasilia was Oscar Niemeyer. The new resting place for Kubitschek was dedicated and his body was transferred there on 12 September 1981.

Ostensibly the form of the Memorial JK was what disturbed some of the more paranoid generals who raised objections to it and tried to prevent its dedication. The monument consisted of a high metal structure, the top of which "loops sideways into what the architect, Oscar Niemeyer, intended to be an abstract rendering of a palm."[8] Under the palm was a fifteen foot bronze statue of Kubitschek weighing 1.5 tons. The palm was intended to protect the statue from weathering. The military protestors claimed that the palm and the statue of Juscelino were meant to symbolize a hammer and sickle. They justified their argument on the basis of Niemeyer's communist past. Between 20-27 August 1981, work on completing the Memorial JK was suspended, while Niemeyer was pressured to change his design. He refused. He commented that "some say that it is a sickle, others say that it is a sword. It is difficult to coexist with mediocrity."[9] He categorized the pressure on him as "political intimidation that casts into doubt my professional good faith, . . . I have decided to resist . . . I want to say that I will not give into threats, that the monument represents only an abstract sculptural form that anyone can interpret as he likes: a sword, a sickle, a rake, or a votive candle."[10]

By 1981 much time had passed since Juscelino's presidency and it is likely that the form of the monument to Kubitschek was the excuse rather than the reason for the objection of certain military men to the Memorial JK. Even though he had been dead for half a decade, Juscelino was still the symbol of the hopes of the Brazilian people for the future of their country; he was remembered as the country's last successful democratic president. Those military men who had no desire to see the restoration of democracy used whatever excuse they could to prevent the establishment of a lasting monument to Brazil's most democratic president in the national capital which he had been responsible for constructing.

The maneuvers of the successors to the hardliners who had persecuted Juscelino many years before were to no avail. The Memorial JK was duly inaugurated, with President Figueiredo in attendance. It thus became a monument to the man who had been the single most important influence in the development of modern Brazil, its greatest practitioner of political democracy, and the founder and builder of the city in which he is buried.

Chapter 19

THE HISTORICAL ROLE OF
JUSCELINO KUBITSCHEK

The historical significance of Kubitschek grows as time passes. His role in pushing forward the economic development of Brazil is all but universally appreciated. The alteration which he brought about in the way Brazilians judged their country and themselves is recognized by Brazilians and foreigners alike. As the demand for an end to dictatorship and a return to democracy grew, Brazilians looked back upon Juscelino's period in office as a model of what a democratic regime could really be, and at the same time as proof that a democratic government was possible in Brazil.

The Accomplishments of Kubitschek

It seems probable that Kubitschek will be seen as the greatest president that Brazil had in the twentieth century. The construction of Brasilia and the transference of the national capital to that city seven hundred miles in the interior is itself enough to give Kubitschek an important place in Brazilian history. This aspect of Juscelino's career is amply recorded in Brasilia itself; his sculptured bust on the marble-faced edifice in the Praça dos Tres Poderes, the quotation engraved on one side of the Palacio da Alvorada, his grave topped by a ninety-foot tall monument with a statue of Kubitschek made by Oscar Niemeyer, are all tributes to his role in having Brasilia constructed.

The memory of Kubitschek's association with Brasilia will certainly go far beyond these mere physical monuments. The transfer of the capital was clearly one of the most important events to occur in Brazil during the present century. The construction of the new capital in three and a half years was a major achievement of modern Brazilians brought about because of the insistence and drive of the man who was president when they took place.

In economic terms, Brazil was a different country when Juscelino left the presidency than it had been when he took office. It was tied together as never before by a network of trunk highways which gave a major push to the opening up of the vast interior to settlement. It had been endowed with an electric power grid which laid the basis for the future expansion of the country's cities and its industries. It had acquired a vastly expanded steel industry and completely new automobile, shipbuilding, and machine tool plants. Kubitschek was right when he said that the economic development programs of subsequent governments, most notably the so-called "Brazilian miracle" of the late 1960s and early 1970s, had been built on the bases which he had laid a decade before.

The push to the west stimulated by the founding of Brasilia, together with Kubitschek's industrialization programs, provided a basis for Brazil to assume a new role in international affairs. Abandoning the traditional attitude of isolation from its Spanish American neighbors, Brazil under Kubitschek took a position of leadership among the Latin American countries. Through Operation Pan America he led them in demanding the cooperation of the United States in providing capital resources and expertise needed for economic development. This aspect of his leadership both complemented his internal policies and reflected the new importance which his economic development program was giving to Brazil. Here, too, the policies of his successors built on pioneering efforts taken by Juscelino.

We have emphasized several times in this volume the important impact of Kubitschek on the popular psychology of the Brazilian people. This impact was certainly one of the most significant and long-lasting heritages of Juscelino to his fatherland. He found its citizens generally pessimistic about their country's future and skeptical about their own achievements. He left them a people who were very proud of what their country had achieved during the Kubitschek period, and boundlessly optimistic about Brazil's future. So basic was this change in popular outlook, that it was not dimmed even by the two decades of troubles which followed Juscelino's exit from the presidency.

Kubitschek provided Brazil with the most democratic government which it had had in its history. He was elected and gave up his

388

post to an elected successor who represented the opposition, something almost unique in Brazil's past. The three branches of government all operated normally during his administration, with the rights and functions of the judiciary and legislature being respected by the executive. Juscelino immediately ended the state of siege which his predecessor had imposed. There was no censorship of the press under Kubitschek. All of this was in contrast both to what had happened before Juscelino became president and to the two decades after he left office. One American observer who studied the attitudes of Brazilian elites in the early 1970s found that some of them were very skeptical about whether economic development could take place within a structure of political democracy; Kubitschek had already proven that this was possible fifteen years previously.[1]

There can be no question about Kubitschek's democratic bona fides during his terms as governor of Minas Gerais and president of Brazil. There remains a question, however, concerning his willingness to serve as mayor of Belo Horizonte during the Estado Novo period. Certainly, the Estado Novo was a dictatorship, and Kubitschek knew it. When I asked him about the question he had no really good rationalization for having served the Vargas regime. His explanation was in terms of his personal friendships. It is clear that the challenge he saw in the post and the satisfaction he enjoyed from meeting that challenge overcame his democratic scruples. That never happened again.

As the result of both the economic spurt during the Kubitschek government and of the freedom which existed under it, Brazil experienced a cultural renaissance during Juscelino's period in office. This encompassed the universities, literature and publishing, the stage and cinema, the plastic arts, and most notably, architecture. These gains made by the country's cultural institutions suffered gravely during the military governments after 1964, although even those regimes were unable totally to destroy the progress made during the Kubitschek administration.

Juscelino the Politician

From his record in all three executive posts which he held—mayor of Belo Horizonte, governor of Minas Gerais, and president of Brazil—it is clear that Kubitschek was not an ordinary politician.

He was that extraordinary combination of a man who had a clear vision of what he wanted to accomplish for his country and an ability to manipulate his political environment so as largely to achieve it. Kubitschek's vision was an economically developed and politically free and democratic Brazil. He used a variety of different attitudes and techniques to achieve his objective. One basic element was to fix his sights on a limited number of specific goals, to the achievement of which he concentrated all his resources and talents. In Belo Horizonte he paid special attention to constructing key street systems, building new neighborhoods, and above all, to the creation of Pampulna, and kind of precursor of Brasilia. As governor of Minas Gerais, he concentrated particularly on his twin programs of transport and energy, adding to these the creation of some key manufacturing enterprises. As president, of course, Kubitschek concentrated on his thirty-one targets. Within those, he gave particular attention to only a limited number of items: electricity, roads, steel, the auto and shipbuilding industries, and above all else, Brasilia.

As a counterpart to his concentration on a limited number of specific objectives, Kubitschek was willing to allow other politicians, with whom he had to work, to achieve their own rather more mundane ends. This involved the adroit use of patronage. As governor, he conferred frequently with the local leaders of the PSD, Republican party, and Labor party, which supported his administration, concerning projects of key interest in their municipalities, with not only willingness but enthusiasm to provide them with local improvements which would enhance their prestige. However, he insisted that these politicians' requests be for public works and similar projects rather than for replacement of local officials, and particularly of teachers.

As president, too, he was willing to allow his political allies to include within the budget items which were of particular concern to them and their constituents once the projects associated with his Target Plan had been addressed. As he pointed out years later, the Target Plan never accounted for more than 25 percent of the budget. Much of the rest reflected the political needs of his allies in Congress. The use of patronage by Juscelino could be punitive as well as positive. For example, when the Partido Trabalhista Brasileiro was threatening to block transfer of the national capital from Rio to Brasilia, Kubitschek informed Vice President Goulart

390

that if the Trabalhistas persisted he, Kubitschek, would break off with them; Goulart knew very well that that would mean their losing the extensive patronage which they controlled in the Labor Ministry and the social security system. The PTB quickly changed its attitude.

Another key element of Kubitschek's political technique was his almost unlimited energy and hard work. This was so not only when he was mayor, governor, and president, but also during the post-Estado Novo period when he was secretary general of the PSD in Minas Gerais. His energy and hard work gave him a considerable advantage over virtually all of the other politicians with whom he had to deal. Most important of his political tools was his close contact with his constituents. As mayor, he went out just after sunrise to visit public works projects or other programs of the city government in different parts of the city and visited the people in the vicinity on a virtually house-to-house basis. As governor, he constantly travelled around the state to keep track of projects of his administration and to confer with local political leaders and citizens. He talked on these occasions with workers and casual visitors, as well as with party members.

As president, he intensified these citizen contacts. He spent a large part of his time visiting his government's projects in various parts of the country; he personally investigated the Northeastern drought crisis of 1958; he virtually commuted back and forth to Brasilia; and he participated in patriotic or other celebrations going on in different parts of the country. On all of these occasions, he made it a point to talk not only with local figures of importance but also with ordinary citizens who were present. He was a good listener as well as a good talker. He asked people about problems in their locality, got their opinions about whatever it was he was inspecting, and listened to whatever it was they wanted to talk to him about. In this way he convinced vast numbers of people that he was really concerned about the things which concerned them. In addition, he was a missionary. Whether in his talks with national political leaders, local politicians, or rank-and-file citizens, Kubitschek always sought to explain to his listeners what his government was doing—whether in the city of Belo Horizonte, the state of Minas, or the United States of Brazil. He also sought to defend what he and his government were doing, and to seek to enlist the support of his audience for those efforts.

His was always an optimistic message. He sought to convince his listeners that what he was doing such as paving the main street of Belo Horizonte, or building a large hydroelectric project in Minas Gerais was not only possible, but was an important contribution to the future of the city, state, or nation. He answered criticisms, he counteracted doubts, he sought to convince people that Brazil was capable of a great deal more than it had so far accomplished, and that they should cooperate in helping the country fulfill its promise. He sought to get people to share his vision and to support his efforts to turn it into reality, even if this meant hard work and sacrifice.

What Juscelino Left Undone

In the five years he was president, Kubitschek left incomplete the process of Brazilian economic development. He was unable to establish the tradition of political democracy on a firm enough foundation to resist the idiocies and incapacities of his successors. Kubitschek concentrated on a relatively limited number of objectives during his time in the presidency. He did not try to do everything at once. In particular, he did relatively little to develop those parts of the country's agriculture which were economically and socially retrograde. Nor did he seek to bring about any fundamental social change in the country. He thought that both of these policies would be more appropriate to a time when Brazil had an integrated manufacturing sector which would be capable of producing the inputs needed for a general agricultural development program, and which would shift the country's political balance sufficiently to make possible fundamental rural reforms which were not politically possible in the Brazil of which Juscelino became president.

It is clear that Kubitschek was not unaware of the problems of agricultural development and reform. He thought that his presidential term of 1956-1961 would not be his only period as chief executive. He was convinced, until the revolution of 31 March to 1 April 1964, that he would be reelected president in 1965. To that end, he had developed a program for his second presidency. This program centered on the expansion of the country's agriculture and on bringing about some land redistribution and other reforms which were needed. Unfortunately Kubitschek was unable to have a second term as president, largely because of the incompetence of his successors, which gave rise to the assumption of power by the military in 1964.

The failures of Quadros and Goulart also resulted in the end of the political democracy in which Kubitschek believed and which he had practiced. This failure brought to prominence one of the ironies of Kubitschek's political career: the diehard opposition of important elements of the Armed Forces. This opposition originated from the division of the military, as well as civilian public opinion, between the supporters of Vargas and his opponents.

Those traditionally opposed to Getúlio were also equally opposed to Kubitschek. Some of them plotted against him when he was president. He fortified their opposition to him when he pardoned those who were court martialed for mutiny, thus depriving them of the possibility of being martyrs. Subsequently, they and some of their hierarchical superiors took revenge on ex-president Kubitschek. After the 1964 coup they brought about the deprivation of his civil rights and then submitted him to humiliating interrogation and other persecution.

Juscelino and Getúlio

Certainly the only Brazilian political figure in the twentieth century who can rival Kubitschek in importance has been Vargas. Thirty-five years after the death of the latter and nearly a decade and a half after the demise of the former, they were still widely regarded as the two most important of the country's political leaders. A public opinion poll late in 1981 revealed that Vargas generally was seen as having been the nation's most important political leader; Kubitschek ranked second. Among the most humble citizens, Getúlio won the support of 48.8 percent of those polled and Juscelino 14.7 percent. Among groups higher in the social scale, Juscelino was seen as being more important than Getúlio.[2]

Of course, Vargas ruled for almost four times as long as did Kubitschek. During much of his period in power, he had complete control over the organs of public expression and was able to deeply impress the humbler citizenry with the picture of himself as their *patrão*, and "father of the poor." He died a martyr's death. His suicide letter pictured his martyrdom as being on behalf of the people of Brazil, and particularly of the most humble among them.

393

This as much as anything else assured his enshrinement in the hearts and memories of the working class of Brazil.

The appeal of Juscelino was different from that of Vargas. He did not seek the support of one particular group among Brazil's citizenry, unless it be that of the candangos who built Brasilia. Rather, he sought to get the Brazilians in general to raise their sights, to come to understand themselves better, to know what they were capable of doing and then to live up to their own best natures and their full capacities. He never appealed to one group of Brazilians against another but sought to find grounds for conciliation so that the nation as a whole could work together for its progress and prosperity.

Looked at from one point of view, the different nature of the attractiveness of Getúlio and Juscelino to the people of Brazil can be seen as reflecting the Brazil of the past, and the Brazil of the future. In his appeal to the lower classes, Vargas was manipulating one of the deepest strains in the Brazilian national character. He did not picture himself as the leader of the Brazilian workers, but rather as their protector, patron, and benefactor. He raised to a national level the old patron-client relationship which had its origins in the slave society of the plantations of colonial and imperial Brazil. He used to his own political advantage the age-old tradition that the weaker members of the nation's society must seek out powerful figures to whom to attach themselves, and with whom to establish the asymmetrical mutual relationship whereby the patrão protects and helps out his dependents in times of need, in return for which the dependent is unalterably loyal to and will rally behind the patrão. Vargas pictured himself as the master of the Brazilian national plantation.

In contrast, Kubitschek sought to fix the eyes of his countrymen on a Brazil which did not yet exist, but which he was convinced could be brought into being. He was much more of a leader and much less of a patron than Vargas. He urged his fellow Brazilians to move ahead under his leadership to create a new industrial Brazil which would occupy its vast territory, and which would put to use its vast but latent resources. The Brazil he saw was one which by increasing its capacity to produce would assure its citizens vastly higher levels of living. A Brazil whose citizens' talents, whether in industry, in science, in the fine arts, in literature, or in a vast number of other fields, would win it a major place among the world's nations. This Brazil would also be a free nation. It would be a country in which government would be in the hands of those whom the citizenry had freely chosen to govern, and in which the government did not interfere with the citizens rights to think, speak, believe, and write as they saw fit, that is, a country in which civil liberties and civil rights would be assured.

Power and its Uses

There is no doubt that the two men who influenced Brazil most in the twentieth century *were* Vargas and Kubitschek. Both brought profound changes to the country. Both sought to foster the economic growth of the nation. Both sought to increase the material well being of its citizens. Both sought to enhance the role of Brazil in the hemisphere and the world at large. Both men had what the Latin Americans sometimes call "the vocation for power." Both Getúlio and Juscelino loved power. They both enjoyed the struggle to achieve it. They both savored the exercise of it. Yet there was a profound difference between them in their attitudes towards power, and to a large degree this was the mark of the difference between the two men as leaders of their country.

Vargas loved power for its own sake and recognized little or no necessary limitations on it once he had it. He believed in no political principles so that he would use almost any methods and ideas to hold on to power. During his first fifteen years in the presidency he could rule with equal ease insofar as his principles and his conscience were concerned, either as a de facto ruler uninhibited by constitutional restraints, a chief executive under a democratic constitution, or a dictator under a fascist constitution, and an ally of the communists.

The attitude of Kubitschek towards power was very different. Although he enjoyed very much the experience of power, he sought to use it for the achievement of certain goals. It is clear that one of those goals was political democracy. He was uninterested in exercising power for power's sake. He felt that there were necessary limitations of power, that his use of power should be circumscribed by the system of democratic government.

In a small book which he wrote after leaving the presidency, Kubitschek discussed democracy:

I consider that a democratic regime is really installed in a country not only when a constitution is promulgated or even when there are functioning juridical institutions providing fundamental human rights. Democracy becomes a fact in an authentic sense of free and dignified social life when every class, every group, every individual loses fear of the State. In truth, the democratic state could not be feared, but must be, to be sure, respected. And only those are respected who know how to be respectful.

I don't consider that we have reached a state of perfect realization of the democratic system. But one thing is certain: there has been definitely planted in the consciousness of the Brazilian people the conviction that there is only one form of government behavior compatible with the dignity of man: that of respect towards popular aspirations and manifestations. A government that turns its back on the people, which seeks to intimidate individuals . . . choosing its own time to distribute benefits, may present itself as having all the external characteristics of a regular democracy . . . but it is, in essence, a totalitarian regime.[3]

Kubitschek also indicated his conviction that he had adhered to his own belief in democracy. He said: "I carried out a government without menaces, because I carried out a government without fear. I had, thanks to God, the courage to experiment with democracy which . . . implies an emphasis on justice and generosity. Liberty is a risk, is an adventure, from which we cannot flee without renouncing our own human condition."[4]

This attitude of Juscelino was brought out most clearly at the time when, as the 1960 presidential campaign was beginning to gather momentum, some of his associates suggested to him that he should run for reelection, in spite of the constitutional prohibition. No one stated Juscelino's position better than he himself. He issued a statement which referred to him in the third person and asserted that "in the government he fulfilled all of the promised goals. Why should there be missing the democratic goal, which he has always considered and considers fundamental? The president of the Republic accepts and will accept no other solution which is not simply this: on the 31st day of January of 1961, he will transmit the post to his successor, freely chosen by the votes of the majority of the people."[5]

Conclusion

Kubitschek's Target Plan and his success in fulfilling its goals which are the best measure by which to judge Kubitschek's place in history. The Plan included the original goals which he set forth when a candidate for president and Brasilia, the one which he added subsequently and which came to be so dear to his heart. The Plan included also three targets which never were formally incorporated into the Programa de Metas: the instilling into the Brazilian people of a belief in themselves and their own capabilities, the gaining for Brazil of an enhanced status in the hemisphere and the world, and the demonstration that democracy is not only abstractly the best system of government, but that it is also the best form of government to obtain all of the other goals which he had set before himself and the nation. Judged by these standards, Kubitschek was, I believe, the best president and the greatest political figure that Brazil has had in the twentieth century.

NOTES

Chapter 1

1. For a study of the struggle over protectionalism, see Nicia Vilela Luz, *A Luta Pela Industrialização do Brasil* (São Paulo: Difusão Europeia do Livro, 1961).
2. For two classic studies of the Brazilian waves of development, see Caio Prado Junior, *História Económica do Brasil* (São Paulo: Editora Brasiliense, 1962) and Celso Furtado, *Formação Económica do Brasil* (Rio de Janeiro: Fundo de Cultura, 1964).
3. For an extensive analysis of the import substitution strategy of industrialization, see Robert J. Alexander, *A New Strategy of Economic Development* (Marymount, NY: Orbis Books, 1976).

Chapter 2

1. See Robert J. Alexander, *Organized Labor In Latin America* (New York: The Free Press, 1965), Chapter 6 and Robert J. Alexander, *Labor Relations in Argentina, Brazil and Chile* (New York: McGraw-Hill, 1962) for discussions of the growth of organized labor before, during, and after the Vargas era.
2. Samuel Putnam, *Marvelous Journey: A Survey of Four Centuries of Brazilian Writing* (New York: Alfred A. Knopf, 1948), p. 207.
3. See chapter 13 on "The Kubitschek Regime and the Brazilian Cultural Renaissance."
4. Putnam, *Marvelous Journey*, p. 210.
5. See Jordan M. Young, *The Brazilian Revolution of 1930 and the Aftermath* (New Brunswick: Rutgers University Press,

1967), particularly chapters 3 and 4, for a more extensive discussion of the Revolution of 1930.

6. Nelson Werneck Sodré, *História Militar do Brasil* (Rio de Janeiro: Editora Civilização Brasileira, 1965), pp. 287-88.

7. Oblique references to the controversy over Getúlio's return to power was made in Dutra's speech turning over the presidency to Vargas. See José Teixeira de Oliveira (ed), *O Governo Dutra* (Rio de Janeiro: Editora Civilização Brasileira, 1956), p. 341.

8. Interview with João Goulart in Maldonado, Uruguay, 5 June 1972.

9. Interview with Alizira Vargas in Rio de Janeiro, 10 January 1966.

10. Interview with João Goulart, see note 8.

11. Interviews with Goulart, Vargas, see notes 8 and 9. Also Jordan M. Young (ed.), *Brazil 1954-1964: End of a Civilian Cycle* (New York: Facts on File, 1972), p. 16.

12. Jordan M. Young (ed.), *Brazil 1954-1964*, pp. 16-17.

Chapter 3

1. Juscelino Kubitschek, *A Experiencia da Humilidade* (Rio de Janeiro: Bloch Editores, 1974), p. 24. References to this work in the text of chapter 3 will use the abbreviation "E.H."

2. Juscelino Kubitschek, *A Marcha do Amanecer* "Bestseller" (São Paulo: Importadora de Livros, 1962), pp. 15-16, 20-21.

3. Kubitschek, *A Marcha*, p. 14.

4. José Moraes, *Juscelino: A Homen, A Candidatura, A Campanha* (Belo Horizonte: Imprensa Oficial de Minas Gerais, 1955), pp. 16-17.

5. Moraes, *Juscelino*, pp. 16-17.

6. Moraes, *Juscelino*, p. 18.

7. Interview with Juscelino Kubitschek in Belo Horizonte, 1 June 1972.

8. Interview with Francisco Negrão de Lima in Rio de Janeiro, 6 April 1966.

Chapter 4

1. Juscelino Kubitschek, *A Experiencia da Humilidade* (Rio de Janeiro: Bloch Editores, 1974), p. 331. References to this work with the text of chapter 4 will use the abbreviation "E.H."
2. Juscelino Kubitschek, *A Escalada Política* (Rio de Janeiro: Bloch Editores, 1976), p. 16. References to this work in the text of chapter 4 will use the abbreviation "E.P."
3. Interview with Juscelino Kubitschek in Rio de Janeiro, 31 May 1972.
4. Interview with Juscelino Kubitschek in Rio de Janeiro, 31 May 1972.
5. Moraes, *Juscelino*, p. 38.
6. Moraes, *Juscelino*, p. 38.

Chapter 5

1. Juscelino Kubitschek, *A Escalada Política* (Rio de Janeiro: Bloch Editores, 1976), p. 41. References to this work in the text of chapter 5 will use the abbreviation "E.P."
2. Interview with Astrogildo Pereira in Rio de Janeiro, 19 October 1965.
3. Interview with José Segadas Viana in Rio de Janeiro, 16 March 1956.
4. Interview with Luís Carlos Prestes in Rio de Janeiro, 27 August 1946.
5. Interview with Agildo Barata in Rio de Janeiro, 20 August 1965.
6. Interview with Juscelino Kubitschek in Belo Horizonte, 1 June 1972.
7. Moraes, *Juscelino*, pp. 46-47.
8. Also Edward Riedinger's interview with Kubitschek in Rio de Janeiro, 13 June 1974.
9. Moraes, *Juscelino*, p. 50.

Chapter 6

1. *Quatro Anos no Governo de Minas Gerais (1951-1955)—Sintese das Realizacões do Governador Juscelino Kubitschek de*

Oliveira (Rio de Janeiro: Livraria José Olympio Editora, 1959), p. 307. References to this work in the text of chapter 6 will use the abbreviation "Q.A."

2. Interview with Juscelino Kubitschek in Rio de Janeiro, 31 May 1972.
3. Juscelino Kubitschek, *A Escalada Política* (Rio de Janeiro: Bloch Editores, 1976), p. 211. References to this work in the text of chapter 6 will use the abbreviation "E.P."
4. Interview with Juscelino Kubitschek in Rio de Janeiro, 31 May 1972; see also Kubitschek, op. cit., pp. 311-12.
5. *Visão da Industria*, São Paulo, May 1954, p. 24.
6. Moraes, *Juscelino*, p. 70.
7. Moraes, *Juscelino*, p. 73.
8. Moraes, *Juscelino*, p. 73.
9. Moraes, *Juscelino*, p. 73.
10. Edward Anthony Riedinger, *Como se Faz Um Presidente: A Campanha de J.K.* (Rio de Janeiro: Editora Nova Fronteira, 1988), p. 45.
11. Riedinger, *Como se Faz*, p. 46.
12. Interview with Juscelino Kubitschek in Rio de Janeiro, 29 June 1973.

Chapter 7

1. Interview with João Café Filho in Rio de Janeiro, 8 June 1966.
2. Interview with Juscelino Kubitschek in Rio de Janeiro, 31 May 1972.
3. Interview with João Café Filho in Rio de Janeiro, 8 June 1966.
4. See article by Azeredo Coutinho "A Traição de Café Filho," in *Panfleto*, Rio de Janeiro, June 1958.
5. Juscelino Kubitschek, *A Escalada Política* (Rio de Janeiro: Bloch Editores, 1976), p. 304. References to this work in the text of chapter 7 will use the abbreviation "E.P." For Café Filho's own account of his life before becoming president, see vol. I of his memoirs, João Café Filho, *Do Sindacato ao Catete* (Rio de Janeiro: Livraria José Olympio Editora, 1966).

6. Juarez Távora, *Uma Vida y Muitas Lutas*, 3rd vol., *Voltando a Planicie* (Rio de Janeiro: Livraria José Olympio Editora, 1976), p. 32.
7. Glauco Carneiro, *Historia das Revolucões Brasileiras* vol. 2 (Rio de Janeiro: Edicões O Cruzeiro, 1965), p. 483.
8. Interview with Juscelino Kubitschek in Belo Horizonte, 1 June 1972; also see Café Filho, op. cit., p. 383.
9. Távora, *Uma Vide*, p. 28.
10. Interview with Juscelino Kubitschek in Belo Horizonte, 1 June 1972.
11. Café Filho, *Do Sindacato*, pp. 470-71.
12. Jordan M. Young (ed.), *Brazil 1954-1964: End of a Civilian Cycle* (New York: Facts on File, 1972), p. 19.
13. Café Filho, *Do Sindacato*, p. 495.
14. Café Filho, *Do Sindacato*, pp. 527-28.
15. Etelvino Lins, *Um Depoimento Político (Episodios e Observacões)* (Rio de Janeiro: Livraria José Olympio Editora, 1976), p. 63.
16. Lins, *Um Depoimento*, p. 65.
17. Café Filho, *Do Sindacato*, pp. 485-91.
18. Café Filho, *Do Sindacato*, pp. 496-97.
19. Café Filho, *Do Sindacato*, p. 497.
20. Café Filho, *Do Sindacato*, p. 497.
21. Café Filho, *Do Sindacato*, p. 497.
22. Távora, *Uma Vide*, pp. 34-35.
23. Interview with João Goulart in Maldonado, Uruguay, 5 June 1972; also see Riedinger, *Como se Faz*, pp. 158-161.
24. Maria Victoria de Mesquita Benevides, *O Governo Kubitschek: Desenvolvimento Económico e Estabilidade Política* 3rd ed. (Rio de Janeiro: Paz e Terra, 1979), Chapter 3.
25. *New Leader*, New York, 27 December 1954.
26. Távora, *Uma Vide*, pp. 36-37.
27. Távora, *Uma Vide*, pp. 60-63.
28. Interview with Nestor Peixoto de Oliveira in São Paulo, 6 March 1956.
29. Távora, *Uma Vide*, p. 71.
30. Távora, *Uma Vide*, pp. 77-78; for Café Filho's version of these events, see Café Filho, *Do Sindacato*, pp. 512-24.

31. Moisés Vinhas, *O Partidão: A Luta por um Partido de Massas 1922-1974* (São Paulo: Editora Hucitec, 1982), p. 181.
32. Riedinger, *Como se Faz*, p. 200.
33. Riedinger, *Como se Faz*, p. 217.
34. Vinhas, *O Partidão*, p. 177.
35. Riedinger, *Como se Faz*, p. 217.
36. See also Távora, *Uma Vide*, p. 90.
37. Riedinger, *Como se Faz*, p. 240.
38. Benevides, *O Governo Kubitschek*, p. 97.
39. Távora, *Uma Vide*, p. 69.
40. See also Távora, *Uma Vide*, pp. 33-34, 74-76; and Riedinger, *Como se Faz*, pp. 222-26.
41. Octavio Ianni, Paulo Singer, Gabriel Cohn, and Francisco C. Weffort, *Politica e Revoluçao Social No Brasil* (Rio de Janeiro: Editora Civilização Brasileira, 1956), p. 104.

Chapter 8

1. Interview with President João Café Filho in Rio de Janeiro, 8 June 1966.
2. Interview with Juscelino Kubitschek in Rio de Janeiro, 31 May 1972.
3. Juscelino Kubitschek, *A Escalada Politica* (Rio de Janeiro: Bloch Editores, 1976), p. 413. References to this work in the text of chapter 8 will use the abbreviation "E.P."
4. For his discussion of the onset of his illness, see Café Filho, *Do Sindacato*, pp. 522-59.
5. Glauco Carneiro, *Historia das Revolucões Brasileiras* vol. 2 (Rio de Janeiro: Edicões O Cruzeiro, 1965), p. 487.
6. Távora, *Uma Vide*, p. 98.
7. John W.F. Dulles, *President Castello Branco: Brazilian Reformer* (College Station: Texas A&M University Press, 1980), p. 55.
8. Carlos Castilho Cabral, *Os Tempos de Jânio e Outros Tempos* (Rio de Janeiro: Editora Civilização Brasileira, 1962), p. 87.
9. Cabral, *Os Tempos*, p. 81.
10. See Távora, *Uma Vide*, pp. 56-58, 62, 64-65.
11. Carneiro, *Historia*, p. 486.
12. Carneiro, *Historia*, p. 487.
13. Cabral, *Os Tempos*, p. 83.

14. Café Filho, *Do Sindacato*, pp. 558-59.
15. *O Cruzeiro*, Rio de Janeiro, 26 November 1955.
16. *O Cruzeiro*, Rio de Janeiro, 26 November 1955.
17. Carneiro, *Historia*, pp. 489-94.
18. Interview with Juscelino Kubitschek in Belo Horizonte, 1 June 1972; see also Carneiro, *Historia*, p. 495.
19. See also Café Filho, *Do Sindacato*, pp. 496-97.
20. Interview with Parsifal Barroso in Fortaleza, 22 April 1966.
21. See also Young (ed.),*Brazil 1954-1964*, p. 27.
22. John W.F. Dulles, *Castelo Branco—The Making of a Brazilian President* (College Station: Texas A&M University Press, 1980), p. 213.
23. Interview of Juscelino Kubitschek by Edward Riedinger in Rio de Janeiro, 26 November 1974.

Chapter 9

1. Interview with Plinio Barreto in São Paulo, 16 April 1956.
2. Celso Lafer, *The Planning Process and the Political System in Brazil: A Study of Kubitschek's Target Plan 1956-1961* (Ph.D. diss., Cornell University, 1970), University Microfilms, Ann Arbor, Michigan, p. 34.
3. Lafer, *Planning Process*, pp. 36-37.
4. Interview with Juscelino Kubitschek in Rio de Janeiro, 31 May 1972.
5. Thomas E. Skidmore, *Politics in Brazil 1930-1964* (New York: Oxford University Press, 1967), pp. 36-37.
6. Interview with Juscelino Kubitschek in New York City, 28 November 1966.
7. O.J. Menezes, "Industry—Preliminary Diagnosis" (MS), August 1965.
8. Alberto Deodato, *Nos Tempos de João Goulart* (Belo Horizonte: Editora Itatiaia Ltda., 1965), p. 25.
9. Juscelino Kubitschek, *Por Que Construí Brasília* (Rio de Janeiro: Bloch Editores, 1976), pp. 364-65.
10. Stefan Robock, *Brazil's Developing Northeast—A Study in Regional Planning and Foreign Aid* (Washington, DC: The Brookings Institution, 1963). p. 95.
11. Robock, *Brazil's Developing Northeast*, p. 97.
12. Robock, *Brazil's Developing Northeast*, p. 96.

13. Interview with Juscelino Kubitschek in New York City, 28 November 1966.
14. Some discussion of the situation giving rise to SUDENE and the role it was designed to play can be found in the chapter "O Problema do Nordeste," in Celso Furtado, *A Pre-Revolução Brasileira* (Rio de Janeiro: Fundo de Cultura, 1962).
15. Interview with Juscelino Kubitschek in New York City, 28 November 1966.
16. Ibid.
17. Lafer, *Planning Process*, pp. 151-52.
18. Lafer, *Planning Process*, pp. 153-56.
19. Skidmore, *Politics in Brazil*, p. 167.
20. Philip Raine, *Brazil: Awakening Giant* (Washington, DC: Public Affairs Press, 1974), p. 165.
21. Eduardo Matarazzo Suplicy, *Política Económica Brasileira e Internacional* (Petropolis: Editora Vozes Ltda., 1977), p. 34.
22. Suplicy, *Política Económica*, p. 35.
23. Leôncia Basbaum, *História Sincera da Republica* vol. 3 (São Paulo: Editora Fulgor Limitada, 1968), p. 223.
24. Interview with Juscelino Kubitschek in Belo Horizonte, 1 June 1972; a synthesis of the Medici development plan can be found in *Metas e Bases para A Ação de Goberno* (Brasilia: Presidencia da Republica, 1970).
25. Ibid.
26. Interview with Gilberto Paim in Rio de Janeiro, 13 October 1965.
27. Robert T. Daland, *Brazilian Planning: Development, Politics and Administration* (Chapel Hill: University of North Carolina Press, 1967), p. 88.
28. Lafer, *Planning Process*, pp. 53-56.
29. Carlos Lessa, "Quince Años de Política Económic en el Brasil," *Boletín Económico de América Latina* 9/2 (November 1964): 102.
30. *As Metas do Governo*, Presidencia da Republica, Serviço de Interesses Estaduals, Serviço Grafico do IBGE, n.d. (1959), vol. 1, Introduction, p. 3.
31. Lessa, "Quince Años," p. 187.
32. Interview with Agilberto de Lacerda Figueiredo Santos in São Paulo, 26 April 1956.

33. Lessa, "Quince Años," p. 188.
34. Lafer, *Planning Process*, p. 68.
35. Lafer, *Planning Process*, pp. 68-70.
36. Interview with Antônio José Chediak in Rio de Janeiro, 6 April 1966.
37. Lafer, *Planning Process*, p. 57.
38. Lafer, *Planning Process*, pp. 58-59.
39. Lafer, *Planning Process*, p. 59.
40. Lafer, *Planning Process*, pp. 60-62.
41. Lafer, *Planning Process*, pp. 64-65.
42. Lessa, "Quince Años," pp. 159-60.
43. Lessa, "Quince Años," p. 162.
44. Lessa, "Quince Años," p. 162.
45. Cited in Werner Baer, *Industrialization and Economic Development in Brazil* (Homewood, IL: Richard D. Irwin, Inc., 1965), p. 66.

Chapter 10

1. Lessa, "Quince Años," p. 164.
2. Lessa, "Quince Años," p. 163.
3. Lafer, *Planning Process*, pp. 167-68.
4. Lafer, *Planning Process*, p. 168-69.
5. Lafer, *Planning Process*, p. 171.
6. Lafer, *Planning Process*, pp. 172-75.
7. Lessa, "Quince Años," p. 164.
8. Lessa, "Quince Años," p. 165.
9. Lessa, "Quince Años," p. 166.
10. Lessa, "Quince Años," p. 166.
11. Werner Baer, *The Development of the Brazilian Steel Industry* (Nashville: Vanderbilt University Press, 1969), pp. 80-81.
12. Baer, *Development*, pp. 81-82.
13. Lincoln Gordon and Englebert L. Grommers, *United States Manufacturing Investment in Brazil—The Impact of Government Policies 1946-1960* (Boston: Harvard Graduate School of Business Administration, 1962), p. 24.
14. Gordon and Grommers, *Manufacturing Investment*, p. 25.
15. See Nicia Vilela Luz, *A Luta Pela Industrialização do Brasil* (São Paulo: Difusão Europeia do Livro, 1961), for a survey of evolution of tariff policy in Brazil.

16. Gordon and Grommers, *Manufacturing Investment*, p. 21.
17. Gordon and Grommers, *Manufacturing Investment*, p. 28.
18. See Lessa, "Quince Años," pp. 192-93 for some further explanation of this.
19. Gordon and Grommers, *Manufacturing Investment*, p. 19.
20. Gordon and Grommers, *Manufacturing Investment*, p. 20.
21. Lessa, "Quince Años," p. 174.
22. Lessa, "Quince Años," p. 178.
23. Lessa, "Quince Años," p. 193.
24. Gordon and Grommers, *Manufacturing Investment*, p. 48.
25. Werner Baer, *Industrialization and Economic Development in Brazil* (Homewood, IL: Richard D. Irwin, Inc.), p. 69.
26. Gordon and Grommers, op. cit., p. 60.
27. Gordon and Grommers, *Manufacturing Investment*, p. 54.
28. Gordon and Grommers, *Manufacturing Investment*, p. 60.
29. *1971 Automobile Facts and Figures*, Automobile Manufacturers Association, 1971, p. 7.
30. Lessa, "Quince Años," p. 168.
31. Lessa, "Quince Años,", p. 169.
32. Lessa, "Quince Años,", pp. 165-66.
33. Comisión Económica Para América Latina, *La Fabricación de Maquinarias y Equipos Industriales en America Latina—II, Las Maquinas Herramientos en el Brasil* (New York: Comisión Económica Para América Latina, 1962), p. 4.
34. Ibid.
35. Lessa, "Quince Años," p. 168.
36. *Jornal do Brasil*, Rio de Janeiro, 31 December 1965.
37. Interview with Juscelino Kubitschek in New York City, 28 November 1966.
38. Lessa, "Quince Años," p. 168.
39. Lessa, "Quince Años," p. 182.
40. Celso Furtado, *Dialectica do Desenvolvimento* (Rio de Janeiro: Editora Fundo de Cultura, 1964), p. 106.
41. Lessa, "Quince Años," p. 183.

Chapter 11

1. Skidmore, *Politics in Brazil*, p. 168.
2. This historical background is taken from the chapter on "A Mudanca da Capital," in Manoel França Campos, *Brasilia 3*

de Março (Rio de Janeiro: Livraria São José, 1960), pp. 139-66.

3. Juscelino Kubitschek, *Por Que Construí Brasília* (Rio de Janeiro: Bloch Editores, 1976), p. 8. References to this work in the text of chapter 11 will use the abbreviation "P.Q."
4. Campos, *Brasilia*, p. 159.
5. See also Campos, *Brasilia*, pp. 202-4.
6. Campos, *Brasilia*, p. 206.
7. Campos, *Brasilia*, p. 215.
8. Betty Wilson, "Brasília, Brazil—The Carving of a Capital Out of a Wilderness," *Américas*, Washington, DC, August 1959.
9. Interview with Juscelino Kubitschek in New York City, 28 November 1966.
10. Speech by Juscelino Kubitschek at New York University, New York City, 5 March 1962.
11. Skidmore, *Politics in Brazil*, p. 168.
12. Interview with Daniel Krieger in Brasilía, 17 March 1966; and with Ernesto Street in Rio de Janeiro, 16 August 1965.
13. Interview with Juscelino Kubitschek in New York City, 28 November 1966.
14. Interview with Juscelino Kubitschek in New York City, 28 November 1966.
15. Interview with Ernesto Street in Rio de Janeiro, 16 August 1965.
16. Raine, *Brazil: Awakening Giant*, p. 166.
17. Interview with Mario Pedrosa in Rio de Janeiro, 24 August 1959.
18. Interview with Juscelino Kubitschek in New York City, 28 November 1966.
19. Brigadier General Vernon Walter et al., "The Road of the Jaguars: Belem-Brasilia Highway, Brazil, January 1965" (Mimeographed), p. 1.
20. Interview with Socrates Bonfim, President of Cia. Siduerurgica de Amazonia, in Manaus, 26 February 1966.
21. Interview with José Maria Alkmin in Belo Horizonte, 6 June 1966.
22. John Dos Passos, *Brazil on the Move* (Garden City, NY: Doubleday and Co., 1963), pp. 52-61.
23. Passos, *Brazil on the Move*, p. 69.

24. Milton Eisenhower, *The Wine Is Bitter: The United States and Latin America* (Garden City, NY: Doubleday and Co., 1963), p. 120.

Chapter 12

1. Oliver Onody, *A Inflação Brasileira*, privately published, Rio de Janeiro, 1960, pp. 117-19.
2. Mario Simonsen, *A Experiencia Inflacionaria no Brasil* (Rio de Janeiro: Instituto de Pesquisas e Estudos Sociais, 1964), pp. 10-11.
3. Simonsen, *Experiencia*, pp. 63-64.
4. For a concise discussion of the monetarist-structuralist controversy over inflation from two alternative points of view, see Roberto Campos, "Two Views of Inflation in Latin America" and David Felix "An Alternative View of the 'Monetarist-Structuralist Controversy'" in *Latin American Issues* ed. Albert O. Hirschman (New York: Twentieth Century Foundation, 1961).
5. Ignacio Rangel, *Recursos Ociosos* (Rio de Janeiro: Conselho de Desenvolvimento, 163), p. 6.
6. Carl Shoup, *The Tax System of Brazil* (Rio de Janeiro: Fundação Getúlio Vargas, 1964), p. 5.
7. Simonsen, *Experiencia*, p. 68.
8. Simonsen, *Experiencia*, pp. 71-72.
9. Gordon and Grommers, *Manufacturing Investment*, p. 151.
10. Simonsen, *Experiencia*, pp. 74-75.
11. Ignacio Rangel, *A Inflação Brasileira* (Rio de Janeiro: Tempo Brasileiro, 1963), p. 56.
12. Rangel, *Inflação*, p. 73.
13. Rangel, *Inflação*, p. 74.
14. Rangel, *Inflação*, p. 73.
15. Skidmore, *Politics in Brazil*, p. 177.
16. Skidmore, *Politics in Brazil*, p. 178.
17. Skidmore, *Politics in Brazil*, p. 182.
18. Juscelino Kubitschek, *Por Que Construí Brasília* (Rio de Janeiro: Bloch Editores, 1976), p. 361.
19. Kubitschek, *Por Que*, p. 362.
20. Kubitschek, *Por Que*, pp. 358-59.
21. Kubitschek, *Por Que*, p. 362.

Chapter 13

1. Gilberto Freyre, *New World in the Tropics: The Culture of Modern Brazil* (New York: Alfred A. Knopf, 1959), p. 18.
2. Samuel Putnam, *Marvelous Journey: A Survey of Four Centuries of Brazilian Writing* (New York: Alfred A. Knopf, 1948), p. 202.
3. Afranio Coutinho, *No Hospital das Letras* (Rio de Janeiro: Edições Tempo Brasileiro, 1963), pp. 63-64.
4. Stefan Zweig, *Brazil: Land of the Future* (New York: The Viking Press, 1941), p. 160.
5. *Jornal do Brasil*, Rio de Janeiro, 1 September 1965.
6. *O Estado de São Paulo*, São Paulo, 10 October 1965.
7. Passos, *Brazil on the Move*, p. 84.
8. Peter Blake, *The Master Builders* (New York: Alfred A. Knopf, 1960), pp. 98-100.
9. Freyre, *New World*, p. 23.
10. Zweig, *Brazil*, p. 144.
11. João Saldanha, *Os Subterraneos de Futebol* (Rio de Janeiro: Tempo Brasileiro, 1963) is the main source of this information on Brazil's most popular sport.
12. Freyre, *New World*, pp. 88-89.

Chapter 14

1. See E. Bradford Burns, *The Unwritten Alliance: Rio Branco and Brazilian-American Relations* (New York: Columbia University Press, 1966), for a study of Rio Branco's long reign as Foreign Minister.
2. Vladimir Reisky de Dubnic, "Trends in Brazil's Foreign Policy," in *New Perspectives of Brazil* ed. Eric N. Baklanoff (Nashville: Vanderbilt University Press, 1966). Reference on page 81.
3. *Revista Brasileira de Política Internacional* Rio de Janeiro, March 1969, p. 152.
4. *Revista Brasileira* (1969), p. 150.
5. *Revista Brasileira* (1969), p. 146.
6. *Revista Brasileira* (1969), p. 139.

7.   Milton Eisenhower, *The Wine Is Bitter: The United States and Latin America* (Garden City, NY: Doubleday and Co., 1963), p. 202.

8.   Juscelino Kubitschek, *Por Que Construí Brasília* (Rio de Janeiro: Bloch Editores, 1976), p. 138. References to this work in the text of chapter 14 will use the abbreviation "P.Q."

9.   Tad Szulc, *The Winds of Revolution: Latin America Today— and Tomorrow* (New York: Frederick A. Praeger, 1963), p. 116.

10.   Interview with Juscelino Kubitschek in Belo Horizonte, 1 June 1972.

11.   Interview with Juscelino Kubitschek in Belo Horizonte, 1 June 1972.

12.   *Revista Brasileira de Política Internacional*, March 1959, op. cit., pp. 152-53.

13.   *Revista Brasileira* (1959), p. 149.

14.   Jerome Levinson and Juan de Onis, *The Alliance That Lost Its Way: A Critical Report on the Alliance for Progress* (Chicago: Quadrangle Books, 1970), pp. 65-66.

15.   *Revista Brasileira* (1959), pp. 154, 158.

16.   Interview with Juscelino Kubitschek in Belo Horizonte, 1 June 1972.

17.   Interview with Juscelino Kubitschek in Belo Horizonte, 1 June 1972.

18.   Speech by Juscelino Kubitschek at New York University, New York City, 5 March 1972.

19.   Interview with Juscelino Kubitschek in Belo Horizonte, 1 June 1972.

20.   *New York Times*, 11 June 1959.

21.   *Hispanic American Report*, July 1960, p. 348.

22.   Interview with Juscelino Kubitschek in Belo Horizonte, 1 June 1972.

23.   *Hispanic American Report*, July 1960, p. 348.

24.   José Honorio Rodriguez, *Brazil and Africa* (Berkeley: University of California Press, 1965), p. 334.

25.   Wayne A. Selcher, *The Afro-Asian Dimension of Brazilian Foreign Policy* (Gainesville: The University Press of Florida, 1974), p. 155.

26.   Selcher, *Afro-Asian Dimension*, p. 154.

27. *Hispanic American Report*, July 1960, p. 566.
28. Selcher, *Afro-Asian Dimension*, p. 155.
29. *Hispanic American Report*, July 1960, p. 566.
30. Interview with Juscelino Kubitschek in Belo Horizonte, 1 June 1972.
31. *Hispanic American Report*, July 1960, p. 652.
32. Interview with Juscelino Kubitschek in Belo Horizonte, 1 June 1972; see also Kubitschek, op. cit., p. 648.
33. *Hispanic American Report*, July 1960, p. 281.
34. Osvaldo Orico, *Confissões do Exílio: J.K.* (Rio de Janeiro: Livraria Francisco Alves, 1977), p. 31.
35. *Hispanic American Report*, July 1960, pp. 350, 421.
36. *Hispanic American Report*, July 1960, p. 421.
37. *New York Times*, 27 July 1968.

Chapter 15

1. Interview with Juscelino Kubitschek in Belo Horizonte, 1 June 1972.
2. Interview with Juscelino Kubitschek in New York City, 28 November 1966.
3. Skidmore, *Politics in Brazil*, p. 171.
4. Interview with Juscelino Kubitschek in New York City, 28 November 1966.
5. Dulles, *President Castello Branco*, p. 110.
6. Benevides, *O Governo Kubitschek*, p. 155.
7. Benevides, *O Governo Kubitschek*, p. 156.
8. Benevides, *O Governo Kubitschek*, pp. 187-88.
9. Lawrence S. Graham, *Civil Service Reform in Brazil: Principles Versus Practice* (Austin: University of Texas Press, 1968), p. 123.
10. Graham, *Civil Service Reform*, p. 195.
11. See Introduction by Afonso Arinos de Melo Franco, to João Café Filho, *Do Sindacato ao Cateta* (Rio de Janeiro: Livraria José Olympio Editora, 1966), p. xxxv.
12. Vladimir Reisky de Dubnic, *Political Trends in Brazil* (Washington, DC, Public Affairs Press, 1968), p. 29.
13. Interview with José Segadas Viana in Rio de Janeiro, 16 March 1966.

14. Interview with Juscelino Kubitschek in Belo Horizonte, 1 June 1972.

15. Interview with João Goulart in Maldonado, Uruguay, 5 June 1972.

16. Interview with Parsifal Barroso in Fortaleza, 22 April 1966.

17. See Robert J. Alexander, *Labor Relations in Argentina, Brazil and Chile* (New York: McGraw-Hill, 1962), pp. 65-66.

18. Interview with Bayard Boiteux in Rio de Janeiro, 25 August 1959.

19. Interview with Edward Riedinger with Juscelino Kubitschek in Rio de Janeiro, 2 October 1973.

20. Kenneth Paul Erickson, *The Brazilian Corporative State and Working Class Politics* (Berkeley: University of California Press, 1977), pp. 102-3.

21. Interview with Parsifal Barroso in Fortaleza, 22 April 1966.

22. Erickson, *Brazilian Corporative State*, p. 33.

23. Ronald Chilcote, *The Brazilian Communist Party: Conflict and Integration* (New York: Oxford University Press, 1974), p. 150.

24. Chilcote, *The Brazilian Communist Party*, p. 151.

25. Basbaum, *História Sincera*, pp. 231-32.

26. Moisés Vinhas, *O Partidão: A Luta por um Partido de Massas 1922-1974* (São Paulo: Editora Fulgor Limitada, 1968), p. 182.

27. Szulc, *Winds of Revolution*, p. 32.

28. Sergio Magalhaes, *Problems do Desenvolvimento Economico* (Rio de Janeiro: Editora Civilizacao Brasileira, 1960), pp. 32-33.

29. Interview with Sergio Magalhaes in Rio de Janeiro, 13 January 1966.

30. Octavio Ianni, Paulo Singer, Gabriel Cohn, and Francisco C. Weffort, *Politica e Revoluçao Social No Brasil* (Rio de Janeiro: Editora Civilização Brasileira, 1956), p. 105.

31. Kubitschek, *Por Que*, p. 216.

32. Kubitschek, *Por Que*, pp. 216-17.

33. Kubitschek, *Por Que*, p. 219.

34. Kubitschek, *Por Que*, p. 220.

35. For a discussion of ISEB, see Frank Bonilla, "A National Ideology for Development: Brazil," in *Expectant Peoples:*

Nationalism and Development by K.H. Silvert (New York: Random House, 1963).

36. Carneiro, *Historia*, pp. 504-16.
37. Edward Riedinger interviews with Juscelino Kubitschek in Rio de Janeiro, 6 April 1974 and 24 October 1974.
38. Carneiro, *Historia*, pp. 519-31.
39. Interview with Carlos Lacerda in Rio de Janeiro, 3 February 1966.
40. Interview with Juscelino Kubitschek in Belo Horizonte, 1 June 1972.
41. Ibid.
42. Interview with José Sarney in São Luiz, 16 April 1966.
43. Orico, *Confissões*, p. 135.
44. Kubitschek, *Por Que*, p. 274.
45. Kubitschek, *Por Que*, p. 200.
46. Kubitschek, *Por Que*, pp. 199-204.
47. Kubitschek, *Por Que*, p. 202.
48. Kubitschek, *Por Que*, pp. 274-78.
49. Kubitschek, *Por Que*, p. 305.
50. Basbaum, *História Sincera*, p. 222.
51. Kubitschek, *Escalada Politica*, p. 501-2.
52. Skidmore, *Politics in Brazil*, pp. 171-72.
53. Young (ed.) *Brazil 1954-1964*, p. 48.
54. Suplicy, *Política Económica*, p. 34.
55. Kubitschek, *Por Que*, pp. 258-59.
56. Interview with Antonio José Chediak in Rio de Janeiro, 6 April 1966.
57. Szulc, *Winds of Revolution*, p. 195.
58. Interview with Juscelino Kubitschek in Belo Horizonte, 1 June 1972.
59. Cabral, *Os Tempos*, pp. 146-47.
60. Interview with Juscelino Kubitschek in Belo Horizonte, 1 June 1972.
61. Kubitschek, *Por Que*, pp. 258-59.
62. Young, *Brazil 1954-1964*, p. 61.
63. Interview with João Goulart in Maldonado, Uruguay, 5 June 1972.
64. Interview with Bayard Boiteux in Rio de Janeiro, 25 August 1959.

65. Interview with Juscelino Kubitschek in Rio de Janeiro, 31 May 1972; see also Kubitschek, *Por Que*, pp. 215-16.
66. Orico, *Confissões*, p. 121.
67. Interview with Juscelino Kubitschek in Rio de Janeiro, 31 May 1972; see also Kubitschek, *Por Que*, p. 238.
68. Basbaum, *História Sincera*, p. 238.
69. Dubnic, *Political Trends*, p. 105.
70. Mário Victor, *Cinco Años que Abalaram o Brasil* (Rio de Janeiro: Editora Civilizacão Brasileira, 1965), p. 66.
71. Dubnic, *Political Trends*, p. 113.
72. Young, *Brazil 1954-1964*, p. 61.
73. Victor, *Cinco Años*, pp. 42-49; see also Young, *Brazil 1954-1964*, p. 63.
74. Victor, *Brazil 1954-1964*, pp. 54-65; Cabral, *Os Tempos*, pp. 169-74.
75. Interview with João Goulart, Maldonado, Uruguay, 5 June 1972.
76. Victor, *Cinco Años*, p. 67.
77. Dubnic, *Political Trends*, p. 108.
78. Dubnic, *Political Trends*, p. 110.
79. Victor, *Cinco Años*, p. 67.

Chapter 16

1. Speech by Juscelino Kubitschek at New York University, in New York City, 5 March 1962.
2. Interview with Juscelino Kubitschek in New York City, 28 November 1966.
3. Cited in *Hispanic American Report*, Stanford University, Stanford, California, August 1961, p. 556.
4. *Hispanic American Report*, August 1961, p. 556.
5. Victor, *Cinco Años*, p. 81.
6. Victor, *Cinco Años*, p. 82.
7. Juscelino Kubitschek, *A Marcha do Amanhecer* "Bestseller" (São Paulo: Importadora de Livros, 1962), pp. 227-28.
8. Victor, *Cinco Años*, pp. 357-58.
9. Victor, *Cinco Años*, p. 446.
10. Victor, *Cinco Años*, p. 446.
11. *Hispanic American Report*, January 1962, p. 1041.
12. Dubnic, *Political Trends*, p. 34.

13. *Hispanic American Report*, August 1962, p. 559.
14. *Hispanic American Report*, January 1964, p. 1103.
15. Interview with João Goulart in Maldonado, Uruguay, 5 June 1972.
16. *Hispanic American Report*, January 1964, p. 1103 and February 1964, p. 1196.
17. Orico, *Confissões*, p. 20.
18. *Hispanic American Report*, January 1962, p. 1041.
19. *Hispanic American Report*, December 1962, p. 961 and April 1964, p. 178.
20. Orico, *Confissões*, pp. 24, 28, 58; see also Young (ed.), *Brazil 1954-1964*, p. 178.
21. Joseph A. Page, *The Revolution That Never Was: Northeast Brazil 1955-1964* (New York: Grossman Publishers, 1972), p. 181.
22. José Honorio Rodriguez, *Brazil and Africa* (Berkeley: University of California Press, 1965), p. 332.
23. Interview with Juscelino Kubitschek in Belo Horizonte, 1 June 1972.
24. Department of State, "American Republics Establish an Alliance for Progress," Washington, DC, September 1961.
25. Jerome Levinson and Juan de Onis, *The Alliance That Lost Its Way: A Critical Report on the Alliance for Progress* (Chicago: Quadrangle Books, 1970), p. 128.
26. Levinson and Onis, *Alliance*, p. 129.
27. Interview with Juscelino Kubitschek in Belo Horizonte, 1 June 1972.

Chapter 17

1. Orico, *Confissões*, p. 25.
2. Dulles, *President Castello Branco*, p. 368.
3. Interview with Juscelino Kubitschek in Belo Horizonte, 1 June 1972.
4. Interview with João Goulart in Maldonado, Uruguay, 5 June 1972.
5. Victor, *Cinco Años*, pp. 564-65.
6. Dulles, *President Castello Branco*, p. 396.
7. Hermano Alves, "A Trilha de Perseguições e Traições na Volta de JK," *Reunião*, Rio de Janeiro, 27 October 1965.

8. Dulles, *President Castello Branco*, p. 414.
9. Alves, "A Trilha de Perseguições."
10. Orico, *Confissões*, pp. 34-35; see also Dulles, *President Castello Branco*, pp. 414-16.
11. Dulles, *President Castello Branco*, p. 416.
12. Orico, *Confissões*, p. 39.
13. Orico, *Confissões*, p. 37.
14. Victor, *Cinco Años*, p. 569.
15. Victor, *Cinco Años*, p. 572.
16. Dulles, *President Castello Branco*, p. 11.
17. See Mauro Borges, *O Golpe em Goias: Historia de uma grande traição* (Rio de Janeiro: Editora Civilização Brasileira, 1965), for an account of Borges' participation in the coup, and in the selection of Castelo Branco, and of his cassação.
18. Dulles, *President Castello Branco*, p. 32.
19. Dubnic, *Political Trends*, p. 51.
20. Dulles, *President Castello Branco*, p. 33.
21. Dulles, *President Castello Branco*, pp. 33-34.
22. Dulles, *President Castello Branco*, p. 36.
23. Orico, *Confissões*, p. 43.
24. Orico, *Confissões*, p. 44.
25. Victor, *Cinco Años*, pp. 585-86.
26. Interview with Edward Lacey in Rio de Janeiro, 31 May 1972.
27. Dulles, *President Castello Branco*, p. 38.
28. Victor, *Cinco Años*, p. 586.
29. Georges-André Frechter, *Brazil Since 1964: Modernization Under a Military Regime* (New York: John Wiley & Sons, 1975), p. 45.
30. Frechter, *Brazil Since 1964*, p. 45.
31. Orico, *Confissões*, p. 49.
32. Interview with Juscelino Kubitschek in Belo Horizonte, 1 June 1972.
33. Dulles, *President Castello Branco*, p. 51.
34. Dulles, *President Castello Branco*, p. 57.
35. Orico, *Confissões*, pp. 50-51.
36. Orico, *Confissões*, p. 52.
37. Victor, *Cinco Años*, p. 591.

38. Interview with Juscelino Kubitschek in Belo Horizonte, 1 June 1972.
39. Dulles, *President Castello Branco*, p. 140.
40. Interview with Juscelino Kubitschek in Belo Horizonte, 1 June 1972.
41. Dulles, *President Castello Branco*, p. 142.
42. Interview with Juscelino Kubitschek in Rio de Janeiro, 31 May 1972.
43. Interview with Juscelino Kubitschek in Belo Horizonte, 1 June 1972.
44. Interview with Cleantho de Paiva Leite in New York City, 13 November 1966.
45. Interview with Juscelino Kubitschek in Belo Horizonte, 1 June 1972.
46. Interview with Juscelino Kubitschek in Rio de Janeiro, 2 August 1974.
47. Interview with José Maria Alkmin in Belo Horizonte, 6 June 1966.
48. Interview with Juscelino Kubitschek in Rio de Janeiro, 31 May 1972.
49. Frechter, *Brazil since 1964*, p. 108.
50. Interview with Juscelino Kubitschek in Rio de Janeiro, 31 May 1972.
51. The foregoing information was related by a friend of Kubitschek who wishes to remain anonymous.
52. Interview with Juscelino Kubitschek in Belo Horizonte, 1 June 1972.
53. The foregoing information was related by a friend of Kubitschek who wishes to remain anonymous.
54. Interview with Juscelino Kubitschek in Rio de Janeiro, 2 August 1974.
55. Interview with Carlos Lacerda in New York City, 15 November 1967.
56. Interview with Juscelino Kubitschek in New York City, 28 November 1966.
57. Interview with Juscelino Kubitschek in Rio de Janeiro, 31 May 1972.
58. Interview with Juscelino Kubitschek in Belo Horizonte, 1 June 1972.

59.	Cited in *Fatos e Fotos Gente*, Rio de Janeiro, 5 September 1976, p. 48.
60.	Ibid., pp. 48, 64-65.
61.	Ibid., p. 48.
62.	Interview with Juscelino Kubitschek in Rio de Janeiro, 29 June 1973.
63.	Orico, *Confissões*, pp. 74-75.
64.	Interview with Juscelino Kubitschek in Rio de Janeiro, 31 July 1975.
65.	Orico, *Confissões*, p. 75.
66.	*Fatos e Fotos Gente*, 5 September 1976, p. 48.
67.	Letter of Juscelino Kubitschek to Robert J. Alexander, 7 April 1976.
68.	Orico, *Cinco Años*, p. 76.

Chapter 18

1.	Kubitschek, *A Experiencia*, pp. 354-55.
2.	*Fatos e Fotos Gente*, 5 September 1976, p. 23.
3.	Ibid., p. 10.
4.	Ibid., p. 14.
5.	Ibid., p. 21.
6.	*Manchete*, Rio de Janeiro, 3 September 1977, pp. 3-10.
7.	*Visão*, Rio de Janeiro, 31 August 1981, p. 20.
8.	*New York Times*, 9 September 1981, p. A12.
9.	*Visão*, 31 August 1981, p. 20.
10.	*New York Times*, 9 September 1981, p. A12.

Chapter 19

1.	See Peter McDonough, *Power and Ideology in Brazil* (Princeton, NJ: Princeton University Press, 1981).
2.	*Isto É*, Rio de Janeiro, 2 September 1981.
3.	Kubitschek, *A Marcha do Amanhecer* "Bestseller" p. 223.
4.	Ibid., pp. 223-24.
5.	Kubitschek, *Por Que*, p. 309.

BIOGRAPHICAL NOTE

In spite of his importance in the history of modern Brazil, surprisingly little has been written about Juscelino Kubitschek as president of the republic and his administration. So far, no full-length biography of him has been published, either in Brazil or abroad. Although halting with his exit from the presidency, his own memoirs are still the best presentation of his career. Of the other books listed in the bibliography, only six deal at some length with any of its aspects.

The volume by the journalist José Moraes is a more or less authorized campaign biography, issued during the 1955 presidential election, and published by the state government of Minas Gerais. The second book, *Quatro Años no Governo de Minas Gerais*, is a rather detailed study of his administration as governor of Minas Gerais. The third, by Manoel França Campos, is a book issued to celebrate transfer of the capital to Brasilia. It contains considerable information about other aspects of the Kubitschek national administration as well. The volume of Maria Victoria de Mesquita Benevides looks at his presidential administration in the light of the interrelationship between his economic development program and the relative political stability of his administration. The recent book by Edward Riedinger deals with Juscelino's presidential campaign, its antecedents, and events immediately following it. Finally, Celso Lafer's doctoral dissertation examines the planning of the Kubitschek development program.

The lack of books on the builder of Brasilia and the father of "desenvolvimentismo" is probably explained in part in terms of what happened to Brazil after he left the presidency. Following the military coup of 1964, his name was anathema to the ruling group, and for a decade the government probably would not have allowed publication of any study of him or his administration which would have cast doubt on the official allegations concerning the "corruption" and "subversion" of his regime.

Although volumes on Kubitschek are relatively scarce, numerous authors of books and articles dealing only tangentially with him and his administration have contained interesting and sometimes valuable information. These include autobiographies of a number of Juscelino's contemporaries. Material on the Kubitschek presidency is more extensive than that on other aspects of his life. Outstanding in this regard is the long article by Carlos Lessa entitled "Quince Años de Política Económica en el Brasil," appearing in the *Boletín Económico de América Latina*, the monthly magazine of the Economic Commission for Latin America, in its issue of November 1964. It contains the best available resume of facts and figures concerning the economic development efforts of the Kubitschek administration, as well as a description of some of the policies and techniques of Juscelino's government in this field.

The book of Mario Victor entitled *Cinco Años que Abalaram Brasil* contains a very extensive account of the country's politics from the end of the Kubitschek administration through the first year of the military regime. It is a valuable source of information on some of Juscelino's activities in the years immediately following his leaving office.

I have made extensive use of the aforementioned sources, as well as of a wide range of other published material touching more or less briefly on aspects of Kubitschek's career. In addition, I have interviewed a number of people with knowledge about Juscelino's life and career, most particularly Juscelino Kubitschek himself. On five occasions, he talked at considerable length with me, and in addition I heard his public lecture at New York University in New York City a little more than a year after he left the presidency. Edward Riedinger has been kind enough to make available to me transcriptions of several of his interviews with Kubitschek.

All of the sources listed below have been cited at least once in the text.

BIBLIOGRAPHY

Books and Pamphlets

Alexander, Robert J. *A New Strategy of Economic Development.* Maryknoll, NY: Orbis Books, 1976.
_____. *Organized Labor in Latin America.* New York: The Free Press, 1966.
_____. *Labor Relations in Argentina, Brazil and Chile.* New York: McGraw-Hill, 1962.
As Metas do Governo. Presidencia da Republica, Serviço de Interesses Estaduais, Servico do IBGE, n.d. (1959), vol. I, Introduction (pamphlet).
Baer, Werner. *The Development of the Brazilian Steel Industry.* Nashville, Vanderbilt University Press, 1969.
_____. *Industrialization and Economic Development in Brazil.* Homewood, IL: Richard D. Irwin Inc., 1965.
Baklanoff, Eric N. (ed). *New Perspectives of Brazil.* Nashville, Vanderbilt University Press, 1966.
Basbaum, Leoncio. *História Sincera da Republica.* vol. 3. São Paulo: Editora Fulgor Limitada, 1968.
Benevides, Maria Victoria de Mesquita. *O Governo Kubitschek: Desenvolvimento Económico e Estabilidade Política.* 3rd ed. Rio de Janeiro: Paz e Terra, 1979.
Benton, William. *The Voice of Latin America.* New York: Harper & Bros., 1961.
Blake, Peter. *The Master Builders.* New York: Alfred Knopf, 1960.
Borges, Mauro, *O Golpe em Goias: História de uma grande traição.* Rio de Janeiro: Editora Civilização Brasileira, 1965.
Burns, E. Bradford. *The Unwritten Alliance: Rio Branco and Brazilian-American Relations.* New York: Columbia University Press, 1966.
Cabral, Carlos Castilho. *Os Tempos de Jânio e Outros Tempos.* Rio de Janeiro: Editora Civilização Brasileira, 1962.

Café Filho, João. *Do Sindicato ao Catete*. 2 vols. Rio de Janeiro: Livraria José Olympio Editora, 1966.

Campos, Manoel França. *Brasilia 3 de Março*. Rio de Janeiro: Livraria São José, 1960.

Carneiro, Glauco. *História das Revoluções Brasileiras*. 2nd vol. Rio de Janeiro: Edicões O Cruzeiro, 1965.

Chilcote, Ronald H. *The Brazilian Communist Party: Conflict and Integration*. New York: Oxford University Press, 1974.

Comisión Económica Para América Latina. *La Fabricación de Maquinas y Equipos Industriales en América Latina—II, Las Maquinas-Herramientos en el Brasil*. New York: Comisión Económica Para América Latina, 1962.

Coutinho, Afrânio. *No Hospital das Letras*. Rio de Janeiro: Edicões Tempo Brasileiro, 1963.

Daland, Robert T. *Brazilian Planning: Development, Politics and Administration*. Chapel Hill: University of North Carolina Press, 1967.

Deodato, Alberto. *Nos Tempos de João Goulart*. Belo Horizonte: Editora Itatiaia Ltda., 1965.

Dos Passos, John. *Brazil on the Move*. Garden City, NJ: Doubleday & Co., 1963.

Dubnic, Vladimir Reisky de. *Political Trends in Brazil*. Washington: Public Affairs Press, 1968.

Dulles, John W.F. *President Castello Branco: Brazilian Reformer*. College Station: Texas A&M University Press, 1980.

_____. *Castello Branco—The Making of a Brazilian President*. College Station: Texas A&M University Press, 1978.

Eisenhower, Milton. *The Wine is Bitter: The United States and Latin America*. Garden City: Doubleday & Co., 1963.

Erickson, Kenneth Paul. *The Brazilian Corporative State and Working Class Politics*. Berkeley: University of California Press, 1977.

Frechter, Georges-André. *Brazil Since 1964: Modernization Under a Military Regime*. New York: John Wiley, 1975.

Freyre, Gilberto. *New World in the Tropics: The Culture of Modern Brazil*. New York: Alfred Knopf, 1959.

Furtado, Celso. *Dialética do Desenvolvimento*. Rio de Janeiro: Fundo de Cultura, 1964.

_____. *Formação Económica do Brasil*. Rio de Janeiro: Fundo de Cultura, 1964.

_____. *A Pre Revolução Brasileira*. Rio de Janeiro: Fundo de Cultura, 1962.

Gordon, Lincoln and Englebert L. Grommers. *United States Manufacturing Investment in Brazil—The Impact of Government Policies 1946-1960*. Boston: Harvard Graduate School of Business Administration, 1962.

Graham, Lawrence S. *Civil Service Reform in Brazil: Principles Versus Practice*. Austin: University of Texas Press, 1968.

Hirschman, Albert (ed). *Latin American Issues*. New York: Twentieth Century Fund, 1961.

Ianni, Octavio, Paulo Singer, Gabriel Cohn, and Francisco C. Weffort. *Política e Revolução Social No Brasil*. Rio de Janeiro, Editora Civilização Brasileira, 1965.

Kubitschek, Juscelino. *A Escalada Política*. Rio de Janeiro: Bloch Editores, 1976.

_____. *A Marcha do Amanhecer* "Bestseller." São Paulo: Importadora de Livros, 1962.

_____. *Por Que Construí Brasília*. Rio de Janeiro: Bloch Editores, 1976.

_____. Memoirs in three vols: *A Experiencia da Humilidade*. Rio de Janeiro: Bloch Editores, 1974.

Lafer, Celso. *The Planning Process and the Political System in Brazil: Study of Kubitschek's Target Plan 1956-1961*. (Ph.D. diss., Cornell University, 1970). Ann Arbor: University Microfilms, 1970.

Lins, Etelvino. *Um Depoimento Político (Episodios e Observaçoes)*. Rio de Janeiro: Livraria José Olympio Editores, 1977.

Luz, Nicia Vilela. *A Luta Pela Industrialização do Brasil*. São Paulo: Difusão Europeia do Livro, 1961.

Magalhães, Sergio. *Problemas do Desenvolvimento Económico*, Rio de Janeiro: Editora Civilização Brasileira, 1960.

McDonough, Peter. *Power and Ideology in Brazil*. Princeton: Princeton University Press, 1981.

Metas e Bases para A Ação do Governo. Brasília: Presidencia da República, 1970.

Moraes, José. *Juscelino: O Homen, A Candidatura, A Campanha*. Belo Horizonte: Imprensa Oficial de Minas Gerais, 1955.

Oliveira, José Teixeira de (ed). *O Governo Dutra*. Rio de Janeiro: Editora Civilização Brasileira, 1956.

Onody, Oliver. *A Inflação Brasileira*. Rio de Janeiro: privately published, 1960.

Orico, Osvaldo. *Confissões do Exilio: J.K.* Rio de Janeiro: Livraria Francisco Alves, 1977.

Page, Joseph A. *The Revolution That Never Was: Northeast Brazil 1955-1964*. New York: Grossman Publishers, 1972.

Prado Junior, Caio. *História Económica do Brasil*. São Paulo: Editora Brasiliense, 1962.

Putnam, Samuel. *Marvelous Journey: A Survey of Four Centuries of Brazilian Writing*. New York: Alfred A. Knopf, 1948.

Quatro Anos no Governo de Minas Gerais (1951-1955)—Sintese das Realizações do Governador Juscelino Kubitschek de Oliveira. Rio de Janeiro: Livraria José Olympio Editora, 1959.

Raine, Philip. *Brazil: Awakening Giant*. Washington: Public Affairs Press, 1974.

Rangel, Ignacio. *A Inflacão Brasileira*. Rio de Janeiro: Tempo Brasileiro, 1963.

————. *Recursos Ociosos*. Rio de Janeiro: Conselho de Desenvolvimento, 1963.

Riedinger, Edward Anthony. *Como se Faz Um Presidente: A Campanha de J.K.* Rio de Janeiro: Editora Nova Fronteira, 1988.

Robock, Stefan. *Brazil's Developing Northeast—A Study in Regional Planning and Foreign Aid*. Washington: The Brookings Institution, 1963.

Rodriguez, José Honorio. *Brazil and Africa*. Berkeley: University of California Press, 1965.

Saldanha, João. *Os Subterraneos de Futebol*. Rio de Janeiro: Tempo Brasileiro, 1963.

Selcher, Wayne A. *The Afro-Asian Dimension of Brazilian Foreign Policy 1956-1972*. Gainesville, University Press of Florida, 1974.

Shoup, Carl. *The Tax System of Brazil*. Rio de Janeiro: Fundaçao Getúlio Vargas, 1965.

Silvert, K.H. *Expectant Peoples: Nationalism and Development*. New York: Random House, 1963.

Simonsen, Mario. *A Experiencia Inflacionaria no Brasil*. Rio de Janeiro: Instituto de Pesquisas e Estudos Socials, 1964.

Skidmore, Thomas E. *Politics in Brazil 1930-1964*. New York: Oxford University Press, 1967.

Sodré, Nelson Warneck. *História Militar do Brasil*. Rio de Janeiro: Editora Civilização Brasileira, 1965.

Suplicy, Eduardo Matarazzo. *Política Económica Brasileira e Internacional*. Petropolis: Editora Vozes Ltda., 1977.

Szulc, Tad. *The Winds of Revolution: Latin America Today—and Tomorrow*. New York: Frederick A. Praeger, 1963.

Távora, Juarez. *Uma Vida e Muitas Lutas*, 3rd vol. *Voltando a Planicie*. Rio de Janeiro: Livraria José Olympio Editora, 1976.

Victor, Mário. *Cinco Años que Abalaram O Brasil*. Rio de Janeiro: Editora Civilização Brasileira, 1965.

Vinhas, Moisés. *O Partidão: A Luta por um Partido de Massas 1922-1974*. São Paulo: Editora Hucitec, 1982.

Young, Jordan M. (ed). *Brazil 1954-1964: End of a Civilian Cycle*. New York: Facts on File, 1972.

————. *The Brazilian Revolution of 1930 and the Aftermath*. New Brunswick: Rutgers University Press, 1967.

Zweig, Stefan. *Brazil: Land of the Future*. New York: The Viking Press, 1941.

Newspapers and Magazines

Américas. Pan American Union, Washington, DC.

Boletín Económico de América Latina. Monthly of Economic Commission for Latin America, Santiago, Chile.

Fatos e Fotos Gente. Rio de Janeiro magazine.

Hispanic American Report. Stanford University, Stanford, California monthly.

Isto É. Rio de Janeiro weekly.

Jornal do Brasil. Daily newspaper, Rio de Janeiro.

Correio da Manha. Daily newspaper, Rio de Janeiro.

L'Espresso. Weekly news magazine, Rome, Italy.

Manchete. Rio de Janeiro weekly magazine.

New Leader. Weekly political and literary magazine, New York City.

New York Times.

O Cruzeiro. Weekly magazine, Rio de Janeiro.

O Estado de São Paulo. Daily newspaper, São Paulo.

Panfleto. Left-wing monthly of late 1950s and early 1960s, Rio de Janeiro.

Reunião. Opposition weekly, 1960s.

Revista Brasileira de Política Internacional. Scholarly publication on international affairs, Rio de Janeiro.

Time. New York City news weekly.

Visão da Industria. Magazine, São Paulo.

Interviews Conducted by Author

Alkmin, José Maria. Long-time friend of Juscelino Kubitschek, Vice President of the Republic, in Belo Horizonte, 6 June 1966.

Barata, Agildo. Ex-Treasurer of Communist party of Brazil, in Rio de Janeiro, 20 August 1965.

Barreto, Plinio. Leader of União Democrática Nacional, deputy in 1946 constituent assembly, in São Paulo, 16 April 1956.

Barroso, Parsifal. Leader of Partido Trabalhista Brasileiro, Minister of Labor under Kubitschek, in Fortaleza, 22 April 1966.

Boiteux, Bayard. President, Sindicato de Profesores do Distrito Federal, Socialist Party leader, in Rio de Janeiro, 25 August 1959.

Bonfim, Socrates. President of Companhia Siderurgica de Amazonia, in Manaus, 26 February 1966.

Café Filho, João. Ex-president of Brazil, in Rio de Janeiro, 8 June 1966.

Chediak, Antônio José. Ex-speech writer of Juscelino Kubitschek, in Rio de Janeiro, 6 April 1966.

Goulart, João. Ex-president of Brazil, in Maldonado, Uruguay, 5 June 1972.

Kreiger, Daniel. Leader of União Democrática Nacional, in Brasília, 17 March 1966.

Kubitschek, Juscelino. Speech at New York University in New York City, 5 March 1962; in New York City, 28 November 1966; in Rio de Janeiro, 31 May 1972; in Belo Horizonte, 1 June 1972; in Rio de Janeiro, 29 June 1973; in Rio de Janeiro, 2 August 1974, in Rio de Janeiro, 31 July 1975.

Lacerda, Carlos. Ex-leader of União Democrática Nacional, in Rio de Janeiro, 3 February 1966; in New York City, 15 November 1967.

Lacey, Edward. English teacher of Juscelino Kubitschek, in Rio de Janeiro, 31 May 1972.

Leite, Cleantho de Paiva. Former Chief of Cabinet of Transport and Public Works Ministry under Kubitschek, economist, in New York City, 13 November 1966.
Negrão de Lima, Francisco. Governor of State of Guanabara, in Rio de Janeiro, 6 April 1966.
Oliveira, Nestor Peixoto de. Editor of *Resenha Socialista*, in São Paulo, 6 March 1956.
Paim, Gilberto. Economist and journalist, in Rio de Janeiro, 13 October 1965.
Pedrosa, Mário. Ex-socialist leader, leading art critic, in Rio de Janeiro, 24 August 1959.
Pereira, Astrogildo. A founder of Communist Party of Brazil, in Rio de Janeiro, 19 October 1965.
Prestes, Luís Carlos. Secretary General of Communist Party of Brazil, Senator, in Rio de Janeiro, 27 August 1946.
Santos, Agilberto de Lacerda Figueiredo. Official of Sindacato de Condutores Eletricos e Trefalcão, in São Paulo, 26 April 1956.
Sarney, José. Governor of Maranhão, former União Democrática Nacional leader, in São Luis, 16 April 1966.
Street, Ernesto. Economist of National Confederation of Industry, in Rio de Janeiro, 16 August 1965.
Vargas, Alzira. Daughter of Getúlio Vargas, in Rio de Janeiro, 10 January 1966.
Viana, José Segadas. Ex-Director General of Labor, organizer of Partido Trabalhista Brasileiro, in Rio de Janeiro, 26 August 1946 and 16 March 1956.

Interviews Conducted by Riedinger

Kubitschek, Juscelino. 25 September 1973, 2 October 1973, 6 April 1974, 13 June 1974, 24 October 1974, 26 November 1974, 2 December 1974.

Miscellaneous Materials

Kubitschek, Juscelino. Letter to Robert J. Alexander, 7 April 1976.
Menezes, O.J. "Industry—Preliminary Diagnosis," (Manuscript), August 1965.
State Department. "American Republics Establish an Alliance for Progress," Press Release, Washington, DC, September 1961.

Walter, Brigadier General Vernon A., Major Jack J. Gardner, Captain Clarke Brinthall, "The Road of the Jaguars: Belem-Brasilia Highway, Brazil, January 1965) (Mimeographed).

MONOGRAPHS IN INTERNATIONAL STUDIES

ISBN Prefix 0-89680-

Africa Series

36. Fadiman, Jeffrey A. *The Moment of Conquest: Meru, Kenya, 1907.* 1979. 70pp.
    081-4 $ 5.50*

37. Wright, Donald R. *Oral Traditions From The Gambia: Volume I, Mandinka Griots.* 1979. 176pp.
    083-0 $15.00*

38. Wright, Donald R. *Oral Traditions From The Gambia: Volume II, Family Elders.* 1980. 200pp.
    084-9 $15.00*

41. Lindfors, Bernth. *Mazungumzo: Interviews with East African Writers, Publishers, Editors, and Scholars.* 1981. 179pp.
    108-X $13.00*

43. Harik, Elsa M. and Donald G. Schilling. *The Politics of Education in Colonial Algeria and Kenya.* 1984. 102pp.
    117-9 $12.50*

44. Smith, Daniel R. *The Influence of the Fabian Colonial Bureau on the Independence Movement in Tanganyika.* 1985. x, 98pp.
    125-X $11.00*

45. Keto, C. Tsehloane. *American-South African Relations 1784-1980: Review and Select Bibliography.* 1985. 159pp.
    128-4 $11.00*

46. Burness, Don, and Mary-Lou Burness, ed. *Wanasema: Conversations with African Writers*. 1985. 95pp.
129-2 $11.00*

47. Switzer, Les. *Media and Dependency in South Africa: A Case Study of the Press and the Ciskei "Homeland"*. 1985. 80pp.
130-6 $10.00*

48. Heggoy, Alf Andrew. *The French Conquest of Algiers, 1830: An Algerian Oral Tradition*. 1986. 101pp.
131-4 $11.00*

49. Hart, Ursula Kingsmill. *Two Ladies of Colonial Algeria: The Lives and Times of Aurelie Picard and Isabelle Eberhardt*. 1987. 156pp.
143-8 $11.00*

50. Voeltz, Richard A. *German Colonialism and the South West Africa Company, 1894-1914*. 1988. 143pp.
146-2 $12.00*

51. Clayton, Anthony, and David Killingray. *Khaki and Blue: Military and Police in British Colonial Africa*. 1989. 235pp.
147-0 $18.00*

52. Northrup, David. *Beyond the Bend in the River: African Labor in Eastern Zaire, 1865-1940*. 1988. 195pp.
151-9 $15.00*

53. Makinde, M. Akin. *African Philosophy, Culture, and Traditional Medicine*. 1988. 175pp.
152-7 $13.00*

54. Parson, Jack, ed. *Succession to High Office in Botswana. Three Case Studies*. 1990. 443pp.
157-8 $20.00*

55. Burness, Don. *A Horse of White Clouds*. 1989. 193pp.
158-6 $12.00*

56. Staudinger, Paul. *In the Heart of the Hausa States.* Tr. by Johanna Moody. 1990. 2 vols. 653pp.
160-8 $35.00*

57. Sikainga, Ahmad Alawad. *The Western Bahr Al-Ghazal Under British Rule: 1898-1956.* 1991. 183pp.
161-6 $15.00*

58. Wilson, Louis E. *The Krobo People of Ghana to 1892: A Political and Social History.* 1991. 254pp.
164-0 $20.00*

59. du Toit, Brian M. *Cannabis, Alcohol, and the South African Student: Adolescent Drug Use 1974-1985.* 1991. 166pp.
166-7 $17.00*

Latin America Series

8. Clayton, Lawrence A. *Caulkers and Carpenters in a New World: The Shipyards of Colonial Guayaquil.* 1980. 189pp, illus.
103-9 $15.00*

9. Tata, Robert J. *Structural Changes in Puerto Rico's Economy: 1947-1976.* 1981. xiv, 104pp.
107-1 $12.00*

11. O'Shaughnessy, Laura N., and Louis H. Serra. *Church and Revolution in Nicaragua.* 1986. 118pp.
126-8 $12.00*

12. Wallace, Brian. *Ownership and Development: A Comparison of Domestic and Foreign Investment in Colombian Manufacturing.* 1987. 186pp.
145-4 $10.00*

13. Henderson, James D. *Conservative Thought in Latin America: The Ideas of Laureano Gomez.* 1988. 150pp.
148-9 $13.00*

14. Summ, G. Harvey, and Tom Kelly. *The Good Neighbors: America, Panama, and the 1977 Canal Treaties.* 1988. 135pp.
149-7 $13.00*

15. Peritore, Patrick. *Socialism, Communism, and Liberation Theology in Brazil: An Opinion Survey Using Q-Methodology.* 1990. 245pp.
156-X $15.00*

16. Alexander, Robert J. *Juscelino Kubitschek and the Development of Brazil.* 1991. 429pp.
163-2 $25.00*

17. Mijeski, Kenneth J., ed. *The Nicaraguan Constitution of 1987: English Translation and Commentary.* 1990. 355pp.
165-9 $25.00*

Southeast Asia Series

31. Nash, Manning. *Peasant Citizens: Politics, Religion, and Modernization in Kelantan, Malaysia.* 1974. 181pp.
018-0 $12.00*

38. Bailey, Conner. *Broker, Mediator, Patron, and Kinsman: An Historical Analysis of Key Leadership Roles in a Rural Malaysian District.* 1976. 79pp.
024-5 $ 8.00*

44. Collier, William L., et al. *Income, Employment and Food Systems in Javanese Coastal Villages.* 1977. 160pp.
031-8 $10.00*

45. Chew, Sock Foon and MacDougall, John A. *Forever Plural: The Perception and Practice of Inter-Communal Marriage in Singapore.* 1977. 61pp.
030-X $ 8.00*

47. Wessing, Robert. *Cosmology and Social Behavior in a West Javanese Settlement.* 1978. 200pp.
072-5 $12.00*

48. Willer, Thomas F., ed. *Southeast Asian References in the British Parliamentary Papers, 1801-1972/73: An Index.* 1978. 110pp.
033-4 $ 8.50*

49. Durrenberger, E. Paul. *Agricultural Production and Household Budgets in a Shan Peasant Village in Northwestern Thailand: A Quantitative Description.* 1978. 142pp.
071-7 $10.00*

50. Echauz, Robustiano. *Sketches of the Island of Negros.* 1978. 174pp.
070-9 $12.00*

51. Krannich, Ronald L. *Mayors and Managers in Thailand: The Struggle for Political Life in Administrative Settings.* 1978. 139pp.
073-3 $11.00*

56A. Duiker, William J. *Vietnam Since the Fall of Saigon.* Updated edition. 1989. 383pp.
162-4 $17.00*

59. Foster, Brian L. *Commerce and Ethnic Differences: The Case of the Mons in Thailand.* 1982. x, 93pp.
112-8 $10.00*

60. Frederick, William H., and John H. McGlynn. *Reflections on Rebellion: Stories from the Indonesian Upheavals of 1948 and 1965.* 1983. vi, 168pp.
111-X $ 9.00*

61. Cady, John F. *Contacts With Burma, 1935-1949: A Personal Account.* 1983. x, 117pp.
114-4 $ 9.00*

63. Carstens, Sharon, ed. *Cultural Identity in Northern Peninsular Malaysia.* 1986. 91pp.
116-0 $ 9.00*

64. Dardjowidjojo, Soenjono. *Vocabulary Building in Indonesian: An Advanced Reader.* 1984. xviii, 256pp.
118-7 $26.00*

65. Errington, J. Joseph. *Language and Social Change in Java: Linguistic Reflexes of Modernization in a Traditional Royal Polity.* 1985. xiv, 211pp.
120-9 $20.00*

66. Binh, Tran Tu. *The Red Earth: A Vietnamese Memoir of Life on a Colonial Rubber Plantation.* Tr. by John Spragens. Ed. by David Marr. 1985. xii, 98pp.
119-5 $11.00*

68. Syukri, Ibrahim. *History of the Malay Kingdom of Patani.* Tr. by Conner Bailey and John N. Miksic. 1985. xix, 113pp.
123-3 $12.00*

69. Keeler, Ward. *Javanese: A Cultural Approach.* 1984. xxxvi, 523pp.
121-7 $18.00*

70. Wilson, Constance M., and Lucien M. Hanks. *Burma-Thailand Frontier Over Sixteen Decades: Three Descriptive Documents.* 1985. x, 128pp.
124-1 $11.00*

71. Thomas, Lynn L., and Franz von Benda-Beckmann, eds. *Change and Continuity in Minangkabau: Local, Regional, and Historical Perspectives on West Sumatra.* 1986. 363pp.
127-6 $16.00*

72. Reid, Anthony, and Oki Akira, eds. *The Japanese Experience in Indonesia: Selected Memoirs of 1942-1945.* 1986. 411pp., 20 illus.
132-2 $20.00*

73. Smirenskaia, Zhanna D. *Peasants in Asia: Social Consciousness and Social Struggle.* Tr. by Michael J. Buckley. 1987. 248pp.
134-9 $14.00

74. McArthur, M.S.H. *Report on Brunei in 1904.* Ed. by A.V.M. Horton. 1987. 304pp.
135-7 $15.00

75. Lockard, Craig Alan. *From Kampung to City. A Social History of Kuching Malaysia 1820-1970.* 1987. 311pp.
136-5 $16.00*

76. McGinn, Richard. *Studies in Austronesian Linguistics.* 1988. 492pp.
137-3 $20.00*

77. Muego, Benjamin N. *Spectator Society: The Philippines Under Martial Rule.* 1988. 232pp.
138-1 $15.00*

78. Chew, Sock Foon. *Ethnicity and Nationality in Singapore.* 1987. 229pp.
139-X $12.50*

79. Walton, Susan Pratt. *Mode in Javanese Music.* 1987. 279pp.
144-6 $15.00*

80. Nguyen Anh Tuan. *South Vietnam Trial and Experience: A Challenge for Development.* 1987. 482pp.
141-1 $18.00*

81. Van der Veur, Paul W., ed. *Toward a Glorious Indonesia: Reminiscences and Observations of Dr. Soetomo.* 1987. 367pp.
142-X $16.00*

82. Spores, John C. *Running Amok: An Historical Inquiry.* 1988. 190pp.
140-3 $14.00*

83. Tan Malaka. *From Jail to Jail.* Tr. and ed. by Helen Jarvis. 1990. 3 vols. 1,226pp.
150-0 $55.00*

84. Devas, Nick. *Financing Local Government in Indonesia.* 1989. 344pp.
153-5 $16.00*

85. Suryadinata, Leo. *Military Ascendancy and Political Culture: A Study of Indonesia's Golkar.* 1989. 222pp.
179-9 $15.00*

86. Williams, Michael. *Communism, Religion, and Revolt in Banten.* 1990. 356pp.
155-1 $16.00*

87. Hudak, Thomas John. *The Indigenization of Pali Meters in Thai Poetry.* 1990. 237pp.
159-4 $15.00*

88. Lay, Ma Ma. *Not Out of Hate: A Novel of Burma.* Tr. by Margaret Aung-Thwin. Ed. by William Frederick. 1991. 222pp.
167-5 $20.00*

ORDERING INFORMATION

Orders for titles in the Monographs in International Studies series may be placed through the Ohio University Press, Scott Quadrangle, Athens, Ohio 45701-2979 or through any local bookstore. Individuals should remit payment by check, VISA, MasterCard, or American Express. People ordering from the United Kingdom, Continental Europe, the Middle East, and Africa should order through Academic and University Publishers Group, 1 Gower Street, London WC1E, England. Orders from the Pacific Region, Asia, Australia, and New Zealand should be sent to East-West Export Books, c/o the University of Hawaii Press, 2840 Kolowalu Street, Honolulu, Hawaii 96822, USA.

Other individuals ordering from outside of the U.S. should remit in U.S. funds to the Ohio University Press either by International Money Order or by a check drawn on a U.S. bank. Most out-of-print titles may be ordered from University Microfilms, Inc., 300 North Zeeb Road, Ann Arbor, Michigan 48106, USA.

Prices do not include shipping charges and are subject to change without notice.